The Radical Redemption Model

EXTREME BELIEF AND BEHAVIOR SERIES

Series Editor
Rik Peels

The Radical Redemption Model: Terrorist Beliefs and Narratives
Beatrice de Graaf

Forthcoming Titles
Conceptualizing Extreme Beliefs and Behaviors: Definitions and Relations
Rik Peels and John Horgan

Explaining Extreme Beliefs and Behaviors: Theoretical, Methodological, and Ethical Challenges
Rik Peels and Lorne Dawson

The Radical Redemption Model

Terrorist Beliefs and Narratives

BEATRICE DE GRAAF

OXFORD
UNIVERSITY PRESS

Oxford University Press is a department of the University of Oxford. It furthers
the University's objective of excellence in research, scholarship, and education
by publishing worldwide. Oxford is a registered trade mark of Oxford University
Press in the UK and certain other countries.

Published in the United States of America by Oxford University Press
198 Madison Avenue, New York, NY 10016, United States of America.

© Oxford University Press 2024

All rights reserved. No part of this publication may be reproduced, stored in
a retrieval system, or transmitted, in any form or by any means, without the
prior permission in writing of Oxford University Press, or as expressly permitted
by law, by license, or under terms agreed with the appropriate reproduction
rights organization. Inquiries concerning reproduction outside the scope of the
above should be sent to the Rights Department, Oxford University Press, at the
address above.

You must not circulate this work in any other form
and you must impose this same condition on any acquirer.

Library of Congress Cataloging-in-Publication Data
Names: Graaf, Beatrice de, author.
Title: The radical redemption model : terrorist beliefs and
narratives / Beatrice de Graaf.
Other titles: Radicale verlossing. English
Description: New York, NY : Oxford University Press, [2024] |
Series: Extreme belief and behavior series |
Includes bibliographical references and index.
Identifiers: LCCN 2024020996 | ISBN 9780197792469 (hardback) |
ISBN 9780197792483 (epub) | ISBN 9780197792476 | ISBN 9780197792490
Subjects: LCSH: Terrorism—Psychological aspects. |
Terrorism—Religious aspects—Islam. | Terrorists—Psychology. |
Terrorists—Religious life. | Radicalism—Religious aspects—Islam.
Classification: LCC HV6431 .G697313 2024 | DDC 363.325—dc23/eng/20240801
LC record available at https://lccn.loc.gov/2024020996

DOI: 10.1093/oso/9780197792469.001.0001

Printed by Marquis Book Printing, Canada

Contents

Acknowledgments   ix

A Paradigm for Studying Extreme Belief and Behavior:
Introduction to the Series   1
   Purpose of the Series   1
   This Volume   3
   What Is Extreme Belief and Behavior?   4
   The Normalcy Hypothesis   6
   A First-Person Approach   7
   Inherent Normativity   11
   Cross-Domain Study   13
   True Interdisciplinarity   16
   Structure   18

1. Terrorists and Their Beliefs   23
   A Place in Paradise   23
   Religion as Moderator   24
   Studying Radical Redemption as a Narrative   31
   Current Literature on the Religion-and-Radicalization Puzzle   37
   Life Histories Approach   41
   Radical Redemption as an Orthopraxis   45
   Scope of the Book   47
   Positionality   49

2. The Desire for Radical Redemption: A Novel Approach   53
   Generative Life Stories   53
   Generative Terrorists?   56
   Radical Redemption as a Way to Cope with Injustice   61
   Redemption as a Religious and Cultural Theme   62
   Redemption as Sacred Praxis   67
   Conclusion   71

3. Radical Redemption in History   74
   The Fourth R   74
   Anarchism: Propaganda of the Deed, 1880–1920   77
      Auguste Vaillant's Act of Redemption   78
      Zinaida Konopliannikova's Urge for Emancipation   80

vi CONTENTS

    Guilt and Atonement in the RAF   84
        Using Their Own Bodies as Weapons   88
        Win or Die   90
        Blessed Are Those Who Hunger for Justice   94
    Freedom from the Yoke of Technology   99
    Conclusion   104

4. **The First Panel: Sensing a Deficit**   107
    A Social and Moral Deficit   107
    Dreams of the Desert   108
    Global Landscapes of Jihad   111
    Viral Times   113
    Enough of My Flatscreen   116
    Grappling with the Deficit and the Desire for Purity and Action   120
    Enough of My Government   123
    The Deep History of Radical Redemption   127
    Conclusion   131

5. **The Second Panel: Devotion and Struggle**   134
    Devotion and Struggle   134
    Earning Points   135
    Purify My Soul   137
    Jihad and the Rifle Alone   140
    I Felt Chosen   142
    Muslim Babies Are Being Butchered   148
    To Syria: It Is My Duty   154
    General Van Uhm   157
    Among the Most Wanted   161
    The Premier League   165
    With Grandmother to the Caliphate   166
    Bad Luck?   170
    Redemption for Stay-at-Home Terrorists   173
    Gökmen Tanis, March 18, 2019   175
    Conclusion   179

6. **The Third Panel: Validation Achieved?**   182
    Validation or Contamination   182
    Redemption Accomplished   183
        The Crime–Terror Nexus   183
        Profit or Redemption?   185
        Offer and Confirmation of Radical Redemption: *Rumiyah*   188
        Penance Paid and Reward Received   190
        I Have Saved the Netherlands   192

Denial and Disappointment 195
   In Denial 195
   No Premier League After All 199
Refutation and Reappraisal 200
   Redemption Frustrated 200
   Delegitimized Redemption—the Counternarrative of bin Laden 203
   The Dream of a Boy from The Hague 207
   Chaos and Infighting 210
Conclusion 213

7. Radical Redemption Narratives in Other Contexts 216
   By Way of Control 216
   Terrorism or Armed Opposition? 217
   Ethnic-Tribal Conflict or Religious Terrorism? 221
      Talking with Terrorists in Africa 221
      A Long History of Injustice and Deficit 223
      Rewards on Earth and in Paradise 225
   Right-Wing Extremist Delusions of Redemption: Saviors
       of Their Own Community 229
      The Fragmented Extreme-Right Universe 229
      Far-Right Redemption Narratives 233
      Far-Right Redemption Narratives in the Netherlands 239
      The Bergden Case 239
      Nobody Does Anything 241
      They Lied to Us 246
      Local Redemption or Revenue Model? 250
   Conclusion 251

8. Toward a Grounded Theory of Radical Redemption 254
   The Grounded Theory Approach 254
   The Recurring Pattern of the Triptych 255
   Radical Redemption as an Orthopraxis 258
   The Role of Religion in the Radical Redemption Narrative 259
   The Rich Varieties of Religious Radical Redemption 262
   Not Validation but Contamination 265
   Recidivism and Reintegration 270
   The Role of Religion in the Process of Disillusionment,
      Disengagement, and Reintegration 272
   Conclusion 276

9. Conclusion 278
   Drawings of the Desert 278
   Believers and Their Communities 279
   Radical Redemption: An Inherently Inconsistent Narrative 280
   A Parasitic Narrative 283

Appendix 1: Interviewees and Profiles — 285
   Table of Interviewees and Their Profiles — 286
   Interview List — 297
Appendix 2: Methods — 301
   Oral History as Research Method — 301
   Limitations of the Life Histories Approach — 302
   Selection of Interviewees — 303
   Source Calibration — 305
   Broadening the Perspective — 306
Appendix 3: Ethics — 309
   Vulnerable Research Subjects — 309
   Ethical Clearance — 309
   Informed Consent — 310
References — 311
Index — 331

Acknowledgments

This monograph is based on the research that came out in Dutch as a popular book for a larger audience: *Radicale verlossing: Wat terroristen geloven* (Prometheus, 2021). Andy Brown helped me to translate that version into English. I then rewrote the entire manuscript, restructured it, and improved it with the input and help of several reviewers of Oxford University Press, my colleagues (among them most notably Kees van den Bos), and Rik Peels, editor of the Extreme Belief and Behavior Series. Mathanja Berger edited the English manuscript for me. When I started the work on this book, I used the translated text from the Dutch volume as a basis (since it contained the original research), rewriting and adding to it systematically as I went through the entire text. Chapters 1, 8, and 9 are newly written, and only very small parts of them overlap with parts in the Dutch volume. Chapters 3, 4, 5, and 6 are the empirical chapters and do overlap with the chapters in the Dutch book, but they have been checked, amended, and edited. Chapter 2 has been substantially rewritten. Finally, this English volume has two new appendices, on methods and ethics.

When writing a book on terrorism, an author imposes a burden on her family, friends, and colleagues. I am grateful to my colleagues of the Security History Network in Utrecht for coming along with me, despite the intensity of the theme, on my journey through the very recent history of terrorism and extremism. Wouter Klem, Erik de Lange, Ozan Ozavci, Trineke Palm, Joep Schenk, Carla Spiegel, Nikki Sterkenburg, and Jossie van Til-Duijsters loyally read the text as I wrote it and helped me to produce a historical narrative that was clear and to the point. Annelotte Janse was an enthusiastic and valuable research assistant from the beginning of the project, as was Jorin Dijkstra, who joined the team later. The students attending the course on terrorism in the History of International Relations Master's program were the first with whom I was able to discuss my findings; I would especially like to mention Tom Schoen and thank him for his input in the research.

The Faculty Ethics Assessment Committee Humanities at Utrecht University worked very closely with me on avoiding all the pitfalls inextricably bound up with research of this nature. I would like to express my enormous gratitude to Mariëtte van de Hoven, Jan Odijk, Desiree Capel, Koen Leurs, Luuk Slooter, Frans de Liagre Böhl, and Joris de Graaf (also Utrecht University's privacy officer) for their critical assistance and guidance.

The original plan arose in consultation with the National Coordinator for Counterterrorism and Security (NCTV). The NCTV provided a grant for the research and gave me crucial assistance throughout the project. Without the essential tips and advice from Cees Kraayveld (PI De Schie), Yola Wanders and Richard Baas (PI Vught), and Jeroen Rempt (PI Alphen aan den Rijn), I would never have been admitted to the penitentiary institutions or been able to speak to the detainees. The Custodial Institutions Agency provided me with the formal opportunity and freedom so essential for researchers to make those visits. Arjan Derksen, leading Enschede police officer, helped me on my way with the research into the Bergden case. The officials and analysts of the police and security services whom I cannot mention by name here also know how grateful I am to them for all their useful tips and advice.

Martijn de Koning, Joas Wagemakers, and Christian Lange were indispensable in providing advice on religious issues and research on Islam and the Arab world. Kees van den Bos helped me navigate the social-psychological challenges. His advice and support were essential in bridging the gap between the social sciences (social psychology) and the humanities (history). Thanks to their critical eye, I could at least try to avoid the pitfalls I would otherwise certainly have fallen into as a non-Arabist and non–social psychologist. (Of course, if that still happened, it was not their fault.)

Rik Peels, as editor of the Extreme Belief and Behavior Series, was unsurpassed in encouraging me to keep going, go the extra mile, and really finish the book. His philosophical perspective helped me to further sharpen the research question and analysis. It is a tremendous honor to have this book appear in his series. I thank Nadina Persaud for her patient guidance in steering us through the trajectory of reviews and adjustments. Without them, it would have been a different book! Andy Brown and Mathanja Berger were of invaluable help in translating the first parts of the research (which came out in Dutch) and editing the final manuscript for me. Mathanja's dedication and perseverance in smoothing out the last folds and untangling the last knotted sentences were unmatched.

Esther Heldenbergh, Myrthe van Groningen, and Susanne Keesman helped me organize the project and relieved me of the day-to-day concerns. Andries Zoutendijk read the text and was, as always, a critical sounding board. Michel Kok of the City of Utrecht and Rogier Donk of the Utrecht police were worthy sparring partners from the early beginning; they put me on the right track and helped me find interviewees and other contacts.

A very special aspect of the research was the opportunity to build bridges across great distances and to remote areas, and to talk to convicted terrorists and their victims in far-off places. Mensen met een Missie had confidence in this project. Frans Davelaar, Ton Groeneweg, Stephanie Joubert, and especially Kees Schilder made it possible for me to include voices from Africa in this book. Unfortunately, due to the Covid-19 crisis, I couldn't travel to Africa myself, but Kees Schilder personally conducted interviews essential to this study in Cameroon and helped me arrange online interviews. My conversations with youth workers, pastoral carers, and victims of Boko Haram violence in Cameroon left a great impression; much more needs to be written about their situations and their resilience.

Carrying out research in Indonesia was another unique experience. Thanks to the people at the Dutch embassy—ambassador Lambert Grijns above all, but also Roel van der Veen, Edwin Arifin, and Brechtje Klandermans—I was given immediate access to a wide range of meetings and individuals, including a nocturnal visit to old Batavia and the Sunda Kelapa (thanks, Roel!). From terrorism victim and founder of AIDA Max Boon and from my Indonesian fellow researcher Solahudin I received indispensable background information and tips for further research. Max Boon's dedication in the field is impressive, and it was an honor to learn from him. Chadijah Saraswati accompanied me through a flooded Jakarta and supported me during all interviews.

In this word of thanks, I would expressly like to thank all detainees and ex-detainees. They were willing to share with me the often painful and emotional experiences of their radicalization processes and their dashed expectations. Some of them genuinely opened up their soul to me; in doing so, they rendered themselves very vulnerable. Despite the great divide between their lives and mine, this book owes its existence to a great extent to their time and openness.

Because of the Covid-19 crisis and other setbacks, it took me much longer than planned to complete this volume. But, as always, my family kept supporting me throughout the setbacks and lows that did occur during the process of doing this research. Whenever I came back from a visit to a PI, from digging around in the archives, or from study trips to far-off places, it was Roland and the children who brought me back to the here and now and stopped me from losing myself in all the compelling and intense life stories.

A Paradigm for Studying Extreme Belief and Behavior

Introduction to the Series

Purpose of the Series

This is the first volume in the Extreme Belief and Behavior Series. The purpose of the series is to defend, develop, and articulate a paradigm for studying extreme belief and behavior that has been insufficiently explored in the literature.

The paradigm is built on five hypotheses that together distinguish this series from other work on extreme belief and behavior:

1. *Normalcy hypothesis*: extreme believers and actors are usually psychologically and psychiatrically as normal/healthy and rational as nonextreme believers and actors.
2. *First-person approach*: to better define, analyze, understand, and explain extreme belief and behavior and the way they relate to one another, as well as to better predict and prevent such belief and behavior, we need to adopt not just a third-person approach—one in terms of, say, an analysis of economic, social, and other broad factors—but also a first-person approach; that is, we need to carefully listen to what extreme believers and actors themselves say about their beliefs, narratives, emotions, desires, and goals.
3. *Inherent normativity*: defining, conceptualizing, operationalizing, describing, understanding, explaining, predicting, and preventing extreme belief and behavior are all inherently normative endeavors that call for being explicit about the underlying moral and epistemic values and norms of the researchers in question and the positions they take, as well as dominant cultural and institutional norms and

various kinds of power structures, for instance, in counterterrorism measures.
4. *Cross-domain study*: we can better understand radical conspiracy theorizing, extremism, fanaticism, fundamentalism, and terrorism if we study them in relation to one another rather than in isolation.
5. *True interdisciplinarity*: we should study radical conspiracy theorizing, extremism, fanaticism, fundamentalism, and terrorism from a truly interdisciplinary perspective that encourages and facilitates conversation between different disciplines and methods.

That the series is built on these fives ideas does not mean they are taken for granted or are considered indubitable. Rather, they provide starting points. At the same time, they will be carefully reflected upon, adjusted, and fine-tuned as we move ahead.

Many readers will be familiar with the seminal five-volume *Fundamentalism Project*, edited by Martin E. Marty and R. Scott Appleby and published between 1991 and 1995. It brought together the very best and state-of-the-art empirical and historical work on fundamentalism in the early nineties. That collection inspired me to start this new series. Yet, this project is crucially different. It does not seek to bring together the best empirical and historical work on extreme belief and behavior per se. Rather, it aims to make progress on *how we should study* extreme belief and behavior by carefully laying out an insufficiently explored paradigm. It addresses deep underlying conceptual, epistemological, and ethical issues in relation to empirical issues regarding such things as describing and explaining extreme belief and behavior that influence how we approach them in the first place. I believe this is more welcome than ever. For even though we have been able to make progress in the study of extreme belief and behavior, several scholars, such as John Horgan, have suggested that a general explanation may not be possible at all (see Horgan 2014, 2024). Others have gone even further and have spoken of a "stagnation" in the field.[1] This series will explore whether articulating the five elements of a new paradigm can help in moving things ahead.

---

[1] Or at least, in certain subfields of the study of extreme belief and behavior. Thus, for instance, Sageman (2014) about terrorism studies.

This Volume

In this first volume in the series, historian and terrorism researcher Beatrice de Graaf looks beyond acts of terrorism and their consequences and explores how convicted terrorists narrate their extreme belief and behavior. To discover what terrorists believe and how those beliefs bring them to commit their deeds, she recorded the life stories of almost thirty convicted terrorists who were in prison over the past ten years. Most were Dutch detainees convicted for jihadist terrorism, but she also includes accounts by non-Western terrorists—Indonesian, Syrian, and Pakistani jihadists, and Boko Haram members in Cameroon—and Western right-wing extremists, who were all in prison over the past decade. First, De Graaf shows that while their stories are all unique, there is nonetheless one common denominator, which is a desire for significance and meaning in lives that are often lacking in prospects and fulfillment. Rather than focusing on orthodoxy (right belief), the detainees mostly speak about their lived *orthopraxis* (right practice)—which, De Graaf argues, does not mean that their beliefs are irrelevant. Second, the study combines a historical perspective with qualitative radicalization studies and concepts from the sociology of religion and social psychology—such as "the quest for significance" and "the redemptive self"—to identify and analyze how convicted terrorists developed narratives of radical personal redemption that combined ideology and praxis (the whole of actions and words), and how these were validated by a perceived group or support base or, instead, became contaminated in the course of time.

This monograph embodies the five core elements of the paradigm this series explores. First, it works from the assumption that the subjects in question are largely normal and rational humans with a certain degree of self-knowledge who acted for reasons. Second, and closely related to that, the book takes it that their behavior can be better understood by listening to them and reconstructing the narratives they share to interpret their lives. Third, De Graaf carefully reflects on her own positionality as a white, female, Christian scholar interviewing white extremists as well as white and colored Islamic subjects, most of whom were detained at the time of the interviews. Fourth, the volume integrates work on extremism and ideas from the literature on terrorism and on fundamentalism. Fifth and finally, it combines a more historical approach with life story interviews and uses theories and concepts from anthropology, history, philosophy, religious studies, social psychology, sociology, and theology.

What Is Extreme Belief and Behavior?

Before we consider each of the five hypotheses in more detail, a short word on what extreme belief and behavior are.

Let me emphasize that "extreme belief and behavior" is just shorthand for a wide variety of extreme phenomena as we find them in conspiracist, extremist, fanaticist, fundamentalist, and terrorist movements. In the *cognitive* realm, we find not only extreme beliefs but also such things as extreme mindsets, extreme cognitive character traits or vices—like dogmatism, narrow-mindedness, credulity, and black-and-white thinking (see Peels 2023b)—and various biases and thinking styles, such as evidential self-insulation (Cassam 2021b). In the *behavioral* realm, we find not only actions, such as violent protests and discrimination against homosexuals, but also omissions, such as opting out of democratic processes. And there are more realms than just the cognitive and behavioral ones.[2] There is, for instance, also the *affective* realm, in which we find extreme emotions like vengefulness and resentment, and there is the *conative* realm, which comprises extreme wishes, goals, and desires, such as the desire to purify one's nation from any nonwhite elements. Moreover, there are extreme *structures* and *symbols*, such as hierarchical and oppressive organization and appeal to infallible authority. A fully accurate title for the series would mention and include all such phenomena. Again, "extreme belief and behavior" is just shorthand for them.

The series will largely confine itself to extreme belief and behavior in the five kinds of phenomena I mentioned: conspiracy theorizing, extremism, fanaticism, fundamentalism, and terrorism.[3] Of course, extreme belief and behavior can be found far beyond these in phenomena that overlap with them—things such as cults, nationalist and traditionalist movements, and insurrections. The series largely confines itself to these five phenomena to limit the scope and bring focus to the debate. In addition, as we shall see throughout the series, despite crucial differences between them, many of the fundamental questions we can ask about them and the challenges we face in doing so are quite similar.[4]

---

[2] For more on these different realms and empirical support for the distinctions between them, see Kindermann et al. (forthcoming).

[3] There is no weight (comparative size, importance, etc.) attached to the order here; it is just alphabetical.

[4] Of course, some scholars already study some of these five phenomena in relation to others; for example, Van Prooijen et al. (2015) when it comes to radical conspiracy theorizing and extremism, and Cassam (2021b) when it comes to extremism, fanaticism, and fundamentalism.

What do I mean by "extreme belief and behavior"? Here are some examples of extreme belief: That there is only moral good and moral evil in the world, nothing in between. That climate change is a hoax invented for ideological or financial reasons. That the Bible (or another holy scripture) is literally and historically true and infallible in its entirety. That there is a divine law that must be obeyed by all and that should replace civil law. That white people are intellectually and morally superior to other races. That evolutionary theory and big bang cosmology are merely wild conjectures driven by atheistic ideological agendas. That the primary function of women is to produce offspring. That apostates ought to be stoned to death.

And here are some examples of extreme behavior: Violently storming the US Capitol on January 6, 2021. Abducting young school girls in northern Nigeria. Killing fifty-two people by suicide bombing in various London city buses on July 7, 2005. Refusing to talk to someone from a different faith. Maintaining racial segregation in public transport across the country. Pursuing moral purity at the cost of taking care of one's family. Forbidding the use of television and social media. Publicly portraying democrats as child-abusing Satanists. Refusing to pay taxes because one believes the secular modern state is the anti-Christ that should not be obeyed.

How should we conceptualize such extreme beliefs and behaviors, specifically as we find them in conspiracy theorizing, extremism, fanaticism, fundamentalism, and terrorism? In other words, exactly what makes them extreme? There are numerous options here. One might suggest that the extreme position and the extreme action are the statistically rare ones; that they are the positionally far-right and far-left ones; that they are the ones formed and done out of vices, such as arrogance, dogmatism, vengefulness, and narrow-mindedness; that they are the objectively (mind-independently) morally and epistemically defectives ones; that they are the ones that conflict with fundamental democratic values and liberal institutions, and so on.[5] Maybe these accounts can even be combined, or maybe one account can serve one purpose, whereas another one can serve another purpose. Here, I will not take a stance on this, since the issue of conceptualizing and operationalizing extreme belief and behavior is itself part and parcel of the project, addressed in detail in the second volume in the series. Using *extreme* as an umbrella term will do for the purposes of this introduction.

---

[5] For some of these options, see Cassam (2021b).

The Normalcy Hypothesis

In the 1980s, explanations of extreme belief and behavior as found, for instance, in terrorism in terms of neuropsychological deficiencies and psychiatric disorders were quite popular among academics. In fact, some of these kinds of explanations can still be found in the literature. Adam Lankford (2013), for instance, claims that people turn to terrorism because they suffer from psychological trauma.

Such psychopathological explanations have come under severe criticism, among others by John Horgan (2003, 2014) and Gaby Thijssen (Thijssen et al. 2023), especially for the lack of empirical adequacy and predictive power. Moreover, many scholars now stress that fundamentalists and terrorists act in various senses perfectly *rationally*; it would not do justice to their rational agency to pathologize them (Baurmann 2007; Crenshaw 2011; Horgan 2014; Sageman 2004, 2014). This is because there is not only *objective* rationality—believing in accordance with the publicly available evidence—but also *subjective* rationality, which has to do with what is rational given the evidence available to a subject, where the exclusion and manipulation of evidence in the course of time may have a substantial influence on that (diachronic rather than synchronic rationality). Fake news, indoctrination, manipulation, epistemic bubbles, and echo chambers are core notions nowadays in epistemology, which increasingly pays attention to how the nonideal circumstances in which people live influence what they believe and know or fail to know (so-called nonideal epistemology).[6]

This series, therefore, builds upon the idea—now pretty widely accepted among academics—that extreme believers and actors are usually relatively healthy and rational people, an idea often referred to as the *normality hypothesis* or *normalcy hypothesis* (e.g., Dawson 2019). This is not to say that some or many of their beliefs are not problematic: they may well be—and in some cases clearly are—false, unwarranted, and irrational in several senses. Some or many of the extreme actions may well be unjustified or even deeply immoral. We study extreme belief and behavior, after all, because we believe much of it is detrimental to the flourishing of our societies, their democratic institutions, and the social cohesion between various groups, and that is why we want to understand, explain, and prevent it. Of course, many extreme believers and extreme actors suffer from psychopathology—as numerous

---

[6] For an introduction to nonideal epistemology, see McKenna (2023).

people who are clearly in no way extreme believers or extreme actors also do—and in some cases, such pathology may even figure in an explanation of their beliefs and behavior. But all that is perfectly compatible with the idea that extreme believers and actors are generally not much more likely to suffer from psychiatric diseases or to be deeply irrational; that they are in many regards much more normal than we would, perhaps, expect them to be; and that a general psychopathological explanation for extreme belief and behavior does not work.[7]

A First-Person Approach

Third-person approaches to extreme belief and behavior have been common in the literature since the onset of academic terrorism and radicalization research in the 1960s and 1970s. By *third-person approaches*, I mean approaches from a perspective external to the extreme believer and actor themself, particularly at a macrolevel. These are explanations in terms of economic circumstances, social factors, and political developments. Manni Crone (2016), for instance, has argued that most terrorists have a criminal background. The failure of various attempts after 9/11 to explain violent extremism in terms of ideology (religion, or Islam specifically) have made such third-person approaches even more prominent, as Dawson (2021a) points out.

Yet, such explanations pay little attention to motivational agency, that is, to the beliefs, narratives, personal reasons, religiosity, and other subjectivities of those engaged in extreme actions (see Jackson 2015). A minority of researchers—such as Lorne Dawson, Beatrice de Graaf, John Horgan, Ayhan Kaya, and Kees van den Bos—have, therefore, begun to develop a somewhat different approach. They believe any fuller explanation of extreme belief and behavior will also have to incorporate, say, the extremist's own reasons, beliefs, narratives, and religiosity. They argue that in qualitative, quantitative, historical, and theoretical research on these phenomena, this first-person perspective ought to be taken seriously. They also take it that there are further reasons for doing so: among other things, how people experience and interpret what goes on in their world can yield an important basis

---

[7] For a nuanced approach to this issue and a historical overview of how the debate on this developed, see Emily Corner's contribution to volume 3 in this series.

on which to analyze what happens when people radicalize and what can be done in terms of prevention and deradicalization.

This trend toward the first-person perspective bases its ideas on already-existing data, such as first-hand accounts in biographies and autobiographies, but also on new data that have often been collected with an eye to this new approach, particularly in interviews and in ethnographic studies (e.g., De Graaf 2021; Harambam 2020). Of course, this trend takes it that third-person sociopolitical and socioeconomic elements *also* factor into a proper explanation. But these authors suggest the first-person perspective approach to extreme belief and behavior has not yet been sufficiently developed—we need a more articulated first-person approach and a synthesis of first- and third-person perspective explanations.[8]

The first-person approach has had some early defendants. Russell Hardin (2002), for instance, argued that extremists have a crippled epistemology, that is, a set of misleading ideas about how to acquire knowledge about themselves and the world. And in earlier decades, historians such as Martha Crenshaw and Bruce Hoffman, pioneers in modern, academic terrorism scholarship, published qualitative accounts of terrorist biographies, albeit not in a systematic fashion.

Only over the last few years, though, has a systematic application of the first-person perspective truly gained a foothold. Due to its variation in topic—extremism, conspiracism, terrorism—and disciplinary background—law, sociology, psychology, and so forth—it takes many different shapes. Quassim Cassam (2018, 2021b) has argued extremists' beliefs crucially factor into any viable explanation of extremism, and I have argued the same holds for the role of beliefs in explaining fundamentalism and radicalization toward extremism (Peels 2020, 2023c; Peels and Kindermann 2022). Lorne Dawson has defended the view that academics in these fields have wrongly neglected the explanatory power of individuals' religiosity (Dawson 2021a, 2021b). Michael Baurmann has argued we should understand fundamentalists' beliefs and preferences in order to explain and potentially even predict their behavior (Baurmann 2007; Baurmann et al. 2018). Mark Juergensmeyer (2017) has interviewed terrorists from many different religions and explained in detail why and how we should enter terrorists' minds (Sheikh and Juergensmeyer 2019). Arie Kruglanski has defended across a wide variety of extremisms that we

---

[8] Thus also De Graaf and Van den Bos (2021).

should take motivations for extremism seriously (Kruglanski et al. 2021). Kees van den Bos (2018) has defended the view that a crucial explanatory factor for radicalization consists of (ultimately subjective) perceptions of and judgments about unfair treatment, deprivation, and immorality. And Beatrice de Graaf has interviewed a significant number of terrorists and developed a radical redemption model—the triptych of the radical redemption narrative—in which their beliefs, reasons, narratives, and orthopraxis play a crucial role. This model is carefully laid out and defended in the volume at hand.[9]

The philosophical and anthropological idea underlying the first-person approach is that humans are moral and epistemic agents with a certain degree of insight into their own beliefs, reasons, motivations, intentions, and purposes, despite their cognitive limitations, their fallibility, and their occasional dishonesty and self-deception. Humans are not merely toys of economic, social, political, and other macrolevel factors—they are beings with reason, a degree of free will, the ability to deliberate, and the possibility of self-knowledge, beings who act for reasons and exercise influence in the world. To fully understand and explain extreme belief and behavior, then, we cannot appeal merely to factors beyond them; we need to involve factors that matter from the perspective of extreme believers and actors themselves.

This turn toward the first-person perspective requires exchange among its proponents and between proponents and critics. Conversation with those who are critical of it is needed, because we can all learn from their hesitations and criticisms. But we also need a conversation among its proponents, because this approach is not without its challenges. Apart from practical challenges, such as how to get ethics committees to accept such research and how to safely do such fieldwork, there are deep content-related challenges. Let me mention five of them here.

(1) Respondents and subjects' reports on beliefs and narratives are no guarantee that those are indeed the beliefs and narratives that explain their actions (the same holds for their affections), as has been pointed out (e.g., Cassam 2021a; Dawson 2019). And although there

---

[9] In her model, De Graaf adds a fourth R (radical redemption) to the three Rs of Louise Richardson's influential approach in terms of revenge, renown, and reaction (see Richardson 2006). See also De Graaf and Van den Bos (2021) and De Graaf (2021) for a Dutch presentation of the main results and the radical redemption model.

are methods for triangulation, they go only so far. The issue of whether self-reported beliefs and other self-reported states can truly figure in an explanation of extreme actions also raises important methodological, ethical, and philosophical questions about the extent and limits of first-person authority in social epistemology, about self-knowledge, about reliability and validity, and about the relation between belief and action as explored in the philosophy of action and experimental social psychology.

(2) Even if one agrees the first-person perspective is relevant, there can be disagreement on exactly which first-person factors are relevant. Some, for instance, explicitly discard ideology and various extreme beliefs as explanatorily irrelevant (e.g., McCauley and Moskalenko 2017a, 279–80). How important are cognitive factors (beliefs, ideology, etc.) in comparison with affective factors (emotions)? How can we move forward here?

(3) Crucial concepts for first-person perspectives, such as belief, rationality, and religiosity, are used in many different senses and are hard to conceptualize and operationalize: Do we focus on the religious community, on dogma, doctrine, and other teachings, on the "image of God," on the "mindset" of the pious, on extreme religious behavior, on extreme religious ideas, or on yet something else?

(4) It is clear that the importance of the first-person perspective does not make the third-person perspective irrelevant, but it is less clear how they are to be integrated with one another. For instance, Clark McCauley and Sophia Moskalenko have argued that people radicalize because of a whole host of factors identified by social-psychological theory, such as group grievance, status, and intergroup competition, but they also acknowledge elements that from a first-person point of view are explanatorily relevant, such as radical intentions and emotions (McCauley 2012; McCauley and Moskalenko 2017a). How can these two kinds of explanations be synthesized?

(5) Finally, some have questioned whether it is ethically desirable or even permissible to try to understand, say, terrorists from the inside, since it seems to require some sort of *Verstehen* or even empathy toward terrorists (Morton 2011; Dershowitz 2002), and some consider it contaminating, as Stampnitzky (2013, 189) points out.

Inherent Normativity

The third core idea in the series is that the study of these five phenomena is inherently normative: it cannot be a purely descriptive matter. By the *study* I mean how, for instance, violent extremism is defined, conceptualized, modeled, mapped, operationalized, described, qualitatively and quantitatively studied, understood, explained, and predicted. More specifically, we cannot do so without assuming certain moral and epistemic values and norms—not just those we generally need in science (coherence, simplicity, explanatory power, etc.) but ones specific to debates on extreme belief and behavior. Let me illustrate this by way of three examples.

First, a debate rages on whether we should even use a term like *fundamentalism*. It has been claimed that it wrongly lumps together phenomena that have little or even nothing in common, that it is too strongly tied to Christian tropes and too Western anyway, that it is offensive to people and easily induces labeling them as extreme or irrational, that it leads to delegitimating the other, and that it is merely a political tool that exemplifies political biases.[10] Some have suggested alternatives to the word *fundamentalism*, such as *conservatism*, *maximalism*, *sectarianism*, and *exclusivism*, but others have argued these are not academically more fruitful and face problems of their own. In any case, it should be clear that both the choice to use the word and the choice not to use it are inevitably intertwined with moral and political values and positions (for more on this, see Peels 2024). The ways in which such terms can be morally and politically laden have already received much attention in other fields, such as feminist epistemology and philosophy of science (see, e.g., Haraway 1988; Harding 1991).

The second example of inevitable normativity concerns extremism, not so much the use of the word as its conceptualization. It is not uncommon to define *extremism* in terms of a position to the political far right or the political far left, statistical rareness, overall societal disapproval, or uncommon/extreme methods. Yet, on such definitions, extremism may rule in not only the beliefs and actions of people like Timothy McVeigh and organizations like the German Red Army Faction (RAF) and the Irish Republican Army (IRA), to mention just a couple of extremist movements, but equally those of Martin

---

[10] For some of these criticisms, see Wood and Watt (2014), specifically the chapters by Simon A. Wood and Khalid Yahya Blankinship.

Luther King Jr., Nelson Mandela, and Extinction Rebellion. This is problematic, for while the latter three might be considered *extreme*, they would be widely considered not to be *extremist*. Rather, civil rights movements are considered to be protest movements, consisting maybe of radicals with extreme views but not of people who have radicalized or people who are extremists. How, then, to properly distinguish the two? One response is that extremism is always relative to a certain set of values and principles. Thus, Martin Luther King Jr. was an extremist *for many Americans* in the 1960s, but presumably not for the readers of this volume. Many who claim that extremism is a social construction seem to prefer this route. Those who feel uneasy about such a response may suggest we should build in normative elements into our definition and conceptualization of extremism, things such as unwarranted preoccupations with one's people, nation, or blood, or things like irrationality or moral and cognitive characteristic traits. An example of such an approach is Cassam's account of extremism (2021b). My point here is that no matter which route we prefer, how we understand extremism is inevitably a normative issue. On the one hand, one could refer to a particular group and designate something as extremist relative to that group—which, of course, raises the question of how we decide on which group is relevant: the majority, society at large, the Western world, the democratic world? On the other hand, one could appeal to norms and values that one takes to be more objective, both epistemic (rationality, open-mindedness, etc.) and moral ones (willingness to compromise, autonomy, freedom, mutual respect, etc.). Of course, this makes a difference to what we classify as extremist and what not—thus, the scope of extremism—and also to how we study it, for instance, as something that is inherently cognitively detrimental or not.

A third example of how the study of extreme belief and behavior is inevitably a normative matter concerns belief in conspiracy theories or, more generally, conspiracy theorizing. There are two main views in the theoretical literature on conspiracy theory belief. According to a view called *generalism*, there is something inherently problematic about belief in conspiracy theories in general, so that we can ascribe a low prior probability to any conspiracy theory simply by virtue of its being a conspiracy theory, while *particularism* says that each particular conspiracy theory ought to be treated on its own evidential merits, and that we cannot assume a low prior probability just by virtue of the fact that something is a conspiracy theory.[11] I think Patrick Stokes (2018, 25) rightly says that particularism is now the consensus in the

---

[11] The distinction was first made by Buenting and Taylor (2010).

literature, defended by such leading figures as Charles Pigden (1995) and M R. X. Dentith (2014). Yet recently, there have been some notable exceptions (Cassam 2019; Harris 2018; Napolitano 2021). Clearly, this makes a crucial difference not only to the scope of conspiracy theory beliefs one studies but also to *how* one studies them—for instance, whether one starts from a general suspicion toward conspiracy theorizing or not, as Dentith (2023) points out.

That these debates are inherently normative does not mean that, say, extremist or conspiracist movements cannot be accurately described or explained, or that one description or explanation would not be better than another. Rather, the point is that we can do these things only from background assumptions about values and norms. It is therefore pivotal that existing empirical work on extreme belief and behavior is brought into conversation with normative approaches—theories, models, arguments, concepts, distinctions, tools—from such philosophical fields as ethics, philosophy of science, and (social) epistemology, as well as from fields like cultural studies and anthropology that have done theoretical work on positionality. We can make progress if in this way we systematically reflect on and explicate how various norms and values play a role in our research and how potential biases that come with them can be countered—needless to say, all of this in continuous interaction with empirical and historical work on extreme belief and behavior.

Cross-Domain Study

The seven volumes in this series will all explore extreme belief and behavior as found in five partially overlapping domains: conspiracy theorizing, extremism, fanaticism, fundamentalism, and terrorism. Obviously, each of these five notions is conceptually complex, and each definition of them will likely prove controversial. In fact, getting a firmer conceptual grip on them and exploring ways to move forward when scholars firmly disagree on how to conceptualize them are part and parcel of this series—it is actually the primary purpose of the second volume. Let me give some provisional definitions, though, to give the reader a rough idea of what I have in mind with each of these five phenomena. *Fanaticism* can be defined as the identity-defining, wholehearted affective devotion to an absolute value that motivates uncompromising action.[12] *Fundamentalism* can be defined as a response to modern developments, such as liberal ethics, evolutionary theory, and

---

[12] See, for instance, the work of Paul Katsafanas, e.g., Katsafanas (2019), and the work of Ruth Tietjen, e.g., Tietjen (2021).

historical-biblical criticism, which seeks certainty by reading holy texts literally and by formulating fundamentals; maintains clear in-group and out-group distinctions; desires to return to an alleged previous ideal state; and maintains a strongly morally dualistic picture of the world (see, for instance, the work of Martin Marty and Scott Appleby). *Extremism* is the belief that one's in-group can never be healthy or successful unless it is engaged in hostile action against an out-group, as well as one's actions based on that belief (see, e.g., Berger 2018). *Belief in conspiracy theories* can be defined as belief in a secret arrangement between two or more actors to usurp political or economic power, violate established rights, hoard vital secrets, or unlawfully alter government institutions (see, e.g., Uscinski and Parent 2014). And *terrorism* can be defined as the use of violence or the threat thereof to further some political, social, religious, or other ideological aspiration (see the work of John Horgan).

If this series had been published ten years ago, people might have wondered why conspiracy theorizing is on this list. However, over the last few years, particularly since the Covid-19 crisis, conspiracy theorizing has taken center stage in the academic study of extreme belief and behavior. In fact, we nowadays see much overlap between conspiracy theorizing and various branches of extremism, even to such an extent that many government agencies and practitioners are concerned with both—think of the role of QAnon supporters in the insurrection at the Capitol on January 6, 2021. Research suggests political extremism is positively associated with a tendency toward conspiracy theory beliefs, the hypothesis being that there is an underlying thinking style that seeks to make sense of societal events (Van Prooijen et al. 2015). Moreover, in academic work on conspiracy theorizing we equally see the elements of a new paradigm, such as the idea that we can only properly understand and explain conspiracy theorizing if we do extensive ethnographic work and listen to what conspiracy theorizers themselves have got to say (Harambam 2020); the idea that conspiracy theory belief should not be understood as a delusion (Bortolotti et al. 2021); the idea that belief in conspiracy theories can be perfectly *rational* in various senses of the word, even to such an extent that we should reject the principle of guilty until proven innocent for conspiracy theories (Dentith 2014); and the idea that the study of conspiracy theory belief is inherently and deeply normative (Peels et al. 2023).

Such cross-domain study is important, for many of the deeper questions about the five phenomena of conspiracy theorizing, extremism, fanaticism, fundamentalism, and terrorism bear important similarities. Take the issue of how to define, conceptualize, and operationalize these notions. Similar questions pop up here: Should we use a stipulative definition, should we employ an exemplary definition, is a definition in terms of necessary and sufficient conditions possible, or should we opt for a family resemblance analysis? Can we define these phenomena in a more or less neutral fashion, or are they inherently normative—and if so, what should we do with that, particularly when it comes to operationalizing these notions? Each of the terms has a troubled history, and they have all been abused for various political purposes. Can we still use them in the face of knowledge of that history? Can and should we conceptually re-engineer them?

Or take the issue of explanation. What is it to *explain* extreme behavior? Does our ability to explain it entail that we can to some extent predict it? What is the relative weight of macro-, meso-, and microlevel factors in explanations of extreme behavior? What semantics should we use for explanations? And when we speak about triggers, causes, reasons, mechanisms, factors, drivers, enabling conditions, preconditions, motives, pathways, indicators, precipitants, accelerators, bases, determinants, and other things, what does each of these notions stand for, and how do they relate to one another?[13]

The trend toward the first-person perspective and the frame of the extreme actor as a normal, healthy, rational person with problematic behavior can be perceived in research in the fields of fanaticism, terrorism, extremism, fundamentalism, radicalism, and conspiracism studies. But the authors of such research are often in different disciplines and frequently publish in different journals, employing distinct methods and using other perspectives. Awareness of this development is, therefore, limited. The purpose of this book series is to bring these divergent analyses into dialogue, explore the strengths and weaknesses of this trend, and further develop it into a full-fledged paradigm—not one that is meant as a rival to third-person approaches, but one that has been insufficiently explored so far and that can be *combined with* third-person approaches.

---

[13] For an early exploration of these issues, see Peels (2023c). I will not try to be exhaustive here, but further clusters of questions that are similar across the five domains concern responsibility for extreme belief and behavior, the relation between individual extreme belief and behavior and that of the group, subjectivity in the extreme believer and actor on the one hand and subjectivity in the scholar on the other, as well as the interaction between these two, and resilience toward extreme belief and behavior.

True Interdisciplinarity

The final core idea of the series is that we need various academic disciplines to study, understand, and explain extreme belief and behavior. If we confine ourselves to, say, social psychology or religious studies, we will miss out on crucial factors. Among the disciplines relevant to the study of extreme belief and behavior are anthropology, communication and media studies, criminology, cultural studies, economics, history, international relations, law, philosophy, clinical and social psychology, sociology, political science, religious studies, psychiatry, and theology and divinity.[14]

I think it is worthwhile to add true interdisciplinarity as a separate pillar, since the diversity in terms of domains—conspiracy theorizing, extremism, fanaticism, fundamentalism, and terrorism—does not guarantee disciplinary or methodological diversity. Social psychology, for example, can and indeed does study each of these five domains.

One reason to think we need each of these disciplines is the growing consensus that any viable explanation of, say, extremism and terrorism is going to be multilevel: it will comprise macrofactors, such as social, economic, and political developments; mesofactors, such as group identity; and microfactors, such as individual grievances and personal religiosity. Of course, it is in theory possible for a single discipline to study phenomena at all three levels, but we will see that to make sense of those phenomena at multiple levels, we usually need numerous disciplines and numerous methods. Some have pointed out that any viable account will be multilevel (Borum 2011, 8; Horgan 2008, 2014). In the literature, we find various explanations that aim to provide such a multilevel account. Gabriel Almond, Scott Appleby, and Emmanuel Sivan, for instance, already argued that a particular fundamentalist movement's shape and form is explained by three kinds of factors: structural factors, like war, conflict with other religions, and secularization; contingent chance factors, like the death of a leader; and more personal factors, like specific individual decisions (Almond et al. 2003, 116–44). They call this approach the *structure-chance-choice framework*. Clark McCauley and Sophia Moskalenko (2017a) provide an account of radicalization into extremism in terms of factors on a macro- or mesolevel—things like intergroup competition and group isolation—but equally in

---

[14] Further disciplines may be relevant more indirectly, fields such as education theory, linguistics, literary studies, and public administration studies.

terms of microfactors, such as love, risk, and status. James Khalil and Lorne Dawson (2023), using the Attitudes-Behaviors Corrective (ABC) model (see Khalil et al. 2022), argue that any viable explanation of ideologically justified violence will synthesize rational choice explanations, social identity explanations, and ideological explanations (cf. Dawson 2017, 39).

Now, clearly, none of the academic fields I distinguished is all by itself sufficiently equipped to address each of these levels—if only because one needs radically different methods to come to anything close to comprehensiveness: quantitative methods from economics, surveys, field experiments, lab experiments, interviews; theological methods like hermeneutics; and philosophical methods like conceptual analysis and reflective equilibrium. The search for a single-factor explanation—for example, the psychological profile of the terrorist—is in all likelihood futile. We can only understand, explain, and prevent extreme belief and behavior if we study them from the different perspectives of these disciplines, using the different methods, and then explore how they can be synthesized.

I said the fifth core idea is not just interdisciplinarity but *true* interdisciplinarity. Interdisciplinarity in the sense of doing interdisciplinary work, rather than talking about it, is already difficult enough—should we do even more? I believe the answer is affirmative. What I mean by *true interdisciplinarity* is threefold. First, it means that in studying extreme belief and behavior, scholars from various fields bring not only their results to the table in order to discuss them with scholars from other fields but also their methods, their background theories, their assumptions, their disciplinary positionality, their models, and sometimes even their paradigms. True interdisciplinarity not just engages findings—sometimes, these simply conflict, and then what do we do?—but also digs deeper by exploring the factors that led to these findings and how they are interpreted in the first place.

Second, true interdisciplinarity does not simply carve up the cake of research into pieces that are each to be taken care of by scholars from a single discipline. That would be *multi*disciplinarity rather than true *inter*disciplinarity. Rather, some pieces of the cake are taken care of by scholars from different disciplines, often using different methods. To give just two examples from this series: the issue of how to operationalize normative notions in the study of extremism, such as cognitive vice, will be addressed jointly by an economist and a philosopher; and a matrix to build conceptualizations of fundamentalism will be construed by two philosophers and a scholar in the psychology of religion.

Third, true interdisciplinarity seeks integration of the results. For example, if poverty and lack of access to resources are more prevalent among right-wing violent extremists in a particular country, and so are psychopathology (e.g., depression) and religious narratives in terms of revenge and redemption, how are those to be synthesized? Is, for instance, economic poverty a dependent variable here, on which psychopathology and religion operate as moderators? I realize that in pursuing true interdisciplinarity, the bar is put pretty high—but I believe in the long run it will be the only way to make true progress.

Structure

Finally, let me sketch the road ahead by describing how the series is structured. It consists of five edited volumes (volumes 2, 3, 4, 5, and 6 in the series) and two monographs (volumes 1 and 7). The five edited volumes tackle five issues that are central to the new paradigm: conceptual mapping (edited by myself and John Horgan); explanations (edited by myself and Lorne Dawson); responsibility (edited by myself, Naomi Kloosterboer, and Chris Ranalli); subjectivity (edited by myself and Quassim Cassam); and resilience (edited by myself, Michele Grossman, and Elanie Rodermond). The two monographs show how the new paradigm works by applying it to radical redemption narratives (the book at hand, by Beatrice de Graaf) and by exploring in more philosophical and interdisciplinary depth the theoretical challenges the new paradigm faces and the opportunities it provides (volume 7, by myself). Since I've already introduced the volume at hand—the first volume in the series—let us directly go to the second volume.

Conceptualizing Extreme Beliefs and Behaviors: Definitions and Relations. This second volume is fully devoted to exploring challenging conceptual issues in defining, analyzing, and operationalizing notions such as extremism, radicalization, fanaticism, and terrorism. The focus is theoretical, but the work is firmly empirically embedded. It explores the following four crucial questions about extremism, fundamentalism, fanaticism, conspiracy theorizing, and terrorism: (1) How can each of these extreme phenomena be defined in a fruitful manner, and what are the desiderata in seeking definitions of each of them? (2) How should the project of defining and conceptualizing these phenomena be undertaken—in terms of necessary and sufficient conditions, family resemblances, or INUS conditions,[15] and based

---

[15] "INUS" stands for an insufficient but necessary part of an unnecessary but sufficient condition.

on data sets, intuitions about particular cases, common understandings in the public debate, or yet something else? (3) What is the role of normativity in defining these extreme phenomena—in other words, what is the proper place of normative or even pejorative concepts and the normative framework of the researcher? (4) And how do the phenomena of extremism, fanaticism, fundamentalism, terrorism, and conspiracism relate to one another and to things such as apocalypticism, nationalism, cults, charisma, and state terror? This volume lays the conceptual groundwork that the other volumes in the series will build on.

Explaining Extreme Beliefs and Behaviors: Theoretical, Methodological, and Ethical Challenges. This edited volume takes a step back from the many specific explanations we find in the literature of extreme belief and behavior as found in such phenomena as conspiracy theorizing, extremism, fanaticism, fundamentalism, and terrorism. It explores the very project of explaining these phenomena. The first part of the volume concerns various fundamental theoretical and contextual issues. What is the relationship between understanding and explaining extremism? What is it about extreme beliefs that challenges our capacity to explain them? What are the pitfalls of current approaches, and why are explanations so urgently needed?

The second part then moves on to explore related methodological issues. What does providing an explanation entail? What are the desiderata for viable explanations—qualitative and quantitative data, macro-, meso-, and microlevels of analysis, first-person and third-person accounts, attitudes and behaviors, or beliefs and actions? The third part explores related empirical issues and challenges. How should we conceive and integrate insights into such related phenomena as the turn to extremism in a particular context (e.g., a country or historical circumstance, such as a conflict), the rise of extremist movements, and the turn to extremism by individuals? What conceptual, theoretical, and methodological resources are available or can be created?

Responsibility for Extreme Beliefs. This edited volume explores various issues in the relations between extreme beliefs and extreme behavior on the one hand, and responsibility on the other. The first part concerns the issue of who is responsible: Should we target the individual, the community, or none—that is, are structural factors to blame? To what extent does one manifest one's epistemic or moral agency in forming or keeping extreme beliefs? What role do group dynamics play? Which environments foster extreme beliefs and behavior?

The second part concerns what kind of responsibility is at issue. For instance, how do legal, moral, and epistemic responsibility relate to each other with respect to extreme beliefs? To what extent is responsibility for extreme belief and extreme behavior relative to culture and time? The third part concerns when responsibility attributions are appropriate and when not. What are excusing or exculpating conditions of individual or group responsibility for extreme belief? How does epistemic agency depend on cognitive and affective capacities, (self-)knowledge and (self-)ignorance, and intellectual self-trust, self-esteem, and self-respect? How should we understand indoctrination, and how much room does it leave for responsibility? Can peer pressure or group ignorance excuse? Do circumstantial factors excuse, such as being in an epistemic bubble or echo chamber, or living in a society dealing with fake news, propaganda, censorship, polarization, suppression, or war? And which conditions are particularly salient for, say, conspiracy theorizing or fundamentalism?

Extremism and Subjectivity. This edited volume zooms in on the subjectivity of individual extremists, conspiracy thinkers, fundamentalists, terrorists, and fanatics, as well as on the subjectivity of academics studying these groups, security practitioners, and policymakers. *Subjectivity* is a widely used but poorly understood notion in the literature, so this volume aims to get a firmer grip on it. Among other things, it answers such questions as the following: What constitutes a person's subjectivity? Why is it theoretically and practically important to engage with the subjectivity of extremists? What is the role of their affections, passions, and beliefs in causing and sustaining their extremism? How should we construe religiosity, and what work can it do as an explanatory factor for extreme beliefs and extreme behavior? What role do cognitive and moral virtues and vices play in a person's subjectivity, and how do these notions help us to understand, say, fundamentalism and terrorism? Finally, which senses of *rationality, justification, reasonableness*, and similar terms can be applied to individual extremists and groups of extremists and conspiracy thinkers, and what does that mean for studying their subjectivity?

Resilience to Extreme Beliefs and to Extreme Behavior. An important idea in the literature on prevention is that we should aim to make communities and individuals resilient toward extreme beliefs and extreme behavior. But what exactly does that amount to—how should we conceptualize resilience? What role do cultural, political, and economic factors play in resilience, and how do they relate to beliefs and character traits of individuals who constitute the community? Is resilience compatible with the radicalization of some members in a community? How do moral, political, and religious resilience relate to one another? Can resilience be operationalized and measured? How does it relate to deradicalization? Are there specific best practices for building resilience toward, say, right-wing extremism and jihadist Salafism that can be implemented elsewhere? What is the role of education in creating resilience?

Synthesizing First- and Third-Person Perspectives on Extreme Belief and Extreme Behavior (provisional title). This monograph draws various threads of the series together and focuses on synthesizing first- and third-person explanations of extreme belief and extreme behavior as found in extremism, fanaticism, fundamentalism, conspiracism, and terrorism. It uses several notions from the existing empirical literature, such as orthopraxis and religiosity, but also philosophical concepts that have not yet been employed in the empirical literature on extreme belief and extreme behavior (such as Lisa Bortolotti's concept of epistemic innocence) to show how third-person approaches, in terms of social, political, cultural, and economic factors, can be combined with first-person approaches in terms of the subject's beliefs, reasons, and narratives. In doing so, this volume will shed light on how understanding and explaining extremism, fundamentalism, and the like relate to one another. Finally, it reflects on various normative issues that come with first-person explanations, third-person explanations, understanding, and explaining (such as the positionality of the researcher), and on epistemic and moral challenges regarding the empathy required for understanding.

The seven volumes are related to one another as follows. This first volume provides relevant empirical data and a model that illustrates the paradigm articulated in the series. The second volume provides the conceptual groundwork for the other volumes. The third volume, building on the theoretical and empirical groundwork in volumes 1 and 2, then moves on to explore explanations of extremism, fundamentalism, and so forth. The fourth volume uses the theoretical insights from volumes 1–3 and the empirical insights from volumes 1 and 3 in moving from the descriptive to the normative. It tackles various issues regarding responsibility for extreme beliefs and extreme behavior. Volumes 5 and 6 take up these responsibility-related issues by zooming in on the subjectivity of extreme believers and extreme actors (volume 5) and exploring how individuals and communities can take responsibility for their beliefs and actions by becoming more resilient (volume 6). Volume 7 synthesizes first- and third-person explanations and, in doing so, sheds light on the relation between understanding and explaining extreme beliefs and extreme behavior.

Of course, the five core ideas are not set in stone: they are tentative, and the underlying research is still ongoing.[16] I hope the series will encourage rigorous empirical, historical, and theoretical inquiry, research that flows from fruitful interaction across disciplines and domains that all concern extreme belief and behavior, and work that takes extreme believers and actors seriously in order to better understand extreme belief and behavior and to make our democracies more resilient.

Rik Peels
Amsterdam, January 2024

[16] For their helpful comments on this introduction to the series, I thank Beatrice de Graaf, John Horgan, and the members of my Extreme Beliefs research group, in particular Allan de Novaes, Julia Duetz, Scott Gustafson, Joe Jaspers, Wilma Kannegieter, Nora Kindermann, Naomi Kloosterboer, Clyde Missier, Chris Ranalli, Ruth Tietjen, and Theo van Willigenburg. Work on this introduction, book, and series was made possible by the project Extreme Beliefs: The Epistemology and Ethics of Fundamentalism, which has received funding from the European Research Council (ERC) under the European Union's Horizon 2020 research and innovation program (grant agreement no. 851613) and from the Vrije Universiteit Amsterdam, the Netherlands.

1
Terrorists and Their Beliefs

A Place in Paradise

One day late 2012, ten young men from Delft, the Netherlands, did not appear in the square where they usually hung out; they had left for Syria. They were part of a group known as the Paradise Gate Boys, after the eponymous shopping mall in Delft where they would often meet. There were some fifty youths in the group, with an average age of 16 years. They were of Moroccan origin and had grown up in the Gillis neighborhood of the city. Some had criminal records, often for drug dealing. City councillor Abdel Maanaoui, who knew many of the boys and their families, said he was dumbfounded. Things had seemed to be going better for them: they were less restless and less recalcitrant toward their parents and the authorities. "When they started showing a fervent interest in Islam, we thought, That's fine, they're taking life more seriously," said Maanaoui.[1] No one predicted that it would be the first step toward joining the terrorist conflict in Syria and Iraq (Kouwenhoven 2014).

The boys were bound together by their shared experiences of clashes with the city authorities and failed work placements. But what really sparked their radicalization was a drama in December 2010 that affected all of them. One of the boys, "Mo," robbed a supermarket in the nearby village of Moerkapelle, together with two friends. They were caught in the act and, after grappling with a supermarket employee, Mo fell from a stepladder and broke his neck. He died of his injuries the same evening. "Many of the young men suddenly realized that they would never get to paradise if they went on living as they did," said Maanaoui. "Then they thought, If we're going to die, let it be on the path of jihad and not as shoplifters." The group members, who had not before been regular visitors to the mosque or noted for their devout behavior, began to dedicate themselves to Islamic faith. They sought answers from increasingly radical preachers, first at the As-Soennah Mosque in The Hague, where Imam Fawaz Jneid was still preaching, and then from Mohamed Talbi

---

[1] All translations of non-English material are my own unless indicated otherwise.

at the Al-Qibla Mosque in Zoetermeer. Radical activists from a group known as Straat Dawah and Behind Bars encouraged them to set out on the path of jihad.[2]

At the end of 2012, Mourad Massali left the Netherlands to join Jabhat al-Nusra, a jihadist organization in Syria allied to Al Qaeda. Nine of his friends followed him. They threw themselves into the fight with full gusto, proud to be a group of friends taking part in the jihad, "by the grace of Allah." In the course of 2013, first Mourad, then Choukrie Massali, Soufian El Fassi, and Abu Jandal lost their lives in the "blessed land" where, as martyrs, they hoped to reach the real paradise.

In this chapter, I introduce my approach to the religious beliefs of terrorists and explain how I arrived at my research question concerning the role of the narrative of redemption in someone's radicalization into violent jihadism and terrorism. My basic argument is that in order to understand what drove so many young men and women, including the ones just mentioned, to become jihadist terrorists, we need to take their religious beliefs seriously. That is no easy task in itself, given all the atrocities committed by terrorist organizations in Syria and Iraq, with Islamic State (IS) at the forefront. Being able and willing to understand transcendental religious motives is a challenge for people with a secularized background whose lives are not structured around such beliefs. And it is perhaps even more difficult for those who are religious—including members of the Islamic religious communities from which the ten young men from Delft came—but for whom the core of their belief lies in the conviction that God is full of love and abhors evil.

Religion as Moderator

Importantly, the causes of terrorism are extremely complex, and it is very hard, if not impossible, to generalize them and put them into simple radicalization charts (Schmid 2013). Terrorism should be studied in the context of time and space, and not be reduced to a single causal pathway (Crenshaw 1995). Moreover, many so-called root causes, such as poverty, inequality, discrimination, or war experiences, are not predictive on their own; as such, they do not suffice for a person to radicalize. In this book, therefore,

---

[2] This group of young Salafist men called itself Straat Dawah when they went out onto the streets to convert people, and Behind Bars when they protested to demand the release of detained jihadists. See Sterkenburg (2014).

I do not aim to delineate an overarching theory or model of radicalization that explains all. Instead, my aims are necessarily more modest: I will start with the empirical evidence that some individuals do radicalize, become extremists, and resort to terrorist violence. Throughout this analysis, I will examine the role of beliefs in the various radicalization processes under consideration.

Before I set out on this path, it is important to briefly define *radicalization*, *extremism*, and *terrorism*. I will use the standing legal definitions, as, for example, provided by the Netherlands General Intelligence and Security Service (AIVD) and the National Coordinator for Counterterrorism and Security (NCTV). *Radicalization* is then considered as a process in which someone experiences a growing willingness to pursue and/or support radical changes in society—if necessary, in an undemocratic manner—that are in conflict with or could pose a threat to the democratic legal order.[3] *Extremism* involves "individuals or groups who deliberately overstep the bounds of the law to commit illegal, sometimes violent, acts" (Van den Bos 2018, 5–6). *Terrorism*, finally, is defined as follows:

> Pursuing objectives or carrying out acts with the aim of inspiring grave fear in the population or part of the population; of unlawfully coercing a national government or an international organization to act, not to act, or to condone something; or of severely destabilizing or destroying the fundamental political, constitutional, economic, or social structures of a country or an international organization. This generally takes the form of violence, or the threat of violence, directed at human life.[4]

In short, we could say that radicalization is the more open process of advocating radical change; extremism is the more rigid, fixed outcome of such a process that also involves an extremist mindset, the acceptance of violence, and the systematic undermining of the legal order; and terrorism is the ultimate willingness to plan, engage in, and carry out terrorist attacks. Figure 1.1, offered by Kees van den Bos (2018, 5–6), is helpful here.

---

[3] See the relevant descriptions and definitions on https://www.aivd.nl/onderwerpen/over-de-aivd/inlichtingenwoordenboek and https://www.nctv.nl/onderwerpen/dtn/definities-gebruikt-in-het-dtn. For a comprehensive and well-substantiated explanation of the definitions of terrorism, radicalization, and deradicalization, see Weggemans and De Graaf (2017, 27–48).

[4] Dutch Criminal Code, article 83/83a, based on similar definitions in EU law. Indonesia has a related legal definition.

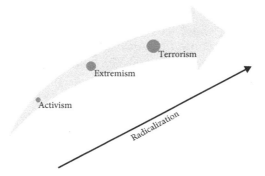

Figure 1.1 The process of radicalization. Reproduced with permission from Van den Bos, *Why People Radicalize*, Oxford University Press (2018).

In this book, I am specifically interested in how religion plays a part in the radicalization toward terrorism. Like so many other factors, religion is a slippery and elusive concept to relate to terrorism. To be sure, there are many instances of religiously informed radicalization. If religious leaders issue fatwas and call for an apostate's elimination, this may really and directly affect the willingness of followers to put this call into action. If religious agendas based on sharia law are imposed, they affect a religious community's embracing of corporal punishment (e.g., hacking off the hands of thieves). If religious leaders suggest apocalyptic readings of political constellations and advocate QAnon-related conspiracy theories, their fellow believers will follow suit in adjusting their political preferences and donations to these extreme beliefs. Yet, it has also been demonstrated that religious leaders can have an attenuating influence on radicalization processes.[5] Religious communities may reject and denounce specific violent readings of holy texts and call for peace and dialogue. Research found that members of mainstream religious communities—for example, the Protestant Church in Germany—were less prone to Covid-19-related radicalization and conspiracy theories than nonchurch, self-reported believers (Pickel et al. 2022, 185).

Religion, therefore, can play a variety of conflicting, complementing, and diverging roles in relation to radicalization and violent extremism, as Van den Bos rightly has laid out. This, of course, has something to do with the fact

---

[5] See the many examples of peacebuilding influences of religious leaders in situations of terror and conflict in Sisk (2011).

that religion is a very broad and spongy concept: it denotes the individual and the communal as well as the practical and the dogmatic dimension, the divine and the worldly realm, the transcendent and the tangible rituals, the moral/ethical and the esthetical domain. The psychologist William James (1902, 27) originally defined religion as "the feelings, acts, and experiences of individual men in their solitude, so far as they apprehend themselves to stand in relation to whatever they may consider the divine," with *divinity* including both deities and other godlike objects and concepts. For sociologists such as Emile Durkheim, religion should also be considered a "unified system of beliefs and practices with regard to sacred things" as upheld and practiced by a specific community, a church, or any other religious denomination (Van den Bos 2018, 206–12).

In this book, I see religion as a combination of both aspects: the feelings, acts, and experiences of individuals in relation to what these individuals consider to be divine, as well as an organized system of beliefs and practices tied to a specific community or institution. Lorne Dawson's concept of religiosity is helpful here. Dawson (2021b, 2) defines *religiosity* as "the salience of religion in someone's life," including such things as "practice, devotion, belief, knowledge, communality, and experience." Importantly, whereas *religion* is a heavy, "thick" concept, *religiosity* seems hard to measure and quantify. As Donald Holbrook and John Horgan (2019, 8) state, "One does not need to 'qualify' with any level of 'expertise' or knowledge in discourses associated with particular ideologies to be affected by them, or for them, to impact on our frames of reference." With these scholars, and with Dawson (2021b, 15), I therefore agree it is paramount to recognize that "ideology is embedded throughout journeys towards terrorism" and that this journey can take different forms: practical, emotional, behavioral, and cognitive.

But there is more to religion than this conceptual catchall conundrum. And that is the gist of my book. In relation to processes of radicalization, religion should not be considered a predictor of radicalization or terrorism as such, but rather as a moderator of sorts. From experimental psychology, we know that attitudes and beliefs are weak predictors of actions and behavior (McCauley and Moskalenko 2017a).[6] Religion, as a set of beliefs, is therefore not suitable for predicting which individual will resort to terrorist violence and which one will go out and serve world peace. Possibly, future research will yield more results in this field, but so far, religion is notoriously

---

[6] Yet, the discussion about how to understand these results is still ongoing; see Dawson (2019, 84).

bad at offering specific, measurable, accountable, and reasonable forecasting results. That is why, in this study, I start with a data set of "given" terrorist convicts and use religion as a moderator rather than as a predictor.

In this volume, I seek to answer a number of related questions. One important question asks how religiously informed beliefs influenced the convicts' radicalization trajectory toward terrorism. Social-psychological research has established a series of seminal factors that, in combination, trigger the radicalization process and pave the road to terrorism: an acute sense of uncertainty, a longing for a pure identity, perceptions of significance loss, feelings of injustice, or the desire to revenge specific grievances. Yet, in view of my earlier remark that terrorism should always be studied in context, these motivating forces toward radicalization need to be imbued with specific meaning, with particular religious beliefs and associated emotions. They need to be made amenable, translated from the realm of abstractions into an actionable direction. Oftentimes, when oriented toward general models and variables that are studied in isolation from their contexts, social-psychological theory and models may appear a bit lifeless and generic. Yet, the theory of grievances, injustices, and worldview defenses needs real-life colorization. Grievances, for example, require a very convincing and precise contextual, historical explanation of what happened. Who are the culprits, and where are they? How can revenge be enacted? What is my moral duty? This is where religion comes in, and history. Religion fills concepts of significance (loss or gain), injustice, meaning making, and mortality salience with a precise interpretation and realization, and inevitably relates them to the individual believer. And history shows how this plays out in time and space, since the process of filling these abstract concepts with specific meaning is always historically contingent.

This is why I understand religion here as a moderator, as depicted in figure 1.2, which is based on figure 1.1. Religion offers specific cognitive, affective, and behavioral assistance and agendas to people involved in a radicalization process. I use the term *moderator*, indicating that between the predictor and the result there is something—religion—that influences this causal process. Religion may also function as mediator, explaining and determining rather than influencing this process (Karazsia and Berlin 2018, 13).[7] The discussion

---

[7] See also the seminal and pioneering article on moderators and mediators by R. M. Baron and D. A. Kenny (1986).

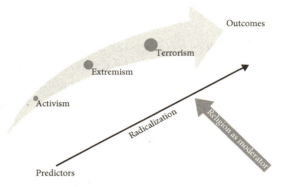

Figure 1.2 The role of religion as moderator

on when and how a mediator may become a moderator or vice versa is still ongoing, and settling the issue requires more theory building and testing, especially in the quantitative and mathematical domain. Therefore, I leave this to others.[8] Here, it suffices to say that religion does not act as a simple predictor but helps to understand the how and why of the radicalization process. It explains the kind of cognitive, affective, and behavioral solutions a person may come to accept and embrace while on a road to terrorism.

Obviously, if religion acts as an agent of influence in processes of radicalization, it can do so in multiple ways. Here, I focus on the level of the individual, albeit as part of a larger offline or online group or community. By conducting interviews with a number of convicted terrorists—predominantly, but not exclusively, jihadist ones—I investigate how these persons used religion to embark on a significance quest that led to participation in terrorism. In particular, as I will explain, I focus on the notion of *redemption*. This religious construct involves all three dimensions—the cognitive, the affective, and the behavioral—that influence radicalization. More mundane notions such as *revenge, renown,* and *reaction* as introduced by Louise Richardson (2006) as models for understanding terrorism may also be read and interpreted through a religious lens. Yet, the term *redemption*, as we will see, is more than that. In its radical form, it is very much part and parcel of a holistic, extremist mindset and worldview that helps us understand how individuals become

---

[8] See also the excellent discussion in Muthuswamy (2021).

engulfed in extreme beliefs and practices and end up committing acts of terrorism.[9]

In short, religion influences processes of radicalization—perhaps not as an original predictor (this needs to be further investigated; the verdict is open and inconclusive) but most certainly as a moderator. In specific situations and under certain circumstances, it shapes notions of unfairness, gives contours to vague grievances, feelings of shortcoming, and uncertainty, offers a direction in repairing one's sense of loss or defending one's cause, and legitimizes violent transgression of the law. It can do this, and does so, in various ways, either by fueling the radicalization process and influencing it with extreme content or by mitigating that process and calibrating it with more moderate content. Here, I focus on the extreme content, in particular on the notion of *radical redemption*. This notion provides a compelling narrative that makes sense of past losses, present grievances, and future action, and embeds them in a broad, metaphysical, ideological, and/or extremist worldview. It offers both an explanatory model and a moral call to action that is very hard to resist once embraced by a group or individual, as we will see.

This research puzzle—that is, how religion and radicalization intertwine, interrelate, and impact each other—leads me to hypothesize that religion serves as a moderator of radicalization and that it can do so specifically—but not exclusively—via the narrative of radical redemption. This brings me to the following research question: To what extent does the radical redemption narrative shape radicalization toward terrorism? This question can be divided in three subquestions: (1) How does terrorism manifest itself as a praxis of radical redemption? (2) How does the redemption narrative—when we encounter it—offer individuals a framework within which they can give their lives meaning? (3) At what point and why does this narrative lose its appeal? In line with Van den Bos's (2020a) proposed sand glass model for research designs in the realm of radicalization studies,[10] this yields figure 1.3.

---

[9] Agreeing with Quassim Cassam and Rik Peels, I consider extremism not just as the willingness to embrace violence as a method ("methods extremism") but also as a mindset, as a set of extreme beliefs, and as a form of psychological and ideological extremism. See Cassam (2021b); on extreme beliefs, see Rik Peels on https://extremebeliefs.com/ and Peels et al. (forthcoming).

[10] Van den Bos presents the model in a manual that he developed for setting up empirical legal research projects, but it is applicable here as well—he even refers to conducting "qualitative in-depth interviews with prisoners" (Van den Bos 2020a, 23–4).

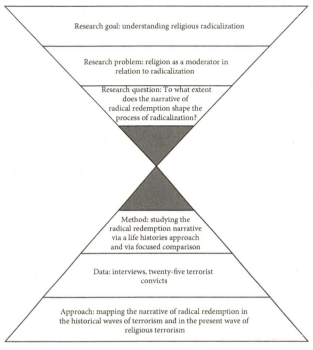

Figure 1.3 The research design

Studying Radical Redemption as a Narrative

I will answer my research question by applying the notion of radical redemption as a narrative. Several pertinent reasons made me decide to take this approach.

First of all, my choice to use this concept to further specify religion's function as a moderator is informed by the fact that the notion of redemption is used both in the literature and in the statements of terrorist perpetrators themselves. The doyenne of terrorism research, Martha Crenshaw, already referred to the "incentive" of redemption, the phenomenon that terrorist violence can "have a personal meaning for the individual. It is a path to individual salvation, regardless of the political outcome for the collectivity in the real world. The motivation for terrorism may be to transcend reality as much as to transform it." She also pointed out that "such redemptive groups may resemble religious cults as much as ideological organization," including the longing for self-sacrifice among nineteenth-century anarchists and members of the Weather Underground of the 1960s (Crenshaw 1987, 20–1).[11]

For the young men from Delft, their friend Mo's death acted as a wake-up call; it made them pay more attention to their soul and score in the light of the Last Judgment. With the summons to a life of purity and moral righteousness in their mind, and the offer of redemption and the fight against injustice in their online inbox, they decided to embrace the narrative of radical redemption and left for Syria. They would rather die an honorable death in the Syrian desert than lead a miserable life of shoplifting and playing cat and mouse with the police in the streets of suburban Delft. For them, religion was not a matter of deep reflection and theological studies—it was a feeling, an epiphanous moment, a stirring. While scholars and citizens in the West often overly rely on religious dogmas and cognitions when contemplating religion, it makes sense to also take religion seriously as an emotion, a duty, and a guiding praxis. Religion combines the emotional, cognitive, and behavioral. It is, in the words of sociologist Douglas A. Marshall (2002), "behavior, belonging, and belief"; thus, as Lorne Dawson also has demonstrated, it relates very well to radicalization, which also touches upon these three domains (see, e.g., Dawson 2021a, 2021b, 2009).

Late 2016, another young man was arrested in Rotterdam and prosecuted for hiding a Kalashnikov and boxes of fireworks in his cellar. He already had a criminal record at the time, but witnesses stated that in the few months before his arrest, he had become quieter, more introspective. Though he did not talk about it much, one of his friends told me that his arrested mate had been looking for redemption for his violent past—for atonement, for something that, in Allah's eyes, would make up for what he had done. He had a Kalashnikov in his cellar, the friend explained, to prepare for such atonement.[12] Indeed, a recent study on the link between crime and terrorism concluded that a substantial percentage of the interviewees had a demonstrable "redemption narrative"—in other words, taking part in a jihadist struggle gave them the opportunity to redeem themselves from their criminal past (Basra et al. 2016). They also indicated that such a violent form of redemption enabled them to satisfy their personal needs, whether that was

---

[11] See also Basra et al. (2016). Bart Schuurman and John Horgan (2016) mention redemption as a "rationale for violence" but discard this as a religious motive and redefine it as a "personal one"—something Lorne L. Dawson (2021b, 8–9) does not agree with (and neither do I).

[12] Interview with a probation officer; interview with Amin*, October 30, 2019, penitentiary institution/terrorist detention unit (PI/TDU). Names marked with an asterisk are pseudonyms, used at the request of the interviewees or the Custodial Institutions Agency (DJI).

a desire for adventure, violence, or atonement. This redemption narrative thus facilitated their transition from criminal behavior to membership of a terrorist organization, both psychologically and in practice.

I have been conducting research into terrorism and political violence since 2004. In this period, I have spoken to dozens of people involved in the fight against terrorism and radicalization, including police officers, public prosecutors, staff members of the General Intelligence and Security Service (AIVD), youth workers, and analysts. I have also spoken to former and detained terrorists and their family and friends, at first mainly in the Netherlands, Germany, and Italy; later in Belgium, France, the United Kingdom, Spain, and the United States; and in more recent years also in non-Western contexts, such as Indonesia and Africa. What became increasingly clear to me was how current and former radicals grapple with their own quest for meaning and their belief that they were called to do something bigger, something higher. They had put their own comfortable lives and, even more importantly, those of others in jeopardy in the full belief that they were angels of vengeance and members of a vanguard, an elite of divine warriors. The latter applied mainly to jihadists, but former members of the Irish Republican Army (IRA), Red Army Faction (RAF), Weather Underground, and Red Brigades also saw themselves as heroic heralds of a new age (see, for example, De Graaf 2011, 2012a; Weggemans and De Graaf 2017).

The notion of radical redemption has influenced the process of radicalization in a great many stories, both then and now. But how did that work? That forms the second reason why I focus on this concept in my book. The term *redemption* has not been investigated systematically in relation to radicalization so far,[13] although it occurs in accounts of both historical terrorism—even back into the nineteenth century—and modern-day terrorism. It is a very gripping narrative that gives coherence to the fight against injustice and its relevance for one's own identity and life: Who am I in the face of such injustices? What is my duty? What does God, or what does history, want me to do? Redemption is the notion that links the more generic, external identification and recognition of evil, apostasy, injustice, and unfairness to the personal commitment of the individual to choose the good, to embrace the just cause, and to serve posterity, one's community, God, and so forth. It combines cognitive beliefs, triggers emotions, and calls to action. With Andrew Beatty, Rik Peels, and Nora Kindermann, I consider the narrative

---

[13] As Dawson states as well (2021b, 9).

method exceptionally well suited to connect emotions, beliefs, and actions and to embed them properly within the context of radicalization:

> [A]n emotion is a judgement, an assessment of the circumstances affecting me. It's also an action in a world made by others: a response—of pleasure, fear or anger—to what lies beyond our control, to what disturbs our equilibrium, our goals and desires. This tension between inner and outer imperatives—to overstate an opposition— ... can only be captured in narratives.[14]

The narrative of redemption is a motive that pops up in various forms in all monotheistic religions and to a substantial extent also in polytheistic religions and political ideologies. Why is redemption such a recurrent motive? One explanation is that it is in itself a narrative that binds the individual to a development in time and space that transcends the here and now. That also holds true for the narrative of *radical* redemption. The epitaph *radical* here implies that redemption is part of and shapes the process of radicalization, including the willingness to accept radical acts—of violence—to achieve the desired redemption. According to Donatella della Porta, radical groups use different frames "to characterize their positions and justify their actions." With their radical and strategic "frames" or "narratives," they "define the problem, identify protagonists and antagonists, and point to particular lines of action." They mobilize their support base for their chosen course of radical action. Their narratives give "explanatory consistency and emotional power" to these actions and "connect the group's collective past to their present situation" (della Porta 2008, 226-7).

A narrative is thus a *storyline* and a *temporal construct*: it connects the past of shortcomings and sin, via the presence of perceived frustrations, to the future of improvement, redemption, and deliverance from evil. It elevates, transforms, and converts individuals; it takes them out of the confines of mundane situatedness and projects them into a more meaningful, metaphysical story. Radical redemption tells a story of the fight against injustice and the possibility of victory for the righteous ones. It is a literary motive, a storyline, and a psychological coping mechanism (see chapter 2 for further

---

[14] Thanks to Rik Peels and Nora Kindermann (2023, 82) for the insight on narratives and the quote from Beatty; see also Beatty (2014).

discussion). It is a combination of thinking and doing, a gliding scale of reasoning and preparing for action.[15]

Thus, we come to the third reason to investigate radical redemption as a narrative: it sits right at the intersection of social psychology, religious studies, and history, and these three disciplines need to work together to make sense of it. The narrative approach is in itself process oriented and historical. It captures the historical lives of the perpetrators in the way they view and portray themselves on the path toward a holy war, captured in time. It touches upon social-psychological mechanisms in their wanting to engage in such a radical struggle. And it also involves religious notions of transcendence, good, and evil as they are applied in real life in an iterative, temporal sense—for example, in responding to past injustices and preparing for concrete future actions.

In chapter 2, I show how Dan McAdams identified and traced narratives of nonradical redemption of perfectly normal, nonterrorist persons by applying a life histories approach. This was for me the inspiration and instigation to test the concept of *radical* redemption and try to couple McAdams's insights with my own historicizing methods and apply these to terrorist convicts. Of course, as John Horgan and others have pointed out, it is very difficult, if not impossible, to discern between motivation and post hoc legitimation here. After all, most terrorists tell their stories, including those of redemption, after the fact. Researchers are hardly ever present to record terrorist self-reflections while the radicalization is ongoing. Yet, as Horgan (2012, 201–2) explained and Dawson (2019, 77) reiterated, this may not matter much. Every story people tell about trials and turns in their lives is open and incomplete, even if they had been able to tell it while they were having these experiences. Whether post hoc or ad hoc, reflections and reconstructions of one's motives and musings are always subjective. The main point here is that subjective interpretation and perception constitute the framework through which all individuals try to give meaning to their lives, to give words "to inchoate feelings and thoughts" (Dawson 2019, 82). And who can decide whether what the terrorists tell us is true or not? Is it factual truth that is at stake here? Or is it about the narrative that people tell, appropriate, and stick to, even if they do not always understand it themselves? Since terrorists

---

[15] See, for example, the literature on framing and collective action, here discussed by Dawson (2021b, 15–16); see also my work on how injustice frames mobilize into collective action (De Graaf 2011) and when such injustice frames and narratives fall short in generating support (Demant and De Graaf 2010).

relate narratives about their actions not only long after the fact but sometimes also shortly after their deeds or even beforehand, and since they demonstrably share such stories among themselves, it makes sense to study them, especially if we take care to avoid deterministic pitfalls and study each of these narratives as a moderator—how it influenced the terrorist's radicalization process—rather than as a predictor or mediator. Moreover, as a historian who has worked with oral history and perpetrators before, I am well aware that oral testimonies are notoriously untrustworthy; I will elaborate on how I dealt with this unreliability objection—which is obviously a well-known one for historians working with historical sources and agents—in appendix 2.

Social psychologists and historians need each other to really fully understand "how people construct mental representations that align with their surrounding social and cultural systems," as psychologist Ryan Lei and others recently made clear (Lei et al. 2023). The historical and societal contexts of these processes of interaction and radicalization matter significantly (Van den Bos 2020b). Indeed, key publications have paid too little attention to the historical context of radicalization processes and their narratives. Kenneth Gergen (1973, 1980) has rightfully criticized social psychology for neglecting the historical processes relevant to understand what people believe, feel, and do in specific, given, historically contingent, social contexts. Terrorism and radicalization, as has been stated before, need to be contextualized—not only in terms of the perpetrator's radicalization process and life course (since there are so many different pathways toward terrorism) but also in terms of the overarching social, cultural, and temporal context that provides the backdrop of this individual process. Every historical period yields its own narratives of redemption. Every time as well as every place offers triggers and events that are used to form a new frame of injustice and a new story of repression that need to be fought. Della Porta (1995) has convincingly shown how the revolutionary terrorists of the 1970s and 1980s used and instrumentalized specific incidents and political constellations to formulate their frames of injustice and mobilize new generations of terrorist recruits (see De Graaf 2011). This is why chapter 3 in my book first goes back in time to indicate how the narrative of redemption morphed and changed in previous waves of terrorism, depending strongly on the particular historical context in place. Only when we fully realize the historical contingencies of the terrorist narratives that are being told will we arrive at a better understanding of the role religion plays in processes of radicalization.

Finally, the main focus of the book is on religious radicalization, particularly that of jihadist terrorists. As will become clear, the narrative of redemption is especially convincing in a religious context. The jihadist terrorists that I have interviewed demonstrate that case. Yet, that is not all there is. The redemption narrative also holds, up until today, in the context of modern political ideologies such as right-wing extremism. It sits well within any ideology or worldview that applies an eschatological and/or apocalyptical perspective and divides the world in good and evil. It resonates deeply with ideologies that advocate a struggle for justice and campaigns against impurity, but less so with the glorification of violence per se or with mass shootings. That is why I also devoted a chapter to the question of how radical redemption plays out in cases of nonjihadist terrorism. Surely, we need to further deepen our understanding of when, how, and under which circumstances the narrative of redemption works and can be identified, and when not. Excluding cases in which radical redemption is not a moderator helps us to better understand the variegating processes of radicalization. This book merely offers a first step on that trajectory of reflection.

In sum, radical redemption is a narrative worthwhile studying in connection to religious radicalization. It is not the only narrative at play for religious radicalization, nor is it for radicalization in general. Furthermore, it is not the only moderator that impacts the process of radicalization. More research on its relation with other moderators and narratives—such as relating to injustice, revenge, fear, and uncertainty, or to capacities of self-control or even pathologies—is certainly needed. Yet, with this study I aim to contribute to a grounded theory on how religion impacts radicalization, in particular how narratives of radical redemption shape a person's and a group's trajectory toward terrorism.

Current Literature on the Religion-and-Radicalization Puzzle

The religion-and-radicalization puzzle—namely, how religion and radicalization intertwine, interrelate, and impact each other—can be addressed, like radicalization in general, on three levels: the macro-, the meso-, and the microlevel.[16] I will make the case that, while our study of radical redemption

---

[16] This section has previously been published in De Graaf and Van den Bos (2021).

starts on the level of the individual, it also needs to take meso- and macrolevel elements into account. But first, let me point out some insights from existing literature that has touched on this puzzle.

Theories on religion and radicalization into violent extremism and terrorism often focus on a macrolevel of analysis. That means that these theories try to explain and map radicalization processes by means of structural factors in society, zooming in on such variables as the occurrence of poverty, discrimination, lack of participation, exclusion, context of war, or failed states (see, e.g., Abadie 2006; Burgoon 2006; Krueger and Malecková 2003). Some studies foreground religion—operationalized in terms of religious representation, religious narratives, or the existence of apocalyptical creeds—as fuel for radical groups. Marc Juergensmeyer is the most recent and influential exponent of this type of analysis. Sometimes, such theories are referred to as *root cause theories* (see Juergensmeyer 2017; Crenshaw 1981; Bjørgo 2005). Yet, while appropriating religion as root cause of radicalization, these theories often fall short in operationalizing and explaining the transition from absolute conditions in society to actual precipitating factors.

Instead of taking the factual state of social or economic oppression or the concrete level of adherents to a specific religious group or sect as indicative of outbursts of radical violence, numerous studies have demonstrated that mesolevel mechanisms of relative deprivation, risky shift, or cognitive dissonance as induced by specific radical groups are far more useful for explaining the emergence of violent radicalization: they are more predictive and more informed by data that allow for causal mechanisms. Macrolevel factors clearly need a chain of translation and interpretation in order to be "weaponized," indicating that prospective theories on radicalization should draw not only from economic, religious, and historical theories but also from social-psychological insights (see Moghaddam 2005; De Graaf 2011; Van den Bos 2018).

Of course, recent approaches on the macrolevel developed by scholars of religious studies, history, and political science have charted important new terrain: they have convincingly traced the changing discourse on martyrdom, miracles, eschatology, and sacred values in jihadist literature, for example (see Armstrong 2014; Cavanaugh 2009; Atran 2010, 2016; Müller 2019). Yet, in order to properly understand processes underlying religiously informed radicalization, we need to bridge the gap between macrolevel factors and individual psychological factors—the microlevel of analysis.

The most recent framework that captures religion in quite a sophisticated manner can be found in the body of psychological coping literature. In place of religious belief as individual difference variable, religious coping strategies and religious appraisals are typically emphasized here (Gall et al. 2005). This literature looks at how specific aspects of religion relate to individual coping processes and examines the relation between specific religious beliefs and capacities of individual appraisals and coping. Such relations require investigations into an individual's psychological makeup, resulting in a microlevel approach to the analysis of radicalization and terrorism. Taylor Newton and Daniel McIntosh propose, for example, that religious beliefs can act as a cognitive schema, shaping cognitive processes, including the perception of stress, through a *transactional model*. This model views cognitive appraisals as the intermediaries between beliefs and coping strategies. For instance, belief in a just and benevolent God correlates with surrendering control to God, which in turn leads to less psychological distress when coping with uncontrollable negative events (see Newton and McIntosh 2010; Lazarus and Folkman 1984; Maynard et al. 2001).

In recent years, this approach has been tested in the field of radicalization. Jacquelien van Stekelenburg, for example, describes radicalization as a process of an increasing acceptance of violence that explains extremist behavior and the exclusion of other groups. In this process, radical groups may begin to reinterpret anger-eliciting situations and reappraise them from a position of moral superiority. They then make the attribution that the outgroup is morally inferior and needs to be eliminated, based on a reappraisal fueled by the emotion of contempt. Here, emotion transformation theory aligns with religious beliefs regarding in-group and out-group identities, since specific religious beliefs may provide a group with a sense of being morally superior to "apostate" or "infidel" others (see Schulten et al. 2019; Van Stekelenburg 2017; Doosje et al. 2016; McCauley and Moskalenko 2017b).

Another microlevel approach looks into how people's motivation and cognition assist them in goal attainment. For example, Arie Kruglanski's goal systems theory has established a threefold interface between cognition, motivation, and action. Within this goal systems approach, a person's quest for significance is a major explanatory factor in understanding processes of radicalization. With respect to religious radicalization, goal attainment can be such a strong mobilizing factor within specific religious groups that patterns of goal shielding enable believers to ignore all other considerations of moderation, empathy, or civil obedience (Shah et al. 2002). Furthermore, when something prevents people from attaining their goals, this elicits huge frustrations and violent emotions or even extreme behavior, as also explained in the appraisal and coping theories I mentioned (Folger 1977; Gurr 1970).

Yet, such microlevel approaches still leave unanswered the question about the content of the goals and beliefs that provide radicals with their quest. More historical—*historical* in the sense of situated in time and space, in cultural, social, and political contexts—research is therefore necessary to combine findings on the abstract and generic social-psychological mechanisms with a better understanding of how *precisely* individuals develop and embrace specific narratives, discourses, and appraisals that serve their radicalization process. Finding acceptance in religious groups provides protection from perceived threat and buffering of social exclusion (Hogg et al. 2010). Furthermore, perceived collective support for one's valued identity and beliefs can motivate group members in developing aggressive behavior against other people. Research indicates strong associations between radicalized religious beliefs and ideologies and violent behaviors, suggesting again that individual coping and appraisal mechanisms, emotions, and sentiments need narrative carriers—such as social discourses of threat, (in)justice, salvation, and significance—in order to be mobilized into processes of cognitive and behavioral radicalization (see Van den Bos 2018; della Porta 1995, 2009; Ferguson and Binks 2015). These processes often take place in groups or other social contexts, both offline and online. For example, research conducted by the International Centre for the Study of Radicalisation (ICSR) examined people's motives for joining IS. Many radicalizing youngsters and foreign fighters who went to join the caliphate in Syria and Iraq reported the search for redemption in extremist religious beliefs and terrorist religious groups as an important motive (Basra et al. 2016).

This overview shows why a combined, multilevel approach is necessary, an approach that ties an individual's need for coping with uncertainty to the group's ideological and religious beliefs, which in turn are dependent on the social, cultural, and political macrolevel context and need to be historicized. An approach that takes the concept of radical redemption as a narrative and as a (religious) moderator in relation to the process of radicalization does exactly that.

Life Histories Approach

In this book I employ a *narrative analysis* of terrorism as radical redemption, which also includes a double historical perspective provided by the life histories of the perpetrators themselves and by the broader context—political, social, cultural—within which the perpetrators operated and from which their narratives originated.

The phenomena of radicalization and terrorism, as many experts have explained, are very complex, and it is complicated and difficult to support research with empirical evidence, especially when embarking on a qualitative, interview-based research design (e.g., Feddes et al. 2020). And yet, that is the methodology I have chosen to apply here: this book is based on a narrative, historical, and qualitative life histories approach, founded on thick description and microhistory—that is, detailed descriptions and life stories—in line with calls made by Peels, Dawson, and Horgan to systematically conduct interviews and involve first-person accounts of terrorist motivations in research (for a more thorough discussion of my methods, see appendix 2).[17] I have chosen this methodology because it enables me to seek deeper explanatory insights into the relation between beliefs, transcendency, and willingness to act. By allowing convicted terrorists to tell their own stories, we can reconstruct their life stories, which we can then combine with available biographical data from other sources, such as the media, court reports, police reports, and, where possible, interviews with third parties. We can triangulate, to some extent, the interviewees' statements and thus create a more thorough and grounded reconstruction of their paths of radicalization than if we just presented the convicts' personal perspectives and narratives.

For this study, I allowed my interviewees to tell their stories in a semistructured manner. People have a tendency to jump back and forth in time, to express their displeasure, frustrations, or emotions about a specific event and then link it to a moment in the past or future. I always steered the conversation back to the chronology, with the passage of their lives as the guiding framework—birth, family, background, upbringing, school, and so on. I focused especially on moments of transition and turning points in their lives, devoting particular attention to those defining moments that,

---

[17] See Dawson (2019); Horgan (2012); Bortolotti (2021). In his Extreme Beliefs research project, Rik Peels makes a case for a systematic philosophical and theological study of first-person accounts of extreme beliefs. See https://extremebeliefs.com/.

according to the interviewees themselves, had led them to embrace radical ideas and participate in terrorist activities. This could be a series of moments that together heralded a sudden change of course in their lives, or a more gradual process of increasing violence and terrorist activity.

My intention was not to attempt to fit objectified life stories of terrorists into the mold of existing radicalization models so as to confirm or negate them. Rather, my radical redemption model arose out of these existing models in combination with various other factors, such as historical research. This study approaches such life stories from a different perspective, namely, that of the extremists and terrorists themselves. How do they talk about their lives, and about the beliefs and motives that led them to commit violent acts? How did their beliefs or opinions change? What did they hope to achieve, and did their acts ultimately give them fulfillment and satisfaction? The stories are, consequently, not statements of fact—though I have checked the facts as far as possible—but accounts of a quest for meaning and significance: they describe how the interviewees themselves interpret the turning points in their lives. While their life stories are based on biographical facts (which can mostly be verified), they do not coincide fully with those facts. They are accounts in which the interviewees talk about the meaning of their lives in the light of a larger, often even eschatological story, and which are driven by imagination, hope, desire, disappointment, and all variety of subjective interpretations.[18]

Of course, I encountered many other explanations for embarking on a radical career, such as addiction, domestic violence, unemployment, crime, and emotional solidarity with minority groups. Many of the interviewees had difficulty distinguishing between their own feelings and those of others. But what concerns me, and what increasingly became clear to me while conducting all these interviews over the past years, is that these convicted terrorists themselves chose to cast their lives, and all their associated frustrations and deficiencies, in the mold of a narrative that I came to see and define as one of *radical redemption*. That narrative became an umbrella under which the other explanations just mentioned, as well as all the entanglements and emotions in the interviewees' lives and in the world, found a place and a meaning and became a part of their identity. It is, after all, much more invigorating, even "cooler," to see yourself as someone called

---

[18] For arguments supporting such an approach, see, for example, Cohler (1982). See also appendix 2. In the Netherlands, Marjo Buitelaar has often applied this approach; for example, to the experience of identity by Islamic women—see Buitelaar (2014).

to take part in the jihad than as someone who is running away to avoid an argument with their parents. But that is not to say that domestic quarrels were not real or that the framing of their lives is fictional. On the contrary, the narrative of radical redemption offered these individuals, who were grappling with life and in search of meaning, a new and appealing perspective for action.[19]

By *terrorists*, I here explicitly mean individuals who have been charged with and convicted for terrorist crimes. I therefore often refer to them as *convicted terrorists*, to indicate that some of them resolutely do not wish to see themselves as terrorists and contest their conviction. In this study, however, I have followed the ruling of the court. Most of the people I spoke with were still in detention. Those I spoke with outside prison, both in the Netherlands and in Indonesia, had also been convicted as terrorists but had completed their sentences. *Radicals* or *radicalizing youth* refers to those who—following the definition given in "Religion as Moderator"—find themselves in a process in which they experience a growing willingness to work toward and/or support far-reaching changes in society—if necessary, in an undemocratic way—that are incompatible with or can pose a threat to the democratic rule of law. A radical, or a radicalizing person, is therefore not necessarily a terrorist. Conversely, almost all convicted terrorists I interviewed went through such a radicalization process.[20] The difference lies in the tipping point at which a radical commits a crime that disrupts society and is convicted as a terrorist. The *radical* in *radical redemption* thus pertains to the fact that adherents to this kind of redemptive belief—and encompassing orthopraxis (see next section)—are willing to enact that belief by means of violence to gain redemption and/or to support acts that are incompatible with or pose a threat to the democratic rule of law.

I started my interviews in the Dutch terrorist detention units (TDUs) in De Schie (Rotterdam) and Vught, which housed around thirty-five terrorist detainees. I met my interviewees in and outside prison and was able to speak with some of them more than once.[21] Questions that interested me

---

[19] This became clear to me and was confirmed in interviews with TDU staff working with detainees, including the heads of the TDUs at Vught and De Schie prisons.

[20] I was unable to determine whether the two Syrian militants that I interviewed had also been radicalized. They have been convicted for terrorist crimes but claim that they joined a militia and took up arms in self-defense. Their situation before they became involved in terrorist activities was in any case clearly different from that of the men who were radicalized in the Netherlands. This is addressed in greater detail in chapter 7.

[21] For a more detailed description of this method and the way I systematized the interviews, see appendices 2 and 3.

concerned, for instance, how they talked about their lives, how they came to join a radical group or movement, and what beliefs and motives led them to commit violent acts. Perhaps their opinions changed? Also, I wanted to hear from them what they had hoped to achieve with their actions, and why they believed in the effect they would have. And did their acts ultimately give them fulfillment and satisfaction? In this book, I attempt to gain a greater insight into the orthopraxis of terrorists, to learn more about how terrorists' religious beliefs and actions are related. In particular, I focus on the desire for redemption of radicalizing individuals and members of terrorist organizations.

To enable a valuable qualitative comparison and to make their stories more universal, I not only visited Dutch detainees convicted for jihadist terrorism but also talked to a number of Indonesian jihadists, indirectly recorded some accounts by Boko Haram members in Cameroon, and spoke to Syrian detainees and one convicted Pakistani jihadist (in detention in the Netherlands). I also interviewed people convicted of terrorism who hold another set of beliefs, namely, that of right-wing extremism. While the focus lies on individuals convicted of jihadist terrorism in the Netherlands, these stories of non-Western terrorists and Western right-wing extremists are important for the identification of patterns that will aid our understanding of perpetrators' beliefs and how they give them meaning. One common denominator in the interviews and life stories is that all the people I spoke with have been convicted or detained in the past ten years. In that sense, their situations are to some extent comparable in terms of the context of the period (9/11, the advent of worldwide jihadism, the Arab Spring, and the caliphate), technology (the spread of the Internet and social media), and major geopolitical changes (the new chaos of the war on terror, the wars in Iraq and Syria, and the great refugee crisis).

I talked to almost all the Dutch terrorism convicts that were incarcerated between 2018 and 2021. Not all of them gave me permission to use their stories. In the end, I could use the life histories of twenty-five convicted terrorists—twenty in Dutch prisons and five in Indonesia—and I interviewed another sixteen people in their immediate circle, including anti-terrorism experts, youth workers, family members, and victims. On the basis of these interviews, supplemented by conversations with staff of TDUs and the probation service, I constructed "accounts of redemption," which I then rendered anonymous and sometimes, in consultation with the interviewees, cut and recompiled to make tracing their true identities as difficult as possible. Finally, I used these narratives to examine the nature of the link between theology/ideology and praxis, exploring the nature of the spiritual landscape of terrorists who depict themselves as heroes and saviors, as the wreakers of vengeance on those they see as unbelievers and oppressors.

Radical Redemption as an Orthopraxis

Obviously, on the basis of just twenty-five in-depth interviews, we cannot make sweeping, generalizing statements on the influence of religion on radicalization. Yet, by combining the insights gained from these interviews with findings on other, historical patterns of radical redemption, we can say something about how this specific narrative may operate in particular contexts.

This study aims to further our understanding of the religious-transcendental aspect of redemption. The argument's empirical foundation is provided mainly by interviews with convicted jihadist terrorists. While that places the jihadist variant of radical redemption at the center of the study, this variant is experienced and explained differently by each individual interviewee. At the same time, my research distinguishes itself from many existing studies of terrorists' ideologies and religions by not taking the postulated documents and theories of terrorist organizations as a starting point for the analysis but rather focusing more closely on the relationship between their beliefs and praxis as described in the radical redemption narrative. What do terrorists believe, how does that belief translate into a specific action, and what do they hope to achieve with that action? Religious beliefs are too often seen as static systems of dogmas and rigid beliefs. Faith, it is said, means taking the Bible or the Koran literally. But holding (extreme) religious beliefs can also mean, for example, that one blindly believes conspiracy theories about "Jews as the root of all evil."[22] I will focus not so much on theological, dogmatic statements as on the narrative, "props," images, and especially the orthopraxis, the search for acts of purity—using a grounded, anthropological, and "lived historical" perspective on religion rather than a bird's-eye perspective.[23]

---

[22] See also Wilkinson (2020), who similarly emphasizes the importance of research into the stories terrorists themselves tell.
[23] This latter perspective is employed, for example, in the excellent macrosociological and macrohistorical studies of Marc Juergensmeyer (2017), Scott Atran (2010), and Karen Armstrong (2014).

Every scholar in religious studies can explain that beliefs of individuals are always related to practice and interact dynamically with the individuals' circumstances and with the people around them. Even the most dogmatic Christians, Muslims, or Jews have adapted their customs and rites to the changing times—to the advent of electricity, motorized vehicles, and so on. Fundamentalism is often described as a reactionary movement to modernity (see Peels 2023a, 740). And in the current era of online preachers and recruiters, the content of right-wing extremist or jihadist beliefs changes from day to day and varies according to platform, recruiter, or imam. This dynamic interaction between belief and practice is known as the *orthopraxis* of a specific religion. Every religion, or, more precisely, every congregation within that religion, pursues its own orthopraxis. Some congregations sing isorhythmically, while others have a live band at the front of the church. Some mosques give women a visible place to pray, in others they are separated from the men. The beliefs of young people today are often far more defined by their social activities and relationships than by doctrines they have been taught (see Day 2009).

I therefore use the term *religious praxis* to refer to all the practices, rituals, and symbols an individual or community utilizes as part of their religious faith in a bigger, coherent metaphysical narrative. Such practices provide coherence for a large group of people and enable the individual to be part of both a metaphysical whole and a real or perceived social community. Orthopraxis is a religious praxis in which the struggle for purity and the correct—mostly in the sense of strict, orthodox, or even fundamentalist— interpretation of forms, rituals, and practices takes center stage.[24] The radical redemption narrative is thus as much a cognitive belief as it is a framework for individual social and emotional practice and collective action, as depicted in figure 1.4.

This figure shows that the narrative of radical redemption includes the orthopraxis, emotions, and cognitive beliefs of terrorist perpetrators. However, these constitutive elements need contextualization—on the macrohistorical level, we need to know how social, political, and cultural

---

[24] The concept of praxis as a complement to dogma was developed in the religious sciences in the 1970s and 1980s; see, for example, Boff (1987) and Gutiérrez (1974). In effect, it builds epistemologically on Durkheim's notion that, besides being a system of faith-based beliefs, religion is always a unified set of practices relative to sacred things and is experienced as a community through rituals and activities (Durkheim 2008). People do not need to be able to read to be religious. Nor do they need to know the catechism or the Koran by heart to lead a deeply religious life. For a fascinating study of a form of orthopraxis within Islam, see Abu-Zahra (1997, 37–50, 75).

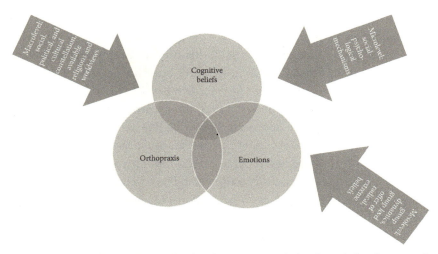

Figure 1.4 The narrative of radical redemption as a hybrid, multilevel approach

constellations facilitate and produce specific narratives; on the mesolevel, how group dynamics foster and disseminate the offer of a particular narrative; and on the microlevel, how social-psychological, pathological mechanisms trigger a narrative and make it stick for the individual. This hybrid, multilevel approach helps us in paying greater attention to what terrorists do, complementary to what they say or write, as their actions contain at least as much meaning and conviction as their words. As I said earlier, I am interested in the exact relation between terrorists' religious beliefs, emotions, and actions. For instance, how does the desire for redemption of radicalizing individuals and members of terrorist organizations play out? And what are the religious narratives that jihadists and extremists listen to and tell each other? Asking these questions enables me to reconstruct the way in which the terrorist individuals I interviewed found a home in the worldwide spiritual and militant landscapes that radical and terrorist ideologies offered them. And, very importantly, it helps me to understand in which context, when, where, and how they threw themselves in the midst of these radical redemption narratives and committed themselves to practices of terrorist violence.

Scope of the Book

The first three chapters offer background and historical context to the theoretical angle. We look in detail at the narrative psychological theory of

Dan McAdams, who is, as far as I am aware, the only psychologist who has established a concrete link between religion and psychology by means of the concept of redemption. As said, this concept deeply resonates with insights on radicalization in existing literature, but it has never been properly operationalized before in this field of research (see McAdams 2006). This is followed by a brief look at the first waves of terrorism from the perspective of the radical redemption approach. I describe how terrorists, individually and collectively, have always embraced the idea and practice of redemption. From these historical precursors of radical redemption narratives, it becomes clear that the degree of intensity with which this motive is legitimized and recognized by an existing group, organization, or constituency is historically contingent, and that the radical redemption narrative has acted as a frame for collective action in many diverging ways.

Chapters 4, 5, and 6 offer findings and patterns based on the interviews conducted in the Netherlands and Indonesia. Empirical and descriptive, these chapters examine the life histories of the interviewed terrorists in terms of radical redemption, from desire to practice, from dreams to action. I explore how this approach helps us understand what really drove them and under what conditions redemption narratives become less persuasive. This process is closely related to events: for instance, the fall of the Berlin Wall and the end of the caliphate undermined the persuasive eschatological power of the respective underlying narratives. Alternative voices can also contribute strongly to the decline of the redemption narrative; for example, when actors within a movement come forward who wish to pursue change by means of nonviolent methods. Or the holy status of the redeemers may be disputed by members of the group who would rather, perhaps, leave redemption to God, Allah, political leaders, or society. Various factors can speed up the process, as we will see when we discuss what is currently happening to Boko Haram and Al-Shabaab members detained in Cameroon and Kenya.

Chapter 7 presents accounts of non-Western, tribal-jihadist, and secular redemption narratives and compares them with the accounts given in the previous chapters. Chapter 8 is reflective and looks for a grounded theory of radical redemption, together with guidelines on how to debunk the power of redemption narratives and thus break the cycle. Chapter 9—a short, concluding chapter—brings all findings and recommendations for follow-up research together. The three appendices outline the challenges and pitfalls of conducting conversations with convicted terrorists and explain how, despite the limitations and disadvantages, such conversations can provide the basis for a solid analysis of what terrorists believe.

Positionality

In light of research into religion and terrorism, conducted in the Netherlands, Indonesia, and indirectly in Cameroon, a few notes on my own positionality are in order at the end of this first chapter and at the beginning of this book. What does it mean that I carried out a research project on religious radicalization and interviewed terrorist convicts, most of them people of color, while being female, Christian, white, highly educated, and from the Netherlands myself? Although disclosing these elements of self-identification makes my position more vulnerable, as has been noted elsewhere (Massoud 2022), I will briefly discuss how my positionality may have influenced my research and data collection, and how I dealt with this.

First of all, as a female scholar, I have noticed before in my interviews with male perpetrators—be it former Wehrmacht and SS soldiers, officers of the East German secret police, or terrorists from the third wave of terrorism[25]—that being a woman made me less menacing to them, and they talked more easily to me. The same happened with the male terrorists I interviewed for this study (when I conducted my study, there were no female terrorist convicts detained). For me, my gender identity—including being a mother, which they often asked about—was therefore largely a benefit rather than a burden.

The same held for being a Christian. Personally, I recognize the desire to live a pure life as well as grappling with the knowledge that everything is not as it should be, that one makes wrong choices every day, and that we are called to live a better, more honest life. With a few of the detainees, I have had highly personal and sometimes deep conversations about sin, desires, suffering, and injustice. In talking with religious interviewees, it helped that I did not discard their stories on miracles, angels, and dreams, and their longing for deliverance, heaven, and paradise, as irrational or delusional. ("Do you believe in angels too?" one detainee asked me at some point. My

---

[25] I conducted interviews with Wehrmacht and SS veterans for Thom Verheul's 2003 documentary *Op de drempel van het grote vergeten*; see https://www.vprogids.nl/cinema/films/film~1903887~op-de-drempel-van-het-grote-vergeten~.html. For my interviews with Stasi officials, see De Graaf (2007); for my interviews with terrorists from the 1970s, see De Graaf (2011).

answer was that I had not seen one myself, but would and could not rule out the possibility on the mere basis of our simple human senses.) What was difficult for me personally—and gave me headaches every time I came back from my interviews—is that redemption was appropriated and perverted to legitimize acts of terrorist violence, whereas in my own faith and the mainstream Dutch Protestant community I belong to, redemption is considered as something that we should leave to God; we cannot bring it about ourselves. For my interviewees, it was enough that I was a religious believer, too, and I had the impression that that made it considerably easier for them to tell me their stories. At the same time, to make sure I did not unwittingly apply conceptual or normative religious biases informed by my own theological upbringing and socialization, I worked with an expert in Arabic and Islamic studies and an Arabist, who reviewed and read my texts.

Interestingly, although I anticipated that being academically educated would make it more difficult for me to set up a conversational connection with my interviewees, who without exception had a different educational background, none of them academic, this was not the case. Instead, it helped that they recognized me from television, where I sometimes comment on issues relating to conflict, terrorism, and war; they knew that I was a professor and were very keen to explain to me that I had got many things wrong and would do well to listen to them. That I was a relatively well-known terrorism expert and a university professor seemed to work in my advantage. "We saw you on television! And now we are going to tell you how things really are," as one interviewee opened the interview. What was more, it prompted reluctant convicts to talk to me.

What was more difficult for me to reckon with is that I am white and from the Netherlands, whereas some of the detainees I interviewed in the Netherlands and Indonesia are people of color and in a position of vulnerability (on the latter, see appendix 3, which explains protocol and integrity standards). Here, let me briefly say a few things about my position as a white person with a Dutch nationality.

It seemed that the Dutch-Moroccan and Dutch-Turkish detainees—constituting the majority of my interviewees—considered themselves just as much Dutch as I considered myself Dutch. As for the Indonesians, I tried to identify their attitudes and sentiments toward me as representing the country that had formerly colonized and oppressed their people. Yet, they explained to me that Indonesia is such a young country, demographically speaking, that there is hardly any public memory of Dutch colonial rule—dating back more than six or seven generations of Indonesians by now—to speak of in today's Indonesian society. It is, and remains, a controversial historical issue, and rightly so: only recently, new official reports were published on the use of extreme violence by the Dutch armed forces and authorities in the war against Indonesian independence.[26] Yet, there are national traumas far closer to the surface of collective memory in Indonesia, such as the anti-communist purges of 1965 and 1966, when around a million people were killed. Moreover, my Indonesian interviewees disclosed how happy they were with the collected works of my "Dutch professor colleague from Leiden," Christiaan Snouck Hurgronje (1857–1936), who, as an adviser to the Dutch colonial authorities, produced numerous works on daily life, customs, and traditions of the early Muslims of the Indonesian archipelago. Precisely these books had helped them in their search for the "purest" forms of Muslim worship in their lands (see chapter 4).

So, although I was very much aware of the colonial heritage of my nationality, it did not seem to play a burdensome role for my interviewees, and my Indonesian colleagues in Jakarta confirmed this. Instead, my outsider status as a foreigner and as a white, Christian woman in Jakarta made it easier for me to ask simple, candid, and sometimes perhaps even seemingly naive questions about the beliefs of my interviewees. That I was, in their eyes, a harmless and neutral outsider also seemed to make them, former terrorist detainees and marginalized people, less wary, more open, and more comfortable while talking to me. Still, to make sure that these elements of my positionality did not unwittingly bear on my research outcomes, I worked with an Islamic and Indonesian female research assistant while collecting the data and asked an Indonesian Muslim colleague to read the texts.

In short, although the reported elements of self-identification were, and are, things to reckon with, on the whole, I have tried to rule out indirect influences by submitting my texts to Muslim and Indonesian scholars. What is more, parts of my research have already been peer-reviewed and published, and have been subject to commentaries from scholars from a wide variety of fields (theology, sociology, philosophy, religious studies, psychology, history), both religious and secular, in academic settings and lay

---

[26] See https://www.niod.nl/en/projects/independence-decolonization-violence-and-war-indonesia-1945-1950.

circumstances, including the terrorist detention centers in the Netherlands, where I discussed the findings with the prison employees.[27] All in all, I therefore consider such elements to be more of a benefit than a burden; and being aware of them and addressing them candidly during the interviews seemed to break down barriers rather than erect them.

---

[27] See, for example, the following publications that were based on this research: De Graaf and Van den Bos (2021); De Graaf (2021); and the special issue "Dossier radicale verlossing" (2023), *Tijdschrift Sociologie* 4, which contains numerous articles discussing and reflecting on this research project, including my response, in Dutch.

2
The Desire for Radical Redemption
A Novel Approach

Generative Life Stories

The notion of radical redemption is crucial to this study and to the approach adopted here. Having borrowed the notion of redemption from narrative psychologist Dan McAdams, I will explain here why and how I use it as a *sensitizing concept*. This means it functions as an "interpretive device" to arrive at a grounded theory of radical redemption, rather than as a full-fledged definition with "fixed bench marks" (Bowen 2006, 13–14).[1] Let me offer some background on the terminology and psychology behind the idea of redemption.

McAdams analyzes the way in which people tell their life stories and thereby create their own narrative identity. In his (2006) book *The Redemptive Self*, he describes how the people he encountered through his practice often constructed their life stories around certain negative, life-threatening situations with which they had been confronted in the past. Remarkably, his clients gave these accounts of disasters and setbacks an explicitly positive twist. After suffering from cancer or drug addiction, losing their jobs or their loved ones, they recovered and were healed, restored. After the experience, they were determined to make something of their lives and to help others. McAdams refers to these people as *generative* personalities: having suffered a significant setback, they wanted to do something good, to contribute to making the world a better place and tell others about their experience. A typical generative life story features a sudden change of course from a negative situation of suffering to one of redemption or liberation. For McAdams (2006, 4), redemption is the psychological experience of deliverance from

---

[1] A sensitizing concept gives direction to an as yet unclear combination of social relations, patterns, and causal links. The notion comes from the methodology of the grounded theory approach, which I examine in greater detail in chapter 8. For a more precise definition of these concepts, see Bowen (2006). On grounded theory, see also Van den Bos (2020a, 40–2).

suffering combined with engagement for a better world. As a result of their experiences, generative people develop specific coping mechanisms in which they devote their energy to promoting the well-being and development of future generations—McAdams (2006, 28–52) sees *generativity* as working to achieve something that transcends immediate self-interest and even the horizon of one's own life. All this becomes a little clearer if we look at what McAdams sees as the opposite of a generative life, which has a *redemption sequence* as its narrative—the opposite is a *contamination sequence*, that is, a sequence of life events seen as contaminating all that is good in a person's life (see McAdams et al. 2001, 474).

Such a psychologically informed, narrative approach to life stories aligns perfectly with Arie Kruglanski's insights on "the quest for significance" and with Martha Crenshaw's findings on how terrorists use narratives of redemption (Shah et al. 2002; Kruglanski et al. 2009, 335; Crenshaw 2007, 153). That is why I apply this approach to the radicalization processes experienced by terrorists. I thus reconfigure McAdams's concept of generic redemption and speak of *radical* redemption instead. Radical redemption links McAdams's narrative psychological insights on generative personalities to the radical and violent or violence-glorifying way in which terrorists look for significance and embrace the idea of redemption as a coping mechanism and strategy. We shall see just how important their narratives of radical redemption were to most of the convicted terrorists I spoke with, as well as how often their life stories ultimately turned into narratives of contamination and disappointment. But first, a little more on generativity.

Almost all of us, of course, occasionally do something for others or do something good that does not directly benefit ourselves. But McAdams speaks of generativity in cases where people explicitly mention this as a motive, tell their life stories explicitly in terms of certain patterns of redemption, and define their identity in terms of it. He identifies a number of recurring patterns. For example, it is a very logical step for his—American—clients to adopt a Christian redemption narrative. These narratives follow a Christian-religious pattern: the person in question seeks atonement for their sins, experiences forgiveness, and feels called to lead a life of gratitude and helping others. The source domain of this type of social appraisal is the Christian religion; the redemptive move (coping mechanism) is the forgiveness of sins. Other kinds of redemption narratives are also conceivable. One person, for instance, was still illiterate as an aging adult; he learned to read and helped ghetto children with their schoolwork. Here, knowledge is the source domain of social appraisal, and elevation through education is the liberating element. Or take the typical American rags-to-riches story: this, too, is a narrative of liberation, of shaking off the shackles of poverty and using one's new wealth to help others (McAdams 2006, 24–5). Finally, another very common narrative is winning the fight against cancer: a career man or woman becomes seriously ill, is cured, and retrains as a nurse out of gratitude.

For generative life stories, it is important that people personally and consciously experience such a crisis and recovery process and that they can talk about it purposefully. Outsiders must be able to clearly identify the subjects' coping mechanisms in the stories. In addition, in these stories, there is a clear qualitative distinction between life *before* and life *after* the redemptive move. Lastly, and not unimportantly, the stories have cost these people a great deal of time, energy, effort, faith, and repentance. McAdams cites many religious and belief-based redemption narratives. That is only natural, because the stories feature many existing and recognizable symbols and motives. They also derive power and legitimacy from the fact that religious and belief-based institutions and organizations—churches, sects, faith communities—often push generative people to the forefront, urging them to tell their stories in religious publications, during services, or at political gatherings. In this way, individual life stories find validation in a wider community or with a higher authority.

McAdams's research thus concerns people who tell redemptive life stories and who want to contribute to a greater good, such as the community. Now, it seems a little cynical to apply this same approach to terrorists, who devote themselves not to generation but to degeneration and destruction. Yet, it is important to acknowledge that terrorism as a movement thrives on a mass of followers who fully believe that a great injustice has been committed in their own lives and in the lives of others and that it is their task to do something about it. In other words, they see themselves as repairing what went wrong and doing a good thing. They often gain a sense of well-being and meaning from their violent actions. Terrorists, too, live lives filled with the "dynamics of redemption stories," and especially with the "arrogance" of individuals who believe in a personal calling and think they are part of a "chosen" group (McAdams 2006, 90–1).[2] Almost all the radical, violent activists and terrorists I spoke with displayed this sense of having been

---

[2] McAdams applies this to life stories of individual Americans, but his psychological insights on the concept of feeling chosen or called can also be applied to radicalizing individuals.

called. They remained thoroughly convinced of their own moral right and could, even in prison, recall the strength of their former conviction that they had been chosen, singled out, to do something big.

Generative Terrorists?

As said, identifying generativity in the life stories of terrorists may seem unnatural, because for McAdams it so emphatically refers to people who want to do good after experiencing redemption. Yet, this generative approach can be connected to the quest for meaning in people's lives in relation to radicalization and terrorism studies. Terrorists do not consider themselves horrible human beings—they view themselves as fulfilling a higher mission in carrying out their deeds. Within a context of religious beliefs about sin, redemption, and salvation, they interpret their acts of violence, martyrdom, and warfare as filled with higher, salvific, and redemptive meaning. For them, radical redemption functions as a cultural worldview that shapes both cognitions and appraisals of certain stressful situations, steers emotions in a specific direction, and facilitates mobilization toward radical and violent behavior (see, e.g., Van den Bos 2020c; Van den Bos et al. 2005).

This insight into radical redemption as a narrative carrier for radical social appraisals fits with the observation that radical violence may buffer the realization that life is unjust, and that fundamental situations of injustice and inequality will continue to exist if one does not take arms against that injustice. In their struggle against injustice and oppression, radicalizing people will turn even more to actions, including violent ones, to confirm their cultural worldviews. This is in line with the ideas of social psychologist Ernest Becker (1971, 1973, 1975), who offered a psychodynamic explanation of specific cultural worldviews that help to make sense of existential uncertainties and fears. In embracing religious beliefs, the individual simultaneously lays down their whole existence to some higher meaning and is able to expand the self as an individual heroic personality. In understanding the willingness to surrender to sacrifice and martyrdom, as some religious terrorists do, Becker's work is key.

Thus, in accordance with the ideas of Kruglanski and Becker, terrorists' deeds of political or religious violence can be seen as a quest for meaning. Their lives, until then lacking in meaning, can be lifted up out of the grind of daily life, misery, or even disgrace and crime, and acquire value in the light of a greater narrative. The terrorist act is the moment, the practice, in which redemption is achieved. This is a radical form of redemption, one that is accompanied by violence and threat, and transcends the existing, conventional frameworks of activism, devotion, and political mobilization. And it is generative: it enables the perpetrator to achieve a higher state of consciousness and to give their banal or criminal behavior a higher meaning. Whether someone is arrested for distributing violent material, for buying explosives, or for being an accomplice to or actually participating in an attack, the act immediately acquires a deeper, metaphysical meaning: from the perspective of the terrorist ideology or religion, it may be seen as punishing evil, eradicating injustice, or restoring law and order.

So, how does this work? How does the idea of radical redemption relate to existing theories of radicalization? The approach chosen here in essence relates to that which motivates the thoughts, feelings, and behavior of terrorists. That is to this day one of the major questions addressed by research on terrorism and radicalization: What drives terrorists? Generally speaking, the psychological literature suggests that people's motives and behavior are driven by goals that they can achieve or hope to achieve (Kruglanski et al. 2002). Redemption can be interpreted both as a way in which one may achieve the greatest goal in one's life and as a frame to appraise one's current life situation. The notion plays a central role in practically all religions and belief systems, including such main secular worldviews as socialism, communism, and even nationalism. People also feel better if they do not pursue their goals alone, but together with others. Collectively working toward a greater good motivates their behavior; it gives them energy, makes them feel good, and focuses their actions.

People thus strive most deeply to achieve important goals. And the closer they get, the more fanatical their efforts become. They engage in *goal shielding*, putting on blinders and focusing only on the finish line (Shah et al. 2002). If they are prevented from achieving their goal at the last moment, they experience enormous frustration; it unleashes strong emotions, perhaps even extreme behavior (Gurr 1970; see also Berkowitz 1993; Folger 1977). The link between these emotions, the social and cognitive appraisal of a specific situation, the application of coping mechanisms to deal with this situation, and the development of a perspective for action to improve it can, in many cases, take on the form of a redemption narrative or experience.

Let us return momentarily to the pursuit of goals. People need cultural narratives and interpretation frameworks to give meaning to their situation during times of stress and crisis, and to their attempts to transcend their situation. We need our culture, in the broad sense of the word, in order to deal with our existential uncertainties and lead meaningful lives (see especially Becker 1973). Why do we get up in the morning and do things? Because life has meaning. In other words, we get up because what we do has meaning: it leads to the achievement of important goals. But people need guidelines to help them decide what is meaningful. They find such guidelines in religion, ideologies, and other beliefs, as well as in highly culturally determined forms and symbols. For instance, some people may maintain a lifestyle-based worldview and transcend personal life crises by taking up running or becoming vegans, repertoires made available to them by such authoritative sources as diet gurus, doctors, or celebrities. Others may burn a candle in church because their grandmother or their parents used to do so.[3]

The same applies to violent political movements and terrorist organizations. Note that I do apply these general insights to terrorists because the normalcy hypothesis still stands, and research has not yet established that terrorists should be considered as abnormal, pathological perpetrators (see, e.g., Victoroff 2005; Horgan 2014). Researchers have shown, for example, that after 9/11, North African Muslims in Britain increasingly felt discriminated against and started to compare their experiences of injustice. They shared certain symbols, stories, and anecdotes with each other, together developing a repertoire of street language and violent behavior to give expression to these feelings of injustice. Creating a group narrative and a collective pattern of behavior tied the members of the group even closer together, and the shared symbols of injustice became even more potent (see Githens-Mazer 2008). A similar collective pattern of language and action was prevalent among left-wing revolutionary activists and terrorists in the 1970s. They customarily expressed their desire for radical liberation and redemption by calling police officers "pigs," referring to their own comrades as "revolutionaries," and glorifying the use of AK-47s in word and deed.

For terrorists and violent radicals, their actions are a solution to and a buffer against the unpleasant and frustrating sense that certain things in the world are not as they should be. Not only is radical violence functional, it also has psychological value: it helps them to come to terms with the fact

---

[3] For the sociological approach to rituals and the cultural determination of human action and interaction patterns, see Blumer (1969) and Mead (1934).

that there are fundamental injustices and that their group and their norms and values are in jeopardy. When people are confronted with all the things that undermine their lives or hinder them from achieving their goals—death, injustice, discrimination, evil—they have a stronger need to confirm their symbols, rituals, and ideological heritage, if necessary, through violence (see, e.g., Van den Bos et al. 2005).

For generative people, it is also important to attribute a deeper meaning to those setbacks or frustrations and then to pursue their goals with even greater effort and engagement. Violence and terrorism cannot be understood in purely functional and strategic terms. In most cases, strategically speaking, terrorists do not achieve much—at least if we do not count instilling fear as a strategic goal. Terrorist organizations that are successful in the medium to long term are very rare. And the ones that have survived have done so because—like the IRA in Ireland and the Revolutionary Armed Forces of Colombia (FARC) in Colombia—they made the transition to a political organization. Therefore, terrorism and radicalization are always also symbolic phenomena—they do something to and for those who pursue them. Violent symbolic actions satisfy the need of terrorists to do something meaningful with their lives. For many adherents of radical and terrorist movements, terrorism is not a political or strategic activity but the execution of a radical, ethical program that provides elevation, punishment, and meaning. In the words of Crenshaw (1987, 20), the incentive to join a terrorist organization or become a terrorist lies in the fact that it offers "a path to salvation," a road to change, and a way "to transcend reality as much as to transform it." While this may sound almost delirious, it is in fact what we observe in the field.

I am thus explicitly concerned here with what drives terrorists to embrace or support violence as an expression of their quest for significance. By proposing the theme of radical redemption, in line with the theory of motivated behavior, and extending McAdams's typologies, I aim to transcend the debate on religious versus political motivations. That is not to say that there is no distinction between religious and political-ideological motives, but their underlying psychological processes are similar. Moreover, drawing an imaginary dividing line between religion, beliefs, and political leanings is senseless in the context of theocratic or totalitarian movements. Whether a redemption narrative is political-ideological or religious in nature is more a matter of availability, scale, and gradation than of psychology. Stories can vary, but human psychology remains the same. Furthermore, it is only by comparing religious, ideological, and cultural expressions of redemption and bringing them under a single theoretical umbrella that we can determine whether and how these factors make a difference.

In this psychological-narrative context, I consider radical redemption as a phenomenon that comprises the following six components: it is a *narrative* that an individual upholds to interpret a stressful, problematic life situation (*appraisal*) and to deal with it (*coping mechanism*), so that it motivates the individual to *sacrifice* themselves or others in a violent or violence-glorifying action in the expectation of a *reward* (redemption) for themselves or for their community. That reward is transcendent but can range from secular (e.g., liberating the working classes) to divine (e.g., paradise, the forgiveness of sins). Redemption is achieved when the sacrifice is made, the perpetrator's own community validates the action (*validation*), and religious leaders accord the perpetrator a higher status—possibly that of martyr—in the group.[4] If that does not materialize, the narrative of redemption becomes one of contamination and disappointment.

Of course, in a religious context, the concept of redemption acquires a connotation that has been described often and in detail: in addition to being an action in the here and now, the act of redemption is imbued with a redemptive-historical, eschatological, and/or cosmological meaning. Yet, acts of redemption are not only to be found among religious extremists and terrorist groups. The transcendental element—an act that rises above the horizon of the perpetrator's own immediate experience—is also important to secular-oriented terrorists, such as ethnic nationalists, anarchists, and right-wing extremists. For them, the sacrifice is a means to transcend their own finiteness or to do penance for a criminal past, or is an attempt to alleviate the lot of their own group.

Blood, which is necessary for redemption, relates to various forms of sacrifice. From their own perspective, terrorists make a sacrifice by jeopardizing their comfort and safety and taking action, putting their own lives at risk in the struggle—or committing a suicide attack, the ultimate act of sacrifice. Furthermore, terrorists are fully prepared to risk and even take the lives of others. They are driven not only by a desire for revenge but also by a willingness to kill people who are not directly seen as the enemy or as targets, thus creating a "theater of fear" and drawing attention to their grievances. Terrorists, as perpetrators, see themselves equally as victims—of the West, of the system, and so forth—and may see their intended victims also as

---

[4] For the psychology, see McAdams (2006).

perpetrators, as representatives of the system they are fighting against. Targets and victims may be selected as symbolic scapegoats—the World Trade Center for Al Qaeda, a mosque for Brenton Tarrant—or because they are considered instrumental; for instance, the young social democrats killed on Utøya by Anders Breivik.[5] A terrorist attack is always generative for the perpetrator; it is violence for a higher cause. Whether they sacrifice their own lives or the lives of others depends on the function and symbolism of the specific attack and campaign. But either way, they put their own safety and lives in danger.[6] In the following section, we take a brief look at various interpretations of the idea and practice of redemption in the religions and ideologies of the modern age.

Radical Redemption as a Way to Cope with Injustice

There is another reason why McAdams's concept of redemption is applicable to terrorism. This has to do with the flipside of generativity, namely, that which touches upon darker feelings and offers a coping mechanism to work through them. The narrative of radical redemption acknowledges and gives voice to perceived feelings of injustice and frustration and subsequently connects them to a specific course of redemptive action. It connects a deeply felt sense of shortcoming and feelings of injustice regarding specific grievances to the decision to resort to terrorist violence to overcome these grievances.

The terrorists I interviewed did not on their own initiative refer directly to personal traumas. They did, however, all speak of experiencing a sense of deficiency, of falling short in some way. This was frequently related to a feeling of injustice. Kees van den Bos has convincingly shown that the perception of personal or collective injustice is an essential component of every radicalization process. Yet, *injustice* is still a remote and abstract concept, referring to things done by others. By contrast, for the convicted terrorists I spoke with, the sense of injustice was very personal: it was about their own emotional

---

[5] Right-wing extremist Brenton Tarrant committed a terrorist attack on March 15, 2019, killing fifty-one Muslims at a mosque in Christchurch, New Zealand. Right-wing extremist and white supremacist Anders Behring Breivik committed attacks in Norway on July 22, 2011, killing eight people by detonating a van bomb in Oslo and killing sixty-nine people in a mass shooting on the island of Utøya.

[6] An abundance of literature has been produced on this issue. See especially Devji (2009); Kahn (2008); Girard and Doran (2008).

appraisal of injustices either done to them or done to others—to children in Syria, for example. When they addressed these injustices, it triggered personal feelings of falling short. They or their group had suffered from injustice, and it was now *their responsibility* to do something about it; it was *their fault* if they stayed at home and did nothing.[7]

Owning that injustice revealed, very often explicitly and sometimes implicitly, a sense of guilt or shame. They had gradually come to the conclusion that if they did not act, they would be guilty of looking the other way: they wanted and needed to free themselves of that feeling of injustice, of a moral or actual deficit. Before any thoughts of vengeance arrived—if they did at all—they felt a moral responsibility to do something about the injustice and the deficit. Almost all the convicts I spoke to had reached a turning point at some time in their lives when they chose violence as a way to "do good"; violence to them was thus not simply a matter of lashing out in anger. That turning point was linked to their desire to redeem themselves from their own sins and/or to deliver their community from evil. Guilt, penance, and responsibility merged to generate a personal desire to act and boost their feelings of self-worth in the face of a real or imagined discriminating or repressive government. Sometimes, this took the form of a political narrative—"The West/Assad oppresses Muslims"—but more often, the narrative was radical-ethical—"It is my duty to help my fellow Muslims in Syria, and I am to blame if I do not." And radical redemption was the frame that shaped this narrative.

Redemption as a Religious and Cultural Theme

Before exploring the provenance of the concept of redemption, we make a brief excursion into the religious studies on redemption. To me, coming from a Christian background, redemption seemed, at first glance, a very Christian concept. In the New Testament, it is usually referred to by the Greek word *apolutrosis*, which suggests atonement or paying a price to be delivered from evil. The English word *redemption* has the same double meaning: dictionaries define it both in theological terms and in terms of

---

[7] Kees van den Bos (2018, 187–212) emphatically notes that, as a component of radicalization processes, injustice not only comprises a "cold-cognitive" process of analysis but is also accompanied by strong feelings ("hot cognition"). I would add that owning injustice and shifting the focus to one's own role in addressing it are also important components, reflecting, in fact, a search for agency, for one's own role in dealing with and combating injustice. It is, therefore, also about a sense of falling short in one's own life.

clearing a financial debt. It therefore implies a debt incurred or a sin committed by one or more perpetrators (offenders, sinners), as well as a judicial institution that determines that a debt has been incurred or a sin committed, the payment of which (atonement, penance) results in redemption.

In the biblical notion of redemption, all people accumulate debts or sins that they cannot ultimately pay off or atone for. That requires an intermediary—an advocate, scapegoat, or sacrificial lamb, supplied by the divine judge himself, who sent his own Son to fulfill that role. In Christian theology, redemption thus refers to the deliverance of humankind from sin through the crucifixion of the Messiah, the Savior (Luke 2:11). In this way, redemption has also become an eschatological concept, building a bridge—in Christian theology—between the creation and the fall, the birth of Christ and his crucifixion, the here and now and the ultimate Second Coming and Last Judgment. Redemption, in its Christian cultural sense (but it also returns in modern secular ideologies and, to a certain degree, in the radical doctrines of jihadists, as we will see), is necessary to the notion of ultimate salvation. And, conversely, the conversion and redemption of an individual is an important event in the whole redemptive history of God's plan with the world.

In addition to its original concrete, biblical-historical meaning, redemption has acquired a metaphorical meaning: it refers to atonement, to paying a price to be delivered from evil. This has been a very strong theme in the history of society and ethics, as described extensively by Max Weber (1922, 301–31). In the literature, culture, and philosophy of the West, the concept has subsequently been secularized and psychologized and has appeared as a recurring pattern in a wide range of novels and stage plays (see Brown 1981, s.v. "redemption").

Despite the forcefulness with which Christian theology and culture have annexed the concept, it also plays a very significant role in other world religions. Enlightenment in the Buddhist tradition and *Prāyaścitta* in the Indian religions are related to atonement and to deliverance and redemption from sin and guilt. Islam and Judaism can also be seen as religions of redemption. Judaism has an abundance of religious rituals and practices that relate to redemption in both senses of the term, such as the *pidyon haben*, a ceremony conducted after the birth of a firstborn son in which the child's obligation to become a priest is "bought off" (redeemed) by presenting silver coins to a kohen, a descendant of the priestly family of Aaron. Much more widely known is the scapegoat ritual performed on Yom Kippur. Described in the biblical book of Leviticus, the ritual entailed sending a kid goat—as a symbol of the sins of the people of Israel—away into the wilderness.

In Islam, various concepts are used to cover the idea of redemption. By submitting to Allah's will and laws ("submission" is the literal meaning of *Islam*), following the true faith (*iman*), and leading a virtuous life, believers will be blessed by Allah. To deliver themselves from their sins, they must turn to Allah, show repentance, and perform new good deeds, such as praying and giving alms. Muslims have no concept of original sin. They do not adhere to the Augustinian idea that humankind and the world have fallen from grace and tend toward evil. The theological anthropology of Islam has a more optimistic and activist view of humankind and thus resembles liberal and free-thinking Christian denominations remarkably closely (Lange 2016).

For that reason, Sunni Islam has no clear central principle of redemption, unlike Christendom. Nevertheless, Muslims have a duty to deliver, redeem, and purify themselves from all evil and sin, and to ensure that they return every day to the correct form of worship.[8] Terms like *inqadh* (salvation, redemption), *islah* (improvement, correction), *tazkiah* (purification of the self), and *kaffarah* (atonement) demonstrate the importance of repentance and the performance of *hasanat* (good deeds) to keep believers on the path of righteousness. The Koran refers repeatedly to sin and to the need for *tawba* (repentance) and to cancel out bad deeds with good deeds: "Allah loves those who turn to Him constantly and He loves those who keep themselves pure and clean" (Koran 2:222; see also 20:82). Widely used and accessible commentaries on the Koran tend to speak of a register or list of all believers' names on which good deeds can cancel out bad deeds until the individual's soul is saved and their sins redeemed.[9] For example, Omar, the second caliph, famed for conquering Jerusalem, was seen as an apocalyptic figure and was rewarded with the nickname *al-Farooq*, which can be translated both as "he who distinguishes between believers and unbelievers" and as "the Savior."

Another important element of redemption in Islam is martyrdom (Cook 2007; Hatina 2014). Choosing to become a martyr is an extreme act of atonement, with redemption as the ultimate aim. The act must be committed with true and pious intentions. A short film entitled *Sawlat al-fida*, made and

---

[8] For a description of Islamic practices of conversion and the associated redemption, see, for example, Mossière (2020).

[9] See, for example, various texts, including Tahir (2018), on the website of the Yaqeen Institute for Islamic Research: https://yaqeeninstitute.org/.

distributed by IS, is in circulation on the Internet. The title can be translated as "the costs of redemption," establishing a direct link between sacrifice and committing violent attacks. *Fida* means "martyrdom" or "sacrifice." In the 1970s, Palestinian terrorists called themselves *fedayeen*, from the Arabic *fida'iyyin*. *Fida* has more secular connotations than *shahid*, which is the term for *martyr* in current use in jihadist circles, and it is interesting that IS is using this word again.

In Salafism, the term *islah* is commonly used to focus on the need for purification, reform, and change, not only in one's own sinful life but also in the wider community and society (see, e.g., De Koning 2018). The concept of *inqadh*, deliverance from godless repression, has more political implications. Salafists often use this terminology in connection with the struggle for truth. Here, redemption lies in a change of course by a godless individual who turns away from worldly concerns and focuses on the source—the Koran and the traditions of the Prophet in their purest form. Jihadist Salafists interpret this personal change, of course, as a violent reversal, an act of martyrdom. Their martyr's death is the ultimate proof of their true belief, of the fact that they have embraced the truth. Redemption is inherent to their martyrdom (see, e.g., Wagemakers 2016; De Koning et al. 2013).

Is redemption, then, a concept that can occur only within religions? Not at all. There is now wide recognition in sociology and cultural anthropology that the quest for meaning, the formulating of goals that rise above the immediate horizon of people's lives, is inherent in all human cultures. Stretching it somewhat, one could even argue that all humans are religious creatures: almost everyone believes in some higher goal—transcendent or immanent—and is willing to make sacrifices to pursue it. Our "altruistic gene," which causes us to work for the good of the community and take part in fundraising campaigns, also leads to exclusion and stigmatization of the perceived enemies of the community. If we see the here and now as imperfect and broken and project an ideal future beyond the horizon, we need to work, invest, pay, bleed, and suffer to bring it closer. In this way, redemption—paying off a debt to secure that future—can be found to a greater or lesser extent in virtually all ideologies. In the past, people have become radicalized to defend their race, nation, tribe, or football club.[10] The question is therefore not whether redemption only plays a role in religious contexts, but how the

---

[10] Religious themes certainly recur frequently in the football world; take Dutch legend Johan Cruijff, who was given the name "El Salvador" (the Savior) in Barcelona.

social experience of redemption is formed. How does redemption as a trope engrain itself in a given culture, how is it imbued with meaning in a community, and by whom? What form does the perceived sin or guilt and the corresponding penance or atonement take, who must atone, and how? It is thus very important to examine how the idea of radical redemption is given shape and validated by a specific community and belief system.

Obviously, religion is often a strengthening factor in this respect: if concrete ethical practices can be dictated by holy texts, or if perpetrators are given the prospect of rewards in the afterlife, these are additional arguments that give the theme of redemption greater legitimacy and persuasive power. But secular belief systems also have their perpetrators in search of redemption. Take, for example, the suicide terrorists of the Tamil Tigers (LTTE), the militant liberation movement in Sri Lanka that committed hundreds of attacks from the end of the 1980s. Their acts were seen as symbols of holy sacrifice, and the perpetrators were buried with full religious rituals and interred in temples. These rituals closely resembled Hindu practices of sacrifice and purification: the Tamil Tigers used them in an attempt to unite their support base in collective mourning, to carry them along in a belief in renewal and resurrection through their martyrs' acts of redemption, and to mobilize new recruits for the struggle. Such explicit religious practices embody a form of transcendence that we also see in various secular national liberation movements. But not all such movements embrace a notion of transcendence—some of them remain firmly wed to existentialism and resist every notion that there is a higher meaning outside of this one life (see, e.g., Roberts 2005).

What also becomes clear from this example is that radicality and the dimension of redemption depend heavily on the extent to which they are recognized and acknowledged by a large group of believers. A radical act of redemption acquires greater legitimacy when it is part of an established, strict, recognized system of beliefs or a clearly delineated organization. Terrorists are individuals who are prepared to go to the extreme in the service of their beliefs: to achieve their goal, they are willing to risk not only their own lives but also ours.[11]

---

[11] Thus, I am not talking here about people who are prepared to die for their beliefs or opinions under pressure of persecution, but about people who use those beliefs to commit violence against others.

Redemption as Sacred Praxis

My next important step links the approach of radical redemption to insights on religious radicalization. I will do so, in good Durkheimian and Weberian fashion, by interpreting religion via the concept of the sacred and connecting it to the notion of praxis. With William Cavanaugh (2009), I argue that it is difficult to distinguish between sacred and religious violence. Religion is often understood as an organized and established form of faith. Yet, many individuals do not adhere to any fixed forms of worship or shared rules for practicing their faith, and they still consider themselves religious or spiritual and entertain sacred beliefs. These are beliefs that are nonnegotiable because they touch on sacred core values. Many radicals, activists, and terrorists have very limited theoretical knowledge of the relevant religion or ideology and, in some cases, have hardly read their holy texts, yet they do acknowledge and advocate sacred beliefs. In such cases, what is relevant is not the orthodoxy or dogmas behind those beliefs, but their praxis. Not every violent radical possesses a solid ideological basis, but all of them are well acquainted with practices of threat and coercion related to their beliefs. They may not belong to a respectable church or mainstream Koranic school or madrassa, but they see themselves as very religious. Lorne Dawson (2021a, 4) introduces the term *religiosity*, defined as "the degree of someone's commitment to the practice of a religion," to delineate such self-reported religious feelings and adherence from institutional, organized, and recognized forms and memberships of religion.

With McAdams, I see redemption as a generative response to the experience of evil; it transforms that experience into a better situation for an individual or group. In this light, acts of radical redemption can be seen as recognizable sacred practices or rites—recognizable, that is, through the lens of the underlying shared beliefs. By seeing religion, with Durkheim and Clifford Geertz, as a sociological phenomenon, and by seeking verifiable sacred practices, I aim to circumvent the overestimation of rational, cognitive steps leading to terrorist crimes on a linear scale. It is not the subscription to a particular faith group, denomination, or church, or the visit to a particular mosque that causes people to become terrorists. Nor does the appropriation of a set of radical religious doctrines offer much in terms of predicting future terrorist behavior—at least, this connection has not been established by sound research. In reality, radicalization often occurs through less direct and unpredictable forms of rationality that do not fit the linear, cognitive models devised by Western scientists. Such rationality may be more praxis oriented and performative than cognitive and reflective.

None of the radicals and terrorists I interviewed for this book became terrorists or joined a terrorist organization because they had first read some holy book or doctrinal manifesto, be it the Koran or right-wing extremist and Klansman Louis Beam's (1992) essay on leaderless resistance. Hardly any of my interviewees had a broad or deep religious knowledge, spoke Arabic, or knew the Koran or Hadith[12] by heart. Some were well educated and widely read in a religious sense. But people carrying a copy of *Islam for Dummies* in their bag were just as likely to find their way to the caliphate as the seasoned ideologists in the jihad support network Behind Bars. The common denominator was, rather, a shared perspective on the right cause of action, undergirded by a specific belief-based radical praxis. It is important to bear this in mind when we read the convicts' life stories: although the differences in the level of cognitive knowledge—in relation to their religion—between the interviewees were sometimes enormous, that did not necessarily mean that the faith and devotion of the lesser schooled were any less intense. While the cognitive dimension does matter, extreme beliefs of various kinds, including religious ones, can go hand in hand with a more spontaneous and praxeological radical engagement that is not grounded in deep ideological knowledge.

That is why these terrorist convicts' search for meaning should not be considered, in the first instance, from the perspective of a study of the texts describing the revelations, prophecies, dogmas, Hadith, or fatwas from centuries past. Terrorist tendencies cannot be predicted from an individual's principles or even their image of God. What is important is that they apply those principles in a specific *praxis* within which their search for meaning takes on a violent form. The key to understanding the beliefs and the violence of the terrorist is not predominantly their ideology but their lived and believed praxis, or rather orthopraxis, in which actions and practices instantiate inchoate emotions and beliefs. Although the scope of this study does not allow me to produce general insights on predictors—I am studying religion as moderator, not as predictor—such insights may be generated by a stronger focus on the orthopraxis of radicalizing individuals. On the basis of the interviews I conducted, we may construct the hypothesis that if someone's orthopraxis involves small, ritualistic, symbolic, yet radical practices related

---

[12] Traditional Islamic accounts of the actions and statements of the prophet Muhammad.

THE DESIRE FOR RADICAL REDEMPTION 69

to a search for conversion or redemption, such practices can be expected in due time to lead to actions that are more consequential and more violent. This is discussed in more detail in chapter 8.

We need to increase our understanding of the origins of violent political activism and terrorism. Countless studies have been published on radicalization processes, on why and how they occur, on moments at which an individual becomes receptive to radical ideas (cognitive openings), and on the loss of such radical opinions or patterns of behavior (deradicalization and withdrawal). But the transition from thought to deed, from theory to violent action, remains a mystery, as recently again outlined by Kees van de Bos (2018, 108, 214–17). Why does one believer resort to violence and another does not? Why do some socialists become violent revolutionaries while others are content with attending peaceful sit-ins? The link between ideology, religion, and violence has been completely annexed by radicalization literature, in which radicalization—with the choice for violence as a possible outcome—is considered a process, a development over time. Even when we depict this process as a pyramid, as Fathali Moghaddam (2005) does, it is still assumed that it consists of a series of steps or phases in which a development takes place. The biographies of present-day terrorists, however, suggest that a radicalization process unfolds so quickly that it can be seen more accurately as a leap in the dark. "Suddenly you get it!" shouted a jihadist poster around 2013, showing a group of Dutch recruits on their way to join the battle: "From musician to mujahid!"[13] The assumption that radicalization is a linear process and involves a conscious and gradual embracing of radical ideas is not consistent with many terrorists' stories. Some terrorists did not need years or months or even weeks to take the step: their transition from radical ideas to radical actions occurred in a moment of instantaneous enlightenment.

The analogy with philosophical, spiritual, and religious moments of enlightenment and conversion is relevant here, as is the comparison with the adoption of rites and practices within the context of a belief system. For instance, it usually does not require a long process of education to see the host as the body of Christ. Believing is often instantaneous. When someone driven by ideology is part of a group of like-minded people who have

---

[13] This jihadist poster alluded to an advertising slogan for the Dutch Railways from 2012 that stated, "Opeens heb je het: je wordt conducteur!" (Suddenly you get it: you become a train conductor!)

already developed and experienced certain radical practices and rites, then participating in ritual slaughter, religious praxis, or propaganda of the deed is a logical expression of their own convictions. Of course, radical, extremist, or terrorist behavior may sometimes emerge gradually,[14] but we see increasingly often that such processes can develop very quickly and unpredictably.

The radical redemption approach allows us to better describe this quick, suddenly-seeing-the-light character of radicalization. Often seen in the past as a divine revelation or epiphany, this phenomenon has been insufficiently recognized by political scientists and social psychologists—possibly because these disciplines have their roots in theories ultimately founded on rational behavior (see, e.g., Fishbein and Ajzen 1975). We see the same problem in the perceived dichotomy between attitudes—evaluations of your thoughts on certain subjects—and behavior. Attitudes often predict behavior very badly. We should not treat behavior and attitudes as equal processes (see, e.g., Strack and Deutsch 2014). Behavior does not automatically follow attitudes—sometimes, it is more likely to happen the other way around. In this context, joining a radical group may lead individuals to think more deeply about and be immersed in extremist ideas and beliefs.

Radicalization scientists are often too assertive in answering crucial but almost insoluble psychological questions. Does moral reasoning, for instance, precede moral emotion, which is then followed by behavior, as Immanuel Kant posited? Or does the intuition about what is good and what is bad come first and the moral justification later, as David Hume believed? This distinction is as simplistic as it is problematic, and it has muddled the discussion on radicalization and terrorism for far too long. It has generated questions such as this: Do all terrorists act violently as a result of well-thought-out ideological considerations, as the definitions of terrorism more or less suggest, or do some terrorists hold beliefs that are less clearly developed? It is often suggested that terrorist leaders have clearly formulated ideological ideas, whereas their followers are simply hangers-on who have no idea what they are doing and why. As a result, much terrorism is reduced to simple motivational categories, such as personal (trauma, pain, loss of honor), ideological, or social motivations (helping the community). But this overlooks the

---

[14] See chapter 1 for the difference between terrorism and radicalization. According to the General Intelligence and Security Service (AIVD), *extremism* means that one actively aims to bring about and/or support far-reaching changes in society that can threaten the (survival of the) democratic legal order, possibly by employing undemocratic methods that can erode the functioning of the democratic legal order. In its most extreme form, extremism can lead to terrorism, but it can also take nonviolent forms. See https://www.aivd.nl/onderwerpen/extremisme.

fact that followers are often true believers and that they express their radical beliefs in a sacred and violent praxis rather than in intellectual, theological rationalization.

I agree with Kees van den Bos, Lorne Dawson, and Rik Peels that we should take the subjects of our research, and the first-person accounts of their motivations and religiosity, much more seriously (Van den Bos 2018, 42; Dawson 2019; Bortolotti 2021). We must pay closer attention to the feelings of injustice that can seduce people into taking the path of radicalization. At the same time, my interviewees not only felt a general sense of injustice but also had a very personal feeling of "owning" a political or moral deficit. Extreme religious beliefs gave direction and shape to a structural feeling of malaise, as well as to what my interviewees thought they—and not others—should do about it. Ideological templates became a lens through which their existing feelings of falling short and of malaise came into focus and were ignited. If terrorism suspects claim to have committed their acts in the name of Allah or for the *Volksgemeinschaft*, we do well not to dismiss their radicalization as strictly psychological and inspired by personal traumas.

This study takes the self-confessed motives and explanations of convicted terrorists very seriously; not so much as statements of fact—as we will see in appendix 2, it is often impossible to verify whether their reported motives are accurate—but as consciously constructed stories that tell us what the terrorists consider sacred and nonnegotiable and what redemption means to them. Redemption is both an ideological and a religious construct that expresses itself as a form of praxis: an instantiation of an ideological or religious system of beliefs in this world by adopting rituals, practices, and performances that rise above direct and material reality and have transcendental value. In this way, they give meaning to both the action and the perpetrator.[15]

Conclusion

In conclusion, we can now describe the model of radical redemption as a triptych of a narrated past plight, present calling and desire for action, and

---

[15] This definition derives from Maslow (1965) and Frankl (2000), who see "the business of self-actualization" as best being fulfilled "via commitment to an important job, that is, to a transcendental cause of recognized societal significance" (Frankl 2000, 84). See also Crenshaw (2007, 153); Kruglanski et al. (2009, 335).

72 THE RADICAL REDEMPTION MODEL

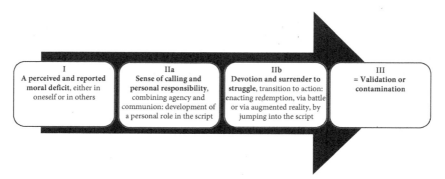

Figure 2.1 The triptych model of radical redemption

future validation. We can formulate this more explicitly as follows: (1) a perceived moral or sociopolitical deficit, including feelings of loss, anger, fear, or revenge regarding past injustices; (2) an immediate sense of calling in the present (including the belief of having been chosen and called to arms), devotion, and participation in the struggle; and (3) the desire for future emotional and cognitive validation of the envisaged redemption, including corresponding rewards—although this validation can also result in invalidation and therefore in denial and "contamination" of the desired redemption. See figure 2.1.

We shall see that adventure and devotion, as well as belief and practice, go hand in hand, and that feelings of falling short and being frustrated about an experienced past injustice become increasingly linked to a desire for purification and action. This model of radical redemption is fulfilled in a series of what can be conceptually and temporally considered as steps or stages, narrated as a storyline by the perpetrators themselves, then and afterwards. This storyline, and the different steps, may be iterated and even amount to a cycle of trying over and over again to gain redemption; see figure 2.2.

Both these notions of the triptych and cycle and the steps that make up this narrative are elaborated in greater detail in chapters 4, 5, and 6, but they can here be narrated as follows. Terrorists believe above all that their state, society, or group has been plunged in a state of absolute, radical evil and injustice. They themselves are a part of that situation, because they live in or identify with that country. They believe that they are personally responsible for the continued existence or termination of that evil, and that they currently live in a state of moral deficit; they feel bad for not doing enough. They experience a desire to radically change the course of their lives. They

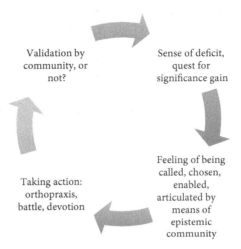

Figure 2.2 The cycle of the radical redemption narrative

feel a vocation, a calling to own their sense of moral or political deficit, and surrender themselves to the fight—the envisaged holy war, the metaphysical battle, and the immediate steps required to join that fight. That action can only be radical: it has to involve violence, sacrificing themselves and others, and participating in the perceived battle that is being waged. They believe that only through such a radical praxis of atonement or revenge can redemption and deliverance be achieved or at least symbolized. If this fails, it can be tried anew.

It should be noted here that specific redemption narratives can be individual or collective. They can entail atonement for a life of sin or deliverance of oppressed fellow believers or group members. The narrative's aim can be redemption from one's own guilt or vengeance for the disgrace suffered by the group as a whole. In all cases, the violence and the redemptive move are part of a greater metaphysical battle between good and evil. Importantly, such a battle must be validated by the (imagined, perceived) support base through recognition and acceptance of the act of redemption. Certain religious or ideological templates must be identified that validate the act of redemption. If the validation is not forthcoming, the narrative of redemption becomes invalidated and contorts into a narrative of contamination and disappointment.

3
Radical Redemption in History

The Fourth R

This study requires a historical chapter that identifies how the narrative of radical redemption works in time and space. To establish similarities and differences between redemption narratives, to look deeper into the meaning of *religious* in these narratives, and to make clearer statements about the last twenty years of terrorism and radicalization, the current chapter takes a look at attacks carried out in earlier waves of terrorism. Since narratives are dependent on historically available incidents and occurrences from which they may infer their frames and storylines, it is important to take these historical contexts into account. With Lei and others, I have already pointed out that any social-psychological account of radicalization processes needs to be contextualized, because "people construct mental representations that align with their surrounding social and cultural systems" (Lei et al. 2023, 2). Thus, the historical context, which is relevant to understand what people believe, feel, and do, should not be neglected (Gergen 1973, 1980).

Moreover, redemption as an act of martyrdom for the perpetrator's own community is by no means a modern phenomenon. Some redemption narratives are strongly individualistic in nature, while others are deliberately associated with existing religious practices, making them collectively recognizable. Since our current thinking on terrorism is strongly embedded in the context of the nation-state, there is little value in studying, say, the narratives of the Saracens or the Indian "thugs." Terrorism is a political and cultural phenomenon that always depends strongly on place and time. A comparison between different forms of terrorism is worthwhile if the contexts are to some extent similar; this was the case in the waves of terrorism that occurred since the end of the nineteenth century. This historical period marked the emergence and consolidation of the nation-state, with its national security apparatus that started to define nonstate actors as terrorists. Terrorism researcher David Rapoport (2004) distinguished the global waves of modern terrorism since that period as follows: anarchist terrorism (roughly, 1880–1914), anti-colonial terrorism (1920s–1960s), new-left terrorism (1960s–1990s), and holy or religious terrorism (1979–present day). Without entering into a discussion on this wave model of terrorism, I will merely say here that the element of redemption can be discerned in each of these waves, albeit to different extents. Some terrorist organizations encouraged their members to sacrifice themselves to free others; others resorted to sacrificing others to achieve redemption for themselves and their own group.

That makes it worthwhile to present an overview of how redemption, as a deep, recurring historical narrative, has shaped past waves of terrorism as well. Thus, although this chapter does not serve as a direct historical context (in time and space) for the interviews I conducted in the Netherlands, Kenya, Nigeria, and Indonesia, it does contain historical cases and references to diverging patterns of radical redemption across time, space, and terrorist organizations. My argument for including such an overview is evidence based, historically informed, and social-psychologically relevant. First of all, it is interesting that, although the first three waves of terrorism are not primarily driven by religious motives or a religious outlook (in Rapoport's distinction, at least), we will see that individuals operating within these waves—whether driven by socialist, communist, anarchist, or a more ethnic-tribal ideology— also displayed elements that are recognizable within the redemption framework. Second, many terrorist perpetrators talked about guilt, sin, and deliverance; used eschatological terminology (last battle, final judgment); and used religiously informed props (Bible verses, prophetic-looking clothing, Christlike gestures). These things indicate that the redemption motive had seeped into their repertoire—perhaps through a lingering religious upbringing, a background steeped in Christian or orthodox culture, or yet another way. Third, this also fed into the way they articulated, played out, and disseminated their narratives of a radical fight and a radical redemption among their support base and beyond.

Historian and political scientist Louise Richardson summarized the waves of terrorism as being propelled by narratives of *revenge, renown*, and *reaction*—the three Rs. Terrorists seek revenge for injustices or humiliations inflicted on them; they aim to make their causes known to the world (or want to bring attention to themselves); and they often design their actions so that they induce and provoke reactions from their perceived enemies (see, e.g., Richardson 2006). These descriptions, though true and compelling, overlook the positive offer of the narrative of a fourth R—that of *radical redemption*. Terrorists are nihilistic and destructive, and they seek religious or political dominance. But terrorism also functions by the grace of the positive offer of redemption presented—in a very ingenious and persuasive way—to potential supporters and recruits. Terrorists see themselves as generative, in the sense described in the previous chapter. To warrant that first-person perspective, I therefore aim to complement Richardson's account of the narratives of revenge, renown, and reaction within the historical waves of terrorism with the narrative of radical redemption. As I said, there may be more narratives, and the three identified by Richardson—although she did not use the narrative method in her analysis—overlap in part with the redemption narrative. Obviously, further research could clarify which narrative correlates best with specific types of terrorism, and this fourth narrative also varies according to time, place, and terrorist group. It also remains to be seen to what extent this narrative is attached to identifiable or even organized religion. Yet, the redemption narrative is such a strong and generative storyline that it can and should be added as a distinct fourth narrative.

Chapter 3 charts these variations for the past waves of terrorism; this will improve our understanding of how the narrative of radical redemption shaped radicalization within the current wave of jihadist terrorism. First, I discuss the fin de siècle anarchists, who wished, with their propaganda of the deed, to avenge the injustice suffered by the oppressed classes and were prepared to sacrifice their own careers and lives for that goal. Next, I leap forward to the anarchists' "distant relatives," the revolutionary terrorists of the Red Army Faction (RAF) in the 1970s. They, too, were motivated by intense anger about injustice and the desire to wreak vengeance on the ruling class, but for them, personal or collective feelings of guilt and the wish to do penance for Germany's National Socialist past played a significant part in their desire to sacrifice themselves for the revolutionary struggle. Interesting parallels can be drawn between the hunger strikes of detained RAF members and those of the members of the paramilitary Irish Republican Army (IRA). Both organizations encouraged their members to sacrifice themselves by starving to death, and so to focus the world's attention on their good cause. But there were differences between the personal motives, the narratives of a quest for meaning, and the extent to which the supporters of these organizations accepted and recognized the hunger strikers' martyrdom. Comparing the RAF and the IRA reveals an important aspect of the redemption narrative: the sacrifice must be recognized and acknowledged, otherwise it has been for nothing. The chapter closes with the story of "Unabomber" Ted Kaczynski, to show how lone wolves can also seek a form of radical redemption. Right-wing extremist and jihadist terrorism, which typify the most recent wave of terrorism, are discussed in the chapters that follow.

Anarchism: Propaganda of the Deed, 1880–1920

The anarchists were the first to commit attacks as propaganda of the deed. The advent of the anarchist movement in the mid-nineteenth century is seen as the first wave of modern terrorism because, unlike earlier terrorist waves or organizations that targeted other opponents or power constellations, the emergence of these groups was directly related to the onset of the modern nation-state (see Jensen 2014; Klem 2020).

Anarchists were early adopters who used the inventions and achievements of the Second Industrial Revolution to compensate for their limited political and nonexistent military power by creating a theater of fear. They achieved that by committing unique acts of horrific violence that generated national and even international attention for their cause. Their innovative talent lay primarily in the field of public relations. They believed in the unity of thought and action, of belief and practice, and took themselves deadly seriously. Anarchism was the libertarian or anti-authoritarian "little brother" of socialism. Russian thinker Peter Kropotkin devised a plan for society in which government and laws were no longer necessary and where people formed a community on the basis of mutual agreements. This nonviolent utopia took a more vitriolic form in the work of Pierre-Joseph Proudhon, who saw all property as theft and, in 1840, proudly called himself an anarchist. Michael Bakunin added the finishing touches to anarchist ideology in the 1870s by calling on his supporters to put the propaganda of the deed into practice and to destroy all remnants of state authority with violence.

Against the background of national revolutions and uprisings in Germany, Italy, and South America, workers' revolts in Spain and France, and unrest in North America, Russia, and India, anarchist propaganda spread rapidly around the world. Anarchists made use of fast steamships and rail networks, published newspapers and magazines, and placed provocative advertisements in the press—"We shall poison the drinking water in Paris," they announced in a French newspaper. Most of all, they were happy to make use of Alfred Nobel's inventions of portable sticks of dynamite. With their "infernal machines" and revolvers, they spread fear among the crowned heads and elites of the West—and horror and glee among the wider population. Tsar Alexander II, the Habsburg empress Elisabeth ("Sisi"), a host of less well-known ministers and police chiefs, and even the American president William McKinley fell prey to anarchist attacks. Through their deeds, the anarchists aimed to provoke governments to overreact so as to tear away the mask of state authority and reveal the true nature of repression and police violence. They then hoped to mobilize the masses to rise up with them in revolt. Among the dynamitards of the late nineteenth century, such high-flown ideas of destruction and resurrection of state and society were always accompanied by highly personal beliefs. We know, for example, that many anarchist bombers believed they had been given a unique individual calling to make their contribution to the worldwide revolution (see De Graaf 2012b).

This was the case with Auguste Vaillant and Zinaida Konopliannikova, two of the French and Russian anarchists who were partly responsible for the tempestuous years of the fin de siècle—the period during which the most anarchist attacks were committed worldwide. We shall see that the anarchist redemption narrative was a combination of personal responsibility, targeted revenge, and collective secular redemption. It contained a sense of personal responsibility and the desire to sacrifice one's own life, a desire to improve and avenge the lot of the oppressed socioeconomic classes by eradicating the bearers of state power so as to punish the repressive and unjust system, but it also was an expression of the hope of a just society.

Auguste Vaillant's Act of Redemption

Auguste Vaillant was born the son of a gendarme in the French Ardennes. His father left him to fend for himself at the age of 12, and Auguste had to steal and do odd jobs to survive. He was not unintelligent, was interested in astronomy and philosophy, and joined the radical socialists. He made his way to Paris and married Virginie Viol in 1883, but was unable to find employment. As a last resort, to support his wife and small daughter, he tried his luck in Argentina, but again without success. He returned to Paris penniless at the age of 32. He took a job in a leather goods shop to try and maintain his family, but sank deeper and deeper into debt. He joined a radical group known as Les Révoltes and discovered anarchism (Merriman 2009, 10–11). On December 2, 1893, he had a photographic portrait taken of himself. A week later, on December 9, he walked into the French parliament building in the Palais Bourbon and threw a nail bomb in among the assembled delegates. Although some fifty people were injured, no one was killed. The attack was world news, as was Vaillant.

A few weeks later, he had the opportunity to explain his acts in court. It was the chance he had been waiting for, and he presented his audience with a compelling account of injustice and redemption. His gospel consisted of denouncing social misery and calling for the prevailing class relations to be overthrown. He told the public in the courtroom that, since the French Revolution, nothing had changed for the class of exploited citizens. Many oppressed people behaved as slaves: they did not rebel and lived out their miserable lives stupefied and numbed. But there were others who refused to accept this and felt called to fight against it. He, Vaillant, was one of those. He could not tolerate the fact that "a few individuals monopolize all the social wealth," while the rest of the people lacked "the bread that is not even refused to dogs" (Vaillant 1894). He presented himself as the representative of all the nameless oppressed people, as the voice of the slave class. Thus, he linked his personal narrative of despair, unemployment, and misery to that of a whole class. And, on behalf of that class, he had "the satisfaction of having wounded the existing cursed society." He acted alone, but not only for himself:

> Tired of leading a life of suffering and of cowardice, I carried this bomb to the people primarily responsible for our social misery. . . . Make no mistake: the explosion of my bomb is not just the cry of the rebel Vaillant but the cry of an entire class vindicating its rights—a class that will soon add acts to words.

At the end of his speech, Vaillant outlined a vision of a renewed society, a society that finally fulfilled the principles of the French Revolution:

> Gentlemen, I conclude by saying that a society in which one sees such social inequalities as we see all around us, where suicides are caused every day by poverty and prostitution is flaring at every street corner—a society whose principal monuments are barracks and prisons—such a society must be transformed as soon as possible, under pain of being speedily eliminated from the human race. Hail to him who labors, by no matter what means, for this transformation!

Vaillant threw his bomb, self-reportedly driven by personal desperation and poverty. It was a deed of individual frustration and revenge on a society whose doors remained firmly closed to him (*Le Petit Journal*, January 11, 1894). On the other hand, through his act, Vaillant raised himself up as a martyr for a whole class, and his single act of destruction was part of a bigger narrative of transformation, of redemption of a society and a class from bonds of oppression and misery. The court was not convinced, and granted Vaillant his sacrifice. He was sentenced to death by guillotine, that infamous instrument of the revolution, despite the fact that no one died in his attack. His young daughter, Sidonie, wrote to the wife of French president Sadi Carnot to ask her to plead for a pardon for her father since, as a martyr, he had been unjustly sentenced to death. In addition, a priest injured during the explosion initiated a petition for Vaillant's death sentence to be rescinded (*New York Times* 1894). But it was to no avail. Vaillant was executed on February 5, 1894. But his cry in court was not silenced; anarchists embraced and perpetuated his offer to act as savior. On June 24, 1894, Italian anarchist Sante Geronimo Caserio stabbed the French president to death during a procession, as revenge for Vaillant's execution.

His attack and death made Vaillant one of the many renowned anarchists who linked their deeds to a wider narrative of liberation and redemption and were not afraid to give their lives for that ideal (Rapoport 2004, 51).

Zinaida Konopliannikova's Urge for Emancipation

Women, too, have embraced this narrative of injustice, sacrifice, and redemption. With them, the contrast between what is seen as female weakness and their total commitment to give their own lives leaves, if possible, an even greater impression.[1]

Zinaida Konopliannikova was born in Saint Petersburg in 1878. Her father was a junior army officer and her mother a peasant. At the age of 18, she was allowed to attend teacher training college and, after qualifying, she started working in Livonia, a region roughly equivalent to what is now Estonia and Latvia. There, she discovered the wretched circumstances in which the people in the Baltic region lived, how poor and how oppressed

---

[1] See also the trial at this time against Vera Zasulich: Schmid (2016).

they were. With its Russification campaign, the tsarist regime tried to eradicate the final remnants of independence and ethnic consciousness. "I pitied the little mites, who were compelled to listen to a foreign tongue," Konopliannikova wrote, "and who looked on me with sad eyes as if inquiring, 'Why are we not allowed to speak here our own mother tongue?' It was hard to hear boys telling me about the Olegs and the Ruriks of Russian history, and knowing nothing of their own national history—so rich in facts and events" (Prelooker 1908, 287). After expressing her concern about this state of affairs on several occasions, she was transferred to a Russian village near Saint Petersburg. But there, too, she continued to identify with the oppressed peasant population, took offense at all the injustice, and tried to mobilize the people. Again, the authorities were not pleased. "If I tried . . . to arrange a most innocent lecture [for the people], the [priest] informed the school inspector that 'the teacher is busy with conversations not concerning her school work.'" Konopliannikova was thwarted from all sides and came to the conclusion that she would get no further in this way.

> I became convinced that it was impossible for me to share with the people even the scanty knowledge which I possess; I was not allowed to open the peasant's eyes to his position and to point out the real reasons of his misery. Under these conditions there was no possibility of an "harmonious development of mind" (which we had been taught in the college ought to be the aim of a teacher), and I came to the conclusion that first of all it was necessary to create fresh conditions. So I became a Revolutionist. (Prelooker 1908, 288)

Konopliannikova decided to join the Socialist Revolutionary Party, set up in 1902 by idealist intellectuals who believed it was their duty, as a privileged and highly educated class, to elevate and liberate the oppressed lower classes, if necessary with bombs and revolvers (Hildermeier 2000, 43). As such, the Socialist Revolutionaries followed in the footsteps of Narodnaya Volya (People's Will), their populist predecessor from the 1880s. The idea was that the violent propaganda of the deed would awaken the masses from their lethargy. Terrorism was a legitimate and essential weapon as long as the conditions for enlightening and elevating the people had not been fulfilled. Until that time, the eyes of the masses had to be opened with violence. Through terrorist attacks, the intellectuals—who could see better just how severe the oppression really was—could challenge the power of the regime from their minority position. Every terrorist attack was in effect a challenge to a duel (Hildermeier 2000, 53, 59). In Konopliannikova's words:

> I clearly saw that the autocratic and bureaucratic government [of Russia] is kept alive only by its acts of violence, only thanks to the perpetual terror exercised by the rulers. And life itself taught me that nothing new can be erected unless the old order is destroyed. If one cannot fight against ideas with bayonets, on the other hand, one cannot remove bayonets with ideas alone. I became a Terrorist. (Prelooker 1908, 289)

After spending two terms of several months in prison for her radical ideas, Konopliannikova decided to commit an act of terrorism. On August 13, 1906, Major General Georgiy Min of the Semyonovsky Regiment was approached by a young woman just outside Peterhof railway station. When he stopped, Konopliannikova shot him through the head, killing him immediately. Under General Min's command, the Semyonovsky Regiment had bloodily quelled an armed uprising in Moscow in 1905 aimed at forcing the tsarist government to introduce reforms. Now it was Min's turn to die. Konopliannikova did not run away after the shooting but waited until she was arrested, after which she was locked up in the Peter and Paul Fortress. Two weeks later, she appeared in court. She refused to stand for a tribunal that she considered a mockery of an independent and impartial court. But she was given the opportunity to read out a statement. As with Vaillant, it was an appeal that became incorporated in the public archives of revolutionary statements. She explained who she was and why she had committed the shooting. She described her experiences in the Baltic provinces and in the heart of Russia itself. Arriving at the end of her revolutionary journey, she had no other choice than to give herself to her cause:

> You may sentence me to death. Wherever I have to die—on the gallows, in the mines, or torture-chambers—I shall die with one thought: Pardon me, my people! I could give so little to you. I have only one life. And I shall die with full faith that days will come when the throne will be demolished, and on the vast plains of Russia the sun of freedom will shine brilliantly. (Prelooker 1908, 289)

Konopliannikova was sentenced to hang, and was executed on September 11, 1906. She refused the offer to send a last written message to her family.

She walked to the gallows herself and, before the executioner had finished reading out the sentence, she put the noose around her neck and kicked the stool away from under her feet.

In many of the attacks that took place during the wave of anarchist terrorism between 1880 and approximately 1920—described by Rapoport (2017) as a "Golden Age of Assassination"—the perpetrators presented themselves as the saviors of their class, people, or group. When we try to establish which redemption narrative they used to justify their actions, we see a number of recurring elements. Both Vaillant and Konopliannikova were concerned with liberating the poor workers in France and the peasants in Russia from oppression and elevating them to a higher state of socioeconomic emancipation. In addition, they wanted to liberate them from a state of ignorance and illiteracy. The oppressed pariahs were often not even aware of what was being done to them. Vaillant and Konopliannikova saw themselves first and foremost as bringers of knowledge.[2] Furthermore, their deeds were instrumental: it was the duty, the ethical responsibility of the highly educated intelligentsia—who may have had no money or power but certainly had knowledge—to challenge the authorities and unleash revolution in the name of the ignorant masses. Lastly, their deeds were intended to liberate the people, mobilize them, and initiate a process of popular redemption.

Their sacrifices were also a way of escaping their own feelings of complete failure and disappointment. Sacrificing oneself for a greater cause gives a tremendous boost to one's feeling of self-worth. It is a badge of honor and an attempt to erase one's insignificance. By committing a highly visible act of destruction, preferably against a recognizable symbol—a parliament building in Vaillant's case, a general in Konopliannikova's—both Vaillant and Konopliannikova were assured a place in the pantheon of revolutionary heroes. That was a better end than a nameless death as an unemployed pariah or a prisoner. In her career and her idealism, Konopliannikova had been frustrated by the obstacles raised by the tsarist regime to thwart reform-minded and engaged citizens. She had nothing more to say to her family. Auguste Vaillant, too, felt that he had nothing more to offer to his family and friends. This life was all that was left to him. They both did not see their attacks as murder but as justified forms of resistance against a government that also ruled through violence. Konopliannikova had the final word:

---

[2] In line with McAdams's "emancipation narrative"; see McAdams (2006, 51).

Who gave you the right to keep us during centuries in darkness? . . . You seized it by might. . . . But now a new right is coming, the right of the people. . . . You declared a war of life and death to this coming right. (Prelooker 1908, 286; see also Crenshaw 2007, 153)

She and her comrades would thus continue to use their language of violence and terrorism as long as it was necessary for them to represent the voice of the people, to join them physically in embracing plight and fright, and to engage in pure, violent action to free them from tyranny. In this narrative of radical socialist redemption, deep feelings of anger over past injustices, a sense of being chosen and called to arms, and a devotion to a battle for a utopian future via the orthopraxis of action were clearly visible.

Guilt and Atonement in the RAF

The[3] organization that embodied the wave of revolutionary left-wing terrorism in the 1970s as no other was the Red Army Faction (RAF). Since there are countless studies on the RAF, I shall not explore its ideas in detail here. What is important for my argument is not only that the RAF was marked by a utopian—or dystopian—belief that state and democracy should be destroyed and reconstructed, but also that its members shared a strong willingness to sacrifice themselves for a good cause. The good cause was a violent struggle against the system of the postwar West German state, which they experienced as a conservative capitalist, even neofascist, straitjacket. In the eyes of the RAF, the federal government had been corrupted by its support for the United States in its war in Vietnam, West German society was collapsing under its addiction to consumption, and the democratic political system had never achieved its own ideals. Acts of symbolic and actual violence were necessary to provoke the system to show its true face and thus to mobilize the working classes, students, and other citizens to rise in revolt (Boterman 2005, 459). For the members of the RAF, it was thus—as with the anarchists—a combination of personal responsibility and the compulsion to act, targeted revenge, and collective secular redemption. They were motivated by a sense of deficit and frustration about the real or perceived capitalist, bourgeois authoritarian, and fascist structures of West German

---

[3] I thank Annelotte Janse for her assistance with the research for this section.

society. They felt responsible for redeeming and punishing Germany's guilt by proxy by taking revenge on the establishment through a praxis of radical violence and, at the same time, by focusing the spotlight on the plight of the oppressed social classes, not only the workers but also the people of Vietnam (as victims of Western, American imperialism). Through their attacks, they hoped—as a vanguard of the revolution—to awaken the masses and mobilize their supporters to also rise in revolt.

Although the RAF was motivated by a secular, left-wing, extremist ideology, the members were aware of and socialized within a Protestant culture (Gudrun Ensslin was a vicar's daughter, and Ulrike Meinhof had had a strict Protestant upbringing), and the RAF emerged from and was steeped in a German culture that was just starting public discussions on collective guilt. These circumstances made some of its core members—though not, perhaps, the RAF as a whole—receptive to notions of atonement, sin, and redemption. Radical redemption can be identified, not so much as an orthodoxy or a holy war, but as a praxis of fighting to redeem oneself and the German society as such from the iniquities of its fascist past (and from its alleged capitalist, imperialist elites). With this effort, the RAF drew on Christian-inspired imagery, discourse, and behavior, albeit more unwittingly than wittingly. This type of radical praxis is still very dissimilar to any type of jihadist holy war, but the religious, metaphysical, and especially eschatological connotations can be made out and were salient.

In the night of April 2, 1968, Andreas Baader and Gudrun Ensslin started fires in two department stores in Frankfurt am Main—the first act of what came to be called the Baader-Meinhof Group, which adopted the name Rote Armee Fraktion (Red Army Faction; RAF) two years later. Historian Frits Boterman uses the concept of *Tatidealismus* to explain the beliefs that drove these radicals to act. *Tatidealismus*, an essentially German concept, refers to "achieving moral purity through action" (Boterman 2005, 459). In this light, the RAF may even be considered a revival of the nineteenth-century anarchist movement with its propaganda of the deed. The deeds—the attacks— resulted, on the one hand, from the frustrations mentioned earlier; on the other hand, they were inspired by the desire to redeem the burden of guilt that the postwar generation of Germans bore on their shoulders. Ensslin's father described his daughter's act as an "act of sacred self-actualization." If the parents did not wish to settle that debt, their children would ensure they had no other choice. In that sense, the RAF members practiced a violent form of *Vergangenheitsbewältigung*, dealing with the traumas of the past.

They tried to process the past of their country and their parents, or rather to deliver themselves of that sense of guilt, through purifying, redeeming violence. According to Wolfgang Kraushaar, the struggle with the past, and against fascism, was the "root of their radicalism" (see Kraushaar 2008, 22). The RAF members not only targeted their immediate victims but, through their "purifying attacks," tried to make an ethical statement. They were better Germans than the generations preceding them because they were prepared to use violence to dismantle the obsolete, authoritarian, fascist structures in society. For the RAF, attacks on representatives of an oppressive state were thoroughly justified (Boterman 2013, 887). The praxis of radical violence was the key to opening society's eyes. The people of postwar West Germany were unfree and imprisoned by the bonds of unchallenged capitalist subjugation; like the farmers and workers of the nineteenth century, they had to be made aware of their state of subjection through violence.

What was different from the nineteenth-century anarchists, however, was that the RAF's statements, texts, and obscure philosophies revealed a deep process of grappling with collective German guilt for the Holocaust and the Third Reich. The first generation of RAF members presented themselves as liberated individuals, but continually spoke of the need to throw off and rid themselves of the remnants of guilt and the burden of history. The correspondence between Gudrun Ensslin and Bernward Vesper, Ensslin's ex-husband and father of her son Felix, is shot through with references to guilt, penance, sacrifice, and deliverance or redemption. On May 2, 1968, Vesper wrote to Ensslin, who was at that moment in prison for the fire attack in Frankfurt:

> Walls, prisons, are the petrified processes of repression in society. Freud's subconscious—where everything is hidden away that cannot be solved rationally . . . I see it by myself—despite the lonely incarceration, I believe, I hope, that I—together with the others who are just as much victims as I am (or you are)—can bring about the change required to break through the vicious circle that holds us prisoner. (Vesper and Ensslin 2010a)

And in July of the same year, Vesper wrote:

> We all wanted to see ourselves as victims—Felix, you, me, the people who hold you prisoner, in the prisons, that petrified suppression of guilt

in society. And to fight the common enemy, more consistently, more resolutely, than until now. (Vesper and Ensslin 2010b)

Ensslin, who had been given a serious Lutheran upbringing, used the same language of guilt, penance, and liberation. But she went further than Vesper. As activists, they were not only victims but also perpetrators. It was they who had to make the required sacrifice, and they were prepared to put not only their own lives and careers at stake but also those of others. In August 1968, she wrote to Andreas Baader, with whom she by then had a relationship, about the need to become the embodiment of the praxis of liberation themselves, no matter how ruthless that was:

> We also treat ourselves ruthlessly. We are forced to. And, as a result, we will treat others just as ruthlessly and cold-bloodedly. Perhaps that was what I lacked, but that's of no consequence, now I understand it, deep in my bones. Hell, YES! Andreas, *Praxis*, your words! (Ensslin and Baader 2010)

Their letters show Ensslin and Baader very much aligned their personal frustrations and feelings of guilt with their social analyses, projecting their radical praxis of destruction both on themselves and on West German government and society.

Dutch activist Ronald Augustin, who joined the RAF later, when the first-generation members were already in prison, also took up this theme of redeeming oneself by fighting against the state. In his writings, the language of alienation and destruction moved even further toward self-justification:

> The core problem facing us in the centres of capitalism was that of alienation. That is to say, consumption, television, dumbing down, indifference to the violence and poverty in the imperialist system. For us, as people who had placed themselves outside society, it was clear we had to change this situation. The discussion was about how we could do something effectively against the system.... We had to shatter the forces of imperialism, as Che Guevara said: "Create two, three, many Vietnams".... I wanted to act effectively; it was already clear to me around 1966 that we could only fight with weapons. We could only bring the system down by attacks from within. As we fought from the inside, liberation movements would attack from the outside. (Janse and De Jong 2016, 205–6)

Using Their Own Bodies as Weapons

The "praxis of liberation" was one of destruction. That destruction was aimed at state and society, but the terrorists' weapons were their own bodies. For such weapons to be used effectively, it was important that the act of liberation was recognized as such by the group for whom it was intended—in other words, this very personal and social desire for redemption required validation. The problem with the anarchists' attacks was that they lacked such impact and support. Auguste Vaillant and Zinaida Konopliannikova may have become notorious for their attacks, but they had no immediate impact in the form of escalating violence; this process took more than a decade. For the RAF members, the search for sympathy and support was a recurring problem. Such support was necessary not only from the perspective of the theory of social and revolutionary mobilization but also from a logistical and tactical perspective. To survive while being on the run from the police and the authorities, for example, the RAF members needed money, help, and safe addresses. Moreover, their supporters had to acknowledge their acts as deeds of liberation and mobilization. These supporters were groups in society with whom the terrorists identified and who were potentially susceptible to their message—and thus could perhaps be persuaded and recruited (Pekelder 2012, 203).

The RAF—along with others, including the IRA—used hunger strikes, among other weapons, to persuade their supporters. The members of the RAF and the IRA were not suicide terrorists. It was not the primary intention of the revolutionary terrorists of the 1970s to die themselves during their attacks—although they were sometimes prepared to take that risk, for instance, when they occupied the West German embassy in Stockholm in 1975. The RAF caused a furor by kidnapping high-ranking figures in the Federal Republic of Germany (FRG), and the IRA used advanced bombs to kill British army officers and members of the public. The victims were selected with some discrimination, and not purely at random. Moreover, the first generation of RAF members still issued warnings before committing a bombing. The 1968 department store fires in Frankfurt were deliberately planned for a time when all staff and customers had gone home. And before the attack on the Springer offices, Ulrike Meinhof called to warn the staff. The intention was to spread fear among the government and specific segments of the population and to draw attention to their message; they explicitly did not intend to alienate left-wing—or, in the case of Ireland, Irish—supporters. The RAF only started its wave of executions after a year, when the first generation of leaders had been imprisoned and the police had used live ammunition on sympathizers. In the case of the IRA, the lethal violence was also the outcome of a longer series of increasingly violent actions and reactions. Nevertheless, the motto of these terrorists was that they wanted a lot of people looking, not a lot of people dead.[4]

Within the context of that process of radicalization, both the detained RAF members and the IRA terrorists in the 1970s and 1980s used their own bodies as weapons—not to kill other people, but to starve themselves. Hunger strikes were emphatically the final means available to terrorists to communicate with the outside world (Sweeney 1993a, 421, 433). The message they wanted to convey through the destruction of their own bodies was to rip off the mask of the state in an impressive and horrific way and to show how monstrous the repression by the government really was. With this strategy, they placed the prison managements and authorities in West Germany and the United Kingdom in a difficult position. If they ignored the hunger strikes, they would be seen as immoral. If they entered into dialogue with the hunger strikers, they would be accepting them as political negotiation partners. And ending the hunger strikes with violence, through forced feeding with probes, would also mean loss of face (Fierke 2012, 327, 329, 339). In other words, if a radical activist or terrorist has no other ways of getting his or her message across, going on a hunger strike is a perfect way to perform an act of sacrifice that is "part of an effort to communicate to an audience the humiliation and injustice that is experienced by the social group he or she embodies" (Fierke 2012, 327).

Hunger strikers sacrifice themselves by refusing to eat, thus making clear to the government and to their supporters that they are prepared to pay the ultimate price to redeem themselves and their immediate peer group. Both the RAF and the IRA resorted to this form of radical martyrdom and communication through action. Between 1972 and 1989, various RAF detainees went on hunger strike, supported by sympathizers from outside the prison walls who followed their situations closely and reported on them to the media (Wright 1991, 39; Passmore 2009, 36–7).

The Provisional Irish Republican Army—the official name of the Irish paramilitary republican organization that resumed active operations in

---

[4] See also Jenkins (2006, 8–9) and De Graaf (2010); the latter assumes that terrorism and counterterrorism can have a symbiotic and reciprocal effect on each other.

1969—was possibly even more effective in maximizing the impact of the hunger strikes of detained members. Between 1976 and 1981, the Provisional IRA organized a large-scale campaign to support the detainees in their claims to be recognized as political prisoners or even prisoners of war rather than as "ordinary" criminals (Dingley and Mollica 2007, 466–8). The organization was particularly successful in getting hunger strikes acknowledged as part of a much longer tradition of passive resistance and martyrdom against British rule (Sweeney 2004).

Win or Die

As a left-wing revolutionary terrorist organization, the RAF was the extreme wing of the protest movement that emerged in West Germany in the 1960s. The movement was driven by deep frustration with the lack of democratic representation and participation in the country's postwar parliamentary system. Moreover, the trauma over Germany's unprocessed wartime past was a major factor, especially because the old National Socialist officials were still in place at universities, in the judiciary, and within government. This made the conflict between the generations in West Germany—and also, for example, in Italy—much more heated than in the Netherlands, Britain, or Belgium. Left-wing revolutionary ideologies found fertile breeding ground in the polarized climate at West German universities. When the RAF committed its first, nonlethal attacks between 1968 and 1971, the movement and its leaders Baader, Ensslin, Meinhof, and Holger Meins could count on a great deal of sympathy. And when that first generation continued their campaign from prison after their arrests in 1972, they found much support among young sympathizers, especially the many trainees and students who had helped in the leaders' defense in court (see, e.g., Pekelder 2007; Gehrig 2011, 238–9; see also De Graaf 2010).

Meinhof and her comrades described in great detail how they were held in what they ominously called *Isolationsfolter*, but what was—for FRG standards at the time—formal solitary confinement. They complained in dramatic terms about the "sensory deprivation" they experienced there and, through their lawyers and assistants beyond the walls of Stammheim Prison, complained loudly about violations of their human rights. Detainee Ingrid Schubert described herself as a "hostage of the state," and saw her confinement in an isolation cell as "Verrechtlichung des Geiselstatus—Vollstreckung staatlicher Totalmacht an wehrlosen Gefangenen—Staatsgeiseln" (the legal formalization of her hostage status, the exercise of totalitarian state power against defenseless prisoners, state hostages) (Schubert 1977).

Complaints were submitted to the European Court. But the detainees' masterstroke was the decision to go on communal hunger strike. At first glance, the strike was intended to improve the conditions of their detention. But the deeper motivation, as indicated, was to place the Federal Republic and the authorities in a bad light. As later became clear, the conditions in Stammheim were not as strict and inhumane as the hunger strikers claimed. It was a prison, not a hotel, but the prisoners had access to a kitchen (Baader roasted chicken for himself), they were allowed to talk to each other and listen to the radio, and they had writing materials. Through their lawyers, they had close contact with the outside world; Baader even succeeded in smuggling out instructions for new operations. He announced the first collective hunger strike in January 1973, in which forty detainees took part between January 17 and February 16 (RAF 1997, 187). The authorities did not respond and left them to pursue the strike. Then, on May 8, the RAF announced a new hunger strike, this time with eighty participants:

> Our hunger strike is nothing less than our sole opportunity in prison to engage in resistance in solidarity with each other. Without the power, the street violence, without the mobilization of anti-fascist citizens who demonstrate for human rights and against torture and whose loyalty the pigs still need, our hunger strike does not relieve us of our powerlessness. (RAF 1997, 189)

A hunger strike was the only way to make that powerlessness visible, as well as the only weapon remaining to them, in their situation of lonely confinement, to draw attention to their plight and mobilize their supporters to action. The West German government again ignored the statement. Between September 13, 1974, and February 5, 1975, eighty detainees went on hunger strike again, this time at the cost of one life: Holger Meins starved himself to death.

Meins, a 33-year-old cinematography student from Munich, was a first-generation RAF member. He had become known in the student movement for producing and showing the film *Wie baue ich einen Molotow-Cocktail?* (How do I make a Molotov cocktail?). His nickname was "Starbuck," after the chief mate on the *Pequod*, the whaling ship from Herman Melville's novel

Moby Dick. Starbuck was the thoughtful crew member who tried to prevent Captain Ahab from taking revenge on the giant whale (Varon 2004, 220; Aust 2008, 45). With his narrow, sensitive face and dark hair (which he grew long in prison), Meins had the look of a guru. This Jesus figure took part in the strike and went further than any of his comrades—unlike Baader, he did not secretly take small bites of food.

In the event that he should die as a result of the hunger strike, Meins had left a short letter behind. In the letter, he launched his final and most effective campaign to strike against the West German state where it hurt the most, in its essence as a constitutional state, by suggesting that he had died not as a consequence of the hunger strike but through the actions of the authorities. His letter, "Notiz für den Fall . . ." (Note, in the event that . . .), was dated March 9, 1974, and read as follows:

> In the event that I die in detention, it was murder—no matter what the pigs claim to the contrary—I will never take my own life, I will never give them a pretext. . . . I am neither a provo[cateur] nor an adventurer. If they say—which looks very probable—that it was "suicide," "a serious health complaint," "self-defense," or "[shot] while trying to escape," do not believe the lies of these murderers. (Meins 1974b)

RAF sympathizers outside the prison took up Meins's battle cry. Holger Meins had been murdered. The Komitees gegen Folter an politischen Gefangenen in der BRD (1974) issued a statement that "Holger Meins fought and died for the liberation of his people from imperialist exploitation and oppression." In that battle, he had been intentionally killed by the West German authorities. Meins had sacrificed himself in the fight. He had in any case not suffered defeat. In Meins's own words:

> either pig or human being
> either survival at any price or struggle until death
> either problem or solution
> there's nothing in between
> victory or death—say these guys everywhere, and that is the language of the guerrilla—even within this small dimension over here:
> because in life it's like in death:
> "people (thus: we) who refuse to stop the struggle,
> either they win or they die,

instead of losing and dying."

...

everybody dies at some point. the question is only how and how you've lived. and that thing is entirely clear: fighting AGAINST THE PIGS as a HUMAN BEING FOR THE LIBERATION OF HUMAN BEING: revolutionary, in the struggle—at all love for life: with contempt for death. that is for me: to serve the people—raf. (Meins 1974a)

Through his martyrdom, Meins had transformed the "failure" of defeat and death into a "victory." His militant sacrifice was new ammunition for the RAF's fight (Varon 2004, 229). Meins's detention and his successful escape—through his death—was intended as a slap in the face of the authorities. He had shown that, if they wanted, people could free themselves of the panopticon of totalitarian control (Varon 2004, 226–7). The images of his emaciated body had been seen around the world. The heap of bones and profuse beard and body hair that was all that was left of Meins was very reminiscent not only of a Christlike savior figure but also of the remains of concentration camp inmates.

And yet, Meins's redemption narrative ultimately had less impact than people initially believed. With his last letter, the remaining RAF members and sympathizers outside prison tried to fuel the conspiracy theory that their first generation of leaders had not committed suicide but had been intentionally killed by the German authorities. But only a few supporters interpreted and recognized Meins's death by hunger as an act of redemption, and only within the RAF itself, where Meins was seen as the *Pequod*'s chief mate Starbuck, who had given his life to save Captain Ahab (Andreas Baader). But beyond the prison walls, the shock of Meins's emaciated corpse soon faded. The RAF's supporters did not know Meins as a senior figure in the movement, nor were they aware of the phenomenon of martyrdom. The support base was also not as strong as it had been; after the violent attacks of 1975 and 1977, people who may have initially felt some understanding or sympathy for the movement wanted nothing more to do with the RAF, its ruthless murders, and its arrogant critique of the system.

The success of Irish militants in their acts of radical redemption clearly shows just how important a solid, territorial support base is, and that it is crucial that the willingness to become a martyr is acknowledged and embraced by a susceptible audience.

Blessed Are Those Who Hunger for Justice

To clearly understand the general history of Irish resistance to British rule, we need to look back a few centuries. The advent of Irish nationalism is often dated around the end of the nineteenth century. The IRA, as a violent guerrilla organization, was the product of the Irish War of Independence that flared up immediately after the end of the First World War and lasted until 1922. Rapoport (2004) locates the IRA, with its narrative of ethnic-national, anti-colonial resistance, in the second worldwide wave of terrorist violence that he sees as starting in the 1920s. That wave was to be long-lasting, as was the IRA itself: in its various fractions and mergers, the IRA survived the end of the second wave and became part of the third—and even of the fourth, to a certain degree. Ethnic-national resistance against foreign rulers is a scenario par excellence for producing martyrs to the good cause, even though that cause acquired a Marxist, revolutionary veneer in the 1960s. Yet, the essence of the IRA was still very much the attempt to use violence instrumentally in pursuit of national self-determination (English 2003; Wilson 2010). In that respect, the IRA had both a completely different pedigree and a completely different aim than the RAF in West Germany, and cannot easily be compared with today's jihadists either.

For this account, however, in an attempt to draw some tentative lines of focused comparison between Irish terrorists and RAF members, we will home in on the very specific acts of hunger strikes in the 1970s and 1980s. We will see that the redemption narrative of IRA members was different from that of the RAF in a number of ways. The most important reason for the members of the IRA to take part in the struggle was their anger and frustration about personally felt oppression and occupation of their territory by British troops. In addition, they wanted to take revenge for the cruelties perpetrated by the British against (innocent) Irish people. Detained IRA members were thus prepared to starve themselves to death to draw the attention of the world media to that oppression and to their struggle for national self-determination; as advocates of the Irish struggle for freedom, they were willing to give their lives for their people. And they were able, far more effectively than the RAF, to channel religious imagery and symbols with their actions, thereby finding resonance within large parts of the Irish population.

In January 1972, a peaceful civil rights demonstration in Derry escalated into a bloody battle. British soldiers fired on the peaceful demonstrators with live ammunition, killing fourteen, all Catholics. The Irish government was unable to control the wave of vengefulness and counterviolence that followed what became known as Bloody Sunday. Northern Ireland was placed under direct control of London, and the British government took the opportunity to introduce a series of emergency measures it had already announced earlier (Faulkner 1971). The police were given powers to arrest individuals without charging them, detain them, and hold them indefinitely. Since the beginning of the Troubles in 1969, the IRA had regrouped and, via internal discussions, disputes, splits, and arguments, reformed as the Provisional IRA, as indicated earlier. They chose armed resistance outside the prison walls. Within those walls, the interned Provisional IRA members chose hunger striking as the ultimate means of applying pressure (Dingley and Mollica 2007, 463).

Under the Prevention of Terrorism Act, political activists had to be treated as "ordinary criminals." This meant that they were not given special status and were not registered as Irish activists, because that would in effect amount to the British government denying its own legitimacy as the highest authority in Northern Ireland. In the autumn of 1980, in an attempt to break through this stubborn British resistance, the detained IRA members announced a collective hunger strike, shortly followed by a second, to allow "the loud voice of the Irish people" to be heard through the willingness of the detained comrades to lay down their lives (Dingley and Mollica 2007, 471). They made the following official statement to the media:

> As further demonstration of our selflessness and the justness of our cause a number of our comrades, beginning today with Bobby Sands, will hunger-strike to the death unless the British government abandons its criminalization policy and meets our demand for political status. (White 1993, 112)

The prisoners demanded the right not to wear prison clothing or to do compulsory prison work, to organize self-schooling and education, and to receive at least one package, one letter, and one visit per week.

The strike received even greater media attention when Northern Irish Catholics elected Bobby Sands to the British parliament. The 27-year-old Sands hailed from a Catholic family from around Belfast, had suffered anti-Catholic harassment throughout his youth, and had joined the Provisional IRA as an active member. Moreover, he was by then well known as the officer commanding of the IRA detainees in the Maze Prison (English 2003, 196–7). This parliamentary political support for Sands and his fellow prisoners allowed the IRA to immediately deny claims from London that the detainees were desperate attention seekers who had no support at all from the wider public. Sands himself was quick to realize that this hunger strike was more than just a tactical move to force the authorities to give the detainees the status of political prisoners. In his diary, he recorded his deeper personal motives:

> I am a political prisoner because I am a casualty of a perennial war that is being fought between the oppressed Irish people and an alien, oppressive, unwanted regime that refuses to withdraw from our land.... I believe I am but another of those wretched Irishmen born of a risen generation with a deeply rooted and unquenchable desire for freedom. I am dying not just to attempt to end the barbarity of H-Block, or to gain the rightful recognition of a political prisoner, but primarily because what is lost in here is lost for the Republic and those wretched oppressed. (Sands 1981, 7–8, "March 1981, Sunday 1st")

As a detainee in H-Block at the notorious Maze Prison, 14 kilometers southwest of Belfast, Sands was robbed of his freedom and autonomy. But this passage shows that, by sacrificing that autonomy, he wished to invoke and put up a symbolic memorial to the loss of autonomy of the Irish people as a whole. He aligned his detention with the oppression of the Irish, under an "oppressive, unwanted" British government. In that way, he contributed not only to the fight for better conditions in prison but also to the greater goal of collective liberation and redemption from British rule in Northern Ireland (English 2003, 194–8).

British prime minister Margaret Thatcher understood that only too well when she emphasized in her response that under no circumstances would she give in to the detainees' political demands. She refused to concede Sands his proxy martyrdom for the Irish people as a whole. In her eyes, Sands was not a freedom fighter. He was in the Maze Prison because he had broken the law and was a criminal:

> There is no such thing as political murder, political bombing or political violence. There is only criminal murder, criminal bombing and criminal violence. We will not compromise on this. There will be no political status [for the detainees]. Of course those convicted of serious crimes and sentenced to long terms of imprisonment should serve their sentences in humane conditions. We will continue to maintain and, if we can, to

improve the high standards which Northern Ireland prisons already provide. (Thatcher 1981)

For Sands, "the issue at stake is not 'humanitarian', . . . improved living conditions"; rather, "[i]t is purely political and only a political solution will solve it" (Sands 1981, 25, "March 1981, Tuesday 10th"). Sands wanted nothing less than self-determination for the Irish and the destruction of Northern Ireland as a whole, and demanded recognition of these aims in London. But after sixty-six days on hunger strike, his body could take no more. Along with nine others, he died of malnutrition and starvation. When his death was announced on May 5, 1981, there was widespread rioting. More than 100,000 people accompanied Sands's coffin on his final journey to the cemetery in Belfast two days later, where he was buried in the "New Republican Plot" (English 2003, 200).

The death of Bobby Sands caused outrage around the world and left a deeper psychological crater than some of the IRA's actual attacks. Everywhere in Europe and North and South America, there were verbal criticisms and street protests against the British government. Students demonstrated, and bishops claimed that Sands's sacrifice had been futile. Both the *New York Times* and *Pravda* called his death a tragedy. As recently as 2001, a memorial to Sands was erected in Cuba. The impact of his death was enormous—much greater than that of Holger Meins's death, six years earlier. At first glance, both the IRA and the RAF had discovered and applied the tactic of the sacralization of hunger. Members of both terrorist organizations had resorted to this weapon against the state while in detention. And both groups had succeeded in leaking images and texts to the media through sympathizers outside the prison (see also Zeilstra 2018).

There was, however, one great difference, and that had to do with the degree to which their supporters accepted and embraced the martyrs' offers of redemption. Saviors can only fulfill their promise of redemption if there is a group or community willing to be saved. And that was emphatically not the case in West Germany. Meins's death, through the widely distributed, piteous, and ghastly images of his emaciated corpse, revived memories of the horrors of Germany's war past. The images may have strengthened the RAF's own sympathizers' belief that the postwar West German state was in no way better than the Third Reich, but they did not reach a wider group of supporters or a grateful public at large (Passmore 2009, 53; Terhoeven 2007, 392–4).

Bobby Sands, on the other hand, was immortalized in murals in Belfast portraying him as a saint on a Catholic prayer card:[5] he lies on a bier, a serene expression on his face, a rosary in his hands, and a halo around his thick, wavy hair. In a direct sense, Sands's hunger strike followed from the exigencies of the prison war (i.e., the IRA detainees' struggle for better conditions and recognition of their status as political prisoners) and the legitimacy of the IRA's campaign against the British. Yet, as a wider echo and reminiscence, Sands's act of defiance invoked a centuries-old Irish tradition of self-sacrifice and martyrdom, implicitly adopting the repertoire of Catholic Irish hunger strikers dating back to the fifth century, the time of the ancient Irish Brehon law and the first missionaries, when serfs could demand their rights through demonstrations of public fasting. Catholic bishops in Ireland had traditionally supported the struggle for independence, and they had done so wholeheartedly in the 1920s, but now, in the 1970s and 1980s, the church was divided. But Sands had no truck with these sensitivities. He justified his hunger strike by quoting the Savior himself in the Gospel of John: "Greater love hath no man than this, that a man lay down his life for his friends" (John 15:13, King James Version).

For many Irish Catholics, it was clear: though they themselves may have disapproved of the path of violence, Bobby Sands was a hero to them. He had not sacrificed himself only for his own personal cause and for his own organization, the IRA, nor had he given his life out of some distorted desire for vengeance against the government or, like Meins and the RAF, to be able to accuse the government of murder. Sands did not describe himself as a martyr; his hunger strike was not in the first instance about his own pain but about the oppression of his Irish Catholic community. For Meins and the RAF, hunger striking was about framing the West German government as new fascists who, through the policy of *Isolationsfolter*, silenced and killed political prisoners. However, as I indicated earlier, it did not enable them to connect to a broader audience. For most West Germans, the death by starvation and suicide of RAF terrorists had nothing to do with making sacrifices for the community (Varon 2004, 229). The RAF detainees convinced only their own direct supporters, who promptly committed new attacks. Sands and his nine comrades, on the other hand, revived a centuries-old Irish ritual that resonated in the community—a historical, symbolic, and religious theme that was immediately recognizable to Irish Catholics.[6] Sands was a

---

[5] For a picture of one of these murals, see Zeilstra (2018, 69).
[6] For the tradition of hunger striking in Irish history, see Sweeney (1993a, 1993b, 2004).

surrogate for the Irish people as a whole, and his suffering was that of his community, which had been oppressed by the British for hundreds of years (Fierke 2012, 449).

That is what made Sands's radical redemption narrative persuasive: it linked individual liberation and emancipation to a community that comprised many more people than just his terrorist organization. It must be stressed that the Catholic halo and the rosary imagery surrounding Sands's death were somewhat unusual in the history of the IRA, owing to the extremity and intensity of the hunger strike campaign as such. The IRA did not systematically train its members to become holy warriors, martyrs, or saints in this fashion. Sands only became a martyr because Catholic priests, his comrades, and his compatriots projected that aura of sainthood upon him; in the murals, he is depicted as a suffering Christ figure. Yet, in the eyes of the public, his sacrifice was highly tangible and unsettling, and his act of redemption inspired new generations to devote themselves to pursuing Irish independence. As Sinn Féin and IRA leader Gerry Sands commented, this "victory exposed the lie that the hunger strikers—and by extension the IRA and the whole republican movement—had no popular support" (English 2003, 200). In fact, Sands had such an impact on the Catholic Church that a number of priests, bishops, and even cardinals actively supported him. While in prison, Sands received visits from various Catholic priests, some of whom pursued his campaign against social injustice with full conviction and supported his family. The cardinal of Armagh and the bishop of Derry both expressed their support for the prisoners' demands for a more liberal prison regime. American cardinals wrote letters of protest to Margaret Thatcher, and priests tried to persuade her to show clemency. Sands was given a Catholic funeral, which was officially denied to suicides—certainly in the extremely traditional Irish Catholic Church. There was, of course, much disapproval and indignation about the way in which the IRA members used their bodies as weapons (see Scull 2016). But Bobby Sands became a folk hero, and his act of radical redemption was embraced and incorporated in the continuing struggle for Irish national self-determination.

Freedom from the Yoke of Technology

Redemption repertoires and motives can be identified in all waves of terrorist violence. The redemption narratives may vary, as may their persuasive power: it makes a lot of difference whether an act of redemption is recognizable to a support base and thereby has an impact, or is a completely obdurate and self-contrived form of devotion to a cause. In the case of lone wolves, there is by definition no support base, at least in organized form. Since there are no followers to save, does that mean that redemption cannot be a motive? The case of Ted Kaczynski is an interesting example in this respect;[7] it is our final stop en route to the current wave of terrorist violence, that of holy terrorism, which will be examined in the following chapter.[8]

Theodore (Ted) John Kaczynski was born in Chicago on May 22, 1942. He was an introvert child who was happiest with his nose in a book and was crazy about mathematics. He proved to have an IQ of 167, skipped a year at school, completed high school with ease, and was admitted to Harvard at the age of 16 (Martinez 2012, 241). In 1967, he was awarded his PhD at the University of Michigan and was appointed assistant professor at the prestigious University of California in Berkeley. But from then on, life began to turn against him. He had difficulty behaving as society expected of him and seemed to be increasingly affected by his latent autism and schizophrenia. When teaching, he preferred to read from his notes and refused to answer students' questions (Greig 2012, 198; McFadden 1996). In 1969, at the age of 27, he resigned from Berkeley and, two years later, withdrew to remote Montana. He built a wood cabin to live in, far away from the inhabited world, without electricity or running water. Occasionally, he would ride his bicycle to the local library to borrow books (Oleson 2005, 212). He slowly came to the conclusion that human dignity was being irrevocably sacrificed to the progressive advance of the "industrial-technological system"—and that it had to be stopped (Oleson 2005, 212).

Kaczynski was a child of his time and, as a scientist, had been enthralled by the warnings of the Union of Concerned Scientists against nuclear energy and the threats posed to nature by technological development (Rome 2003, 552). His concern grew exponentially during the 1960s (Rome 2003, 527). Kaczynski devoured such militant publications as Jacques Ellul's *The Technological Society* and Edward Abbey's *The Monkey Wrench Gang*. Abbey was a source of inspiration for the radical group of environmental activists who had united in the Earth First! movement in 1979 and had been labeled

---

[7] With thanks to Tom Schoen, who researched this story in my MA course Terrorism as Radical Redemption for his (2019) paper "Theodore Kaczynski: A Radical Redeemer?"
[8] The example of "school shooters" also comes to mind, but whether they seek redemption or complete destruction—also from their own perspective—is a question I do not explore further here.

ecoterrorists by the FBI (Jarboe 2002). These ideas helped to form Kaczynski's radicalization process. But what drove him to act was not the books he read but the immediate threat to his living environment from loggers in Montana:

> If nobody had started cutting roads through there and cutting the trees down and come buzzing around in helicopters and snowmobiles I would still just be living there and the rest of the world could just take care of itself. I got involved in political issues because I was driven to it, so to speak. (Kintz 1999)

From the moment he heard the rumble of approaching loggers, Kaczynski decided it was time to act, if necessary, with violence.

> It's kind of rolling country, not flat, and when you get to the edge of [the plateau] you find these ravines that cut very steeply in to cliff-like drop-offs and there was even a waterfall there. It was about a two days hike from my cabin. That was the best spot until the summer of 1983. That summer there were too many people around my cabin so I decided I needed some peace. I went back to the plateau and when I got there I found they had put a road right through the middle of it.... You just can't imagine how upset I was. It was from that point on I decided that, rather than trying to acquire further wilderness skills, I would work on getting back at the system. Revenge. (Kintz 1999)

Kaczynski saw it as his duty to take revenge on the system and to combat the forces of technological destruction on behalf of the natural world—even if it would cost him his own life. He made a conscious decision not to join the left-wing environmental movement, which he found too politically correct. Conservative, right-wing ideas held just as little appeal: despite paying lip service to the purity of an unspoiled past, they gave free rein to capitalism and commercial exploitation of that same natural environment. The situation called for different tactics:

> To a large extent I think the eco-anarchist movement is accomplishing a great deal, but I think they could do it better ... The real revolutionaries should separate themselves from the reformers ... And I think that it would be good if a conscious effort was being made to get as many people as possible introduced to the wilderness. In a general way, I think what has to be

done is not to try and convince or persuade the majority of people that we are right, as much as try to increase tensions in society to the point where things start to break down. To create a situation where people get uncomfortable enough that they're going to rebel. So the question is how do you increase those tensions? (Kintz 1999)

Between 1978 and 1995, Kaczynski pursued a unique campaign to "increase tensions in society." It was unique, because he succeeded in eluding the FBI for many years, during which time he sent sixteen mail bombs, killing three people and injuring sixty. He selected the victims because they were partly responsible for the further expansion of the "industrial-technological system" (Kaczynski 1995, 1). Those he killed were the owner of a computer store, an executive of a large advertising agency, and the chairman of the California Forestry Association, a timber industry lobbying group. It was necessary to sacrifice these people to stop the advance of that system, and to devote his life to achieving that goal. Someone had to do it. The FBI hunted the sender of the mail bombs for eighteen years. He was given the code name "Unabomber" (University and Airline Bomber) because he sent bombs to universities and placed one on a commercial airline flight. Although that bomb did not explode, it showed that Kaczynski was prepared to sacrifice more people for his campaign. He was arrested in 1996, thanks to the cooperation of his brother David, who had shown letters from Ted to the FBI. Kaczynski was sentenced to life imprisonment.

In 1995, at Kaczynski's request, the *Washington Post* published his manifesto "Industrial Society and Its Future," in which he explained his motivations: "The Industrial Revolution and its consequences have been a disaster for the human race. They have ... destabilized society, have made life unfulfilling, have subjected human beings to indignities, ... and have inflicted severe damage on the natural world." The only way to rectify that injustice was revolution, "a revolution against the industrial system" (Kaczynski 1995, 1). And to get that revolution off the ground, "we've had to kill people" (Kaczynski 1995, 12). They had to be sacrificed to free the human race as such from exploitation by technology and politics. For Kaczynski it was about revenge, achieving publicity for his cause, and provoking a response, but also about redemption—for the people, for the natural world, with himself fighting as a proxy warrior for the ignorant masses. Redemption can be seen as both a motive and a goal and should be interpreted as "a deliverance from suffering to a better world," in McAdams's words (2006, 7). For

Kaczynski, radical redemption was the only means to bring about system change, and that could be achieved only through violence and revolution.[9]

Did Kaczynski's campaign against advancing technology have any impact? He and his manifesto became famous and infamous around the world. The *Washington Post* allowed itself to be blackmailed by Kaczynski, printing his manifesto in exchange for his promise to stop sending the mail bombs (Taylor 1998, 310; Moen 2019, 223). But Kaczynski, of course, failed to achieve the "permanent changes in favor of freedom" from technology that he had aimed for. True, his manifesto made a great impression because it was seen as the first act of ecoterrorism. But as a lone wolf, he had distanced himself completely from existing left-wing environmental movements and other activists. His act of transformative redemption fits into McAdams's category of emancipation from slavery, of freedom from (technological) oppression (McAdams 2006, 42). Kaczynski's manifesto and offer of sacrifice were not accepted and adopted until many years later, by Anders Behring Breivik, who copied large parts of it for his own right-wing extremist, white supremacist manifesto (Hough 2011). Breivik recognized Kaczynski's transcendental dimension. For Kaczynski—and for Breivik—it was not only about taking revenge, provoking an overreaction, and increasing tensions in society. His goal was also a kind of transcendental liberation of society from dark forces, a redemption from the tentacles of technology—or in Breivik's case, from *Umvolkung* and the extermination of the white race—through his own proxy devotion to the great cause. To set the revolution in motion, sacrifices had to be made—of others, but sometimes of themselves. They were ultimately prepared to expend time and effort on the great cause, and Breivik even sought a form of martyrdom (Kaczynski 1995, 13; 2010, 11).

The Unabomber was, however, a perverted savior. He selected other people to sacrifice to the destructive technology of his mail bombs, kept potential supporters at a distance, hid from sight, and eluded arrest for almost twenty years. It is thus no surprise that only a person like Breivik followed him and that, in prison, Kaczynski became friends with Ramzi Yousef, one of the main perpetrators of the bomb attack on the New York World Trade Center in 1993, and Timothy McVeigh, who bombed a government building in Oklahoma City in 1995 (Bailey 2017). There was no question at all of

---

[9] In this way, Kaczynski's development process precisely fits the definition of violent radicalization. See Schmid (2013, 8).

Kaczynski's act of redemption being validated, accepted, or acknowledged by a broad group of followers or supporters.

Conclusion

There is a consistent thread running through the history of terrorism and political, ideological, and religious violence, namely, the juxtaposition of the great narrative of the struggle between good and evil with the highly personal dedication, commitment, and sacrifice in service of that great cause. Not all terrorists are equally well educated, well read, or even well spoken. For some of those convicted as terrorists, ties of friendship, adventure, or coincidental complicity lay behind their involvement in attacks and violence. Yet, action and message will at some point come together. The narrative of radical redemption helps to shape that process.

We can observe variations on this theme throughout history, sometimes only as a faint echo or a reminiscence, which may be imbued with veritable religious imagery. The radical redemption narrative could be, for example, purely personal or part of a collective campaign. It could be a form of atonement or penance for a life of setbacks and failure, but also a combination of sacrificing one's own time and life and taking revenge for a perceived injustice. These injustices could be projected on a minority, a socioeconomic class, or the nation as such. The calling felt by the perpetrator could be perceived as a holy act, intended to bring the perpetrator closer to a god or gods, or it could be phrased in more secular-transcendent terms. The battle could be considered a class struggle, an eschatological holy war, or a freedom fight for an oppressed community. The praxis adopted could also assume various forms and involve various methods, weapons, and objects. Interestingly, validation or rewards for the attempted redemption lay mostly outside the perpetrators' scope of control and depended above all on the level of support and resonance they achieved. Table 3.1 presents a breakdown of the narratives with respect to the notion of redemption.

The persuasive power of the narrative of radical redemption varies according to time, place, and type of terrorism. Sometimes, as with Ted Kaczynski, it was purely idiosyncratic. At other times, as in the case of Bobby Sands's hunger strike and the fight for Irish independence, the redemptive efforts were very much validated by a broader community. Sands was able to align his life as a revolutionary and his suffering in prison with the greater,

Table 3.1 Breakdown of various redemption narratives

	Perceived injustices	Orthopraxis	Projected battle (political, metaphysical)	Validation of redemption?
Auguste Vaillant, Zinaida Konopliannikova	Oppression of workers, farmers, Baltic people	Stand up, join farmers, throw bombs, shoot government representatives	Class struggle, anti-capitalist, anti-government freedom fight	Sacrifice acknowledged by support base
Gudrun Ensslin	Collective guilt for fascist past, capitalist oppression of society	Adopt anti-bourgeois lifestyle (steal cars, rob, thwart civil norms), set fire to warehouse, engage in shoot-outs and bombings, use own body in hunger strikes	Anti-imperialist, anti-fascist class struggle	Sacrifice acknowledged only by hard-core sympathizers
Bobby Sands	Oppression of Irish community	Join IRA, engage in hunger strike, use Catholic props	Pro-Irish, anti-British freedom fight	Sacrifice acknowledged by broader Irish community (including global resonance)
Theodore (Ted) Kaczynski	Destruction of nature by capitalist system	Live a "pure" life as a hermit, withdraw to nature, send bombs	Anti-capitalist, anti-technology war fight, restoration of state of nature	Loner, not much validation, no large support base

centuries-old narrative of the oppression of the Irish people by their British rulers. What was more, his story was reinforced with Catholic symbols and rituals: the rosary, the Bible verses, and the Messianic suffering.

From these historical examples, it certainly transpires that narratives that are enriched with or supported by distinctive religious elements offer a more tangible, more recognizable, and therefore more effective interpretation framework in terms of their reach and recruiting power than the abstract philosophies adhered to by, for example, the RAF. That also holds true for ethnic-national narratives, especially when they conflate with specific religious articulations and adherences that are characteristic of that ethnic community, as in Ireland, Sri Lanka, Palestine, and South America. In these cases, the frame of radical redemption establishes an explosive link between a deep—partly invented, partly historical—*past* of rich traditions and crude injustices, including recognizable and existing sacred practices; a *present* of ongoing repression, frustrations, and feelings of injustice; and a projected *future* of liberation. The redemption narrative endows personal frustrations with a transcendent meaning, and places the fight of the individual in a broader eschatological setting, culminating in deliverance, the last battle, final judgment, and/or simply the apocalypse. What is more, these past examples also show the importance of the active role of a support base in making the narrative stick. Take the stories of Vaillant and Konopliannikova. Their executions marked the end of their life stories, but not of their narratives. Their sympathizers used their martyrdom to mobilize new campaigns of violence in Russia and Europe.[10] In this way, the individual sacred practice of redemption of these two anarchists became part of a broader plot and fueled future narratives of revolutionary resistance against a repressive government (compare Lakoff 2002; Lyotard 1984).

Throughout history, we see various kinds of redemption rites, symbols, and sacred practices being embraced. A narrative of radical redemption is, however, most effective if it explicitly brings act and message together, linking personal frustrations to the greater struggle between good and evil, and if the narrative can be communicated and understood as such. That is why the narrative seems to flourish best if it is embedded in and reinforced by deep traditions, rich practices, and a wide acknowledgment and dissemination of an existing religious community that gives a language and an orthopraxis to the eschatological battle between good and evil.

The question now is, how well does the narrative of radical redemption sit with the fourth wave of terrorism, especially in the movement of the worldwide jihad, and in what way does this narrative compare to others? I address this question in the following chapters. In chapter 7 this question is also answered—though in less detail—in the context of right-wing extremist terrorists.

---

[10] The execution of Vaillant inspired anarchist Emile Henry to commit a bomb attack at the Terminus café in Paris. See Klem (2020, 56).

4
The First Panel
Sensing a Deficit

A Social and Moral Deficit

This chapter focuses primarily on the stage in the lives of current and former detainees in which they begin to form images and dreams about the fight against injustice and compare those dreams to their daily lives. We will see that adventure and dedication, extreme beliefs and practical action, fit together well, and that a sense of social and moral deficit and feelings of frustration become increasingly linked to the desire for purification and action. If we see the model of radical redemption as a triptych—sense of deficit, dedication and fight, and validation—this chapter outlines the first panel of the triptych (the other panels will be examined in chapters 5 and 6), addressing the following aspects of this panel as explained in chapter 2: Terrorists believe above all that their country or group is in a state of absolute, radical evil and injustice. This state of injustice makes them feel bad. They then see themselves as part of that situation, because they live in or identify with the group's territory.[1] They believe that they are responsible for the continued existence or termination of that evil, and that they live in a state of moral deficit. They do not do enough: they should radically change the course of their lives and adopt a different (ortho)praxis.

I conducted the first interviews for this study in 2018. I had not expected the interviewees to be so open in talking about their lives. They were a little cautious at first, and started by asking me about my background and beliefs. In all the interviews, I applied the life histories approach, tracking the events of their lives. Most of the men started to talk when I asked them about their

---

[1] Jihadists interpret the area in which they live or that they identify with as a "territory of war" (*dar al-Harb*) or a "territory of Islam" (*dar al-Islam*). When they see the country they live in as a *dar al-Kufr* (territory of disbelief), and they believe that those disbelievers are unjustly conducting war against an Islamic country (and thus make their country a *dar al-Harb*), it is their duty to take action. See, for example, Badara and Nagata (2017).

father, what he did for work, and what kind of relationship they had with him. After that, the conversation would usually proceed quite naturally, passing through their biographies in chronological order. I tried to uncover the most important turning points in their lives and to find out how their ideas, beliefs, and actions had changed over time. All interviewees mentioned one or more transcendental moments in which they felt the desire for another life and an end to injustice or frustration. Upon reaching such a point, they realized they wanted to take a completely different path, help other Muslims, and join in the fight.

In the interviews, I worked on the basis of the Durkheimian insight explained in chapter 1 that religious beliefs or ideologies are not always necessarily linked to strict dogmas but can be much more determined by how a community or an individual experiences them in (social) practice. Many of the interviewees convicted for jihadist crimes did not know the Koran by heart, had not been brought up particularly religiously, and could not speak Arabic. And yet, they had constructed their own faith-based reality and developed their own rituals and practices. They had radical dreams and could sometimes describe the spiritual landscape of their dreams in great detail.

Dreams of the Desert

Sofyan Tsauri was born in 1976 and grew up in Depok, a busy suburb on the southern side of Jakarta dominated by enormous concrete apartment blocks rising above rampantly spreading kampongs.[2] Sofyan's father was a policeman; his family were moderate Muslims, rarely visiting the mosque and not observing regular times of prayer. While at secondary school, Sofyan joined a gang and became involved in petty crime. He was arrested on several occasions, much to his father's anger and his mother's sorrow. "Why is my life always a struggle, a fight?" he would ask himself.[3] When he was 18 years old, a friend gave him a book about Islam. The friend was a member of the Muslim Brotherhood, which was active at many public secondary schools in Indonesia. Although most Indonesian secondary schools are state schools,

---

[2] Sofyan Tsauri was sentenced to ten years' imprisonment in 2010 for several terrorist offenses, including giving military training, possessing weapons, preparing for battle, and being a member of a terrorist organization, in this case Jemaah Islamiyah. He was involved with the group that carried out the attacks on the Ritz-Carlton and JW Marriott Hotels in Jakarta in 2009, although he did not take part in the actual attacks.

[3] Interview with Sofyan Tsauri, February 24, 2020, Jakarta.

almost all have a mosque and a prayer room. From the 1990s, members of the Muslim Brotherhood often set up libraries in schools, where they could invite pupils to take part in prayer or discussion groups.

From the mid-1990s, Sofyan found increasing support and solace in books about Islam. "I started to read about the lives of Muslims around the world, about Muslims in Palestine, who are oppressed there. About Muslims in Bosnia and Afghanistan, who are attacked by Western countries and their factions. The books of Sheikh Azzam and Qutb opened my eyes." Sayyid Qutb, one of the leaders of the Egyptian Muslim Brotherhood and a founder of modern political Islam, was executed for his ideas in 1996 by the Egyptian regime of Gamel Nasser. Sheikh Azzam, Abdullah Yusuf Azzam, was a Palestinian Sunni Islamic scholar who elaborated on Qutb's ideas and expanded on the concept of defensive and offensive jihad. He combined theory and practice in the jihad, was a scholar and cofounder of Al Qaeda, and inspired bin Laden. He was killed by a car bomb in 1989. Qutb and Azzam are the spiritual fathers of the global jihad. Their influence extended far beyond the Middle East, to Indonesia, the Netherlands, and elsewhere (see, e.g., Hegghammer 2019; Calvert 2010).

"I read the books [by Qutb and Azzam]," Sofyan told me, "and discovered that my personal struggle and frustrations were nothing compared to the suffering of countless Muslims in countries where they are not given the opportunity to practice their faith." He followed intensive after-school lessons in the "right doctrines and practices of Islam," and read all the books he could find. And slowly he started to realize that he had to change the way he led his life: "I had to cleanse my soul of all the wrong things I had done. I was known at school for my aggression and anarchist behavior. When I was about 18 or 19, thanks to the religious teaching, I decided that I had to lead a better life: I should not fight out of egoism and recalcitrance, not think only of myself, but direct my energy and aggression for the good of others."

From then on, he started to dream: "I dreamed of rocks, of the desert. I had never been there, but imagined I was in Afghanistan, where I fought faceless enemies on mountainous hillsides. We hid in caves. And we had hand grenades and machine guns that always found their mark. And my ammunition never ran out." Although, a few years later, Sofyan would join guerrilla groups in Aceh that ran military bases and training camps in the jungle, his first images of the holy battle were determined by the landscape he had read about in the books and texts of Arabic and Wahhabist Muslim scholars—the desert. The landscape of the jihad was Arabian, Middle Eastern, wild, and empty. "It was the landscape of the Prophet. Just as the Prophet left Mecca in 622 and fled to Medina, to better prepare himself for the battle, so must we do the same—spiritually and later also physically."[4]

Notably, other convicted terrorists I spoke with, both Dutch and Indonesian, described similar dream images. When one detainee in the Netherlands invited me to take a look in his cell, I saw beautiful drawings on the wall, made with felt-tip pens that lay on his desk. The drawings depicted all kinds of scenes from the desert: mountains and rocks, caves, and oases, drawn in many shades of brown, grey, and yellow. The man told me he had never been there. "This is what I dream of," he said. "Of going there and seeing it for myself. But I am in prison and have never been further than Germany."[5] Fadil*, who came from the Schilderswijk, a deprived district of The Hague, told me of the dreams he had after watching more and more film clips of the war in Syria. "Allah called me. He showed me images of fighters, of the desert, of people hiding behind rocks and ambushing their enemies, who they defeated with guns and swords."[6] He, too, had at that point never been to Syria. But the universal images of the jihad, the stories of the *hijra*,[7] and YouTube clips by IS and other groups merged together to form a vision of the holy battle, of a place where true Muslims could fight the good fight— and win.

Whether my interviewees had seen such images on YouTube or other Internet channels or had only read about them made little difference. They generated the same notions of a universal jihad against the background of a Middle Eastern landscape and of the life of the Prophet and his followers interpreted by the militant Muslims of today. There is now a recognition in the literature that these dreams are frequently part of jihadist radicalization processes, and that it is sometimes difficult for the dreamer to distinguish between nocturnal and day dreams, between wishful thinking and visions and hallucinations caused, for example, by drug use or by injuries and traumas incurred on the battlefield or on the run. Either way, such dreams play an important role: they are shared and passed on, and they create the illusion of being close to the divine—they are considered proof that an individual is on the right spiritual path and divinely directed in their actions (see, e.g.,

---

[4] Interview with Sofyan Tsauri, February 24, 2020, Jakarta.
[5] Interview in PI/TDU, 2019; further details are omitted because this detainee did not wish my account of his drawings to be linked to his name.
[6] Interview with Fadil*, March 6, 2019, The Hague.
[7] The migration of the Islamic prophet Muhammad from Mecca to Medina in 622, which marks the start of the Islamic calendar and is of crucial significance in Islam.

Edgar and De Looijer 2017, 140-1, 149-50). In addition, it is common for jihadists—and thus for jihadist detainees—to ask each other about their dreams and talk about what they mean.[8]

As Haroun* from Amsterdam, who had spent two years in Syria, put it: "That dream of the jihad is everything. You set off on the adventure. You leave your parents and family behind. It is a way of dedicating yourself to something beyond yourself and of structuring your life differently. You carry it with you day and night. To fight injustice and devote your whole life to Allah. It is faith, but it is everything. It is the air you breathe, your daily life, and your dreams—how you experience all that."[9]

Global Landscapes of Jihad

The fourth wave of terrorism—holy terrorism—which Rapoport (2004) dates as starting around 1979, is characterized by the concurrence of ideological and religious violence with the emergence of mass media and the Internet. Holy terrorism occurs in all major religions: Buddhists, Hindus, Jews, and Christians have also been guilty of attacks and killings in the name of their god or gods, with the intention of establishing the Kingdom of God, expediting the coming of the Messiah, or bringing about the End of Days. But jihadism, the violent and armed form of the Islamic struggle, is the most extensive in terms of followers, attacks, and killings (see, e.g., Carson and Suppenbach 2018).

What was new in the fight conducted by Al Qaeda was that the battles were not restricted to local theaters of war, as in Afghanistan between 1979 and 1989, but that, thanks to financial injections by bin Laden and other sheikhs, the radical ideas of Azzam and Qutb were widely propagated in countless publications. In the 1990s, it was the Muslim Brotherhood who distributed these writings worldwide, including in the Netherlands and Indonesia. Similarly, television network Al Jazeera broadcast images around the world of jihadists fighting in Afghanistan, Bosnia, and Israel. At that time, bin Laden's men had to go to a great deal of trouble to record their emir's speeches on videotape and drive through the desert in a jeep

---

[8] This was reconfirmed in a background discussion with an analyst from the General Intelligence and Security Service (AIVD), July 6, 2020.
[9] Interview with Haroun*, January 16, 2020, PI/TDU.

to take them to a television studio in the hope that they would be broadcast. But even then, Al Qaeda's message was already universal. It may have been about injustice and the struggle of Muslims in specific locations and against specific enemies—apostate regimes in the Middle East, corrupt Western powers that refused to stop interfering in the lands of holy places—but it was a struggle that concerned all Muslims—the worldwide *ummah*—and thanks to the advent of mass media, it could be followed all around the world.

It was also a struggle embedded in traditions, rituals, and symbols presented as ancient stories passed down through the generations. Faisal Devji (2005) has convincingly explained that the narrative of the jihad is unique and strong due to that link between the local and the global. The jihad is everywhere, but it is also explicitly somewhere specific. The dreams of the desert can be dreamed anywhere, but they can also be put into concrete practice. The jihad embraces political military campaigns against the communist Soviet Union in Afghanistan, Christian Serbs and the Western coalition in former Yugoslavia, and Zionists in Israel. At the same time, it is an ethical duty for all Muslims in all countries, who can fight that fight without weapons but with conviction and the right orthopraxis (Esposito 2002, 140).[10]

The universal violent jihad was fought on various battlefields in Afghanistan, Bosnia, Israel, Algeria, and Africa, where the fighters presented themselves as advocates of pure Islam and offered to save or deliver their supporters from apostate regimes (see, e.g., Deeb 1992, 55).[11] Those jihadist battlefields, until then primarily regional, found their global apotheosis in the attacks of 9/11. The images of the collapsing towers of the World Trade Center are burned into our collective memory. The attacks established Al Qaeda as a brand name. A few years later, the emergence of social media ensured that the power of the jihadist narrative became a permanent fixture on the Internet and part of the experiential background and horizons of expectation of new generations of radical youth.

---

[10] John Esposito (2002) has rightly pointed out that the neo-orthodoxy or the neo-Salafism that has been dominant since the 1980s is not so much about the right orthodoxy, the right doctrine, and the right principles, as about adhering to the right practices, the pure orthopraxis of Islam.

[11] Mary-Jane Deeb (1992) describes how jihadist groups in Tunisia and Algeria embraced this theme of redemption.

Viral Times

Facebook was launched in 2004; by 2011, it already had 700 million active users. This number has now grown to 2.5 billion. Users can have up to 1,000 virtual friends on each friend list, and each user can appear on or create 100 lists. Eighty percent of Facebook users are between 15 and 29 years old and live not only in the West but also, and more so, in less developed countries or countries where the official media are less efficient or are not trusted. In Egypt, for example, and in Tunisia, some 90 percent of the people prefer following the news on their smartphones and social media to following it via the state media. After Facebook came Twitter (rebranded as X in July 2023). Set up in 2006, this platform had, by 2012, 200 million users worldwide, who sent 340 million tweets a day. By 2018, 321 million people were active on Twitter. At crucial moments, such as during the US presidential elections in 2016, it was the primary source of breaking news (Ritchie et al. 2023; Ortiz-Ospina 2019; Van Deursen et al. 2015, 264).[12]

The emergence of social media had far-reaching consequences. Historically, innovations in information and communications technology have continually caused trend breaks. With the advent of steamships, the radio, and the telegraph, people on different continents could feel connected to each other for the first time. Emigration and exile no longer had to be final. Contact could be maintained with distant trade posts and overseas missions and family members elsewhere in the world. These innovations launched the Second and Third Industrial Revolutions.[13] In hindsight, the advent of the Internet proved to be of greater significance than the end of the Cold War. Technological revolutions have always had direct political and social consequences: new means of communication offer a platform for people who were until then ignored or oppressed. At the time of the Reformation, this applied to printing and the distribution of the Bible and Protestant pamphlets in different languages. In the twentieth century, this process of worldwide expansion went even further. Radio and television gave the fight for independence in colonial regions a great boost after the Second World War. Without the speeches and images broadcast everywhere, Che Guevara

---

[12] In the Netherlands, for example, in 2020, there were 2.5 million Twitter users, with just under a million using it daily.

[13] The Second Industrial Revolution embraces the accelerated industrial and technological development between approximately 1870 and 1910; the Third Industrial Revolution refers to the digital revolution and the transformation of the information and communication processes that emerged at the end of the twentieth century.

would never have become a superhero in the 1960s, nor would Nelson Mandela have become one in the decades that followed. In the 1990s and after the millennium, the emergence of the Internet and social media made the Orange Revolution and the Arab Spring possible and helped to increase the pressure to democratize on authoritarian regimes in Russia, Egypt, and even China and India.

Of course, this is only half the story. Viral times are not necessarily a force for good. Technology, including new information and communication technology, can always be used for good and for bad. The application of technology has rarely been neutral. A society may benefit from technology to promote democracy, quality, and emancipation—or it may not. New technologies based on big data make use of algorithms—a finite series of automated instructions applied for a specific purpose. Those instructions naturally represent underlying values, aimed at increasing profits: by definition, they are not neutral, and they can be pursued at the expense of truth and reliability. The CEOs of the five tech giants (the Big Five) are currently under great pressure to come to grips with this.

There is, however, an even more targeted and malign form of abuse of and through social media, namely, the way in which terrorists have embraced the Internet and the new opportunities it offers. At the end of the nineteenth century, anarchists used the discovery of dynamite to construct small, compact "infernal machines" that they could smuggle along with them to kill kings, tsars, and police chiefs, after which the newspapers described their attacks in all their gory detail. Revolutionary terrorists in the tumultuous 1960s and 1970s were early adopters when it came to machine guns and the use of television to draw the world's attention to their hijacks and kidnaps. Today, jihadists and right-wing extremists have perfected their use of the Internet. While bin Laden had to make do with videocassettes, IS became past masters at using vloggers and creating their own YouTube channels. In 2015, jihadist organizations reached 2 billion individuals with their video messages, ran 10,000 active websites, and, through YouTube or glossy magazines like *Inspire* and *Dabiq*, instructed potential recruits on how to make a homemade bomb or organize an attack (see, e.g., Ingram 2017, 358; Weimann 2010, 50; Farwell 2014, 49; Nanninga 2019; Awan 2017, 139).

My research showed that, with the exception of the convicted terrorists who had grown up in the 1990s, the current generation of terrorists obtained their radical ideas and images almost exclusively from the Internet and social media. Almost all the detainees I interviewed told me they had become entrapped in the net of increasingly radical ideas by watching IS film clips on YouTube. "Just like Hollywood, man!" and "Sick!" they exclaimed.[14] Clicking on innocent clips about clothes or how to act with girls, they were almost automatically—through the perverse YouTube algorithms—exposed to steadily more radical terrorist films. With their criminal or gaming backgrounds, they found it difficult to resist the exciting images of adventure, shootings, fast cars, and willing women waiting for them in the caliphate. Media images have always had an impact, but present-day online messaging goes much further—it is quicker, the images are better, the clips more convincing. With fast, widely available Internet, a much broader audience has become captivated by radical sites—they do not seek them actively, but they find them anyway. The use of social media enables terrorists from around the world to be in constant contact with potential sympathizers and recruits, to arouse their emotions and mobilize them in a way that was unthinkable via the post, telephone, or radio. The online world can draw them into that bubble and keep them there. What is more, that bubble can be made almost impenetrable for those combatting terrorism; that is why, for example, IS often communicated using Telegram, an app that makes it possible to set up recruitment campaigns through encrypted chat rooms. The Internet facilitates the creation of epistemic bubbles, in which individuals can be drawn into increasingly radical content and "normal news" can no longer be found (see, e.g., Bloom et al. 2019, 1242; Prucha 2016, 55).

Importantly, after potential sympathizers switch off their computers, the films keep playing in their heads. The dreams of the jihad and of the desert are addictive and clearly very appealing—not only to radical Muslims in the Netherlands and Western Europe but also to young Muslims in Cameroon, Kenya, and Indonesia. The worldwide jihad was, of course, adapted to the specific local context. But what is conspicuous about this wave of holy terrorism is that the jihadist doctrine devised and elaborated in Egypt and the Middle East by Qutb, Azzam, and bin Laden had such an enormously strong and unifying impact. That was due to the power of the images of the struggle in Afghanistan and even more of the 9/11 attacks on the Twin Towers, as well as to the logistics and infrastructure of rich financiers who sponsored these writings and film clips and helped distribute them. These were not only jihadist organizations but also Salafist and orthodox Islamic

---

[14] Interviews with Amin*, October 30 and November 27, 2019, PI/TDU, and with Fadil*, March 6, 2019, The Hague. See also Hafez (2007).

foundations, who did not themselves incite violence but who did show the stories of the struggle and dedication of the jihadists in mosques, *pesantren* (Islamic boarding schools in Indonesia), *madrassas*, and after-school centers worldwide.

Enough of My Flatscreen

Back to my interviewees, whose dreams of the desert began to chafe with feelings of deficit, injustice, and frustration in their daily lives.

Take Fadil, who was born in Morocco in 1985 and came to the Netherlands at the age of 12 to be reunited with his family. He and his family lived in the Schilderswijk in The Hague, where he attended a local school. He told me his parents were "not very religious"; his father prayed at the prescribed times, but his mother rarely prayed at all. Fadil was allowed to decide for himself whether he went to the mosque. Sometimes he did, but he preferred to go to taekwondo lessons on the weekends. "I was always torn in different directions," he said. "I wanted to be a Muslim, but my daily life and my sports activities made it difficult for me to stick to the compulsory praying times."[15] He did learn Arabic, so that he could recite from the Koran and converse in the language of the Prophet. "Faith is like a burning coal," Fadil said, in his typical ornate language. "You try not to drop it, but it's also difficult to keep hold of it."

As a teenager, while a pupil at the Johan de Witt College in The Hague, Fadil became involved in petty crime.

> The community center was only open twice a week, there was nothing to do at home, so I hung around outdoors, on the street. We were street kids and stole for fun. I tried to carry on studying after I finished school: sports and physical activity management, because that's what I was good at—sports and physical activity. But I didn't make it; I failed the tests, even though the placements at schools were what I enjoyed most of all. I was really good at motivating kids and young people. After that, I went into fruit import and export. I wasn't really aware of the invasion of Iraq. I was busy earning money. I already had a house for myself, with a nice sofa and a flatscreen television. And I had a Dutch girlfriend, who had become a Muslim for me.

---

[15] Interview with Fadil*, March 6, 2019, The Hague.

As for many other interviewees of the current generation of convicted terrorists—born roughly between 1980 and 1995—the Arab Spring was a turning point for Fadil.

> I was sitting on my nice sofa in 2011 and saw what was happening in Syria on the news—on the Dutch news and on Al Jazeera. That war was my wake-up call. All the atrocities were just shown on television! I followed the demonstrations, saw children being abducted, and heard that they were being tortured. Just for writing "piss off Bashar" on a wall. I remember being immobilized by the shock. I said two prayers, to ask forgiveness for my own inability to do anything. Imagine a young Dutch guy hearing that there's a tyrant doing terrible things in Finland; that he sees children being oppressed, people being buried alive—things the Nazis did. Everyone would understand it if the Dutch and other Western European nations went to their rescue, just as they received help in the Second World War, wouldn't they?
>
> So I sat there on my nice sofa, feeling frustrated. This was unfair. I did nothing for Allah, for the community; I was useless. I had a good life, a fantastic life, with a lot of friends. I also felt welcome in The Hague. The people there are really friendly. I always voted for GroenLinks [a green, left-wing political party], the Socialist Party, or the Labour Party. They're on our side. Femke Halsema [then leader of GroenLinks] is a nice, friendly woman. Wouter Bos [then leader of the Labour Party] isn't. He became director of a bank. But I came to see how my life, life in the Netherlands, is far too good. Our problems are so small. In Syria, people were being oppressed; that was really bad. That's what politicians should be trying to solve, what I should devote my life to. I wanted to play a role, do something meaningful, and became more and more dissatisfied.

Personal circumstances that prevented Fadil from leading a happy life and caused him existential confusion played a role, too. Around 2011, he was diagnosed with cancer.

> It was Allah's will. I had testicular cancer and had to have chemotherapy. One testicle was removed, and I donated it to medical science. But I couldn't have children. I had really wanted to be a sports teacher, but that proved impossible. And I wanted a family, but now I couldn't have children. And while I was having the chemo, I saw on the television how children in

Syria needed help. I'd been to Turkey that year, on holiday. There, I saw how refugees lived on the street, with their children. I saw a young boy begging, and I swear, I could have taken him with me and taken care of him. At home, I could no longer sleep. Everything spun round and round in my head. Allah was in my head. I had everything I wanted: holidays, a chic coffee machine, delicious tart from the supermarket. Everything. If I wanted a PlayStation 2, I could buy one. I had to do something, but what? I asked my friends, but they didn't know either. What could I do for those kids in Syria, and for my own life? What could I give back to Allah? I had had enough of my flatscreen.[16]

This was a recurring theme for many of my interviewees of Fadil's generation: they had led lives that were not strictly pious. They had often been involved in petty crime. They had jobs, but not the careers they had dreamed of. They earned enough to buy what they wanted—flatscreens, sofas, and coffee machines were frequently mentioned. The Arab Spring and the war in Syria coincided with a small crisis in their young adult lives. They were between 20 and 30 years old and should—according to the expectations of their families or communities—be settling down, but they sensed a deficit; they felt that something was missing. The images of oppression and misery, of repression of Islamic women and children, spoke to them very clearly. Interestingly, the images also triggered their latent religious beliefs and convictions. By identifying with the injustice inflicted on other Muslims, they began to see themselves more as Muslims and to feel solidarity with and a sense of shared responsibility for the suffering of their fellow believers in Syria.

Amin* tells a similar story. He was born in Amsterdam North in 1989. His father used to work in the mines. "I didn't know that," he said. "I thought it was just a made-up story, but I found out later that it was really true. It left him with a bad back, and he later found work in horticulture. There were four of us kids at home. I was the youngest."[17] Amin did well at school, leaving with an MBO (secondary vocational education) diploma. He soon got a job in the retail sector, where he was responsible for the financial administration of a large chain store.

---

[16] Interview with Fadil*, March 6, 2019, The Hague.
[17] Interviews with Amin*, October 30 and November 27, 2019, PI/TDU.

> That was my goal, going to work—unlike my father—in a smart suit, with a laptop and a leather attaché case. But it turned out to be a lot less interesting than I thought, that office job. When I was young, I saw people in chic suits and with cool lease cars who worked in high-rise glass office blocks. But when I did that myself, for an energy company, it was a disappointment. You have to be cut out for it, sitting at the computer all day. It was pleasant enough—we sent post and packages to all kinds of clients. But then there was a reorganization, and I ended up in the call center. That was terrible, such depressing work. I had people on the phone all day, crying and complaining. So then I thought, No, man. I asked for redundancy pay and took a job at a transport company. Loading and unloading trucks. That was at least a bit more varied.

So, Amin also initially desired a life of wealth and well-being. Furthermore, Islam did not play a great role in his upbringing, and he also felt that something was not right.

> My father went to the mosque, but he did not really read the Koran. And I didn't have to go either. We did pray, but only because it was normal to do so. I would not say that we were practicing Muslims. I did things that were actually not permitted. I watched immoral programs, even though I had read that it wasn't proper. I listened to hip-hop music and had piles of CDs. I could have started my own music library. And that was of course also un-Islamic rubbish. I had read in *The Gardens of the Righteous*.[18] That is about remorse and pure intentions. But it doesn't say anything specific about music. The Prophet, of course, didn't say that rock or hip-hop is not allowed. I said to my imam: "You can be a Muslim 24 hours a day, but you can't be preoccupied with Islam 24 hours a day." And that isn't necessary either, because Islam teaches us that everyone needs their time. Allah gets his time during prayer, and you get your time when you watch films and when you feel good. My intentions were not so lofty that I could sit and read the Koran all day. And that hasn't changed. I want to do what I like doing.

For Amin, too, the war in Syria was an eye-opener.

---

[18] By Muhammad ibn Saalih al-Uthaymeen, a well-known Salafist scholar who lived in Saudi Arabia from 1925 to 2001.

> I had one foot in the faith and the other on the street. If I could earn 300 euros by selling a stolen telephone, I'd do it. Sorry, but for 300 euros, I was happy to break the rules. Anyway, then the war broke out in Syria. Everyone was talking about it—my friends on the street. And I wasn't always home. I was married. I even had two small children. But I didn't want to be a stay-at-home husband; I wanted to keep my old life and my old friends. I talked to them about Syria. I searched for film clips to learn more about it. Yes, I like fine things, and IS had the best films. They had the biggest video network. Once you started looking, you got to see more and more videos, and I became addicted to them. I can't read Arabic, so when I click on something, I don't know straight off what it is. But that makes it exciting. And in full HD on my big television, it's even more exciting. It was top Hollywood quality. Yelling in Arabic, fighting, fighting, fighting. It did get a little monotonous, though. IS showed it as it was, how it should be, what Muslims had to do. These clips showed what real, pure Muslims with guts do. They don't stay at home looking at their flatscreens.[19]

As described in chapter 2, we see here how extreme interpretations of religious dogmas made available through the Internet gave form and direction to a sense of malaise: the IS propaganda identified everything that was wrong with the world and detailed what had to be done about it.

Grappling with the Deficit and the Desire for Purity and Action

Karim* was born in 1987 and lived with his family in the Overvecht district of Utrecht. He explained to me how his older brother Hassan (1983–2015), who was killed in Syria, "had run up against a wall on all fronts."[20]

> We come from a family with nineteen children. My father had children from his first wife in Morocco, and after that started a family in the Netherlands. Here in the Netherlands, Hassan and I had four sisters. Our sisters are really clever, you know. But we were good at football. Hassan had a dream,

---

[19] Interviews with Amin*, October 30 and November 27, 2019, PI/TDU.
[20] Interview with Karim*, April 17, 2020, Utrecht.

to become a professional footballer. We lived in the Vijgeboomstraat in Utrecht and often played football there with Wesley Sneijder [a Dutch international footballer] and his older brother, Jeffrey. Hassan was really good. And at school, too. He was really good at maths, was charming but also very temperamental and always had something to say about everything. I was quieter. I read a lot and was interested in the faith from a young age. Hassan did his very best, but Wesley and the other boys from Overvecht and Ondiep were chosen to join Ajax, while my brother wasn't. That was an enormous disappointment. Then, he started hanging out with young guys who had a bad influence on him. He was demoted to a lower grade level at secondary school, while he was actually much smarter. He tried to take a step toward a career by applying to join the police. But that didn't work—they thought he was too enthusiastic, had too much of a temperament as well. When he was 18, he applied to join the army, where he was accepted and sent straight through to Roosendaal, to the commandos. He passed the admission tests with excellent results! We were so proud. But then it all went wrong again.

Hassan spent a year with the commandos but was detained on suspicion of committing an offense. He swore resolutely that he had not done it and had been framed. He found it very humiliating to be behind bars. He was eventually cleared of all charges and was invited to rejoin the commandos. But he had had enough and had closed that door behind him. Through contacts he had made while in prison, he found his way into the criminal circuit. By then he was married. His wife was well educated, and together, we tried to keep him on the straight and narrow. But without success.

After a year, Hassan's marriage broke up. His wife's business was doing very well, but that made him feel increasingly marginalized. The war in Syria was his wake-up call. "He wasn't even that religious," said his brother. "He knew no Arabic, almost nothing about Islam, and only three small *suras* [chapters of the Koran]. And if I tried to explain something to him, he didn't even listen." But the desire "to show who he was and what he could do, to present himself to his brother, his wife, and his family as a real man and Muslim drove him into the arms of IS Internet recruiters, through chats on Telegram and so on."

He spent more and more time on the Internet, searching for YouTube clips on the war in Syria, and through chats and fora, he came into contact with IS recruiters. "I tried to convince him that it was all bullshit," said Karim.

But he was completely brainwashed by all the so-called brothers. They tried to convince him that he could perform a heroic act if he took part in the jihad in Syria and Iraq, and that he would be accepted by the almighty Allah as a martyr. He also had to distance himself from everyone who was against IS, like me or the local imams. And it went further: he was given a route and logistical instructions, and he received proper training to prepare him for his departure. It was very likely that small group from Arnhem that was recently rounded up, but I'm not sure. Hassan kept that concealed from me. He was so paranoid that he left his telephone at home when he went to the mosque or met the members of the group in some attic room. They took Hassan away from us and persuaded him to make his terrible choice. It was nothing less than a form of theological mind control.

In July 2014, Hassan left for Iraq, at the request of and encouraged by his IS Internet friends. He sent a few photos from Iraq and a farewell film clip, urging his wife and sisters to live a pure life, to not smoke or drink, and to adhere to the prescribed times of prayer; but above all, he called on them to adhere to pure religious practices as much as possible. He was killed during the battle for Fallujah on January 1, 2015.

According to his brother, what caused Hassan to participate in the jihad was a combination of circumstances and a deep feeling of failure in his work, in his career, in his marriage, and as a Muslim. The narrative that IS offered him, plus the chance to prove himself on the battlefield, particularly in the "final battle," proved too seductive. "It wasn't money, adrenaline, or adventure—it was his wish to do something good, to give his life as a martyr and by so doing to wash away the sins and failures of his own life. In effect, he stepped into an alternative life in which he played his part in the final battle."[21]

Almost all the current and former detainees I spoke with had a similar story: they had had a moderate Islamic upbringing, more often than not had little knowledge of Arabic, and had not had a Salafist education. That latent identity as a Muslim was massively triggered by external events in 2011. The war in Syria and the Arab Spring broke violently through the prosperity bubble of my interviewees. The images of the conflict that most of them first encountered through the regular media threw their relationship to their own identity, community, and religious beliefs into sharp relief. That led them

---

[21] Interview with Karim*, April 17, 2020, Utrecht.

to seek more information on the Internet, YouTube, and all kinds of jihad channels. This applied to all of the Dutch-Moroccan and a few of the Dutch-Turkish detainees I talked to. They felt challenged and compelled to reflect on their lives: What did their lives look like in the light of the suffering that was being inflicted on Muslims elsewhere? In all cases, such reflection caused strife and uncertainty. Their life situation—leading a life of material prosperity, yet feeling torn in different directions, "with one foot in the faith and the other on the street"—started to make them feel trapped. They wanted to break out.

We will look at this in more detail later. First, a culture check is in order: Are these stories typical of Dutch Muslims, of young men from the Dutch-Moroccan and Dutch-Turkish communities? Is their experience of religion culturally determined by the context of a thoroughly secularized, prosperous Western society, or did convicted terrorists from a non-Western context share this sense of deficit and desire for purity and action? Did the non-Western radicals' religious beliefs develop traditionally, or eclectically and only when they were older? And did the war in Syria and the suffering of Muslims elsewhere also play such a prominent role in throwing their faith and sense of deficit into great relief?

Enough of My Government

While there are some 1 million Muslims in the Netherlands, which has a total population of 17 million, in Indonesia there are more than 200 million Muslims, constituting 87 percent of the population. The situation in this expansive country of 17,000 islands is completely different politically, sociogeographically, culturally, and demographically. Muslims do not suffer from discrimination, are represented in all social classes, are as diverse internally as Indonesian society as a whole, and, since the end of the Suharto regime in 1998, have a strong voice in policy and politics. Indonesia is a country with severe socioeconomic inequality and power concentrated strongly in the center. It is also a very collectivist society. Origins, tribe, family, and community count for more than the individual, according to Hofstede's practical but controversial model (see Hofstede Insights, n.d.). Indonesia is not a secular country, and everyone is required to be a member of one of the five officially recognized religions: Islam (87%), Christianity (Protestantism 7%; Catholicism 3%), Hinduism (1.7%), Buddhism (0.7%), and Confucianism

(0.05%). Indonesia has a long history of violent conflict involving Islamic movements. Since the emergence of the Padri movement at the beginning of the nineteenth century, political Islam in Indonesia has at various times been engaged in revolt, civil war, and violent resistance—against Dutch colonial rule, against other, more moderate Islamic or non-Islamic factions, and against the centralized governments of Sukarno and Suharto after 1949. From this perspective, the foundation of the Islamic resistance movement Darul Islam in 1942,[22] the emergence of the terrorist organization Jemaah Islamiyah in the 1980s, and the serious bomb attacks on Bali and in Jakarta—in 2002, 2004, 2005, and 2009—can be seen as key moments in a much longer process of violence and radicalization (see Pringle 2010).

The long and tumultuous history of Islam in Indonesia was a recurring theme in my conversations with convicted terrorists. I was struck by the comparison with Dutch detainees: while the radicalization processes of the latter were strongly individualistic and Internet driven, the Indonesian convicts placed themselves much more emphatically in existing historical traditions—though, perhaps, reinterpreted as such by them—of jihad and rebellion against the powers that be. I was particularly interested to find out to what extent a sense of personal and religious deficit played a role when they were confronted with accounts and images of the suffering of oppressed Muslims in Afghanistan and Syria. Did they, like the Dutch interviewees, seek purification, personal redemption, and deliverance? In addition to the life histories approach, I explicitly kept these questions in mind while interviewing the Indonesian convicts. As table 4.1 shows, the number of departees and convicted jihadist terrorists in Indonesia is relatively low, considering the size of the population and the number of Muslims. In the spring of 2020, when I was conducting the interviews, there were a little over 600 terrorists in detention in Indonesia, with some 100 in custody awaiting trial. More than 800 had been released. I was able to speak with five of the jihadists detained between 2015 and 2020.

"Ramli" was born in Lampung, in South Sumatra, in 1981.[23] His father worked for a tobacco company, and his mother had her own business. He was the youngest of five boys and girls. His parents were not strictly religious,

---

[22] Darul Islam was an Indonesian resistance movement with a strong Islamic foundation that fought against the Dutch and Indonesian armies from 1945 to 1962. The name comes from *dar al-Islam*, meaning "territory of Islam."

[23] "Ramli" is the self-chosen nom de guerre of this interviewee, and he was known as such by his comrades. He did not wish to be referred to by his real name.

Table 4.1 Numbers of convicted terrorists and detainees in Indonesia and the Netherlands

Convicted terrorists, departees, reintegrated former detainees	Arrested and convicted 2013–2020	In custody, awaiting trial	Detained in 2020	Sentence completed, reintegrated	Repeat offenders	Departees: individuals leaving to join the jihadist fighting	Returnees
Situation in Indonesia in May 2020[a]	1,160	114	1,400, 613 of whom after 2015	825	<100; approx. 8% of total	1,437[b]	126 on their own initiative; 570 deported from Turkey
Situation in the Netherlands in 2020[c]	approx. 130	approx. 5	36	approx. 90[d]	6; approx. 5% of total	300[e]	60

[a] Interview with Solahudin, February 26, 2020, Jakarta; interview with staff of the Indonesian National Counter Terrorism Agency (BNPT), February 27, 2020, Jakarta. Figures supplemented on the basis of emails received on June 5, 2020, regarding the situation in May 2020.

[b] To Syria, Iraq, Afghanistan, and Mindanao.

[c] Own figures, reports from Public Prosecution Service, court reports, AIVD reports, and media reports. See also table with own figures in De Graaf (2019, 118–29).

[d] Since 2004, when suspects could be convicted under the Crimes of Terrorism Act for the first time.

[e] To Syria and Iraq.

though his mother was a member of Muhammadiyah, an Islamic organization very well known in Indonesia.[24] Ramli attended a public primary school; later, his parents sent him to a secondary school run by Muhammadiyah in Lampung, where he was trained as a mechanic. He proved to be so clever and good with his hands that he became eligible for a "Suharto scholarship"; these scholarships were renowned at the time. A number of universities offered him a place, but he wanted to try and gain admission to the prestigious University of Indonesia in Jakarta.

In 1999, he found a room in Jakarta, but after months of hard study and extra lessons paid for by his family, he narrowly failed the entrance examination. He intended to sit it again, but in the months that followed, everything went wrong. He became disillusioned and spent his time speeding around on his motorbike. "I was good at that," he said. "I won all the street races."[25] On his own in the metropolis, he sought contact with others in a mosque in Cipayung, the district of Jakarta he lived in. He joined a group that discussed the situation on Ambon, which at that time was the scene of a bloody ethnic and religious conflict. After the fall of Suharto's 31-year rule, Indonesia was in an extremely unstable political and economic situation, which had disturbed the fragile balance between the various population groups, islands, and religions. In January 1999, a shouting match between a Christian minibus driver and an Islamic passenger sparked riots and fighting throughout the Maluku archipelago. In the course of 1999 and early 2000, some 2,000 people lost their lives. "I was astounded," Ramli told me. "I knew hardly anything about all this, but now I saw images on television of Muslims being slaughtered. At the mosque, we spoke of nothing else. Why didn't our government do something? Why did Habibi and Wahid [Indonesian presidents at the time] support the Christians? Suharto had been corrupt, but now everything seemed to be getting even worse."

He began to search for information himself. There was as yet no YouTube—it was not launched until 2005—but he heard stories through Internet fora, and friends gave him videocassettes. He also saw more and more friends and fellow Muslims from Cipayung going to Ambon to join the fight. Some returned and were admired and listened to as experts and veterans.

---

[24] Muhammadiyah is a large, nongovernmental Islamic organization, set up in 1912 as a social-religious movement. It has now grown to be the largest reformist platform in Indonesia, focused on organizing and providing religious and secular education and aid programs for young people and the needy. See Ricklefs (2001).
[25] Interview with "Ramli," February 26, 2020, Jakarta.

I heard the stories of friends who had fought there, and could stand it no longer. I was sitting here practicing grammar and brushing up on mathematics, while my friends were fighting. I was good with my hands. I could repair cars and motorbikes, and I was strong and fit. I wanted to be a good Muslim, like my friends. I would make my parents proud of me. I would become a better Muslim instead of wasting my time, and at the same time, put my talents to good use.[26]

Sofyan Tsauri's story, too, was dominated by frustration about the injustice suffered by Muslims elsewhere. He became aware of this injustice at a time when he was also grappling with his role in life, in the mid-1990s, when Suharto was still in power.

I read more and more books that I got from the people of the Muslim Brotherhood. They told me that the West had always oppressed Muslims, and that our government cooperated with America and was actually just as corrupt and apostate. I could borrow videos from the library in the mosque at my school about the struggle in Afghanistan and the Palestinian conflict. I acquired an increasingly great aversion to Suharto and his regime. What did he do for Muslims in Afghanistan or in Palestine? Nothing! What did he do to introduce the sharia? Nothing![27]

Sofyan became increasingly angry—at his parents, at the government, at America, and at Israel, where, although the first intifada had ended in 1993 with the Oslo Accords, the Palestinians continued to protest Israel's settlement policy. Furthermore, he was frustrated about his own selfishness and the unfaithful way he was living his life. "I was always one for *aksi-aksi*, quick with my fists. But I wanted to use that *aksi-aksi* for a good cause. To start leading a new, good life."

The Deep History of Radical Redemption

Although Muslims in Indonesia enjoyed a high level of representation in society and politics, that was not enough for my interviewees. They reproached

---

[26] Interview with "Ramli," February 26, 2020, Jakarta. See also Arnaz (2013).
[27] Interview with Sofyan Tsauri, February 24, 2020, Jakarta.

the Indonesian government on two counts. First, Indonesia was not a holy state, and the sharia had not been introduced. In 1945, Darul Islam had tried to get the Jakarta Charter incorporated in the constitution; under the charter, Indonesia would explicitly embrace the sharia and place Allah above the law. But Sukarno managed to prevent that by substituting the word *Ketuhanan* (God) for *Allah* and getting the sharia obligation scrapped from the preamble of the new constitution. All of my interviewees referred to this missed historical opportunity. It also appears in all the official statements of the various reformist Islamic associations and movements. In 2004, Islamic parties tried, unsuccessfully, to get the charter incorporated in the constitution (Pringle 2010, 68–70). In 1990, however, Islamic courts were recognized in Indonesia; they now exist alongside their secular counterparts (see Van Bruinessen 1996; see also Solahudin 2013).

The second criticism was that the government did too little to help Muslims under threat. In Indonesia itself, according to my interviewees, the government offered insufficient protection to Muslims attacked by Christians on Ambon. Nor did it help Muslims fighting elsewhere—in Palestine, Afghanistan, or Syria. Moreover, all Indonesian presidents continued to maintain relations with and cooperate with the West, including the United States, the "Great Satan." The impure and apostate practices of the president and various ministers, such as living in excessive luxury, also fueled the belief that the government was thoroughly corrupt and that democracy was not compatible with the sharia.

Interesting in the stories of the Indonesian radicals is the combination of, on the one hand, personal frustration and their own search for identity and meaning and, on the other hand, the expression of that search in frames that were both universal jihadist Salafist and yet very Indonesian. As with the Dutch jihadists, radicalization was an individual process, in the sense that the adoption and operationalization of violent and radical acts was an individual process—albeit one facilitated by the awareness, or online presence, of a global community of fellow believers. The Indonesian radicals' own frustrations and feelings of failure were a crucial catalyst in the process of embracing the jihadist narrative of radical redemption. Where they differed from the Dutch jihadists is their greater anger against their own government: they apparently had higher expectations of the government and of Islamic parties. For Dutch radicals, political parties across the board in the Netherlands were by definition corrupt.

Another striking factor in Indonesia was the enormous range of powerful, centuries-old stories and traditions of Islamic activism and rebellion. Sofyan, Ramli, and the others all told me their parents, grandparents, or even great-grandparents had fought in Aceh or had won their spurs with Darul Islam. Kurnia Widodo, born in Medan in 1974, told me that for him, it had all started with the books of the Muslim Brotherhood, of Azzam and Qutb.

> But after that, we started to relate those stories to our national history. We looked up to the sheikhs and scholars, de *ustads* from the Middle East.[28] But we also learned to appreciate our own historical Islamic heroes differently. Like Prince Diponegoro or, even better, Tuanku Imam Bonjol! I had a friend who could tell me all about them. Imam Bonjol already fought the colonial rulers, the Dutch, 200 years ago. And the first real pan-Indonesian independence movement was not Budi Utomo, but Sarekat Islam.[29] We have our own Islamic history of liberation and redemption from the yoke of the oppressors. We have to preserve and continue that history, and each time it becomes more powerful.[30]

During the interview he told me, to put my mind at rest,[31] that

> the Netherlands is not and has long not been our enemy. After 1949, it was the Indonesian government, and America. They are the real enemies. What's more, we are very grateful to Snouck Hurgronje for recording our norms and customs and the history of our religion in such detail. Thanks to the Dutch colonial rulers, those stories have been preserved! I come from five generations of Muslim fighters. My grandparents had Snouck's *De Atjehers* in their bookcase, and I used to read it a lot.[32]

---

[28] *Ustad* is a title of respect used by Muslims in the Middle East and Southeast Asia for someone who is considered a great teacher or master.

[29] Kurnia's interpretation is not entirely accurate. Sarekat Islam fought not for independence but for self-governance; it was initially more an anti-Chinese movement than an Islamic one. That many members and activists in the organization were Muslims does not make it pro-jihadist. See Van der Wal (1967); Kwantes (1975); see also Ricklefs (2001).

[30] Interview with Kurnia Widodo, February 25, 2020, Jakarta.

[31] For more on my positionality of being Dutch in an Indonesian context, see chapter 1, "Positionality."

[32] Interview with Kurnia Widodo, February 25, 2020, Jakarta. See also Gobée and Adriaanse (1957–65); Snouck Hurgronje (1888, 2006, 1893); Steenbrink (1991); Suminto (1985); Dobbin (1983).

This combination of individual awareness, indigenous traditions of resistance, and universal jihad constituted in almost all cases the prelude to joining in the fighting or becoming a member of a terrorist organization. Influences from the Middle East have made themselves felt in Indonesia since the early nineteenth century, when returning *hadj* pilgrims brought a more puritan and fundamentalist Islam and spread it throughout the island kingdom. In the twentieth century, Saudi Wahhabist influences became stronger as anticolonial pan-Islamism gradually took hold in Indonesia. Sarekat Islam and Muhammadiyah—both established in 1912—were strongly influenced by this development. Pan-Islamism continued to exert its influence after independence, although Indonesian Islam always retained its pluralist character and remained a combination of moderate Islam, mysticism, and traditional beliefs. The repression by the colonial rulers and later by the nationalist regimes of Sukarno and Suharto drove radical, fundamentalist movements to seek more religious forms of expression for their plans for reform. They started to practice *dawah* (*dakwah* in Indonesian),[33] and set up organizations that promoted a stricter Islamic lifestyle in schools, pesantren, and mosques. The Muslim Brotherhood organized *usroh* (discussion groups) on various campuses in Indonesia, in which many Indonesian jihadists took part. In the 1990s, a million Salafist books and texts made their way to Indonesia, sponsored by a Saudi foundation (ICG 2004, 6–10).[34]

A final point for consideration is that many interviewees experienced that phase of radicalization when they were far from home and at a distance from their old networks. Ramli was the only one to study in Jakarta; most of the others attended a pesantren, where they were steeped in the doctrine of the holy struggle, of the *fard ayn* (individual duty) of every Muslim. They would talk deep into the night about what it means to be a good Muslim and measure their own radicality against that of their contemporaries. In the dormitory, they would dream of the jihad together. They watched film clips and familiarized themselves with Salafist and often jihadist propaganda.

These boarding schools play a prominent role in expansive Indonesia. For parents, they are an indispensable link in their children's upbringing and education. Good schools are often far away; in such cases, it is simpler and cheaper for parents to send their children to a pesantren, where they know their children will enjoy a sound Islamic education and be thoroughly

---

[33] Islamic proselytism; *dawah* officially means "inviting others to embrace Islam."
[34] The title of this ICG report, *Indonesia Backgrounder: Why Salafism and Terrorism Mostly Don't Mix*, is somewhat misleading. Mostly they do not mix, but sometimes they do. See also Eliraz (2004).

prepared for their working lives. Besides their schooling, the pupils often work on the land, growing their own fruits and vegetables. For a long time, it was not feasible, not to mention politically extremely undesirable, for the government to monitor the curricula and especially the extracurricular education at the pesantren. Most of the schools have functioned perfectly well for centuries. But a small number of them have developed into a kind of archive of and outlet for radical Islamic repertoires; according to researchers, they amount to less than 1 percent of the pesantren, which as a whole account for a fifth of the education system in Indonesia. The International Crisis Group (ICG) states that some fifty of the 14,000 pesantren propagate violent extremist and jihadist ideas, while more of them may have facilitated the spread of terrorist groups like Jemaah Islamiyah (ICG 2009a, 2009b). The most notorious radical pesantren was the Al-Mukmin school in Ngruki, near to Solo on Central Java. Since its establishment in 1972, several generations of radicals and jihadists have been educated at this school (Noor et al. 2008; see also Van Bruinessen 2002). For young people, including some of my interviewees, who found themselves in such an environment, far from home and with little previous religious instruction, schools like Al-Mukmin were breeding grounds for radical desires for redemption.

Conclusion

Faisal Devji (2005) has convincingly explained the power of modern jihadism. His explanation seems to concur with what I extracted from my conversations with current and former detainees in the Netherlands and Indonesia. According to Devji, Islam has been radically transformed since the 1990s. With the help of financiers from the Middle East and the Persian Gulf States, the jihadist narrative has been spread around the world in book form and through mosques, foundations, and imams—it has become a global brand. In addition, the jihadist variant of Salafism has experienced a revival worldwide as a hyper-individualist yet universal ethical program. As a radical doctrine for action, the jihad of Osama bin Laden and, later, of IS leader Abu Bakr al-Baghdadi has become a direct competitor to other, more complex and inaccessible philosophies of political Islam—such as the Muslim Brotherhood's philosophy—and has great appeal for many young people. As my interviewees explained, it's difficult to see why one should wait for gradual political transformation and continue to follow the difficult path of negotiation and reform if the same can be achieved much faster through a radical, holy struggle.

That doctrine of action, that radical narrative, fitted perfectly with the dreams of fame, liberation, and heroism that so many young, alienated, and frustrated Muslims around the world dreamed of. Almost none of my interviewees had enjoyed a thorough education in the doctrine, customs, and practices of Islam. Most could not speak Arabic and had, by their own admission, "little knowledge." With their frustrations and their sense of deficit, they were susceptible to the offer of a clear, pure, radical doctrine of action, a jihadist orthopraxis. That radical doctrine of action tied in perfectly with their desire to combat the deficit in their own lives and "to do something good." Thanks to the "pure" jihadist doctrine, their desire for *aksi-aksi* acquired an eschatological meaning and became embedded in a concrete struggle. With the pure doctrine of action in their pockets—their orthopraxis—they could explain and fight against everything.

Fadil considered the Arab world a chaos. Kurnia thought the government in Jakarta was corrupt. Omar felt that the West did nothing or "just made everything a lot worse." Noureddine* thought his own life was bad. The *ummah* was kept small and was humiliated, exploited, and bled dry by the great powers, by America. The Arab Spring developed into a drama for young Muslims around the world. Assad was the great tyrant who strangled the reform movement in the Arab world, and thanks to the "infidel" governments of the United States, Turkey, and Russia, he remained in the saddle. The European Union was a toothless tiger. After 2001, against this background of war and conflict, the general, universal narrative of the jihad was profiled on the Internet; from 2001, it spread like wildfire on social media. Those Internet images provided perfect material to make the dreams of young Muslims come true and to enable them to star in their own movies. For them, the holy struggle was both a powerful narrative about oppressed Muslims and a unique personal opportunity to take action themselves. Jihadism was an orthopraxis, a doctrine of action: you could do things with yourself, with your own body, and in your immediate living environment that promised salvation and redemption for your own soul. In addition, these things also helped the *ummah* and undermined corrupt and faithless governments. The arena—Syria, Iraq—was tangible and accessible but at the same time part of the world of their religious myths and dreams. What it came down to was a new *hijra*, trials and tribulations in the desert—the final battle.

It should be noted that martyrdom was not necessarily their goal. The most important thing to the radicals I spoke with was "to contribute something to the struggle." If they were killed, that would of course be the ultimate sacrifice, and they would be admitted to paradise as martyrs. But it is important to emphasize that, by their own admission, these fighters were not driven by a death wish—nor did it appear, as far as I could ascertain from their files and from conversations with the authorities, that they had a death wish.

For Muslims from non-Western contexts—thus, for my Indonesian interviewees—the radical narrative of the jihad was also balm to their tormented souls. For them, too, it provided an opportunity to compensate for or even conquer their personal deficit or failures. In that respect, they differed less from my Dutch interviewees than I initially thought—young Indonesian and Dutch Muslims sought a similar hyper-individualist and unique way to interpret Islam and the Koran correctly: they abandoned the moderate Islam of their parents' generation and cobbled together a radical doctrine of action on the Internet and from their friends. That said, the Indonesian radicals I spoke with were more deeply rooted in their own national history of Islamic rebellion. Almost all the convicted terrorists I interviewed stood in a tradition of grandfathers and even great-grandfathers who had contributed to Islamic revolts and rebel movements in the past, attended pesantren, or participated in radical *usroh*. For them, the narrative of radical redemption was the product of a long, collective history, which they now gave a shape of their own.

In the following chapter, we examine how these aspiring fighters put their words into action and their desire for redemption into practice.

5
The Second Panel
Devotion and Struggle

Devotion and Struggle

In chapter 2, we looked at the phenomenon of appraisal—the way in which people assess situations of stress and uncertainty, the emotions and explanations they attach to them, and how they act on them. Dan McAdams (2006) has shown how generative individuals can transform experiences of past suffering and injustice and embed them in a higher, all-embracing narrative. This narrative gives meaning to their doubts, their pain, and their suffering, and it motivates them to make a greater effort and take action to achieve their goals. Radical redemption is an example of a narrative frame within which a series of diverse and strong emotions and experiences—such as stress, pain, compassion, and anger—are connected to articulated beliefs and to projected actions. Such narratives are especially appealing when offered by an influential organization with strong credentials and substantial funds.

In this chapter, we will see how the pull factors of such an appealing organization—including an accessible conflict zone—joined with the push factors of young people looking for meaning and a better and purer life and who were keen to earn points for the afterlife. For some, the main goal was redemption on behalf of others. But what appealed to all my interviewees was the ethical opportunity that radical redemption offered to purify their own lives and give them greater meaning, not only in their own eyes but also in the eyes of their parents, the community, the worldwide *ummah*, and, ultimately, Allah.[1]

---

[1] *Ethical* refers here to the offer of morally pure and good actions. Underlying religious-dogmatic considerations and political strategies were also relevant, but at this stage, they were less important to the individual. We are speaking here of the orthopraxis of radical redemption, not of the dogmas or theology behind it.

This chapter thus offers a historical and political context to, and substantiates and elaborates qualitatively on, the phenomenon of appraisal as psychologists have demonstrated it in experimental and quantitative research settings.[2] We follow the desire for redemption and explore how the available options to achieve this redemption in practice changed over time, beginning with the first wave of international jihadists, who went to fight in Afghanistan, and ending with the last generation, who sought redemption in Syria and Iraq.

Returning to the radical redemption model explained in chapter 2, this chapter focuses on the second panel of the triptych. Since emotions regarding sufferings and injustice in the past have led to a sense of deficit and urgency in the present—the first panel—there must be a change of course, and it must be radical: it must be violent and involve sacrificing oneself and others and joining the struggle.

Earning Points

"I did it for my community," said Fadil*, as he told me of his decision to travel to Turkey and take part in the fight against Assad in Syria. "I wanted to help those small children. [I didn't do it] for the seventy virgins—that is fake, not pure. If you don't do it for pure reasons, you don't earn any points. How do you get to paradise? The Hadith tells us how. If you have a drop of *iman*, pure faith, in your heart, you can enter paradise. I was not afraid of ending up in hell—I was doing a good thing. I went there to liberate Muslims and finally do something good myself and earn points."[3]

For many young Muslims around the world, the quest to acquire the points required to get into paradise is a popular pastime. They talk about it endlessly and exchange tips on Internet fora about *hasanat* (good deeds) that Allah records in his book, about the *thawab* (reward) they can get for performing them, and about the *ajr*, the reward they get in the afterlife,

---

[2] In such research settings, people are subjected to tests to determine their feelings regarding violence. In these experimental settings, large numbers of test subjects are studied (by asking them to complete questionnaires, respond to photographs, etc.) who are not themselves terrorists or radicals but whose responses help determine general social-psychological patterns. Such studies enable social psychologists to determine, for example, under what conditions people respond more quickly to injustice, when they are willing to take action, or when they approve of violence more quickly.
[3] Interview with Fadil*, March 6, 2019, The Hague.

the "bonus points for paradise." Salafists have developed an elaborate doctrine of action around this subject, based on their interpretation of the *fiqh* (Islamic jurisprudence). Islamic doctrine distinguishes five categories of action: *fard* (compulsory), *sunna* (recommended), *halal* (permitted/neutral), *makrooh* (disapproved of), and *haram* (forbidden). Many young Muslims, especially Salafists, share forms of behavior and good deeds according to this typology and attribute points to them (see, e.g., Roex et al. 2010, 58; Van der Velde 2011). My interviewees had also adopted this manner of acting and thinking. In their frustration and feelings of deficit, almost all of them felt the need to earn points, do something good, purify themselves, and build up *ajr* for themselves or even for the members of their family.

In contrast to most young Muslims, the point-counting of my interviewees was inspired by very puritan, fundamentalist ideas of what the right forms of behavior should be. For almost all the convicted terrorists, it started with adapting their own lifestyles: they wanted to stop drinking alcohol, and grappled with addiction, reckless driving, rock music, and television. "I was crazy about Guns N' Roses and didn't want to get rid of my cap and my heavy metal T-shirts," Kurnia recalled, and Amin* told me he had "a whole library of hip-hop CDs."[4] All this had to go, and not all of them succeeded in giving these things up. But then, an offer was made to them—through the Internet, through friends, at the mosque, or at school—that would enable them to link their desire to live more purely to action: to the fight for a higher goal, and to the fight *against others*. Their focus thus shifted from their own bodies and lifestyle to the pursuit of purity, to doing something for others,[5] even if that meant emigrating to Syria or Iraq as *hijra* and taking part in the fighting themselves, possibly sacrificing their own lives in the process. This transformation could happen very quickly and take the form of an "instant conversion," complete with a one-way ticket to Istanbul. But it could also be the result of a long process of radicalization and preparation by family members and friends, spanning years or even generations.

---

[4] Interview with Kurnia Widodo, February 25, 2020, Jakarta; interview with Amin*, October 30, 2010, PI/TDU.

[5] Desiring and pursuing a life of purity is a recurring phenomenon in many religions and belief systems. See Neiman (2008); Wiltermuth and Newman (2018).

Purify My Soul

The Salafist emphasis on individual struggle and the system of types of behavior and associated points they merited were not yet widespread in the 1980s and 1990s. But the general concept of reward and punishment for certain forms of behavior, including judging oneself and others, was already typical among radical Muslims. Almost all my interviewees experienced a moment at which their quest for purity, for a better life, was aligned with an offer of radical redemption that crossed their path, be it via a preacher at a pesantren, a friend, or an online recruiter. Such offer was usually very tangible and physical: they had the opportunity to go and fight. This was an easy route to take for aspiring Indonesian jihadists: they could go to Ambon, Sulawesi, or Aceh. But in the 1980s, the most appealing destination was Afghanistan. At that time, Indonesia was flooded by an enormous influx of literature, ideas, and stories from the Middle East, Egypt, and Saudi Arabia, distributed by several fundamentalist and radical groups. Having a war zone within actual reach—that is, Afghanistan—was an opportunity too exciting to resist. It offered action that was inseparably linked to the doctrine of purity of head and heart and promised reward and redemption.

What also played a role was that migration to a place where you could live and fight as a Muslim could be interpreted as a form of *hijra* and thus as following in the footsteps of the prophet Muhammad, who traveled to Medina in 622 to create an Islamic society. This theme of assigning significance to the decision to go to Afghanistan and, much later, to Syria or Iraq, thus combines the opportunity to engage in *hijra* with taking part in actual violent conflict (see De Koning 2020; Masud 1990).[6]

Farihin was born in Jakarta in 1966. His grandfather was a good friend of Kartosuwiryo, the founder of Darul Islam. "I was his oldest grandson," Farihin told me. "And he loved me very much."[7] Farihin's father was also active in Darul Islam and was imprisoned from 1957 to 1960 for being involved in a failed attempt to assassinate Sukarno. After that, he started a business. Farihin's mother was active in Aisha, the women's section of Muhammadiyah, and had learned Arabic at her pesantren. Farihin's brother and his wife both attended the pesantren in Ngruki, where they were taught

---

[6] For the way in which IS explicitly takes advantage of the desire for *hijra*, see Sarat-St. Peter (2019).
[7] Interview with Farihin, February 25, 2020, Jakarta.

by Abu Bakar Bashir, the founder of Jemaah Islamiyah (JI). Farihin himself attended a different Islamic school.

> I was brought up on the ideas of Hassan al-Banna, Qutb, and Azzam from a very young age. I also learned at the school that only Islamic fighters and heroes fought for the true independence of Indonesia. The Dutch, the Indonesian nationalists, and the communists were all the same. The Padri were our first examples,[8] but they were still very regionally oriented. Darul Islam went a little further, but it was the war in Afghanistan that brought the concept of worldwide jihad to Indonesia. In that time, everything was about Afghanistan; such a small country, invaded by communists. We read everything we could find about it, and watched it on television.

At secondary school, Farihin went off the rails. "I was a gangster," he told me. "My parents saw what I was doing, but were helpless. My grandfather said that, as long as I said my prayers at the right times, the rest didn't matter." Through his grandfather and father, Farihin was eventually approached by Abu Bakar Bashir and Abdullah Sungkar, who asked him if he wanted to join the struggle.

> At that time, they approached three kinds of young people: the children of Darul Islam leaders, pupils at the Al-Mukmin pesantren in Ngruki, and kids who already attended Darul Islam mosques. I grasped the opportunity with both hands, because I was just wasting my time causing trouble and wanted to do something good, and help other Muslims. I arrived in Afghanistan in 1987. But, to my surprise, I was first assigned to a sort of training camp and had to attend school. I first had to learn more about the jihad. Jihad is not only about war; it's about knowledge, about the philosophy of fighting. I felt very close to Allah there. For the first time in my life, I enjoyed learning, and I acquired deeper knowledge. I went from a recalcitrant young man, a rebel, to a real jihadist—with a pure heart.[9]

Sofyan Tsauri also found in Azzam's books on Afghanistan a way to transform his violent past into something pure:

---

[8] Nineteenth-century Sumatran Islamists who wanted to impose sharia law.
[9] Interview with Farihin, February 25, 2020, Jakarta.

> I had a lot of aggression in me. My friends talked to me about it and gave me books to read about pure Islam. Those books gave direction to my hatred. After secondary school, I attended a pesantren, where I learned Arabic and read books about Islam. The books were full of hatred of the West. I learned about the *ghazwa*, the military expeditions that the Prophet undertook, and which present-day Muslims still have to take part in to protect and expand their kingdom. Only then will they receive a real reward. A Muslim must sometimes go to war. The question is how, when, and against whom? What is the right *fikr*, theory, of war?[10]

Sofyan's favorite book in the 1990s was *Ayaturahman fi jihadil Afghan* by Abdullah Azzam,[11] which is about the heroic acts of the mujahideen in the war against the Soviet Union in Afghanistan, in which Azzam himself had participated. After leaving the pesantren, Sofyan joined the police. That was what his parents wanted, as his father and brother were also police officers.

> It was what my mother wanted. I went to the police academy during the day, and the rest of the time, I learned more about Islam. By then, I had become a member of the Muslim Brotherhood. My hatred of the Indonesian government and the West grew more and more. During the day, I was a policeman; on the weekends, I dreamed of the jihad. My friends from the pesantren had already fought in Pakistan. I was given Arabic lessons by Afghanistan veterans. I felt as if I had dried up spiritually. I found the Muslim Brotherhood too cowardly. They just talked and had too much patience. They were weak and did nothing. In 2007, I left the Brotherhood and joined my friend Dulmatin, alias Joko Pitoyo, in Jemaah Islamiyah. When Dulmatin asked me to help him set up a jihadist training camp in Aceh, I didn't need to think about it for very long. I stopped going to work and left for Aceh. I didn't tell my parents; they had already distanced themselves from my radical ideas.

In 2006, Sofyan—together with Dulmatin—joined a group of twenty-four men in Aceh who set up a branch of Jemaah Islamiyah, the Al Qaeda cell in Indonesia, with the aim of preparing a large-scale attack. "Now I could purify my soul," he told me. "Now it was starting for real. I no longer had to pretend

---

[10] Interview with Sofyan Tsauri, February 24, 2020, Jakarta.
[11] Published in English as *Signs of ar-Rahman in the Jihad of Afghan* (Azzam, n.d.).

during the day. We set up a military base, arranged weapons from Java, and smuggled people and ammunition from the Philippines. My friend had already escaped from the authorities before via the Philippines. We organized military training." His dreams returned in their full fury. "I dreamed that I was shooting in the desert, and in the mountains—but now in the jungle, too, because that was where we were. I was very good and quickly became an instructor. I had my *aksi-aksi*, and with that, my redemption."[12]

Jihad and the Rifle Alone

The search for a good escape valve for aggression and feelings of frustration was channeled extremely effectively through the stories of the jihad in Afghanistan. From the 1980s, these stories reached increasing numbers of young Muslims around the world. The ways in which my interviewees viewed the wars in Afghanistan, the Palestinian territories, Bosnia, Kashmir, Chechnya, Ambon, and Libya reflect what researchers call the Islamization of ethnic and separatist conflicts, a phenomenon that became widespread from the 1980s onward (see, e.g., Fox 2004; Litvak 1998; Sikand 2001; Wilhelmsen 2004). With the writings of Azzam in their pockets, the fighters against the Soviet Union in Afghanistan, for example, became mujahideen who were taking part in a holy battle and who saw proof of their divine calling in miracles and signs on the battlefield. In this process of Islamization, military strategy went hand in hand with a strategy of ethical warfare. It was a battle to purify their own lives and those of the members of their group. As Azzam wrote:

> The Ummah is in a state of moral decadence and has distanced itself from the Sunnah. A programme of Islaah (moral rectification) will have to be completed before we, the Ummah, are prepared for this category of Jihaad. (Azzam, n.d., 59)

This Islamization changed the perspective on the *jus ad bellum*. Azzam saw the armed jihad as permissible and even as an obligation for all Muslims, rather than as a last resort in the case of a physical attack. He wrote:

---

[12] Interview with Sofyan Tsauri, October 24, 2020, Jakarta.

> If the kuffaar [unbelievers] attack an Islamic state, then Jihaad in defence of the state is Fardh [compulsory]. This is referred to as "Difa'ee" (defen[s]ive) Jihaad. This Jihaad first becomes Fardh on the armed forces of the state. If the armed forces are unable to halt the advance of the enemy, or due to indifference, do not take up this duty, it then becomes Fardh on all the healthy male citizens of the state to take up the Jihaad. If they too are unable to prevent the enemies' assault, then Jihaad becomes Fardh-e-Ain upon all the Muslims of the state. This includes women and children.... If the citizens of the Islamic state are unable to repel the enemy, or due to some reason do not engage in the Jihaad, the duty then devolves on all those Muslims who are closest to the Muslims under attack.... This will continue until Jihaad becomes incumbent on all the Muslims of the world. (Azzam, n.d., 59–60)

To radical, puritan Muslims with a penchant for violence, Azzam was a hero. He gave words to their desire for redemption and struggle. Convicted Dutch terrorists Samir A. and Yehya K. quoted his motto "jihad and the rifle alone" in 2004–5, the period in which the Hofstad Group was active.[13] My Indonesian interviewees were also devoted to Azzam's writings and liked to read to me from them. Azzam translated pure faith into demonstrations of pure commitment to violence:

> He, the Almighty, Who has created human nature, has made it such that it is more [a]ffected and moved by realities and actions than words and speeches. An environment wherein one sacrifices and suppresses the impositions of personal pride is the most virtuous environment in which the soul may reside. In it the carnal self is nurtured, the soul refined and elevated. It is for this reason that seeing a living example is more beneficial [than] spending many years buried in books. (Azzam, n.d., 66)

This was nothing more than the jihadist interpretation of the propaganda of the deed, in which jihadist ethics and expressive violence replaced political intentions and the desire for strategic effect. This ethic demanded sacrifice, blood, sweat, and tears:

---

[13] The Hofstad Group, or Hofstad Network, is the name given by the General Intelligence and Security Service (AIVD) to a group of young radicalized Muslims. Some members of the group were convicted for terrorist activities. Mohammed Bouyeri, who killed Dutch film director Theo van Gogh in 2004, was also a member of this network. See De Graaf (2014). See also Schuurman (2018); Bessems (2005).

> The life of Jihaad is based on toil and exertion, on sweat, blood, tiredness, sleeplessness, difficulties and pain. Jihaad is built on the human flesh that has to be burnt so that the flame of Jihaad may stay alight, just as oil has to burn to keep a lamp alight. Jihaad binges on grief and fear. The flowing of the blood of the innocent Shuhadaa [martyrs] and scattering of corpses are all complementary to Jihaad. All these are the fuel of Jihaad, and water for its garden. (Azzam, n.d., 76)

With this theory—or rather, with the forceful slogan "jihad and the rifle alone"—the jihad could be put into practice, both on an existing battlefield in a war zone and at home in what was, in principle, a peaceful country. It became a code of conduct, more a series of ethical guidelines than a feasible or concrete political program. After all, if Azzam's reasoning was pursued consistently enough, it was the duty of all Muslims to participate in the struggle and therefore ultimately to engage in that struggle in their own countries against their own governments if the latter did not embrace the sharia or help oppressed Muslims elsewhere. Whether that duty actually produced results was not the main point—what mattered was the purity of the intention and taking the right action.

I Felt Chosen

How did the redemption that these jihadists longed for work in practice? Many of them spoke of an initial euphoria in which dreams, thought, and action came together in preparing for and taking part in the struggle. Their sense of being on the right path was confirmed by victories or miraculous experiences. Farihin, for example, told me about the miracles he experienced during his time in Afghanistan, from 1987 to 1990.

> I felt chosen. We had military training in the mornings, education in the afternoons, and during holidays and longer breaks we were deployed in the fighting. Our battalion experienced all kinds of miracles [*garoma*]. That's how I knew that I was behaving purely. Once, a bomb exploded, leaving a crater several meters wide and deep, but no one was hurt. Allah protected us. Another time, the Russians were bombarding our camp, but the bombs only exploded next to our tents and houses. Nothing was hit. Shortly after that, I met Osama bin Laden, who came to visit our camp. The Indonesian

mujahideen had joined the faction of al-Ittihad al-Islami, around Rasul Sayyaf, of the Hanafi school. The Saudis followed Salafist teaching, but Osama bin Laden also helped us. He was still very young then; he gave speeches, but he was not yet as famous as he would be later. He spent most of the time racing around in trucks. He distributed money and provided funds to lay roads and buy vehicles. He liked to deliver the trucks to us himself. He worked very hard and was extremely kind.[14]

There was some discussion about where they could and should fight, and against whom.

In Afghanistan, we adhered to the concept of the defensive jihad. We were permitted to fight there, because the Russians had started the conflict by invading the country. Indonesia was a different story; there, we first had to do *dawah*. It was not yet a *dar al-Harb* [territory of war]. As long as the government did not attack us Muslims, we were not allowed to fight but had to spread the jihad orally and in writing. When I returned to Indonesia in 1990, I wanted to continue on to Kashmir, Chechnya, Bosnia, or Palestine. But Abdullah Sungkar and Abu Bakar instructed me to help build up Jemaah Islamiyah and teach in Central Jakarta, giving lessons in the jihad doctrine. I had a small shop, and taught in the mosque after closing time.

In 1993, Farihin married a pupil of Abu Bakar from Ngruki. They had seven children, but he still felt the need to play an active part in the struggle, albeit in Indonesia itself.

In 2000, I was sent to Central Sulawesi, where pesantren were being attacked by non-Muslims. Two hundred Muslims were killed. I went there to train Muslims in self-defense, and to tell them about the correct way to engage in the jihad, how to keep themselves pure, and how to resist their enemies. I did that together with other Afghanistan veterans. In that year, I was arrested and spent a short term in prison. In 2002, I was arrested again and spent a longer time behind bars. With hindsight, that was a blessing.[15]

---

[14] Interview with Farihin, February 25, 2020, Jakarta.
[15] Interview with Farihin, February 25, 2020, Jakarta.

The continuing influence of Afghanistan veterans needs no further argument. After the Soviet Union declared the war over in 1989, it was impossible for many Arab veterans to return home. They would be arrested and tortured, and some of them would be banned from entering or staying in the country. At the insistence of the United States, jihadist fighters were driven out of Peshawar; as a result, the mujahideen spread rapidly across the world. Azzam was killed in 1990, and bin Laden founded Al Qaeda in 1993. Many Afghanistan veterans came to Europe, to the Balkans, and some to the Netherlands. Others went to Indonesia and continued their militant activities.

"Ramli" left for Ambon in February 2000 to help Muslims there who, according to the jihadist stories he heard through the JI network, were being persecuted and oppressed.

> I arrived in Batumera and was assigned to a house whose residents had fled because they were afraid of the war. Our trainers were Afghanistan veterans from Negara Islam Indonesia and JI. They gave me training, not only military but also religious, as a jihadist. I learned about the *dawah*, but also had lessons in cartography, how to use weapons and explosives, and in fighting tactics. That was a new world for me! I went there to do something good. And now I had the feeling that, in Allah's eyes, I was becoming a better Muslim. In the mornings, I trained to be a killer, and in the afternoons, I learned how to be a good Muslim. None of my mistakes and failures mattered anymore—my soul had been purified. I wanted to be a real *shahid*, a voluntary martyr and fighter for the faith. I still wore my baseball cap. I didn't start dressing differently, but on the inside, I had been purified.
>
> Azzam was my spiritual guide. And, like him, I also had dreams. I dreamed of the desert, that I was fighting there and was surrounded by enemies. Instead of with a machine gun, like in the real world, I was fighting with a sword. And I won. During the day, I experienced all kinds of miracles. If we were attacked by government troops, we fled to the mountains. Up there, in some miraculous way, we always found food. Once I found a package of bread. And we found honey we could eat without the bees stinging us. So, we knew we were on the right path. Allah was protecting us. When my friend was killed, I carried his body back to the camp. The whole time, I could smell musk, just as Azzam wrote about the *shahid* killed in Afghanistan. I never smelled musk again after that.[16]

---

[16] Interview with "Ramli," February 26, 2020, Jakarta. For a reference to Azzam and the smell of musk on martyrs, see Cook (2017, 157).

Ramli was by now a member of the Komite Aksi Penanggulangan Akibat Krisis (LSM Kompak), a group that was affiliated with Negara Islam Indonesia (NII) and JI. In 2000 and 2001, he fought on Ambon; after that, he trained new recruits in Poso in Central Sulawesi. When those conflicts ended, he returned to Jakarta to study Arabic. In 2002, he heard that fighters in his network had committed an attack on Bali. For him, at the time, the attack was part of the jihadist fight against nonbelievers and was, in a certain sense, a continuation of the struggle in Afghanistan. "We had heard that Australian soldiers would be coming to Bali to rest after their tour of duty in Afghanistan and thought that justified an attack on the island. I was proud that the attack had been carried out using bombs made by my instructors and by jihadists who had taught me." After the attack, LSM Kompak gave him responsibility for keeping the perpetrators, including Abdullah Sunata and Umar Patek, out of police hands. He first found them safe locations to hide on Java, and then made it possible for them and their families to flee to the Philippines. He accompanied them and joined the Philippine terrorist organization Moro Islamic Liberation Front (MILF), where he passed on the military knowledge he had gained in Afghanistan to new recruits and ran training camps for JI and MILF. In 2005, he was arrested while transporting weapons to Indonesia and sentenced to seven years in prison.[17]

Finally, Kurnia's radicalization story also points toward Afghanistan, as well as to the influence of redemption narratives and examples from around the world: through the Internet, a fully globalized jihadist narrative emerged in Indonesia, which further merged with historical and local examples to form a very convincing narrative. Kurnia linked his knowledge of the history of radical resistance in Indonesia and the traditions of the Padri, Tuanku Imam Bonjol, and Sarekat Islam to Azzam's present-day call to take up arms again and drive out the colonial powers. In the 1980s, the colonial power was the Soviet Union; in the 1990s (Kurnia's younger years), it was Israel and the Philippines; in the first decade of the twenty-first century, it was Indonesia. "For me, and for our group," Kurnia said, "Indonesia had become a *dar al-Harb*, a place where believers had to resist the government with violence. It was now our *fard ayn* [duty] to take up arms against the *kufar* [nonbelievers]—like the Padri in the past, but now more internationally."[18] Kurnia had sworn his *bayat*, his oath of loyalty, to the emir of NII in 1992 and

---

[17] Interview with "Ramli," February 26, 2020, Jakarta.
[18] Interview with Kurnia Widodo, February 25, 2020, Jakarta.

had joined an NII group in Banda Lampung. "Until that time, I belonged to the *jahiliyyah*, the unknowing. After swearing my oath and performing my *sjahada* [Islamic confession], I felt special. I had been chosen in the eyes of God; I was different from the others." After that, he trained as a chemical engineer, together with a friend who had studied pharmacy. From 1994, he tried to gather all the information he could find on explosives.

> We were preparing an attack on the national government. First, we experimented in our house, but we caused an explosion. After that, we practiced in the mountains to the north of Bandung. Timothy McVeigh was my inspiration; when I heard in 1995 how powerful his bomb attack had been, I wanted to copy him. I published my findings on jihadist sites like Ar-Rohmah.com, At-Taubah.net, and Muhajirun.com. I was too late for Afghanistan, and my leaders would not allow me to go to Bosnia, but when I heard about the bomb attacks on Bali in 2002, I was very proud. The bombers had used TNT with chloride and a combination of sulfur, carbon, and aluminium powder to push the temperature up. That was my formula!

Kurnia had married in 1999, and by then (in 2002) he had five children. His wife was one of his students: "She knew all about the sharia." After Bali, he moved into the mountains of Aceh, "just like our forefathers," he said. "We set up a camp, Wilayah Amniyah, and prepared new attacks. I gave lessons in how to use explosives, together with trainers who had fought in Afghanistan. I was really part of the group." In August 2010, he was arrested, after his group Jemaah Anshorut Tauhid (JAT), consisting of former JI and NII members, had blown up a military base. "That was the end of my mission," he told me.[19]

Farihin, Kurnia, and Ramli adhered to a theory that was popular among Indonesian jihadists in the 1990s and the decade that followed: a Muslim was permitted to take up arms after he had given the country and the people in question the opportunity to perform their sacred duty themselves; only then was he himself chosen for the struggle. On this theory, Indonesia, for example, was *dar al-Dawa*—a country that still had to be fully converted to Islam. But if the government and the people did not listen, then the country could be designated as *dar al-Harb*, in which case *fard ayn* applied, the obligation of every Muslim to take up arms. "We had endless discussions about questions like this, in closed chat groups," Sofyan Tsauri told me. "I sought

---

[19] Interview with Kurnia Widodo, February 25, 2020, Jakarta.

my answers on the Internet, on Forum Jihad. There you could ask the leaders of Jemaah Islamiyah, Imam Samudra, and Noordin Top questions. For a long time, it was the most popular forum for everyone in Indonesia who wanted to know something about the jihad."[20]

Almost all convicted terrorists embraced the principle of the jihad, but there were differences in their beliefs with respect to how it should be applied and where. This even became one of the major points of dispute between the first and second generations of JI in the years after 2002, and between Al Qaeda, Ahrar al-Sham, and IS in the years following 2011. The generation of Farihin, who had fought in the Afghanistan war, had different, more conservative ideas about this than the generation of Sofyan, Kurnia, and Ramli and the JI supporters responsible for the attacks on Bali. There was also a difference between the wave of departees who left between 2011 and the beginning of 2014 and joined Ahrar al-Sham and the jihadists who joined IS. That difference lay not so much in their embracing the armed jihad as such as in the choice of where to fight and who their victims should be. In all cases, radical redemption involved their own souls and bodies, but the question was who else's blood should flow and where attacks were considered permissible.

In the years following 9/11, Ramli, Kurnia, and Sofyan Tsauri's group took a substantial step further than the network of Farihin in the 1980s and 1990s. Sofyan joined JI in 2007 and, together with his friend Dulmatin and a group of others in Aceh, prepared a series of attacks. Dulmatin had already been involved in the attacks on the Australian embassy and the bomb attack on Bali. Noordin Top, the brain behind and leader of the attack on Bali in 2002, joined the group. "The time of *dawah* was past," Sofyan told me.

> We were in contact with Al Qaeda and Osama bin Laden. After all, we were his allies in Indonesia. It was time to teach the government a lesson and to put a stop to the presence of godless Westerners; it was time for the jihad of attack. We were ready for it. We would free our country of faithless Westerners and put our government to shame. I was willing to give my life to help achieve that purification; and there was a great reward awaiting me.

With his background in the police, Sofyan organized military and weapons training and arranged supplies of firearms for the group. And yet, his comrades did not trust him fully, because he had been in the police force.

[20] Interview with Sofyan Tsauri, February 24, 2020, Jakarta.

Eventually, they committed the attacks on the Ritz-Carlton and JW Marriott Hotels in Jakarta on July 17, 2009, in which nine people lost their lives, without Sofyan. "When I heard about the attack, I was astounded that they had done it without me," he said. "What was I to do? I kept my head down in Aceh for a few months. But on 6 March 2010, I was arrested, together with my wife. My wife knew nothing and was released after a week. But I got ten years. I was released on good behavior in 2016."[21]

Muslim Babies Are Being Butchered

While Afghanistan was the focus of jihadists in the 1980s, in the 1990s, new arenas of war emerged that appealed to the imagination and inspired a younger generation to dream of the jihad. It was, however, still fairly complicated for potential jihadists to travel to Chechnya, Afghanistan, Kashmir, or Iraq. Many were arrested at the border in Russia or elsewhere and sent back or even shot on the spot (see, e.g., Abels and Bessems 2002; see also AIVD 2002, 5, 11). There was as yet no organization that operated as a kind of jihadist travel agency to help aspiring fighters reach the war zone. Only after 2011, after the Arab Spring and the war in Syria, did a new hot spot emerge for the international jihad. The relative ease with which the war zone in Syria could be reached through Turkey was crucial. From 2014, other pull factors emerged, with IS utilizing its recruiting power and funds to call on Muslims to help fight the good fight and to perform *hijra*, to leave their hypocritical homelands behind and help build a pure Islamic state. Push factors included, besides all the socioeconomic and psychological factors, the power of the radical redemption narrative.

That narrative was triggered by dramatic moments of injustice and repression against Muslims and the harrowing images of these events seen around the world. This happened in all waves of terrorism, including the wave of holy terrorism. Videocassettes depicting bloodbaths in Bosnia and Chechnya were popular among members of the Hofstad Group in Amsterdam and The Hague. DVDs of atrocities in Chechnya and of the second intifada circulated in Jakarta.[22] But the Arab Spring of 2011, and the cold-blooded and ruthless response of Assad's troops to the demonstrations and protests in Damascus

---

[21] Interview with Sofyan Tsauri, October 24, 2020, Jakarta.
[22] Interview with Kurnia Widodo, February 25, 2020, Jakarta; interview with Farihin, February 25, 2020, Jakarta; interview with Sofyan Tsauri, February 24, 2020, Jakarta.

and elsewhere, led to a new shock wave. There was collective indignation and horror in the mainstream media and among Western television viewers. Young Muslims grew increasingly frustrated with an American president who did nothing. The unrest and frustration with their own lives merged with their indignation about what was happening to Muslims in Syria.

Ilyas* was born in Morocco in 1976. In 2004, he came to the Netherlands to train as a car mechanic. He completed the course successfully, found a job, and married a Dutch girl, with whom he had three children. Then things started to go wrong—his wife left him and applied for a divorce. "I had a dreadful time," Ilyas said. "I missed my children. For nine years, I tried to gain access to them through the courts. I didn't have a criminal record or a history of violence. I really wanted parental access, but my wife kept the kids away from me. The Netherlands is a bad land for fathers with children going through a divorce."[23] From that time, Ilyas started to project his own unhappiness onto the fate of Muslims in general. "More and more, I found the Netherlands to be a country where discrimination is widespread. Women are not permitted to wear a veil. Everything works against us here. I understand Muslims preferring to live in an Islamic country. But I hadn't got that far yet. I just wanted my children back. But I did start to see patterns." Then the civil war broke out in Syria. "I could stay at home and cry about my own suffering, but that didn't help. So I started helping refugees, giving them lessons. I speak fluent Arabic and French. I am a good cook, and I had money, so I could give them things. That way, I could at least do something. Our people are suffering all kinds of injustices in Syria. In this way, I could give something back."

After 2011, Ilyas—who had by then become a Dutch citizen—increasingly identified with Muslims worldwide, whom he called "my people." He started to look more and more on the Internet for explanations, for information on what was happening in Syria. "I have a lot of knowledge; I've always read about Egypt, about the Taliban, about the Middle East. People in the Netherlands know so little about what happens there. Why did the West, the CIA, work together with the mujahideen in the 1980s, why is the United States now negotiating with the Taliban, and why are we, then, terrorists if we go there to help?" Personal misfortune, frustrations, and the search for some direction in his life merged with a concrete narrative of oppression and the need for resistance and redemption. "Your faith allows you to defend your

---

[23] Interview with Ilyas*, January 16, 2020, PI/TDU.

country and your family. Our country is being attacked there. I searched for all the facts, watched hundreds of film clips, watched YouTube. I know what's happening. Muslim babies are being butchered, and the Netherlands does nothing, America does nothing. We have to help them."

Although Ilyas was active in voluntary work in The Hague, he felt that was not enough. "I saw film clips made by IS," he said. "Were they propaganda? I don't know. I believe in the final battle. If you see what the Peshmerga and other rebels have done there, it wasn't IS that started the beheadings, but the Kurds." A good friend of his left to join IS and kept Ilyas informed of what was going on. And yet, he still did not want to go out there himself. "I couldn't leave. I still hoped that I would be able to see my children. My place is here. But I support the struggle there."

What exactly Ilyas was planning to do never became clear. At the beginning of 2018, the police raided his home and found guns, ammunition, and videos and documents "glorifying armed struggle." He had also taken photographs of himself with a gun, posing as an IS fighter. In prison, Ilyas was placed in the highest security section, where Gökmen Tanis and Mohammed Bouyeri were also detained, and where a maximum of five detainees could be held.[24] That became clear to me when I wanted to interview him. It took some time to comply with all the security regulations and pass through all the air lock doors, and then I only saw Ilyas from a distance, behind a thick metal grating. Ilyas was able to look at his situation with a kind of black humor. "Do they think I'm a terrorist or something?" he asked me, as I tried to conduct a meaningful conversation with him from my barred chicken run.[25]

Ilyas's question was certainly not rhetorical. He vehemently denied being a terrorist and planning an attack. At the same time, during our conversation, he tried to defend IS and justify their actions. A remarkable fact about Ilyas was his age. Unlike my other interviewees, he was in his late thirties when he radicalized. It was as though the war in Syria offered him a "change of course," enabling him to give his own personal suffering a place in his life story and to link his fight against the injustice he had suffered—his children being taken away—to the physical struggle of Muslims in Syria. It was also striking that he referred to people in Syria as "my people, my family." In the

---

[24] Gökmen Tanis and Mohammed Bouyeri were convicted of terrorist attacks in the Netherlands; see later in this chapter.

[25] Ilyas is detained in the highest security section of the penitentiary institution. This terrorist detention unit has an inner yard where the detainees, who also include Gökmen Tanis and Mohammed Bouyeri, can take exercise. There is a kind of gallery around the exercise yard, separated from it by a barred fence. Because Ilyas likes to be outside, I interviewed him there, from the gallery.

context of the final battle, Ilyas felt that it was his duty to help—he should not keep complaining about his own life but help liberate others and win the final battle. "I had my peace of mind back once I knew what the situation was, and could take part in the final battle, for other children."[26]

The war in Syria also triggered Amin to seek clarity in his life. "Why is all this happening?" he asked himself. "Why are my fellow Muslims being oppressed around the world? I didn't have the guts to go there myself, but I kept on looking at the videos."[27] Amin started helping Islamic voluntary organizations.

> My whole hallway was full of clothes. I was constantly taking clothes to the mosque. So many—it was incredible what we collected. I felt that I had to do it. It was my duty to do good deeds. But clothes alone can't stop bombs, can they? You can't destroy Assad's troops with clothes. IS hadn't emerged yet, at that time, around 2011. But I knew that violence was going to be necessary. So, when IS declared the caliphate and started distributing film clips, I was greatly impressed by my comrades who were fighting there.

Amin kept on watching video clips and distributing them in his network. "I didn't dare to go myself, but through the clips, I was with them in spirit. That gave me the feeling that I was taking part in the fight."

Amin was eventually sentenced to eight years in prison on the basis of his Internet behavior and because he distributed jihadist ideas and possessed a Kalashnikov and ammunition, which were found in his storeroom. He had an IS flag hanging on his wall. According to the public prosecutor, he was not an average criminal; he was planning an attack and wished to spread death and destruction. Amin himself claimed he did not plan to use the Kalashnikov and was keeping it for friends whom he did not want to betray. "It was bad luck for me that, just before my trial, those idiots started shooting in Paris and, with those attacks in their minds, the judges of course thought I was a scary terrorist, too." From my conversations with Amin, it was not possible to determine just how radical—or unradical—he was around 2012. A picture does emerge, however, of a man who was dissatisfied with his life, became involved in petty crime, and was deeply affected by the war in Syria. He was obsessed with the idea that "Muslim children were being oppressed"

---

[26] Interview with Ilyas*, January 16, 2020, PI/TDU.
[27] Interview with Amin*, October 30, 2019, PI/TDU.

and that "the West did nothing." Once IS had placed the war in the context of the final battle, Amin went along with that narrative. Collecting clothes and helping Islamic voluntary organizations was no longer enough: "It was time for violence."[28] His fascination with radical redemption took him a long way down the road of radicalization, but he did not see himself departing for Syria, and he—fortunately—never got as far as preparing an actual attack.

Abdelkarim*, born into a large, happy family in The Hague, is the youngest convicted terrorist I interviewed in the Netherlands. At the time of his arrest at the beginning of 2014, he was still under 18. For him, the war in Syria was a turning point—"though not the only one"—at which he started to learn more about Islam. He already went to the mosque, where his father was also active; Abdelkarim had taken Arabic lessons there. But his parents were "not at all" devout, he told me. "My fascination and efforts to learn more about my faith didn't come from my parents but from the injustices suffered by Muslims in Syria."[29]

Abdelkarim was a good student: he started secondary school at the highest—pre-university—level. However, he was demoted to a lower grade level because of his recalcitrant behavior. "Then I started to feel guilty," he said. "I was rebellious. I had a good life; I could get anything I wanted. But on the news and social media, I saw that people on the other side of the world were fighting to survive until the next day. That touched me deeply. I started looking at film clips, about Islam, and then about the struggle. There was too little information about it here, and I wanted to know more. I had good contacts."

After secondary school, Abdelkarim started studying theology at a vocational university and taught at the mosque. That went so well that he was invited more and more often to give lectures, both in person and over the Internet. In the meantime, he had built up a group of friends with whom he started to share his frustrations: "I wasn't really a Salafist like some of the others, but the injustice being inflicted on Muslims brought us together. Those friends and I slowly started wearing different clothes. I increasingly wore a *djellaba* [loose-fitting robe] that came down to my knees. It was a *salwar kameez*, a Pakistani version that dated back to the war of the Taliban. Salafist jihadists wear them, too." His network in The Hague was notorious for all kinds of actions, the strong proselytism of its members, and the fact

---

[28] Interview with Amin*, October 30, 2019, PI/TDU.
[29] Interview with Abdelkarim*, June 11, 2019, The Hague.

that a number of them had left for or wanted to go to Syria (Bahara 2013). Abdelkarim took on a *kunya*, a new name. With his long curly hair and his white robe, he attracted a lot of attention from young Muslim women in the network. "I was still only a young boy in 2012/2013, but my lectures attracted a lot of attention," he said.

> In hindsight, I think that wasn't very good for me. But I felt more and more self-confident. I thought, I can do this. I have a lot to say. I read all the writings of Anwar al-Awlaki and Abu Muhammad al-Maqdisi,[30] and I followed Jabhat al-Nusra. They at least were doing something. And I wanted to share that with the world. I wanted to show the world the injustice being inflicted on the people of Syria, that there were people fighting it and that other people—we—should also do something.

Abdelkarim in particular grappled with his own role in the struggle:

> Deep inside, everyone felt that going there was the absolute maximum that you could do. But I didn't want to do that to my parents. I had such a good relationship with them. They would find it terrible if I went there. That's why I started giving a lot of lectures. You feel guilty, and you want to get rid of that sense of guilt. I wanted to pass on the knowledge I had acquired and that people gave me through the Internet to other people here in the Netherlands. Keeping myself busy with the struggle the whole time reduced my sense of guilt. I was now devoting my time and energy to the good cause. I might have been a spectator and not one of the cooler guys who went to fight, but I was a preacher—and, yes, about the jihad.

Abdelkarim preached increasingly often about theological issues. "I gave lessons on various religious matters, about the End of Days and the Day of Judgment but also about other normal theological questions. But now, with Jabhat al-Nusra and the fight against Assad, it all came very close to home. The Levant—that has always been the most important region within Islam, and that's where the final battle will be fought. So I made that link, too."

---

[30] Anwar al-Awlaki (1971–2011) was an American-Yemeni imam who was seen as a spiritual leader; he was an Al Qaeda ideologue and created the English jihadist magazine *Inspire*. He was killed by a drone strike in Yemen in 2011. Abu Muhammad al-Maqdisi (b. 1959) is a Jordanian-Palestinian writer and jihadi ideologue who popularized many common themes within radical Islam and declared the Saudi royal family and everyone who believes in democracy an apostate. See Wagemakers (2012).

154   THE RADICAL REDEMPTION MODEL

Thus, Abdelkarim became the center of a network of jihadists in The Hague, some of whom left for Syria. He distanced himself from the network at the start of 2014, but was still arrested in June of that year and sentenced to a little less than a year in prison for spreading hatred and recruiting for the armed struggle. He was given a short sentence, because he was not a follower or supporter of IS. "I was for the struggle against Assad and for Jabhat al-Nusra, but not for the kinds of attacks IS was committing, there or in Europe. Above all, I wanted to do something, give some of my time and energy, because I felt guilty" (see Tieleman and Rosman 2017; Van der Laan and Sterkenburg 2015).[31]

To Syria: It Is My Duty

Ilyas, Abdelkarim, and Amin found an outlet for their personal frustrations, feelings of guilt, or simply bad luck in their own lives by helping other Muslims: they collected for Syria, supported Syrian refugees in the Netherlands, preached about the End of Days, and called on people to join the fight against Assad. Doing these things gave them a sense of relief, redemption, and direction. They felt unable to go to Syria themselves for various reasons, but they expressed their drive for redemption through other forms of action.

Several other detainees did take that step—they departed for the war zone. The young people who left for Syria between 2011 and early 2014 did not go to join IS or the caliphate, as Abu Bakr al-Baghdadi did not announce the establishment of the caliphate until June 2014. According to the Dutch General Intelligence and Security Service (AIVD), this first batch of departees mainly joined Jabhat al-Nusra and similar organizations, and not IS, though the latter did already exist.[32] The big difference for departees between the situation before and after 2014 is that before June 2014, IS had not yet started widely flaunting its public beheadings and other horrific acts,[33] had not yet committed any major attacks in Europe, and was not yet engaged in attracting new recruits through its international office and propaganda channels. In 2011–13, the war in Syria was not about IS but about Assad. It

---

[31] Interview with Abdelkarim*, June 11, 2019, The Hague.
[32] See AIVD, "Uitreizigers en terugkeerders," accessed March 15, 2020: https://www.aivd.nl/onderwerpen/terrorisme/uitreizigers-en-terugkeerders.
[33] That only happened after 2014: see Friis (2015).

is worth noting that none of those who went to Syria to fight in these years joined the Free Syrian Army; they clearly wanted to join jihadist groups in the Aleppo/Idlib region—which were later incorporated into Jabhat al-Nusra. This batch of departees was thus also fighting for a future Islamic state.[34] But the timing is important in light of the extent to which they embraced the attacks and violent revenge fantasies of IS.[35]

"In Syria, they stood up for their rights, for their freedom. Assad was bad. They wanted to live there, and they demanded their rights."[36] Haroun* is fired up again as he describes how the people of Syria rebelled against the regime. Haroun was born in Rotterdam in 1988 and later had two younger sisters. His parents were not well off, and they lived in a small house. He had a vocational education, "something to do with administration," but "it didn't really interest me," he said. He experienced a number of setbacks, but he told me: "It was also my own fault." He stopped studying, and his parents told him to move out. "It was simply too full there," he said. He found himself on the street, homeless. "I drifted around for a while, stayed with friends. I played video games a lot; that calmed me down. Then I was placed in an assisted-living project, and things got better for a while. But that went wrong, too: I messed up and missed appointments, and I ended up back on the street." In that same period, the revolution broke out in Syria. "At friends' houses, I started looking up more and more things on the Internet, watching film clips. There was bombing the whole time, but no one did anything." One of Haroun's friends left for Syria in 2011 and started calling and emailing him that he should go, too. In that way, the desire to "do something useful" with his life and the opportunity to do so came together. After that, everything went very quickly.

> It was my duty. For Allah. It is loving your neighbor, doing good for others. If I see you being attacked on the street, I come and help you. If I see Muslim children dying, it's the same principle. Other than that, I didn't know much about the situation. We watched the Dutch news and Al Jazeera, and I became addicted to all the film clips. But I didn't know what was really going on, because no one had left for Syria yet at that time. My friend was one of

---

[34] See, for example, the jihadist Internet publication "De Nederlandse Muhajideen in Bilaad As-Shaam" (2013); De Koning et al. (2020, 241–2).
[35] IS did not start attracting potential recruits with its new caliphate narrative until mid-2014, and only strengthened its narrative of revenge and victory by committing major attacks in the West in 2015. See AIVD (2016, 3). See also Doornbos and Moussa (2016).
[36] Interview with Haroun*, January 16, 2020, PI/TDU.

> the first, and I followed him shortly afterwards. You could say the penny dropped. I left my parents behind and went off to join the fighting. It was my way of devoting myself to a good cause and changing the course of my life. It was faith; it was everything—it is the air that you breathe, my whole life. I had to change my life and sacrifice myself for the cause.

Haroun's words, his interpretation of his life, and the choices he made reflect the theme of the *hijra*: he gave up his comfortable life in a godless environment to go to a region where he could—in his eyes—mean something as a Muslim.

At the same time, his account echoes the jihadist-Salafist account of Ahrar al-Sham. From that perspective, the war in Syria was not an opposition of minority groups against an authoritarian regime but a struggle of Sunnis against a godless and apostate government. In that light, it was the duty of pious Muslims to join the struggle, given that the Syrian Muslims could not do it alone, and neighboring countries and other powers did not do enough to help them. In that situation, *fard ayn* applied—it was the individual duty of every Muslim to help in the struggle.

> It was about doing something good. Children who wrote things on the wall were killed; unarmed citizens were shot; Sunnis were oppressed. What could I do? I had friends who had been criminals, who had experience with weapons, and who were well suited to fighting on the front. I was no good with weapons, but I did want to help my brothers and sisters there. Here I was just a troublemaker. I wasn't allowed to live with my parents any more, I couldn't keep on sleeping on my friends' couches, and I hadn't found a job. Now I could still do something good. I wanted to transport goods back and forth and help smuggle them across the border with Turkey.

Within a week, Haroun had left the Netherlands and, in 2012, crossed the border from Turkey into Syria with no problems. He was given training and attached to a battalion of Ahrar al-Sham, in which his friend from Rotterdam also fought. "But my friend was killed after a couple of weeks," Haroun told me. "He left one day and didn't come back. The other guys buried him; I saw his grave." With each passing month, the situation deteriorated. "Assad's army set fire to our houses, sealed off all the roads, and arrested anyone who demonstrated, including women and children. The women were raped and the kids tortured. I had seen films about that in the Netherlands, but it was much worse in reality." For Haroun, the war was not about revenge but about liberation—not only political and military but also religious and even eschatological liberation. "We didn't want revenge," he said. "We really wanted to free Muslims, to fight in the final battle." It was more redemption than revenge: redemption from his own unemployed, homeless existence in the Netherlands, devotion to Allah, and doing his duty to his fellow Muslims.

And yet, the constant stress of war soon became too much for Haroun. He tried to get away from the front and perform other duties for his unit, such as trading and smuggling. He also found a local girl; he married her, and they had a child. "At the end of 2013, I had had enough. I called my father and told him that I wasn't cut out for fighting. If you have been brought up in the Netherlands, this is too much for you. I didn't have the patience or the perseverance, and my Arabic wasn't good." With the help of friends, he managed to smuggle his wife, their child, and himself back into Turkey. But he was arrested there and sent back to the Netherlands. His wife and child still live in Turkey. Because he left on time, did not fight for IS, and had tried on his own initiative to come back at the end of 2013, he was sentenced to only four years in prison. Still, he said, "It's a bitter pill to swallow. Assad started the war, not me. I now have such a problem with panic attacks that I don't want to talk about it anymore. I hope to see my family again soon, and to get off my medication."[37]

General Van Uhm

Bilal* was inspired by similar motives. He was born into a close Moroccan family in Amsterdam in 1988. His brother and sister did well at school and went on to university. Bilal successfully completed a secondary vocational education and became a youth worker in Amsterdam. But then, his career ground to a halt.

> I started having the usual problems, you know, that all minorities have. I did a placement somewhere, and was promised a contract that I never got. Here in the Netherlands, people see me as a Moroccan, and in Morocco, they see me as Dutch, so nothing happened automatically. Doors just wouldn't open for me. That might be partly my fault, because I didn't feel I was being

---

[37] Interviews with Haroun*, January 16, 2020, and February 5, 2020, PI/TDU.

treated like a normal Dutch person. I felt I had the right to all the things that native Dutch people have; maybe that's why I made less effort—because, you know, as a member of a minority, you have to work even harder.[38]

In that situation—Bilal was now 22—the war broke out in Syria. It is worth letting Bilal tell his story in his own words:

> I wasn't disappointed with life or anything like that, but I did have an attitude of, like, fuck everybody. And then, in 2011 and 2012, all the images started to come in: of dead children, slaughtered babies, kids from 6 months to 3 years old, killed, just like that. And that was exactly the age-group I was working with in a day care center with kids from 1 to 8. And then I saw all those children lying dead, on a plastic sheet. I thought, That can't be happening; what is this? So, I started to find out what was going on. I couldn't speak Arabic or Turkish. I hadn't been brought up particularly religiously, and we rarely went to the mosque, if at all. But I recognized a couple of words. *Hürriyet*, the people in Syria were crying out, for freedom and justice. They were also asking for help: "Where is the world? Help us!" And then I saw General Van Uhm on the television. He called the people who fought against Assad, who stood up to help the repressed children, heroes. That was of course long before the caliphate, and IS.
>
> I decided I wanted to help. I started by collecting clothes. But then I wanted to go along with the aid convoys to Turkey. I was arranging something through an uncle in Belgium, but my father forbade me to go. I found that very selfish. How hypocritical can you be? My dad didn't want me to go there and help, but said I had to stay here and find a job and continue studying. The world was on fire, and he thought it was more important for me to get a good job . . . But that's not what I was like; I wanted to make my own decisions. I tried to set up a foundation with my brother, so that I was doing something myself, but that didn't work out. So I up and left for Istanbul. I wanted to do something good if I could. Then I would be helping, not for the media or for my parents, but for myself. And for my faith. No one was doing anything—the United Nations, America, nobody. You saw all the people in the camps. They had nothing. So that's why I went: not necessarily to become a martyr, but to do something practical,

---

[38] Interview with Bilal*, February 5, 2020, PI/TDU.

to help liberate people. At that time, that was no problem at all, and with my Dutch passport I crossed the border without any trouble.

In Syria, I joined Ahrar al-Sham. I had crossed the border with a friend, and a Syrian who had helped us took us to the group. They gave us a house in Idlib, where there was plenty of space. I'd come from Amsterdam and didn't know much about fighting. So, I had to do my training first, and help distribute goods. And that's what I wanted to do. If people there were suffering, I would suffer along with them. If I could help, I would help. And I was fit and healthy. But I wasn't allowed to use a gun at first because I hadn't learned how, and ammunition was very expensive. And I'd called my parents, who'd begged me not to fight and to stay and help in the camps. But then, around the end of 2013, early 2014, the geopolitical game started, and chaos erupted. My organization suddenly received a lot of support, weapons, tanks, ammunition, from the West, from America. I've been convicted as a terrorist, but my organization was supported by the West and wasn't even on the list of terrorist groups! By then, I had a wife and small child there. I smuggled them into Turkey, because it was getting far too dangerous. In Syria, everyone was fighting everyone else. Our group was fighting against IS. We wanted nothing to do with the caliphate; that was all about territory, weapons, and power. We just wanted to help the Syrians.

And yet I saw wonderful, beautiful things. We were living in the middle of a war zone, but there was plenty of food. That was a real miracle. I think Allah did that for us. After so much bombing, we still had huge supplies of fruit and meat. That was just like in the old stories. The Levant and Sham are blessed lands, I've seen that with my own eyes. Not like it was in Afghanistan, where people had to eat leaves. We could still buy a whole chicken for 80 cents. I called my mother, who was panicking because she saw the whole of Syria being bombed on television, and reassured her. I told her that the shopping center was still open and people were getting married, just as usual. We knew how to deal with the situation—we all had a walkie-talkie and let each other know if a fighter plane had taken off in Homs, for example. Our house was never bombed. We even had an olive orchard and a small business selling olive oil. We were spared. My children were a gift from Allah, too.

But in 2015, I'd had enough of it all: the infighting, the chaos, and the power struggle between the different groups, and Russia and America interfering. So, I left Ahrar al-Sham and drifted around for another two years, before smuggling my wife and child—and finally myself, too—back into Turkey.[39]

In Turkey, Bilal was ultimately captured and deported to the Netherlands. In 2018, Ahrar al-Sham was added to the list of terrorist organizations; as a result, Bilal was convicted of membership of a terrorist organization in 2019 and sentenced to six years in prison.[40]

What all the detainees who went to Syria have in common is the overall narrative of redemption, in which geopolitics combines with Salafist beliefs about purity and justice and a sense of personal responsibility, duty, and, sometimes, even guilt (see Cassam 2021b). "I would have felt like a hypocrite if I hadn't gone," Bilal told me. They believed it was their duty to endanger their own lives by throwing themselves into an armed struggle, or at least to go to the war zone and help in some way, because they felt that everyone else had failed to support the rights of repressed Muslims. The regimes in the Middle East had failed in their religious duty and let Assad do as he wished. The major powers only intervened because of the oil. "Your democratic regimes want only one thing," said Asaad*: "To divide and repress the Middle East. Of course the Arab uprising was a failure; how naive could you be to think otherwise?"[41]

For Bilal and others, the persuasive power of the geopolitical, jihadist-Salafist narrative lay in the fact that they no longer had to rack their brains trying to understand the complex context of missed reforms, corruption, and inequality in the Arab world, and that they no longer needed to think about setting up political parties or the difficult process of organizing opposition and legal changes. Instead, they could pursue an ethical program of purification and struggle, and they could do it immediately. In their own, highly specific redemption narratives, the insoluble complexity of the inequality in the Middle East and the situation of Muslims worldwide could be brought together and flattened out into simple, apocalyptic conspiracy theories. Altruism, impatience, conspiracy thinking, and empathy with Muslims in Syria merged symbiotically with deep feelings of injustice and frustration about their own lives. Because of the concrete opportunity of the war in Syria

---

[39] Interview with Bilal*, February 5, 2020, PI/TDU.
[40] Ahrar al-Sham was considered a terrorist organization by the Dutch Public Prosecution Service, but it was not on the UN or EU sanctions lists. In fact, it received support from EU countries in 2015, and the Dutch Ministry of Foreign Affairs described it in the same year as "moderate." Bilal was added to the terrorism sanctions list in July 2016. See also Dahhan and Holdert (2019).
[41] Interview with Asaad*, January 16, 2020, PI/TDU.

and the propaganda and logistics of groups like Ahrar al-Sham and the Free Syrian Army, those feelings of frustration, powerlessness, and guilt could be channeled into armed jihad. Moreover, their own small lives, with all their banal frustrations, became part of a cosmic struggle, an eschatological narrative of the End of Days. And this applied even more to the young people who took a well-considered decision to join IS.

Among the Most Wanted

Ahmed*, born in Delft in 1995, was the eldest child, with three younger brothers and two sisters. He was difficult to handle at home and ended up at a special school. His story is also one of a series of bad choices and wrong turns. "I wanted to join the police," he told me. "But that wasn't possible, because I didn't have good enough qualifications. So, my parents sent me to a secondary vocational school to learn about trade and hospitality. But it just didn't work out. I had a placement at Lidl, that sort of thing. I hated it. A bit stupid if I think about it now, but that's how I felt."[42] Ahmed dropped out of school and started hanging around at home and on the street. He became involved in drugs and got into debt. "Then my parents sent me to my uncle in the north, where I could get a job at the supermarket where he was the manager. I could have trained for that, too. But I had bad luck. I took something to eat from the store, because my boss said I could do that now and again—and I was sacked. Then I started smoking weed and watching film clips on YouTube, that sort of thing." When some people he owed money to were hot on his heels, Ahmed no longer felt safe. In his situation, going elsewhere to fight in the jihad was a logical alternative:

> I wasn't very religious. Nor were my parents. My dad wasn't interested in Islam at all. I didn't pray, and I smoked weed every day. But then one day, sometime in the middle of 2012, I saw pictures of the war in Syria, and they affected me so deeply that I started to pray. That was spiritual guidance; I saw that as spiritual guidance. I started to think more and more about death. I knew I was Islamic, and that there is a hell and a heaven. You Christians believe that too, don't you? And I started to think about it. I watched all kinds of film clips about it. I was really behaving badly,

[42] Interview with Ahmed*, February 5, 2020, PI/TDU.

man. I just sat around doing nothing, getting fat and spaced out, so to speak, while out there, people were dying every day. I started praying for them and, in 2013, I started going to the mosque more often. Sometimes I'd smoke a bit of weed, but I tried my best to avoid it. And I watched more and more videos, and through them, I felt that I, too, was being called—to the jihad. I was really happy when I saw that rebels and jihadist groups had taken another city from Assad. Those two things came together in my head: I was trying harder and harder to practice Islam and, out there, they were winning battles. And I kept thinking, Why am I still here? What have I got to lose here? There was a general who said that they were heroes, those fighters. And I thought, That's what I want, too. Just like it used to be in Afghanistan, but now the fight was here, much closer to home.

I left just before the caliphate was declared. I had money, and within three days, I was in Syria, no problem. I had asked around a bit: whether there was enough to eat, what clothes I would need; all very simple. I'd worked at Lidl and then in the greenhouses, where I earned 250 euros a week, so I just took all my money with me. It's a big decision. But what would you do if your children were in danger? Those kids there, they could have been my kids. Those women could have been my mother, the young girls my daughters, the sisters my sisters. And, in Islamic terms, they *were* my family. Everyone had their reasons—I wanted to defend my family, and with the most wanted, the really cool guys, who did the real fighting. That was just before the caliphate. Crossing the border in Turkey was no problem at all. When I told them I was from the Netherlands and wanted to go and help in Syria, they just said, "Go ahead," and literally kicked me across it. That was a big surprise. After that, I traveled on to Iraq.

Because his trial was still under way, Ahmed did not want to go into detail about his battle experiences. But he did tell me he was involved in serious fighting.

I experienced a lot of things there. Terrible things, but also wonderful things. Friends who died smelled of musk. And I dreamed that angels spoke to me, and that it was very light. I'm not going to say that it was awful there, because it was also an adventure. I didn't want to kill innocent people, but you have the right to defend yourself. And I was willing to give my life to defend my brothers and sisters there. If I died in the process, so be it. I don't know if I will get a reward for that. I hope so, but only Allah knows that. I think good things about Allah, and He about me, so I will be rewarded for the good deeds I have done. It was not revenge for me. It was a response, a matter of self-defense.

Ahmed was not willing to say much about the countless war crimes committed by IS against innocent women and children, Yazidis, and many other inhabitants of Syria and Iraq. For him, they fall under self-defense and "collateral damage." He did, however, want to say something about the horrific execution of 26-year-old Jordanian pilot Muath al-Kasasbeh, who was burned alive in February 2015. Ahmed was at that time fighting for IS.

Take that pilot. Shortly before, he had bombed an apartment block. Burning him alive was terrible, but it was a justified punishment. He was executed close to the building he'd bombed, as a punishment for all the people, including children, he had killed in the attack. The person who performed the execution had lost his own family in the bombing. So yes, it was a justified act of revenge.

There are many different kinds of martyrdom. I would prefer to live for a thousand years, but I was also prepared to give my life. And I put that into practice. I saved people from burning buildings or from the rubble of destroyed buildings. I protected my comrades. I have no regrets. We did our best to help out there. I thought it was terrible when it all became so chaotic in the course of 2015, with everyone in the opposition fighting each other. But I am not sorry, only that I caused my parents such sorrow. But if they asked to defend my Islamic brothers and sisters again, in Myanmar, for example, and I was able to do so, I'd get right back on the plane. That is my goal; that's what I have to do with my life.[43]

Not everyone was, and is, as certain of where they stand as Ahmed. Omar*, for instance, became friends with Ahmed in 2014 through social media and left for the caliphate together with him. The two of them tried to recruit other young people for the armed struggle. But for Omar, the dream of radical

---

[43] Interview with Ahmed*, February 5, 2020, PI/TDU.

redemption proved a deception, and his quest to sacrifice himself for the cause ended in disappointment and failure.

Omar was born in Utrecht in 1994. His mother had various health problems. His mother and father came from very different backgrounds and had conflicting ideas about faith and how to bring up their children. Omar and his sisters also clashed regularly. All of this led to considerable tension within the family. Omar had difficulty completing primary school, and he dropped out of secondary school without finishing his vocational education. He ended up on the streets, homeless, and started smoking weed. His parents split up, and his mother converted to Christianity. After that, Omar was not welcome anymore at either of his parents' homes. He survived by engaging in petty theft; in addition, his father gave him a small amount of money from time to time. He had a smartphone and, after 2011, started to develop an interest in what was happening in Syria. After meeting Ahmed, he came completely under the influence of IS. Like Ahmed, he was captivated by the stories of the final battle and wiping out the sins of his past life. Omar, too, had not been brought up particularly religiously, but he started to cobble together his own pick-and-mix Salafism. In IS's offer of the opportunity to take part in the final battle, Omar saw the possibility of giving his life meaning and sacrificing himself for his fellow Muslims. His father told the local police officer that Omar was becoming radicalized, but it was too late: Omar and Ahmed had already left.

After a year, however, Omar had already had enough and tried to escape from the caliphate. During his trial, he said that he had found it awful there, and that he had an aversion to fighting and blood. His hopes and expectations had turned into frustration and fear. His second attempt to flee the caliphate was successful; he was subsequently arrested in Turkey and deported to the Netherlands. He was charged with being a member of a terrorist organization and planning and carrying out terrorist crimes. When the public prosecutor showed him images in which he posed laughing next to crucified victims in IS territory, Omar said he had done that so as not to be revealed as a deserter, because he was already making plans to escape. In court, he expressed his regret about his time with IS. He was sentenced to seven years' imprisonment.[44]

---

[44] Interview with an official of the Utrecht City Council who was Omar's case manager, December 9, 2019, Utrecht.

The Premier League

Like Ahmed, Farhad*, from Utrecht, became very much captivated by the offer of radical redemption presented by IS. He was born in 1991, the oldest of two children of Iranian parents who had fled to the Netherlands and went to live in Utrecht when Farhad was 5 years old. His father was a bookkeeper, and his mother worked at Douwe Egberts, a coffee producer. "I discovered my faith around 2004, after the murder of Theo van Gogh.[45] I wanted to know what drove Mohammed Bouyeri and when it was permissible for Muslims to take up arms. I started going to a mosque and praying more often. The stories in the Koran fascinated me. But the Arab Spring was a shock. When IS emerged, I couldn't stop watching their film clips. That was the real thing."[46]

A supporter of the Rotterdam football club Feyenoord, Farhad liked to speak in football terms. "IS was the Premier League," he told me. "Their film clips were better than Hollywood. They took on the United States and Russia—and they won. When they established an Islamic state, I felt called to go and join them. I dreamed of the caliphate." Farhad had completed secondary school, but he had trouble getting into further education and finding a job because of a personality disorder.

> I had become addicted to weed and was unemployed. I wanted a new life, a real life, with an Islamic wife. Via Facebook, I came into contact with people in the caliphate, who urged me to go out there. That was the solution—for my own life, and also to be able to do something for others, and for Allah. I loved history books and thought I could maybe become a history teacher there. Baghdadi was at least a leader who was not corrupt. And because they were winning, I wanted to be on that team, and win the final. Allah called me. Now, I could finally do something worthwhile.[47]

Farhad started distributing film clips himself and praised the beheadings by IS on Twitter. By then, he had saved enough money and had made his travel arrangements. But when he wanted to leave, in April 2016, he was arrested at Utrecht Central Station, with his suitcase, ticket, and everything else. His

---

[45] Dutch film producer who was murdered by Dutch-Moroccan Islamist Mohammed Bouyeri on November 2, 2004; Bouyeri objected to Van Gogh's controversial position on women and Islam.

[46] Interview with Farhad*, December 5, 2019, Utrecht.

[47] Interview with Farhad*, December 5, 2019, Utrecht; media reports (not specified because of the risk of the real name of the interviewee being traced).

father had told the police of his plans. The police found images of beheadings and pictures of Farhad posing in front of an IS flag on his telephone, together with a lot of cash and an IS death list. Farhad was sentenced to 300 days in prison—242 of which were suspended—and to following a course of discussions with his therapists and a theologian.[48]

With Grandmother to the Caliphate

Interestingly enough, many of those who left for Syria or Iraq traveled in pairs or groups of friends, or they followed friends who had already departed earlier. Very few went alone and completely on their own initiative; in that respect, Farhad was an exception. One of the most notable groups was the family of Indonesian detainee Syarafina Nailah, who left for the caliphate in a group of twenty-four, including her old grandmother. In this account, individual patterns of radicalization driven by the Internet merge with the collective tendency of Indonesian Muslims to adopt certain practices—in this case, to leave for the caliphate—as a family. Syarafina is the only convicted female terrorist I spoke with: in the Netherlands, there were initially no female detainees, and in Indonesia, they were often released and only the men were sentenced. While that makes her story unique in this book, Syarafina also displayed the same patterns of moral deficit and the same desire for redemption as the male terrorists.

Syarafina was born in 1996 on the Indonesian island of Batam, in the Riau archipelago to the northeast of Sumatra. She was the eldest daughter of wealthy parents. Her mother was a housewife and her father the director general of the regional government on the island. After completing primary school, Syarafina was sent to an Islamic school in Malaysia, because her parents thought she would get a better education there, and Java was too far away and too expensive. Her family was not very religious: "My mother did wear a headscarf," she told me. "But we hardly ever went to the mosque. And they let me decide for myself whether I went or not. Our school was Islamic, and I just went with the flow. I was a very obedient girl and was mainly concerned with working hard at my studies."[49] After secondary school, Syarafina

---

[48] Because Farhad refused to talk to the therapists and the theologian and expressed mistrust of the government, he ultimately spent 152 days of his suspended sentence behind bars.
[49] Interview with Syarafina Nailah, February 24, 2020, Jakarta.

was admitted to the State Polytechnic on Batam, where she started studying information technology.

    Then things went wrong. My father was always away for his work, my mother was busy with my youngest sister, I was living on the campus, so my middle sister was always at home on her own. She started to feel increasingly lonely and depressed, and spent more and more time surfing the Internet. My uncle, my mother's eldest brother and a strict Muslim, told her about IS and the caliphate. My sister got more and more interested in it and, through Tumblr, established contact with people there. She became addicted to Diaryofmuhajirah, a blog by a Malaysian woman in the caliphate who described how wonderful it was there and how you could lead a perfect Islamic life. She told my sister that we, her family, did not love her enough and that she could fill that hole in her heart, that loneliness, by leaving for the caliphate.

    From that moment, my sister started to become more and more radical. She told me everything about the caliphate. She played truant and wanted to be expelled from school. One day, she ran away from home but, fortunately, my mother found her at the house of one of her teachers. Together with my uncle, my sister started trying to impose her beliefs more and more on us. IS promised her, and us, that we could study there, that my father could get a job there. My aunt had cancer, and my uncle did not have enough money to pay for good medical care. IS promised that my aunt would be given free chemotherapy and other treatment. That Malaysian woman showed all kinds of wonderful images on her blog. I also had a cousin with a personality disorder—he was bipolar—and IS promised us that they could provide us with the very expensive medication required for his treatment. What's more, in 2014, my uncle's company was doing very badly, and he almost went bankrupt. My sister had already convinced my mother. I was skeptical at first, but gradually got used to the idea of going to the caliphate. I was extremely dissatisfied with the corruption in Indonesia and, for example, the inequality and injustice with which women were treated. The caliphate seemed to be the real answer to all those problems.

    If we went, we would be able to save our sister. Otherwise, she would certainly have gone on her own. We could hardly keep her captive, and she would have escaped anyway. And we could save our aunt and our cousin. Our uncle would have no financial problems anymore. I myself was convinced that life would be fairer and purer there. In other words, we would be free of all our troubles here in one fell swoop. And we could begin a new life out there, as a family, in a pure, Islamic community.

By now, my father also saw it as an option. He was unhappy with his work. And we had also learned that the jihad is not only about fighting but also about taking care of each other. Looking after your family is also a form of jihad. By August 2015, he and my uncles had everything arranged. We had money and tickets, and we all left together for Turkey. We took my grandmother; she could hardly stay behind on her own. We divided the family into four groups, otherwise we couldn't be smuggled across the border. One group unfortunately got caught and sent back to Indonesia, but the rest of us—eighteen in all—arrived in Syria, ending up in Raqqa. There, we were split up, the women sent to a women's house and the men elsewhere. At first, my aunt received the treatment she needed. I went to the hospital with her, and learned how to give her basic care, including injections.

But I actually knew from the start that it was all a sham. Everything was incredibly dirty. And that is wrong. Islam requires that you keep yourself and your surroundings clean. But the women's house and the hospital were simply filthy. What's more, IS didn't keep its promises. When our father and uncles and cousins didn't want to fight and be sent to the front—they had after all told us that you didn't have to if you didn't want to—they were thrown in prison. And we no longer got our allowances. In addition, we weren't allowed to study at all. Everything was a lie. The caliphate was a complete mirage. At first, we tried to point all that out to the IS people, all the mistakes and abuses. But it was difficult to communicate, because the Arabic we had learned at school in Indonesia was completely different to the dialect they spoke there. We tried to explain to the people of the caliphate that they weren't living according to the Koran, that how they treated people was wrong, but they didn't listen. My other aunt had glasses and couldn't get a burka over her eyes. So she was picked up, put in a bus, and taken away. I myself experienced how meanly IS treated women and children. Mothers were separated from their children for no reason. My other uncle saw IS people encouraging children to play football with a chopped-off head. Luckily, I didn't see that, but he did. Another uncle was killed during a bomb attack in Raqqa. And the worst was that, when my grandmother died, they just threw her body in a mass grave somewhere at the hospital and we weren't able to bury her properly. That's not Islamic either.

After a few months, all we wanted to do was get away. Fortunately, we had exchanged our jewels for money, which we still had with us. Our first attempt failed, because the man who was going to smuggle us out ran off with the money. Then we had to stay another year to earn money again. To do that, the women made clothes to sell. The men stayed indoors, because we didn't want them to be picked up again. Finally, we managed to save 4,000 American dollars, enough to smuggle the whole family—now only sixteen of us—to the territory of the Syrian Democratic Forces [the Kurdish-Syrian militias fighting Assad] by truck. We arrived there in 2017 and were placed in a refugee camp. Via a journalist, our story made its way into the media and, two months later, the Indonesian government arranged for all of us, everyone, women and men, to be repatriated. The men are still in prison, but we women were allowed to go home.

I asked Syarafina about her sister, and she said:

She has terrible regrets about it all and will feel guilty about it for the rest of her life. But I will, too. We let her be radicalized and went along with it ourselves. We actually had quite a good life in Indonesia, and that is now ruined. We allowed ourselves to be brainwashed by IS. Now, we have lost all our money, and I can no longer study. We try to earn money by selling snacks and clothing, to gather together enough money for the three of us—myself and my two sisters—to go to college. But we still have each other, my mother and my sisters. And my father will also be released one day.[50]

I asked my colleague Solahudin, Indonesia's foremost specialist on terrorism and radicalization, about Syarafina's story. Solahudin works with the Indonesian authorities on developing deradicalization and reintegration programs for convicted terrorists. He confirmed her story—he has met and questioned the family through his work—but explained that, in relative terms, few Indonesians—some 1,500—left for the caliphate. In percentage terms, this is fewer than in the Netherlands, which had a little under 200 departees in a population of 17 million, 1 million of whom are Muslims. Indonesia has a population of 260 million, 85 percent of whom are Muslims. According to the Indonesian National Counter Terrorism Agency (BNPT),

---

[50] Interview with Syarafina Nailah, February 24, 2020, Jakarta; interview with Solahudin, February 27, 2020, Jakarta.

who is responsible for international cooperation with other counterterrorism agencies, Indonesia decided in 2020 not to repatriate the remaining 600 Indonesians still in Syrian camps. Syarafina's family was thus lucky to get out at the last minute. Syarafina and her sisters are currently participating successfully in a BNPT deradicalization and reintegration program. The male members of their family are receiving supervision and counseling in detention and will be released in two years.

According to Andhika and Solahudin, the influence of the Internet and of Al Qaeda–inspired jihadist Salafism are serious problems in Indonesia. While the number of departees remains small, the jihadist-Salafist influence through the many pesantren, the unbridled growth of conspiracy theories, and the susceptibility of Indonesian Muslims to such stories are a considerable cause of concern to the Indonesian government, especially in light of the long history of armed resistance, religious conflicts, and ethnic tensions in the expansive island kingdom. Solahudin and Andhika suspect that, unlike in the Netherlands, discrimination and inequality cannot be an important factor for Muslims in Indonesia because Islam is the majority religion, and Muslims are given every opportunity to practice their religious beliefs and live according to the rules of Islam. And yet, the desire for purity and the appeal of worldwide jihadism, together with local grievances, remain a persistent source of radicalization. But Solahudin and Andhika both believe that religion—especially what they call the "unfounded, uninformed, hyperindividualist interpretation of Salafism"—is the main cause of many young people's fascination with the jihad. "That's why we don't want to bring back any more veterans from the caliphate," says Andhika. "Because then we will get the same phenomenon as in the 1990s, when Afghanistan veterans laid the basis for Indonesian jihadist training camps and organizations here."[51]

Bad Luck?

Not all Indonesian and Dutch individuals who went to Syria after 2014 were confirmed or even trained jihadists. This is clear from Syarafina's story. But the following accounts of Anwar* and Noureddine* show that the decision to join the armed struggle could also be uninformed and naive, the process

---

[51] Interview with Solahudin, February 27, 2020, Jakarta; interview with Andhika Chrisnayudhanto and Zainal Ahzab (BNPT), February 26, 2020, Jakarta. See also Gartenstein-Ross et al. (2020); Solahudin (2013, 192–202).

of joining the fight unpredictable, and the motives of injustice, struggle, and redemption vague and abstract. However, this does not change the fact that religion plays a role, and that a desire for purification, redemption, and justice can cause people to make strange and dangerous choices.

Anwar, born in 1991, and Noureddine, born in 1990, grew up in the Schilderswijk in The Hague and knew each other from a young age. Noureddine, whose father was at home through ill health, completed a secondary vocational education in retail. Anwar told me that he came from a happy family and had qualified as a car mechanic. His family observed Ramadan. But neither the boys nor their parents visited the mosque regularly. They both did kickboxing and took part in competitions. "Our parents had passed on the faith to us," Anwar said. "And we knew that there were rules you had to follow: being polite, not doing bad things to others. But it's a struggle, isn't it? Not to do bad deeds. If you do good, Allah will reward you. But what is good, and what is bad? For some Muslims, it's bad to smoke. I don't know. I was just kind of restless."[52] Anwar had his own car and was a cabdriver, but after 2011, Anwar and Noureddine had both had enough of their jobs. And Noureddine also had to deal with problems at home, because his parents were in the process of getting divorced. "We had already seen what was going on in Syria," Anwar told me. "That was bigger than our lives. It was painful for me. Nobody did anything."

At first, the two friends only felt a partial personal engagement with the suffering of the Syrian people. In the first instance, they went to Turkey for a holiday and "because we had had enough of life at home." Noureddine met a girl there in a bar, Dilah, and decided to return the following year with his friend. At the end of 2014, they were back in Turkey, but Dilah had moved to the southeast of the country. "We were there for two or three months, but it was crap," Anwar told me. He felt like the odd one out, and got talking to Syrians who had fled across the border. "I just sat there, waiting, and wanted to see for myself what it was like in Syria. You heard all kinds of things, but I wanted to see it with my own eyes." Anwar left and entered Syria with no problems, but he fell badly in the mountainous terrain while crossing the border and could not walk anymore. With money that he had taken with him, he rented a house and had surgery on his knee. Noureddine had, in the meantime, split up with Dilah, and he followed Anwar "to help him out." "We were in the territory of the Free Syrian Army, and because we had to wait

---

[52] Interview with Anwar*, November 27, 2019, PI/TDU.

until Anwar's knee was healed, I started a small oil-refining business. Thanks to IS, there was good-quality oil available, and we made a good profit."

"I had finished with Dilah," Noureddine told me. "She wasn't the kind of woman I wanted to marry. I soon met another girl there, the sister of the business partner we had set up the refinery with. So I married her. She is called Sarah." They soon had a son, but then Noureddine had a motorbike accident. "Anwar's knee had healed in the meantime, but now I was out of action. I had broken my leg and got jaundice. I hadn't been involved in the fighting, just had a stupid accident." But they were in the war zone. Deeply concerned because they had been away for more than a year, Noureddine's mother had told the police in The Hague about their disappearance. They were placed on the sanctions list. Whether they were taking an active part in the fighting or not, they were in territory controlled by terrorist organizations.[53] Anwar picks up the story:

> We had actually come to Syria with no clear idea of what we were going to do there and, thanks to pure bad luck, we were stuck there longer than we had planned. My parents thought we had joined Jabhat al-Nusra, but that wasn't true. We had our small company and did business with the Free Syrian Army and with Jabhat al-Nusra, but we ourselves didn't fight. Once we were there, it was the perfect place and time to investigate our faith and the war there. What was the right path for a Muslim? Exactly the question we had asked ourselves before. War is always about money and self-interest. Which side should we fight on? The Prophet gave us rules, and we started to think about them more deeply. But at the same time, there was a war raging around us. We had our oil business, but when the Kurds started to win territory back from IS, that also started to go less well. And we both now had a wife and children.

Noureddine told me that he was also starting to doubt whether the Salafist-Sunni interpretation of Islam was right, and that put him in danger. "I spoke to a lot of people there, and read more. I found it easier to talk to Sufis and Shiites. They understand that sense of moral deficit better, that you don't have to carry that heavy load around with you everywhere. Salafists do that; they impose a really heavy burden on themselves and others. Sufis, Shiites, and moderate Sunnis are more forgiving. When I realized that, I felt more

---

[53] Information from the police.

at peace, but I wanted to get out of there." After two years, in 2017, Anwar and Noureddine decided it was enough and tried to get back to Turkey with their wives and children. "This was not our war. There, we couldn't build up a good life; it was all wrong." They got their wives and children safely back to Turkey, but they themselves were arrested and deported to the Netherlands. Once there, they were sentenced to five years in prison (Berkelder 2018).

For Anwar and Noureddine, radical redemption was only part of their motivation. Their stay in Syria was the outcome of a series of ill-considered decisions, bad luck, curiosity, and the misplaced hope of becoming "better Muslims" in Syria and leading good lives, with obedient wives and their oil business. "IS was there," they said. "But we didn't have much to do with them. We were against injustice, but it all quickly became much bigger than ourselves. IS had little patience with human weakness; they were much too strict, with all those punishments. But try explaining to a judge why we were there, then."[54]

Redemption for Stay-at-Home Terrorists

The final section of this chapter looks at the radical young people who did not leave for the war zones but put their jihadist desires into practice at home in their own countries. What comes clearly to the fore in these accounts is that after 2013, the dominating aspect in the radicalization processes of these stay-at-home terrorists was not altruism or a desire to help but a desire for revenge that was inspired and even driven by the caliphate. This applied to jihadists like Mohamed Merah (Toulouse, 2012), Mehdi Nemmouche (Brussels, 2014), the *Charlie Hebdo* attackers (Paris, 2015), and Anis Amri, who drove his truck into the crowd at the Berlin Christmas market in 2016, as well as to a number of convicted terrorists in the Netherlands.

A striking detainee in one of the penitentiary institutions' terrorist detention units (PI/TDUs)—in that he is very assertive, intelligent, and talkative—is Asaad, who was arrested while traveling through the Netherlands en route elsewhere. Asaad showed no signs at all of loving his neighbors, only of anger and a desire to take revenge for the injustice that he saw Muslims suffering at the hands of the West (*NOS nieuws* 2019a).

---

[54] Double interview with Anwar* and Noureddine*, November 27, 2019, PI/TDU; interview with Noureddine*, February 5, 2020, PI/TDU.

Asaad was born in the Middle East in 1989 as the son of a high-ranking army officer. His parents moved to Scandinavia, where, according to Asaad, he grew up in a "pro-European, secular, and liberal climate." "I was active in the social democratic party, and I'm formally still a member of the party," he told me.[55] But he was unable to secure a high position in the party. In his view, that was because of populist tendencies in Scandinavian society, which obstructed him in his career. He studied civil engineering but decreasingly saw himself as having a future in Europe: "With all the right-wing media, people like me have no chance at all." For Asaad, the war in Syria was an eye-opener. His narrative was not Salafist but anti-imperialist and anti-Western. "I used to be pro-NATO," he told me. "But look what happened in Libya, where NATO intervened. Mohammed Morsi came to power in Egypt, but General Sisi deposed him, with the help of the West. And then the uprising broke out in Syria, and the West did nothing. No one lifted a finger to help my brothers and sisters. French neocolonialists intervened in Tunisia and Libya. But no one dared to do anything against Assad. And in Iraq, too, it went from bad to worse with President Maliki." In 2012, Asaad decided to visit his half-brothers in the Middle East and take a look for himself at the situation in Syria and Iraq. "My cousins were intelligence officers, and my family belongs to a well-known Sunni tribe. They told me about the corruption and how Sunnis were oppressed."

IS was by now also active. I asked Asaad how he saw the jihadist struggle. "I was not brought up religiously," he said. "But in Iraq, I realized that I have four things in common with IS: I am a Sunni, I share the nationality of many IS leaders, even their tribal loyalties, and I abhor the corrupt regimes of Assad and Maliki. I realized that it was my duty, like my cousins, to resist those regimes, take up arms, and go and fight."

However, Asaad did not stay in Iraq but returned to Europe. There he resumed his studies, but he also became much more active on the Internet. He increasingly identified with IS, translated propaganda material and films into English, and distributed them on the Internet, which was not yet an offense in his country (Sandelin and Olsson 2019). He was not clear about his exact plans. "I told my contacts [in IS] in Iraq and Syria that they should not commit any attacks in Europe," he claimed during our interview. But monitored conversations show that he accused the West of having "double standards," considered Dutch and Scandinavian people as "infidel dogs," and

---

[55] Interview with Asaad*, January 16, 2020, PI/TDU.

was planning "to achieve justice for Muslims." It had become his personal quest to expose the real state of affairs, break through the conspiracies, and name and avenge the injustices. He especially singled out the Netherlands for his revenge because Dutch troops, together with the British, had bombed innocent Muslims in Mosul.[56] When he flew to the Netherlands shortly before Christmas in 2017, he was arrested by the Dutch police after a tip from their Scandinavian colleagues and sentenced to three years' imprisonment. Searching his effects, police found a will, videos by IS, and instruction books for carrying out attacks; the only thing missing was a concrete plan for an attack (*NOS nieuws* 2019a).

For Asaad, contributing to the struggle—albeit in the form of distributing Internet propaganda for IS and not through violence—clearly acted as an escape valve for his personal frustrations about his derailed ambitions, and it was a way in which he could identify with a group that put their words into deeds. "It was revenge," he repeated. But it was "also redemption, because it was my duty as a Muslim to help liberate my fellow believers and devote my time and energy to doing that."

At the same time, of all the interviewees, Asaad was best able to make the link between the larger international, geostrategic situation and a religious narrative of struggle and redemption. When I noted that he had made a thorough study of the history and politics of the Middle East, he answered:

> I told you that I have a clear overview of the situation, that I know how it all fits together. None of you understand that. To me, it is all one. After all, for Muslims, there is no separation of church and state. Geopolitics, the conflict between Saudi Arabia and Iran, the intervention of the West, and the final battle of IS—they are all part of the same big story. It is my duty to unmask lies and to tell that story, and to make people aware of it—if necessary, with violence.[57]

Gökmen Tanis, March 18, 2019

Another redemption narrative driven by revenge and rage unfolded in 2019. It was a much more disturbing one, because it had lethal consequences.

---

[56] Interviews with TDU staff, October–November 2019, PI/TDU.
[57] Interview with Asaad*, January 16, 2020, PI/TDU.

On Monday, March 18, Gökmen Tanis opened fire on passengers in a tram in the Dutch city of Utrecht, killing four people and seriously wounding several others. On his gun, he had written: "He who follows the sharia goes to paradise. He who follows democracy goes to hell. You kill people who are Muslims. And Allah allows me to kill you . . ." He had probably been triggered by the terrorist attack of right-wing extremist Brenton Tarrant, who had killed fifty-one Muslims three days earlier at a mosque in Christchurch, New Zealand. Tarrant referred in his texts to victories over Ottoman armies and to other attacks. Turkish president Recep Tayyip Erdoğan used images of the Christchurch attack in a rally in Antalya that weekend (Wintour 2019). According to the Dutch National Coordinator for Counterterrorism and Security (NCTV), Gökmen watched jihadist film clips and images of IS and listened fanatically to Erdoğan's inflammatory speeches.[58] He seemed indeed to have been triggered by Tarrant's attack: on the day of the attack, police found a sheet of paper in Gökmen's escape car that read: "I am doing this for my faith. You are killing Muslims and want to take our faith from us, but you will not succeed. Allah is great."[59]

Experts were quick to claim that Gökmen Tanis was not fully accountable for his actions, while neighbors thought him more likely a disturbed person than a terrorist (*Panorama* 2019). During his trial, the judge asked him if he was "a part-time Muslim and a part-time drug addict" (see Huisman 2020). And yet Gökmen repeatedly showed that he adhered to a deeply radical, anti-democratic, and coherent jihadist doctrine, albeit one expressed in rather simple terms. A 2011 video clip circulated on Dutch blog site GeenStijl showed Gökmen verbally abusing a scantily clad female journalist and Playmate of the Year who was conducting street interviews. He said it was obvious that she was a "democrat" and not from the "sharia" (GeenStijl 2019). Such radical anti-democratic comments did not come out of nowhere: in Gökmen's broken family, his two brothers were also known for their strong religious opinions, and at least one of them was a member of the radical Turkish Islamic organization Kaplancılar (Caliphate State) (Rosman 2019).

Irrespective of how intellectually or behaviorally disturbed Gökmen may have been, his trial showed that he consistently adhered to his earlier standpoints and that he held the Dutch system and Dutch society in contempt. An image emerged of a man addicted to drugs who had an extensive

---

[58] Interviews with NCTV staff and police officers, 2019; see also NCTV (2020, 30).
[59] Interview with Utrecht police and with Sebas Diekstra, the victims' legal representative. See also Houterman and Wetzels (2020).

criminal record—Gökmen had served time in prison for various offenses, including rape, illegal possession of weapons, and theft—and who had difficulty in relating to those around him. One day, he would challenge his neighbors for their—in his eyes—sinful behavior and proclaim his intention to be a pious Muslim; the next, he would walk through the streets drunk and aggressive. He made use of his right to speak at the pro forma hearing in July 2020 to describe his murders as acts of retaliation, of revenge for the injustice suffered by Muslims worldwide at the hands of the West: "'I allow no one to mock our faith,'" said the judge, quoting Gökmen. "'I wanted to show that you are made of diamonds and we of sand. If I had a thousand lives, I would give them to Allah.'" Gökmen also said that "the Prophet is humiliated by caricatures; the Koran is written on naked women and filmed. Muslims are being killed by Dutch soldiers in Libya, Syria, Chechnya, Afghanistan, everywhere. Did you really think we would not do something in return?" (*NOS nieuws* 2019b).

At the same time, through the killings, he seems to have wanted to force a break in his stagnated life and his immense anger. Someone had to do something, and he had nothing more to lose. He was temporarily free, but would very probably be convicted for another indecency offense in July 2019 and be sent back to prison. On March 18, he therefore chose a twisted path of radical, religious redemption, to ensure that "he would go to heaven after all."[60] In terms of what we discussed in chapter 3, Gökmen Tanis seems to have been driven by Louise Richardson's three Rs (revenge, renown, reaction) and my fourth R (radical redemption). Gökmen saw himself as the herald of Allah's judgment over democracy and was willing to sacrifice his failed life by attacking people who in his eyes represented Western democracy: the innocent women and men of Utrecht (see also De Graaf et al. 2019).

Gökmen Tanis's surrender to radical redemption was accompanied by severe behavioral disorders, drug addiction, and intellectual disabilities. There was little evidence that he had further reflected on his narrative or had thought it through. Besides the texts found in his car and on his gun, a few earlier comments, and his behavior in court, he has made no statements to speak of. He does not appear to possess any deep religious or theological knowledge. Yet, being in a state of "confusion" and responding to the appeal of extreme religious ideas can go together very well (De Graaf

---

[60] Information provided during the trial of Gökmen T., March 2–6, 2020, Utrecht. See also NU.nl (2020).

et al. 2019).[61] Embracing the narrative of radical redemption—including the encompassing praxis and acts—can be the outcome of a well-considered process of thought, but it can also be an instinctive reflex, the spontaneous embracing of martyrdom and vengeance as the ultimate solution for all feelings of deficit and injustice in one's own life and in the lives of others. The narrative of redemption facilitates the coming together of radical emotions, radical beliefs, and the desire for action. Perpetrators can commit an act of redemption while in full possession of their mental faculties, supporting their act by theological arguments, or they may surrender to it intuitively and impetuously while in a state of confusion. The latter does nothing to invalidate the logical coherence between the sense of deficit, the religious or extremist offer of redemption, and the accompanying practice.[62]

Gökmen's act must be classified among the most abhorrent and horrific jihadist attacks. It is the deadliest terrorist attack to date in the history of political and terrorist violence in the Netherlands.[63] In March 2020, the court sentenced Gökmen to life imprisonment without psychiatric treatment, since "psychiatric treatment is aimed at recovery and reintegration in society, whereas this prisoner shows no signs at all of remorse or repentance, and there is a very real threat of him committing such offenses again."[64]

Gökmen's motivation in committing his attack was clearly a very selfish, narcissistic, and primitive form of redemption. He came no further than "You are killing Muslims" and "I live by the sharia and will be admitted to heaven." And yet it is important to end this chapter with this attack, because it shows how terrorists and violent loners can employ the theme of radical redemption destructively and nihilistically to justify their acts, forgetting that in all the major global religions, narratives of redemption are intended to

---

[61] For the discussion on the link between psychopathology and terrorism, see Schulten et al. (2019). This combination of confusion, criminality, and behavioral disorders on the one hand, and consistent single-mindedness and conviction on the other, in the case of Gökmen Tanis was also observed by TDU staff; conversations 2019–20, PI/TDU.

[62] As noted earlier in this book, terrorism and psychopathology cannot be explained monocausally: a multilayered, multidisciplinary approach is required to understand these phenomena. Such an approach should offer scope for psychiatric, social-psychological, religious, and cultural explanations. See also Sizoo et al. (2022).

[63] *Deadliest* in the sense of one perpetrator killing the most people. Actions by Moluccan extremists in the 1970s cost more lives. In 1975, they killed three hostages. In 1977, eight lives were lost during the hijacking of a train, but these deaths were caused by the violent ending of the hijack and included six hijackers. Attacks in Apeldoorn (2009) and Alphen aan den Rijn (2011) resulted in seven and eight deaths respectively (in both cases including the perpetrator), but these were—and still are—not considered terrorist attacks.

[64] See district court Midden-Nederland, verdict in case 16/659055-19, "Attack Utrecht Tram Shooter," ECLI:NL:RBMNE:2020:1046, March 20, 2020.

save and liberate, not to increase suffering. In terms of motivation and argumentation, Gökmen Tanis stands entirely on the side of destruction and sadism. Most of the other interviewees who implicitly or explicitly embraced the theme of radical redemption supported it with more nuanced, even "social" or "altruistic" arguments—all of course still within the framework of armed struggle and terrorism. Clearly, terrorists and radicals come in all shapes and sizes and allow themselves to be seduced into committing violent acts of varying severity.

Conclusion

This chapter has considered a wide range of redemption narratives. If we look at the narratives as a whole, three common aspects stand out.

First, all of the convicted terrorists discussed in this chapter described their inspiration and actions to a greater or lesser extent in terms of a *strong religious theme*. Their radicalization process was driven by all kinds of push factors: personal frustrations, failed careers, social or economic isolation, or rage at the injustices suffered by other Muslims. At the same time, the narrative of religious purity and redemption from guilt or injustice was of decisive importance for all of them. This narrative gave them a framework in which to place their personal life stories, their personal quest for meaning in their lives—which they had not looked for very hard before, given the fact that most interviewees reportedly "were not that religious at all."

Second, this religious theme manifests itself in many different ways but is always expressed in a *very practical, even physical, way*. The radicalization process of both Indonesian departees for Afghanistan and the first batch of Western European radicals and "foreign fighters" departing for Syria was driven by their desire to help in a practical way, at first through collecting or providing clothing or medical care, but later by training for the armed struggle and actually taking part in the fighting. Training together from the early morning and sitting around the campfire late in the evening exchanging stories about the battle are very physical, social activities. The same holds true for collecting money, which all Muslims see as a way of expressing their love for their neighbors, a pious duty. As one of the pillars of Islam, the *zakat* is familiar and gives them a sense of satisfaction.

Besides these physical experiences, the interviewees often talked about their sensory and spiritual experiences. Many men told me about the dreams they had, about the desert or the fighting, and some even saw angels. Others experienced miracles: food supplies that did not run out, bombs that narrowly missed them, and olive trees that bore much more fruit than normal. Moreover, they smelled musk on the lips of their dead comrades. In Islam, musk is a mythical aroma, coming from paradise, which symbolizes a "purified" form of blood. According to the Hadith, the bodies of dead martyrs exude the sweet smell of musk (King 2017, 325–65; see also Lange 2016, 104, 133, 142). Whether they trained and fought in Southeast Asia, on Ambon and in Aceh and the Philippines, or in Syria and Iraq, the dreams and tales of miracles were the same and seem to have been strongly inspired by the writings of Azzam—texts that were, and still are, widely distributed at the pesantren by veterans or via the Internet.[65]

Indonesian jihadists, who had actually taken part in the fighting, spoke openly of the desire to become a martyr and to put the ideals of purification and redemption into practice in the most radical way by surrendering their bodies completely to the battle. Some were jealous of their fallen comrades. Obviously, the Dutch detainees I spoke with had failed to sacrifice their lives. Their lack of success may explain why they spoke of martyrdom less willingly. And yet, the physical aspect just described certainly played a role for them, too. But as I mentioned before, the choice to interview convicted terrorists detained in the Netherlands naturally implied a certain selection: I did not speak to those who lost their lives fighting in Syria or Iraq, or to those who stayed there. Suicide terrorists like Sultan Berzel and Lotfi S.—who made a conscious decision to join IS in 2014, called on Muslims in a farewell video clip to commit attacks, and then blew themselves up in Baghdad and Fallujah—were not among my research group, for obvious reasons.[66] The majority of those I interviewed left for Syria in 2011–13 to fight against Assad. They explicitly sought to join jihadist groups and not the Free Syrian Army. Among the militias of Jabhat al-Nusra, martyrdom was primarily to be found in the fight against Assad and not in suicide missions. Others may have once had the desire to become martyrs, but later changed their mind and were ashamed of their earlier ambitions. And yet, among this group, martyrdom in some form was an important desire and driver, because

---

[65] This was confirmed by staff of the BNPT that I spoke with in Jakarta, as well as by an AIVD analyst I talked to in the Netherlands; background discussion, July 6, 2020.

[66] These two jihadists are probably the most violent terrorists from the Netherlands so far. At least five people were killed during the attack by Lotfi S., alias Abu Hanief alias Abu Abdurahman al-Hollandi; the suicide attack by Sultan Berzel claimed between ten and twenty victims. See *RTL nieuws* (2015); Van de Beek and Van Dyck (2017).

committing suicide attacks is by no means the only form of martyrdom. Any effort undertaken in light of the holy battle can be seen as an act of sacrifice. As one interviewee told me: "If I die in the Netherlands as a result of my good intention to help someone cross the road, I am also a martyr, because I died performing a good deed."[67] Of course, the jihadists I talked to had radical, often violent acts of redemption and purification in mind rather than good deeds such as collecting rubbish or helping someone cross a road. But my point is that martyrdom embraces a much wider range of activities than only suicide attacks, and that less violent and radical detainees also mentioned the desire to sacrifice their bodies through their physical efforts.

Third, *armed struggle* presented an excellent opportunity *to deal with and remove their sense of deficit*. Chapter 4 described how that deficit was expressed in terms of the holy struggle and the desire for redemption. In this chapter, we have seen how convicted terrorists translated that desire into action by sacrificing their own bodies and lives in the holy struggle; they took up arms in their own countries or elsewhere. For instance, Haroun's path to radicalization ran from a sense of deficit and frustration about his own failures, through the search for meaning, to surrender to the holy struggle by devoting his life to saving his fellow Muslims. He found this redemption narrative on the Internet, and within a short time, with the help of a friend, he had departed to participate in the fighting. This account clearly features the altruistic aspect that was a decisive factor in the first generation of departees' decision to leave. In the narratives of this first generation, there is also a clear link between the sense of deficit, their devotion to the cause, and the reward—the points you can earn. For the generation of stay-at-home terrorists in and following the IS period, by contrast, revenge plays a greater role—perhaps to compensate for their own failings. For them, redemption is primarily something external: they reflect very little on their own spiritual development or their own sense of deficit, and guilt and penance are projected predominantly on others, who have to be punished.

In the following chapter, we will examine whether the convicted terrorists I interviewed believe that their search for radical redemption has been successful, and if so, to what extent. Has their desire for redemption been fulfilled? How do they look back on their devotion to the cause and the struggle? When do they consider their search for redemption successful, and when do they feel it has failed?

---

[67] Interview with Ahmed*, PI/TDU, February 5, 2020.

6
The Third Panel

Validation Achieved?

Validation or Contamination

This chapter examines the third panel in the triptych model of radical redemption: we explore whether the acts performed to gain radical redemption have been successful and validation has been achieved. The third panel comprises the following aspects: First, only through a radical praxis of atonement or revenge can redemption and deliverance be achieved or at least symbolized. Specific narratives of redemption can be individual or collective. They can entail atonement for one's own life of sin, or deliverance of oppressed fellow believers or group members. The aim can be redemption from one's own guilt or vengeance for the disgrace suffered by the group as a whole. Second, in all cases, the violence and the redemptive move are part of a greater metaphysical battle between good and evil—a battle that must be validated by the constituency or group through recognition and acceptance of the act of redemption. There must be certain templates, religious or ideological, that validate such act. If validation is not achieved, the narrative of redemption becomes a narrative of contamination and disappointment.

As will transpire, very few of the convicted terrorists I spoke with accomplished their act of redemption. This is partly due to the nature of the sample, as mentioned before: I did not speak to those who died in or did not return from the war zone. On the other hand, some of the interviewees did fight and were prepared to become martyrs. But they ultimately turned their backs on that path. For most of them, their dreams of the desert came to an end. The quest for meaning through devotion and struggle resulted primarily in disappointment and deception, sometimes because their own understanding changed, but much more often because parents, friends, or the community refused to acknowledge their acts of radical redemption and urged them to return home.

When their act of redemption failed, was not acknowledged, or did not bring them the sense of fulfillment they had expected, my interviewees experienced disappointment and, sometimes, denial. In a small number of cases, it led to a reappraisal of other forms of engagement. In the following sections, I will examine these three positions from the perspective of the convicted terrorists: redemption accomplished; transformation of the redemption narrative into a narrative of contamination or deception; and refutation and reappraisal.

Redemption Accomplished

The Crime–Terror Nexus

Ahmed* from Delft, whom we met in the previous chapter, told me he was in a rut, working in a supermarket and having a drug addiction. What he did not initially tell me on his own initiative but what was clear from his files was that he went to his uncle in the north of the country because he was afraid of the people he owed money to. He had taken to crime to pay for his addiction and had ended up in the hands of drug dealers, to whom he owed 4,000 euros. When I asked him about it directly, he admitted that remorse about his sinful life coincided with his decision to flee from his creditors. But he still believed that leaving for Syria was the right decision. When he departed for Syria in 2014, he told his father: "I'm finally doing something good. I'm finally on the right path."[1] Ahmed was fully prepared to give his life for the good cause. That he ended up in prison did not change that. He was even willing to see his time in detention as a sacrifice. "Allah sees at least that I am on the right path," he said. He told me he would be willing to go and sacrifice his life again in the fight against injustice, because martyrdom is "the highest virtue." Also, it would redeem him from his worldly debts and feelings of guilt.

This pattern was recognizable in Ahmed's case, as well as in the cases of Gökmen Tanis and various other interviewees. It is a theme that has been picked up in the literature and is seen as part of the *crime–terror nexus*: the desire to seek redemption for a sinful, criminal past through a deed of complete devotion and martyrdom (Basra et al. 2016; see also Stoter Boscolo 2016). Such a redemptive move is identifiable in many cases of people who

---

[1] Interview with Ahmed*, February 5, 2020, PI/TDU.

Table 6.1 AIVD statistics on terrorist departees

Number of adults (18+) who departed for Syria and Iraq (numbers are rounded off)	
Killed in the fighting	100
Returned from the war zone	60
Still in Syria with jihadist intentions	120
In Turkey	15
Other	5

leave their homes to join IS. Unfortunately, I was unable to speak to many of this generation of departees as they either have been killed or are still in Syria or Iraq. In the period of my research (2018–20), most of the convicted terrorists in detention in the Netherlands were of the generation that left in 2011–13. As we saw in the previous chapter, that group of departees was driven more by altruism or by a wish to redeem themselves from a criminal past than by the desire for revenge. For those who departed between 2014 and 2017, the desire to seek redemption for a life of crime was, perhaps, a stronger motive—stay-at-home terrorist Gökmen Tanis, for instance, made it clear in the courtroom that, despite his substantial criminal record, he was convinced that he would "go to heaven."

According to the statistics of the General Intelligence and Security Service (AIVD), as of March 1, 2020, some 300 adults had left for Syria or Iraq, a little over 100 of whom were women (see table 6.1). The majority joined Tahrir al-Sham, a terrorist organization affiliated to Al Qaeda, between 2011 and the start of 2014. Returnees were convicted; they are now in detention or have been released. In March 2020, thirty-six detainees—the total number of convicted terrorists in the Netherlands—were in prison in the terrorist detention units (TDUs) in the Netherlands. Of the adult departees, 120 men and women were still in Syria, Iraq, or Turkey. The majority of them left in the course of 2014 and joined IS. In addition, in March 2020, 205 children were still in refugee camps in Syria and Turkey; more than three-quarters of them were born there and are thus under 4 years of age.[2]

---

[2] See AIVD, "Uitreizigers en terugkeerders," accessed March 15, 2020: https://www.aivd.nl/onderwerpen/terrorisme/uitreizigers-en-terugkeerders.

Several male departees have a history of petty (and sometimes serious) crime, including drug-related offenses (see Thijs et al. 2018). Because I was unable to interview individuals who are still in Syria or Iraq, I here examine the phenomenon of the crime–terror nexus on the basis of secondary literature and terrorist biographies in the media.[3] A prominent aspect of this nexus—the choice for terrorism as a form of penance for sins committed in the past and a way of seeking redemption for a guilty life—is most markedly present in this group of departees, not only from the perspective of their own motives but also in IS's explicit offer of reward for and validation of the redemptive act.

Profit or Redemption?

Research into crime and terrorism often identifies a fundamental distinction between the two phenomena: criminals pursue profit, whereas terrorists are said to be driven by ideology. Academics refer to this as the *profit-versus-ideology dichotomy* (Roberts 2016). Between the two extremes of this distinction, there is a gray area that depends on the type of terrorist or criminal organization involved, and the type of terrorist or criminal concerned (Makarenko 2004; Shelley and Picarelli 2005; Hutchinson and O'Malley 2007; Roberts 2016). There are certainly some similarities between criminal and terrorist networks at the organizational level; for example, both demand complete fidelity and loyalty from their members and use violence for illegal purposes. In addition, their activities are often interrelated. The Irish Republican Army (IRA), Revolutionary Armed Forces of Colombia (FARC), and the Basque separatist movement Euskadi Ta Askatasuna (ETA) were active in the arms and drugs trade (Curtis and Karacan 2002, 7–9). In Afghanistan, the Taliban profited from the opium trade for many years. And in the more recent past, before it had to relinquish the oil fields in the Kirkuk region of Iraq, IS is estimated to have earned some 1.5 million dollars a day through extracting and selling oil. The money was used, for example, to pay foot soldiers, commanders, engineers and other technical support personnel, and doctors (Solomon and Chazan 2015; Solomon et al. 2016). By way of comparison, Al

---

[3] Because this is such a strong redemption theme, it needs to be explained in greater detail, even though this means departing from the method of basing this empirical part of the study exclusively on my own field research.

Qaeda was primarily dependent on donations from wealthy foreign sponsors (Keatinge 2014; Zehorai 2018; Del Cid Gómez 2010). Finally, criminal and jihadist networks can overlap. Perpetrators work together, recruit from the same pool—the Paradise Gate Boys from Delft are a good example—or supply each other with goods and services. For individual group members, crime and terrorism can sometimes be even more closely intertwined.

Our focus here is this final element of the crime–terror nexus—individual criminals crossing over to terrorism and being actively encouraged to do so by a terrorist organization. British militant group Rayat al-Tawheed (Banner of God)—a subdivision of IS—distributed a propaganda poster bearing the slogan "Sometimes people with the worst pasts create the best futures," thus praising a criminal past as an advantage in taking part in the holy struggle.[4] The poster was specifically aimed at young people seeking purification and redemption for their criminal past by promoting the opportunity of devoting their criminal and violent tendencies to a good cause rather than using them for their own benefit (Basra et al. 2016, 26). In a video clip, the group describes how the transformation from gangster to jihadist can be achieved by taking part in the armed struggle. A member of Rayat al-Tawheed in a balaclava loads his gun and releases a few shots to lend his words greater force:

> The reality is, you're all in sin. Because deep down, you know what you're doing, and you're not changing. You're still going around, you know, I'm a Muslim at heart, I'm a Muslim in my heart, *iman*'s in my heart. . . . Where are you when we need to start taking heads off? Where are you when they are slaughtering our children and our fathers, not to say our women, after they get raped? . . . And you still walk around boasting that you are in the West, boasting that you lead this so-called gangster life. . . . Come on! (Gadher et al. 2014)

The only way to be a real Muslim was not to sit around on the couch at home but to "take off" enemies' heads.

Researchers Rajan Basra, Peter Neumann, and Claudia Brunner have observed this desire to transform from criminal or some other kind of sinner to terrorist in various European countries. Individuals who desired this transformation did not actually have to go to Syria or Iraq to take part

---

[4] "Jihad is a purification no matter who you are or what sins you have [committed]; no good deeds are needed to come before it. Don't let anything hold you back" (Roussinos 2014).

in the armed struggle—it was possible to undergo the transformation at home in the West. Mohamed Merah, who shot three French soldiers and four Jewish civilians dead in Toulouse in March 2012, is a good example. Redouane Lakdim and Benjamin Herman, who in 2018 killed several people on the street in Carcassonne/Trèbes and Liège respectively, before being killed themselves, also had criminal pasts and had become radicalized in prison. Saïd and Chérif Kouachi, who committed the 2015 attacks on the satirical magazine *Charlie Hebdo*, and Amedy Coulibaly, responsible for the attack on a Jewish supermarket in Paris in January 2015, as well as the perpetrators of the attacks in the city in November 2015, were all "gangster-jihadists." Abdelhamid Abaaoud, the operational leader of the attacks, had a criminal record. Brahim Abdeslam, who blew himself up in front of the Paris café Comptoir Voltaire, had been involved in drug-related crime, as had his younger brother Salah Abdeslam. Many more examples can be given, such as the perpetrators of the attacks on the Christmas markets in Berlin in 2016 and in Strasbourg in 2018. The Strasbourg attacker, Chérif Chekatt, had as many as twenty-seven convictions to his name. According to Basra, Neumann, and Brunner, such perpetrators came from the same recruiting pool as criminals, creating "synergies and overlaps that have consequences for how individuals radicalise and operate" (Basra et al. 2016, 11).

In the Netherlands, the Paradise Gate Boys mentioned at the beginning of this book also fitted this profile, although they were not gangster-jihadists. The people around them had not noticed the boys were being radicalized because these young men, a number of whom had been involved in a supermarket robbery, were considered petty criminals. The blurring of the lines between crime and terrorism was identified too late: they had already left to join the jihad (Kouwenhoven 2014).

It is clear from all these examples that criminal or gangster behavior by no means precludes conversion and transformation to a religious terrorist attitude and practice. On the contrary, accounts of such jihadists with a criminal record show that young people with little or no religious baggage were most susceptible to the appeal of joining the holy struggle. They were inspired in no time at all—often while in prison—to make the transition from crime to terrorism.[5]

The narrative of radical redemption played a clear role here. According to Inge Versteegt and her colleagues, who compared radicalized young people

---

[5] See also the account of a Danish-Moroccan jihadist in Kester (2014) and Khaja (2014).

with criminal records with a control group, there was no evidence of a greater sense of discrimination, a stricter religious background, or personal trauma. The radicalized criminals—or radicalized individuals involved in crime—were more often addicted to drugs or had become involved in drug-related crime. They were also more fervent in examining their own roles in and responsibility for perceived injustice (see Versteegt et al. 2018).

The International Centre for the Study of Radicalisation (ICSR) in London even speaks explicitly of a reported "redemptive narrative": by joining the jihad, radicalizing young people found redemption and forgiveness for their crimes, while taking part in the armed struggle fulfilled needs they already felt, such as a need for adventure, adrenaline, rebellion, and comradeship. Through this narrative, these needs acquired religious legitimacy and even meaning. It gave radicalizing young people an escape valve for and direction to their feelings of hatred, injustice, and alienation. Joining a jihadist network gave them something to hold on to; it was a coping mechanism for dealing with stress and fear of loss of meaning, and it provided a way to do penance, earn points, and achieve redemption (see Basra et al. 2016, 23–4).

Offer and Confirmation of Radical Redemption: *Rumiyah*

Young people with a criminal record and a surplus of criminal energy who seek radical redemption are a recurring phenomenon in the history of terrorism and political violence. Many members of the Red Army Faction (RAF), and Andreas Baader in particular, took pleasure in robbing banks and stealing expensive cars. Members of the FARC and Palestinian terrorist organizations were also known to be drug criminals. But IS focused more than any other terrorist organization on the criminal milieu as a pool of new recruits, employing the most up-to-date lobbying and PR techniques. By packaging ideological justification for criminal behavior in a narrative of glorification, IS successfully utilized the theme of personal redemption to build a robust bridge between crime and terrorism. At the same time, it could draw on existing Islamic traditions of guilt, penance, reward, redemption, and, of course, the *hijra*; the terrorist organization deployed these very recognizable themes and practices for Muslims specifically to persuade radical young people to join the cause. This, together with the narrative of the final battle and the End of Days that appeared to be unfolding in Syria, proved for many an irresistible combination.

The IS digital magazine *Rumiyah*, published in nine languages, confirmed, extolled, and underpinned IS's offer of redemption. According to *Rumiyah*, it was permitted (*halal*) not only to shed the blood of nonbelievers (*kufar*) but also to rob them of their prosperity. Deception, in the form of fraud, and theft from nonbelievers, polytheists, and idolaters were lauded as legitimate ways of engaging in jihad. "There should be no misunderstanding about the excellence of this deed, as taking this wealth [from nonbelievers] is in accordance with the command of Allah" (*Rumiyah* 2017b, 14).[6] A fifth part of the *ghanimah* (wealth taken from an enemy in times of war) had to be given to the caliphate, but the jihadists themselves were permitted to keep a large portion. This message was picked up and disseminated by Dutch Syria departee Marouane B.: "It is an eye for an eye, a tooth for a tooth. Conduct the jihad in the Benelux by committing robberies with the aim of sending part of the money to IS" (Van Helden 2018). By conducting the jihad in this way, including criminal practices, perpetrators were assured of their reward—one that was paid out in tangible benefits in this life while also retaining its "heavenly value."

When jihadists lost their lives in the holy battle, *Rumiyah* did not fail to glorify their deeds and to profile them as martyrs. That, too, was a form of reward: recognizing and publicizing heroic deeds acted as a stimulus to other jihadists and potential recruits. These tributes made special mention of the martyr's transformation from criminal to jihadist. The obituary for IS fighter Abu Mujahid al-Faransi alias Macreme Aboujui is a good example. Aboujui, Tunisian by origin, grew up in the suburbs of Paris. He had led a life of "disobedience and sins," but as a fighter for IS, he was generous, noble, and brave. *Rumiyah* went on to praise his criminal skills, elevating them to an ideal and ambition for all fighters. The martyr was a "fierce gangster" whom everyone was afraid of. Through his heroic deed, he had not only redeemed himself but also served Allah and shown others the way to true devotion and belief. According to *Rumiyah*, Aboujui had used and honed his violent and criminal talents in the struggle. He and his associates had "entered into the world of robbery and gangs in their previous lives, but the assault this time

---

[6] IS was not the first jihadist organization to legitimate criminal practices in this way: in the 1990s, jihadists in Algeria engaged in similar practices.

differed as it was a form of worship by which they sought to draw closer to Allah" (*Rumiyah* 2017a, 46).

The phrase "previous lives" is crucial here and clearly refers to the intended redemptive move and transformation. IS fighters, former criminals driven by greed, disobedience, and corruption, experienced a rebirth. Abroujui adhered to the true faith, "repented to Allah . . . , and resolved to begin a new life as a true Muslim" (*Rumiyah* 2017a, 46). In this way, *Rumiyah* confirmed that transformation and redemption had been achieved and completed, that "worst pasts" had been turned into "best futures" through the holy practice of devotion and struggle. Previous excesses were forgiven while—or rather, because—criminals could continue with the same violent practices, albeit now purified through the jihadist motive and blessed by IS leaders. This made the caliphate the first terrorist organization to perfect the crime–terror nexus through the offer of radical redemption for its own recruits and for propaganda purposes. With that offer, its validation and legitimation through *Rumiyah*, and obituaries like the one for Abroujui just described, the caliphate attracted countless young people whose lives had become bogged down in petty crime and drugs and who hankered after concrete, practical purification and meaning, through *hijra* and the struggle.

Penance Paid and Reward Received

Because it is difficult to conduct interviews with active IS fighters and fugitive criminals, and because the literature sometimes provides an exemplary case, we will briefly examine the way in which Abderozzak Benarabe lost his belief in radical redemption. His story is a classic example of the crime–terror nexus, which in his case worked in two directions: Benarabe was a criminal, became a terrorist, and ultimately went back to being his old criminal self (see also Basra et al. 2016, 23–5).

In August 2012, Benarabe—a Danish-Moroccan born in 1994—flew from Copenhagen to Istanbul with the intention of crossing the border from Turkey into Syria and joining the jihad against the Syrian government. Benarabe had almost no prior knowledge of Islam and knew very little about the complex conflict in Syria, but he was hoping to escape his criminal past. "I hope that Allah can forgive us for what we have done," said Benarabe in an interview, "because I did many bad things back at home" (Khaja 2014). Benarabe was better known in Copenhagen as "Big A," a feared gangster and leader of the criminal organization Blågårds Plads, named after the square where he and his fellow gangsters gathered. He had already spent eleven years in prison, convicted of shootings, mutilation, drug dealing, and extortion.

Benarabe's "cognitive opening"[7] presented itself when he heard that his brother had been diagnosed with cancer. "I said to God, 'If you make him healthy, then I'll get my act together.'" A promise to Allah is not easily broken. So, when his brother's tumors proved not to be malignant, he turned his back on his criminal life, stopped smoking marijuana, and started attending the mosque. But that was not radical enough for him: several months later, he joined Ahrar al-Sham and left for Syria. "Maybe I'm gonna die there," he told an interviewer. "So what?" But because he had killed people, he was afraid that meeting Allah would be "a big problem." Given all the bad things he had done, praying was not enough. In Syria, he hoped to do more—he wanted to make a difference, to do penance, and to purify himself from all his sins in the eyes of Allah.

At the frontline near Daraya, a bulwark of the Free Syrian Army, Benarabe proved well able to defend himself. Unlike many other foreign fighters, he knew straight off how to use different kinds of weapons. At the same time, it was a horrific experience. In houses and cellars, his troops regularly encountered the bodies of civilians summarily executed by Assad's troops (*NRC Handelsblad* 2012; *Het Parool* 2012). During his first day of fighting, one of his comrades was blown up by a mortar grenade, losing "half his head. That was really bad to see" (Khaja 2014). Benarabe led several attacks, volunteering to do so himself. His comrades hoped that he would stay and lead their unit. But after four days, his equipment was destroyed, and he returned to the camp.

Benarabe had initially planned to buy a house in Syria and use his money to maintain and equip his comrades. But his commander ordered him to return to Copenhagen to collect more money and supplies and smuggle them into Syria. He flew back, furious. With a little under 60,000 euros in donations and "taxes" paid by local drug dealers, he bought three minivans, which he loaded up with medical supplies and high-tech fighting equipment, including night vision goggles, bulletproof vests, and heat sensors. The material eventually reached his troops, but Benarabe had had enough of fighting.

---

[7] A cognitive opening is "the moment when an individual who faces discrimination, socioeconomic crisis, and political repression is trying to understand life events and suddenly his previously accepted beliefs are shaking and he becomes vulnerable and receptive to the new way of thinking—radicalized ideology" (Trip et al. 2019, 2).

When his gang members in Copenhagen asked him to come back and lead his old organization in a fight against rival groups, he could not refuse. He was still religious, he said, but his duty lay in Copenhagen: "These are my brothers, the people I grew up with, and when they need me I must do whatever I can for them" (Khaja 2014).

What is striking about this account is the pact that Benarabe made with Allah. As thanks for his brother's healing and as penance for his own past of manslaughter and murder, he promised to make a difference by taking part in a holy struggle, in this case in Syria. In that struggle, he could continue to use his talents, such as his knowledge of weapons and smuggling money. He did not need to renounce his old behavior—he could legitimate and purify it in the fight against Assad. As a criminal with a guilty conscience, he found redemption on the battlefield in Daraya. On the other hand, he did not stay there for very long. His pact did not extend to sacrificing his life. After doing his penance, Benarabe felt released from his obligation. He had earned his points on the battlefield and with his large-scale smuggling operation; he felt he could now return to Copenhagen. And he had a new narrative to legitimate his criminal activities: in Copenhagen he could also help his brothers and fit his activities into his new-found piety. That his assistance took the form of leading a criminal organization was apparently not a problem; he had, after all, been redeemed. The transformation from radical redemption through the jihad to a slightly less radical redemption as a gang leader was, in his mind, complete. With the support of his brothers-in-arms and his brother's cure, he felt that his choice had been validated and legitimated by both Allah and his own community.

I Have Saved the Netherlands

A striking example of perceived fulfilled redemption can be seen in the case of Pakistani Jibran*, who was arrested in August 2018 and sentenced to ten years' imprisonment for planning an attack on populist and anti-Islam Dutch politician Geert Wilders. Despite all the evidence to the contrary, Jibran denied intending to attack Wilders, saying he wished only to issue a warning. He believed that his actions were successful and that he "saved the Netherlands."

Jibran was born in Pakistan in 1992 in very needy circumstances. He had a younger brother, and his father died when Jibran was 17. Jibran hardly had any schooling. He told me he had completed primary school and had continued to attend secondary school for nearly four years, but that was all. Two years later, he left Pakistan to try his luck somewhere else. He ended up in Italy and had some success as a pizza baker. "Only after I arrived in Italy did I start thinking more about religion," he said. "I was brought up as a Muslim, but in Pakistan we never went to the mosque. In Italy, I was working for an Islamic pizza baker and wanted to know all about what was *haram* and *halal*. There was no pizza with salami."[8] He quickly discovered the value of social media for communicating with his mother and little brother and also for making film clips of his pizzas. He soon had quite a large number of followers. "I enjoyed my life in Italy. I smoked joints and cigarettes; I could drink and do what I wanted. None of that was allowed in Pakistan. Earlier, as a child, I had seen films about cities in Europe; now I could go to them myself. I started making film clips of those visits and put them on the Internet. And I gathered even more followers."

Jibran traveled around, visiting sixteen different countries, and worked at twenty different pizza bakers around Europe. By now, he was following the video channel of Indian doctor Zakir Naik, who was making waves as a strict Salafist preacher and whose lectures had been forbidden in various countries because they were considered to encourage terrorism and incite hatred. Naik was a fervent supporter of conspiracy theories. According to him, 9/11 was an "inside job," and the mainstream media were Islamophobic. Although Naik condemned IS for killing "innocent people," in some of his lectures he expressed approval of suicide attacks in certain situations. "Thanks to Dr. Zakir, I understood my faith better," Jibran told me. "He spoke in my own language [Urdu]. I didn't learn to speak English until recently, here in Europe. Back then, my English wasn't very good."

In 2018, he met a friend in Paris, an old classmate from Pakistan. "He told me about Geert Wilders, and about his sacrilegious cartoon competition." In June 2018, Wilders offered a prize of 10,000 dollars for the best cartoon of the prophet Muhammad. The announcement led, especially in Pakistan, to large demonstrations, death threats to Wilders, and threats of attacks in the Netherlands (*NOS nieuws* 2018; Inayat 2018; see also NCTV 2020, 13). Affected by the draconian punishments for blasphemy in Pakistan, and the strong Islamization in the country since the 1980s in an orthodox sense,

---

[8] Interview with Jibran*, February 5, 2020, PI/TDU.

Jibran was immediately enraged (see, e.g., EFSAS 2020). He saw it as a social media challenge.

> I saw that everyone was talking about it. On the Internet, all kinds of Islamic scholars were discussing the competition. But no one did anything, while it is our responsibility as Muslims, and, therefore, my responsibility too. If you are 100 percent Muslim, you have no choice. Wilders had to understand that. And I'm sure he did. He knows so much. I had no problem at all with Wilders, but I did with his blasphemous plan. If someone showed no respect for Jesus, I would say something about it. If someone shows no respect for the Prophet, I have to say something about it. I'm not a terrorist; I wasn't a member of a terrorist organization. But it was my duty to do something. And I could do something because, thanks to all my followers on social media, I had some influence. What's more, I'd been hanging around too long in Europe, had smoked too much weed, and had not lived a sufficiently pure life. I learned that from Dr. Zakir.

That summer, Jibran traveled to the Netherlands. "The protests in Pakistan hadn't helped," he said. "The protests on Facebook hadn't helped. The protests at the Dutch embassy hadn't helped. So I thought I had to do something. After all, I wasn't that far away. It was my duty to be a good Muslim, for the full 100 percent—to be pure." To Jibran, *purity* meant in the first place the right religious praxis, as presented to him by radical preachers on the Internet. By becoming more radical and performing a spectacular act, Jibran hoped not only to prove his purity and earn points for the afterlife but also to gather more followers and likes for his film clips. For him, worldly fame and heavenly rewards went hand in hand.

Jibran had no friends or acquaintances in the Netherlands, but survived that summer on the street. "Through my social media pages, I tried to recruit supporters, people who wanted to demonstrate with me, or who could give me money to organize protests. I prayed five times a day; I had no friends, nothing. So that's why I decided to make that video, to collect money and to wake people up." In the video that Jibran posted on social media, he called on people to send Wilders, "that dog, that uncivilized one, to hell." According to the judge, Jibran made it clear in chats with friends that he was willing to kill Wilders. He just needed more money.

In August, Jibran was arrested at The Hague Central Station. The day before, he had placed a film clip on his Facebook site announcing an attack on

Wilders or the Dutch parliament. The video was watched 153,000 times and shared 14,000 times (*Hart van Nederland* 2019). On the basis of this video and his chats, he was sentenced to ten years in prison. According to Jibran and his defense lawyer, it was never his intention to kill Wilders—the video was just a rash attempt to provoke people into following him and providing money for demonstrations in the Netherlands. Jibran showed no remorse for his actions. On the contrary, he felt that they had been successful and said, "I have saved this country."

> I didn't come here to take revenge. I am not a jihadist. I came here to warn people, to save them from awful blasphemy. And I did that. 153,000 people watched my film clip; 14,000 shared it. And Wilders canceled the competition and withdrew the prize! I didn't even have to use violence. I didn't need to embrace the black flag [of IS]. Allah knows what he is doing. You see in prison what happens to people who do not respect Allah and the Prophet. Allah does not suddenly appear from behind the clouds to punish them, but they will disappear. Where are they now? What is the reward for people who do not believe? I was proud when the judge sentenced me, because I did it for God. Perhaps someone will say in 100 years' time: "He saved this country." Many of my brothers tried to stop Wilders. I did it.

Jibran was satisfied with what he had achieved. He did not appeal against his sentence. The only thing that made him uneasy was the pressure from his fellow detainees to embrace the black flag: "They want me to join IS. Otherwise, I'm not a real Muslim. I don't want to do that. I'm a Pakistani. I've done my duty. I am already a good Muslim. I have no interest in IS, and I'm not a jihadist. Hopefully, I can do my time here in peace."[9]

Denial and Disappointment

In Denial

My interview with Jibran was an exception in that he readily admitted he had threatened Wilders and wanted to stop the cartoon competition (although he denied intending to kill the politician). By contrast, almost all the other

---

[9] Interview with Jibran*, February 5, 2020, PI/TDU.

detainees I interviewed tried to convince me that they were innocent of the crimes for which they had been imprisoned. What they wanted above all was to give their own account of what they saw as their unjustified detention and treatment by the police and the legal authorities. It is important to note here that detained Islamists and jihadists proclaiming their own innocence is a narrative propagated by jihadist groups worldwide. Organizations like Behind Bars—and, to a lesser extent, Facebook groups like Project A—attempt to dismiss the arrest and conviction of jihadists as anti-Muslim discrimination. The insistence on their own innocence as proof of repressive and discriminatory governments, especially in the West, can thus be an intentional component of a strategy well known among jihadist detainees around the world. In the Netherlands, the jihadist movement is currently very fragmented, and organizations of sympathizers such as Behind Bars, set up in 2011 to draw attention to Muslim detainees, are no longer active in the country. Yet, in its regular review of the terrorist threat in the Netherlands published in May 2020, the NCTV warned of "network forming" among jihadist detainees, suggesting they share and coordinate their accounts, including those of their detention.[10]

Nevertheless, it was sometimes difficult for me to see some of the detainees as terrorists as such. Many had been arrested and convicted for preparing attacks or intending to leave and take part in the armed struggle. In other words, they had not yet been involved in actual attacks or violent acts. This in no way detracts from the justness of their convictions, but whether suspected terrorists have committed violence and killed or wounded others, or have progressed no further than activity on the Internet, provocation, and possession of arms, does have a substantial effect on their narratives of radical redemption and the associated gratification and validation. Possession of arms is, of course, a criminal offense, but of a different order than wounding and killing people. And even if someone is arrested for actually committing acts of violence, it makes a difference whether those acts were committed in the context of war, in Syria or Afghanistan, or were prepared or carried out in a country that is not at war and where self-defense and widespread radicalization of public life are not the order of the day.

Thus, with his film clips and a machine gun in his storeroom, Amin* committed a different kind of crime than Gökmen Tanis, who actually committed murder. It made their forms of devotion and struggle—and the way

[10] See NCTV (2020, 6, 8–9); background discussion with an AIVD analyst, July 6, 2020.

they looked back on their acts of radical redemption—substantially different. Perpetrators with blood on their hands had more to lose, had invested much more, and consequently clung more tightly to the idea of reward and fulfilled redemption. Gökmen, for instance, continued to terrorize the families of his victims even in the courtroom by showing his contempt for them in every way he could. Convicted terrorists Amin, Noureddine*, and Anwar* were an exception in this regard: they had not committed an attack or done some other heroic deed, they had not given their lives for Allah or for their Muslim brothers in Syria, but they were nevertheless now behind bars for several years.

The bitter mix of wrong choices, failed plans, and long convictions made it difficult for the detainees to talk about their original intentions. It took some time to get them to return to their radical ideas and beliefs and to reflect on their radical practices, which they could not fully disclaim. As one prison official sighed: "Most detainees still lay the blame outside themselves, point to others, and try to trivialize the IS material they had on their computers and propagated, or the weapons they had in their possession."[11] In Dan McAdams's terms, it cost considerable mental energy to get the detainees to reflect on the transition from a narrative of redemption to one of contamination or deception.

That initial denial and difficulty with or lack of explicit reflection was also related to the fact that, in a number of cases, the interviewees were still waiting for their appeals to be heard and were therefore unable to speak completely freely. For those whose legal procedures were over and who appeared to have completed the process of deradicalization and disengagement, and even to have abandoned their terrorist past, it was particularly painful to be confronted with their earlier radical statements and activities.

The initial attitude of denial is understandable in light of the theological and psychological notion of radical redemption. These terrorists had to justify to themselves their decision to jeopardize their lives, the welfare of their families, and their future for something so impalpable as redemption, bonus points, or purification, when the hoped-for reward proved to be a mirage or even a fiasco. Denial was for them the least stressful way of dealing with the deception.

Haroun*, who fought with Ahrar al-Sham between 2011 and 2013, revealed a little of that bitter awareness. He indicated he might be willing to

---

[11] Interview with one of the PI/TDU leaders, October 30, 2019.

talk about his radicalization and departure for Syria, but that it was now "so painful that it gave him traumas" and that he had to take medication to keep his depressions and fears under control. He told me he had gone to Syria to help liberate repressed Muslims. But the dream had turned into a nightmare. For him personally, it was "not about revenge but about redemption"—of others and of himself. Still, his return from Syria had been the best decision of his life:

> I couldn't stand it there. It was too difficult. And it didn't work, either. We achieved nothing against Assad's troops. And the opposition troops started fighting amongst themselves. Those who could use weapons could make something of their lives there, but I couldn't. I couldn't do anything at all. I don't want to think back on that time and don't want to talk about it anymore.[12]

And yet, as a result of that "best decision," he was now in prison and could not see or help his wife and child.

Clearly, Haroun was aware not only of personal failings (he had no idea how to use weapons) and of organizational and strategic failings (the opposition troops achieved nothing against Assad's army) but also of psychological failings: he had made the wrong choice and was in prison for acts motivated by radical beliefs he no longer held. According to the prison staff, thanks to that awareness Haroun gradually opened himself up to reflection, discussion, and treatment.

Amin's reflections on the fighting in Syria and Iraq, on the other hand, continued to be completely defined by bitterness. His life story stagnated, at least for the time being, in disillusion and failure. "In the end, it was all for nothing," he told me. The collections, donations, and attempts to support the struggle "all led to nothing. All the stuff ended up with Assad and his shit family." Amin had largely supported the struggle digitally by distributing IS propaganda film clips, and he was also convicted for possessing a machine gun.

> I will never abandon my faith, not even if I am sentenced to 180 years. But those videos—I'll never watch them again. It was all a failure, the whole war. I no longer believe in all those things you say to make yourself feel

---

[12] Interview with Haroun*, January 16, 2020, PI/TDU.

better. And the Internet can be wound up, as far as I'm concerned. My children are only allowed to watch Polish and Russian cartoons. It was all a deception. I don't want any deep discussion any more. I'm going to do my time, and then I'll see what happens. It could always be worse."[13]

No Premier League After All

The Iranian-Dutch detainee Farhad*, whom we encountered in chapter 5, made it easier for himself, in intellectual terms. Shortly after he was arrested in 2016 and sent to prison, the caliphate started to lose ground. By the end of 2017, it was clear that IS was not winning the final battle he had dreamed of—in fact, it was not even fighting that battle. "IS was better than all the others. They beat Syria and America. I thought that was wonderful. But they weren't the real fighters, that caliphate. That was wrong. Because they lost. Everything is lost."[14] This implied that Baghdadi could not be the caliph, and that the struggle in Syria and Iraq was not the final battle.

"With hindsight," Farhad said, "I was lucky to have been captured in time. I never went there. Now I am free, and I can go the mosque again and build up a normal life." That did not mean that Farhad had abandoned all his old ideas: "Baghdadi may not have been the caliph, but he was an ideal leader. He was at least not corrupt. And violence is permitted, as long as it is defensive violence, against countries that attack you. Look at that so-called coalition. What did that achieve? It was better in North Africa and the Middle East when Muammar Gaddafi and Saddam Hussein were still in power. Now there is just more misery." The difference with his attitude in 2016, however, was that he no longer linked these geopolitical beliefs and frustrations to a personal quest for redemption and his own participation in the holy struggle. "There is nothing for me there. I just want to build up a good life and, preferably, to stay in the Netherlands."[15]

Thus, Farhad's faith and, perhaps, also his belief in redemption were not destroyed by the fall of the caliphate. But he did lose faith in the specific redemption that IS offered him and others. So, for this football fan, there was to be no Premier League after all.

---

[13] Interview with Amin*, October 30, 2019, PI/TDU.
[14] Interview with Farhad*, December 5, 2019, Utrecht.
[15] Interview with Farhad*, December 5, 2019, Utrecht.

Refutation and Reappraisal

Redemption Frustrated

The redemption narratives described in this book could take on mythical proportions. For my interviewees, these narratives were fueled by all kinds of religious experiences: they could take the form of dreams and miracles, or their experience of reality in Afghanistan, Syria, and Iraq could seem to tie in with what prophets and religious texts said about the End of Days and the final battle. In the same way, the redemption narratives could be negated: through dreams of their hometown in the Netherlands (as a kind of *heimwee*), through conversations with other believers, and through actual events such as defeats, as well as through an understanding that taking action to achieve radical redemption could be transformed into less radical forms of engagement. Such a refutation and transformation, however, required a whole arsenal of resources, people, and experiences; none of the convicted terrorists I interviewed could achieve that transformation on their own. Roughly speaking, belief in radical redemption among radicalizing young people or already active terrorists could be undermined in three ways: through their constituency, through history, or through their own core network. Of course, deradicalization and counterterrorism policy also played an important role: the extradition of Syrian departees back to the Netherlands, detention and interrogation, and organized confrontations with victims or family members can really undermine belief in radical redemption.

To understand the process of deradicalization and abandonment of ideals, we need to look more closely at the concept of *constituency*.[16] To function effectively, a radical redemption narrative relies on two forms of dynamic, one individual and one collective. The individual component comprises belief, a personal radicalization process, and the embracing of a personal redemption praxis. The collective element concerns the recognition and acknowledgment of the individual choice for and devotion to radical redemption by a constituency. IS fighters felt supported and validated by the praise

---

[16] This concept is often used in radicalization and terrorism literature to describe the concentric circles of potential recruits, sympathizers, and supporters of "real"—that is to say, wanted or convicted—terrorists. For perpetrators, the logistical, tactical, and also idealistic support of such a constituency is crucial in sustaining their convictions and for their own perception of their successes and failures. For the importance of constituency and sympathy with respect to terrorism, see also Pekelder (2012).

and encouragement that reached them through their glossy magazines *Dabiq* and, later, *Rumiyah*, by the widely propagated obituaries and digital shrines for their fallen comrades, and by the help, support, and admiration they received from groups back home in the West, such as Straat Dawah, Sharia4Belgium, and Behind Bars.

If the perceived or projected constituency does not recognize the redemption narrative, the perpetrators have a problem. If a constituency rejects the radical narrative and does not recognize the praxis, issues fatwas against this praxis and distances itself from it publicly, or even condemns certain perpetrators and acts, the legitimizing element of that narrative and praxis dissipates. The orthopraxis of radical redemption is then no longer sanctioned as the right form of practice, which can lead to doubt and changes of mind; in any case, it loses its appeal for potential recruits. The perceived community that supports an individual's radical identity falls away, making that identity unstable. Chapter 3, for example, described how the death of Bobby Sands by starvation was recognized and "adopted" by his Catholic constituency and led to an increase in support for the IRA. Holger Meins, on the other hand, achieved little with his "sacralized hunger strike." Many Germans recognized in the images of Meins's emaciated body a historical memory of concentration camp victims, which alienated them rather than encouraging them to embrace the RAF's fight against the "new fascism" of the Federal Republic.

Much has been written about attempts to refute the narratives of terrorist organizations by using, for example, counternarratives. From these examples, we know that effective counternarratives have to come from within the movement itself if they are to have any chance of success (see, e.g., Van Eerten et al. 2017, 151). It can have an effect if radical activists announce that they are going to pursue change with methods other than violence, as in the latter days of the FARC and the IRA, when political leaders proclaimed they would lay down their weapons and were prepared to enter into negotiations. For many Muslims, King Mohammed VI of Morocco is an example of an effective propagator of counternarratives: he said that anyone who joins IS or takes part in the armed jihad shall receive no redemption but will "end up in hell." The king's words, however, will have no impact on veteran jihadists—they will see such statements as proof of his apostasy.

Furthermore, convicted terrorists can lose their belief in radical redemption and its associated praxis as a result of concrete, spontaneous events in global history. The anti-capitalist narrative of the RAF and related left-wing, revolutionary terrorist organizations, for example, lost its persuasive power after the fall of the Berlin Wall. The fear they propagated, the force of their narrative, and their practice of murdering representatives of the "imperialist" and "neofascist" capitalist establishment were undermined by the end of "real, existing socialism." The implosion of the Soviet Union and communism as a world system put an end to the socialist myth of revolution and insurrection, thus debunking the myth of radical, revolutionary redemption. Financial sponsors and facilitators disappeared, such as the Stasi, which for many years provided RAF members with safe houses in communist East Germany. The anti-capitalist narrative was exhausted, not only as an attractive positive narrative of seduction but also as a terrifying dystopia.

The fall of the caliphate at the end of 2017 undermined the eschatological persuasive power of IS, as Farhad's story shows. The jihad state proved not to be the ideal society where you could live a pure, safe, and peaceful life as a Muslim with your wife and children. IS also proved far from invincible militarily, which reduced fears in the West of an advancing desert ideology with its associated regime of terror and, at the same time, discredited the conqueror's narrative of IS. This did nothing, however, to weaken the appeal of the spiritual, individual side of the radical redemption narrative for individuals wishing to upgrade their lives as "losers." But the practical appeal of being able to take part in a real battle in Syria and Iraq in any case disappeared after 2018. This development made a real impression on several interviewees and caused them to change their views.

Finally, if members of a terrorist network heard doubts or criticisms from their own leaders or close circle of comrades and officers, this could also have a deep impact. Examples of such impact have already been described earlier. If, as was often the case in Syria and Iraq, the envisaged final battle erupted into infighting between rival factions, this caused deep disappointment and led various departees to abandon the struggle. For them, the chaos of the internal strife was incompatible with their belief that they were fighting for a good and pure cause. When Osama bin Laden himself said that Al-Zarqawi and Al Qaeda in Iraq—a precursor to IS—had lost their way and were guilty of injustices against innocent Muslims, the effect was shattering. It did not mean that jihadists suddenly became nonviolent and peace-loving citizens, but it did mark the start of a process of reappraisal and reorientation in terms of their role and duty.

If well supervised and embedded in deradicalization and reintegration programs, such a process could even lead to reappraisal of their religious convictions and of redemption itself. In what follows, we examine these latter forms of withdrawal and reappraisal in greater detail: internal criticism, reorientation regarding the necessity of jihad and the nature of radical redemption, and, eventually, transformation to other forms of engagement.

Delegitimized Redemption—the Counternarrative of bin Laden

It is striking that during our interviews, almost all of the convicted Indonesian terrorists referred to statements by some of their leaders who, after the attacks on Bali or with the advent of IS, spoke out against attacks on innocent Muslims.

Farihin, born in 1996, is an Afghanistan veteran who trained terrorists on Java and Sulawesi. He was convicted in 2000. Although he was a member of the same network as the perpetrators of the attacks on Bali, and his own brother was involved in the attack on the Philippine embassy, after 2002, Farihin gradually saw the error of his ways. "When I was in prison," he told me, "I heard how the older generation of Jemaah Islamiyah leaders condemned the attacks on Bali. Innocent Muslims had been killed in the attacks, innocent civilians. That is not permitted." In his eyes, Indonesia was a country where Muslims should be able to lead good lives, where they could try to introduce the sharia and take advantage of the opportunities democracy offered them to do so. "In a country like that, you shouldn't use violence but do *dawah*," Farihin said. While in prison, he underwent a transformation in his thinking: he started to believe in propagating Islam and the sharia through nonviolent means. He abandoned the notion of radical, violent redemption. "It's about *dawah*, more study, and more education, and not about violence. And certainly not about a caliphate. Allah builds his own *Khilafa*; it's not up to people to do that."[17]

Farihin's statements reflected the course adopted by Jemaah Islamiyah (JI) and Neo-JI (the rebranded JI) in the years from 2002 to 2009: more and more Indonesian Muslims spoke out against terrorist violence, and they even started turning in radical JI members to the police. The question was—and still remains—whether JI's new, nonviolent course was genuine or merely a temporary tactical choice while the group conducted clandestine

---

[17] Interview with Farihin, February 25, 2020, Jakarta.

preparations for armed conflict in the future (Satria 2019). According to Farihin, violent radical redemption was in any case no longer an option in 2020, and people first had to be brought to the pure faith through *dawah*.

"Ramli" came to the same realization. He had been trained by Afghanistan veterans, fought on Ambon and in Central Sulawesi in 2000, and was a member of LSM Kompak, a group affiliated to JI. At first, he was proud that his comrades had committed the attacks on Bali and that so many tourists and Western soldiers had been killed. But when he heard that the victims had included Muslims, he began to have his doubts. "I was still active in LSM Kompak, and in 2005, I was given the order to kill a brother who had converted to a more liberal and nonviolent movement within JI. But I couldn't do it. The man was after all still a Muslim and could return to the right path."[18] Ramli's views on violence continued to be radical, but he started to wonder more and more whether it was the right way to change people's ideas. And there was another, more mundane reason for his change of heart: "I was married by then, and saw that my work for LSM Kompak was going nowhere. I wasn't making a career, wasn't achieving anything, but had to take care of my family. In prison, I had time to think and talk to others. I came to the conclusion that it was wrong to be too quick in condemning people as infidels, to be too keen to do *takfir*."[19]

The final step that made Ramli turn his back on violent jihad for good came about in 2013 when, after serving his sentence for terrorism, he was arrested for arms dealing.[20] According to Ramli, this was when he really came to his senses: "After [bin Laden's] death, all kinds of letters and statements from him were made known through the regular media. We were able to follow that and read everything in great detail." Partly due to the efforts of Solahudin, the Indonesian specialist in terrorism and radicalization, Indonesian penitentiaries devoted considerable attention to the counternarratives emerging from the jihadist community itself. Detainees were even given the opportunity to read the Abbottabad files, which were released on the Internet. For Ramli, this was the last nudge he needed.

---

[18] Interview with "Ramli," February 26, 2020, Jakarta.
[19] Declaring a pious Muslim *kafir*, an infidel; this is a controversial practice, with potentially serious consequences for the suspected infidel.
[20] Ramli was convicted for arms dealing; he himself claimed that he did not know the weapons were to be used for terrorist purposes. Information from an expert of the Indonesian National Counter Terrorism Agency (BNPT).

Bin Laden himself had expressed his reservations about jihadists who condemned everyone as *takfir* too quickly and too radically, striking out wildly in all directions. When Al Qaeda in Iraq and, later, IS in 2013/2014 committed all that slaughter, that went too far for us. Bin Laden had already warned against it. That was not the way to do *dawah* and mobilize Muslims. If America were to launch a crusade against Indonesia and attack our country, yes, then you can fight back and kill infidels, or unleash a jihad against Washington. But Indonesia is a country at peace. There is no war here. I am still a Muslim [of Salafist persuasion], but now I see my work differently.

When Ramli left prison in 2016, he and his wife started working to propagate Islam peacefully. "I am now a bringer of peace. I try to warn young people about radicalization. I tell them what wrong choices I made myself." In 2017, Indonesian IS sympathizers tried to kill him, but the attempt failed. "I know that, to the jihadists, I am a traitor, but that's just the way it is. I now work with an NGO called Circle of Peace, which cooperates on deradicalization programs. That means I can do something for a good cause after all."[21]

The Indonesian deradicalization programs, as set up in the terrorism department in Cipinang (Java), for example, made good use of the Abbottabad files after 2011. Sofyan Tsauri and Kurnia Widodo were also given the opportunity to read the bin Laden letters that researchers had put on the Internet and told me that they, too, had been influenced by them:

> We could easily access the Internet in prison, as we had smuggled laptops into our cells. But we were allowed to read the letters openly. That was a shock for us: Osama bin Laden denouncing needless bloodshed. There was—and is—thus no redemption in shedding innocent blood. We didn't feel guilty for a long time, as our beliefs were wrapped up with religion. Now, we learned and discovered that that wrapping was foolishness. As Ibn Rusdi said, you can commit any kind of foolishness as long as you wrap it in religion. And that's what we did. And now, we had to strip away that wrapping, piece by piece, abandon the foolishness, and retain the pure core. And being in prison gave us the time and opportunity to do that.[22]

---

[21] Interview with "Ramli," February 26, 2020; interview with a BNPT official, February 27, 2020, Jakarta; Arnaz (2013).

[22] Interview with Sofyan Tsauri, February 24, 2020, Jakarta.

What helped strengthen the understanding that it is wrong to spill the blood of innocent Muslims was that, in 2013 and 2014, IS showed what such killings could lead to. Kurnia Widodo, who was imprisoned in 2010, emphasized that the emergence of IS strongly divided opinions.

> I discovered in prison, by talking to other detainees and with prison guards, how many different opinions there actually were. Everyone quoted their own *ustad* [scholar]. So, who was right? Before, I had followed my leaders blindly, wishing to follow those with the most radical—that is, pure— practices. But now, I discovered that there were convicted terrorists who were much milder in their ideas than the young IS sympathizers. Whether you were for or against IS became a real source of division between the detainees.
>
> We followed everything in the news and talked about it continually, also with the guards. Most of us came to the conclusion that IS was going too far. After all, bin Laden had also said that. It even made the people from Noordin Top [who was behind the Bali attacks] less radical. You can't just declare everyone *takfir*, or behead people. Take our guards. They were Muslims, too, but they were very moderate and liberal, and very friendly toward us. They weren't infidels, were they? And that got us all thinking—step by step, not all at once. Once, a man called Feby, a survivor of the attack on the JW Marriott Hotel, came to visit us in prison. He told us about his pain and sorrow. That made an impression on us. I offered him my apologies, even though I wasn't involved in the attack. Others did the same.[23]

Many jihadists began to feel guilty when they realized that innocent Muslims had been killed; sometimes, they were able to go further and extend those feelings of guilt and compassion to non-Muslim victims. But this remains a sensitive and difficult issue in Indonesia, and elsewhere.

After meeting and talking to people from the NGOs Search for Common Ground (SFCG) and Alliance for a Peaceful Indonesia (AIDA),[24] Kurnia abandoned his jihadist beliefs. When he was released from detention in 2017, he joined AIDA to tell his story to young people and give lectures to warn them of the dangers of an overly rigid orthopraxis and violent jihad.[25]

---

[23] Interview with Kurnia Widodo, February 25, 2020, Jakarta.
[24] AIDA is led by Dutch businessman Max Boon, who survived the attack on the JW Marriott Hotel in 2009.
[25] Interviews with Max Boon and Solahudin, February 24 and 26, 2020, Jakarta. See also the website for AIDA: https://www.aida.or.id.

The Dream of a Boy from The Hague

Fadil* from The Hague, whose story was told in chapter 4, decided at the last minute *not* to join IS. At first, he wanted to. The caliphate offered him a way of compensating for his very personal, physical shortcomings and failures, as well as a way to do something for a good cause, to participate in the fight against injustice. Fortunately he allowed himself, just in time, to be persuaded by an older and wiser Islamic man to return home. We could say that someone from Fadil's own constituency—the *ummah* in the Middle East and Asia that he perceived as oppressed—had lifted the scales from his eyes and shown him that his choice for "devotion and struggle" was foolishness and would bring him no redemption.

As described in the previous chapter, Fadil was fully convinced he could do something meaningful in Syria or Iraq and that joining IS would offer him redemption from his failed life.

> I'd had testicular cancer and had been treated, but I no longer felt like a man. With its films on Facebook and Paltalk, Daesh [IS] showed me that there was plenty of work for me to do in the caliphate. I became convinced that the stories were true, that the caliphate was real. Islam was being fought with bullets, with the pen, and with lies; no one could deny that. I saw how people from all over the world were going there—people from Africa, China, America, Australia—to build a new life, just like in the caliphates of old. Life wasn't that bad back then in Al-Andalus, was it? Under the Abbasids, even the donkeys got a pension. It was a genuine modern utopia there, in the caliphate. And I was so sad and dissatisfied about how I was seen here in the Schilderswijk, or rather not seen. I could do everything. I am good with my hands. But everything I tried was a failure. I had already been to Turkey with the aid convoys, but that wasn't enough. I wanted to get away, to fight, to save the children who were suffering there.
>
> To avoid the Dutch authorities, I packed all my stuff and took a train to Germany. I had a contact in the caliphate who was prepared to vouch for me. But once I arrived in Gaziantep in Turkey, he proved to be a swindler. My money was gone, and I had to think of something else. I found another smuggler and deposited some money, but again the papers you needed back then to travel to Syria did not materialize. So I was just waiting there, eating seeds, with a few other guys, Belgians who I'd met through the Internet. I was staying with a 72-year-old Turk, the father of the guy who

was going to smuggle me into Syria. I got talking to the old man, and he opened my eyes. He was sharp with me, saying: "You come from paradise; why do you want to go to hell? What are you doing here? Go and do something good in your own country, where it's possible." Then, I started to have doubts. And the atmosphere by then, in 2015, had turned pretty grim. That man got me thinking, and set me on a different path.[26]

Fadil talked more with his host and the man's family, and he became convinced he should indeed return to the Netherlands.

A couple of days later, I called my younger brother and asked him to send me 150 euros. I gave all my things to my Belgian friend Ashraf: nice shoes, a good waterproof jacket, a laptop. And I bought a lot of food for the family of my guide and his old father. They were very poor. Ashraf did go to Syria with the guide, smuggled across the border via a safe house and through a tunnel. But when he stepped out of the tunnel, he stood on a mine and was blown up. He had been wearing my clothes. I only heard about that later. But that night, I had a dream. I dreamed that I was back in the Netherlands, in the Blauwe Aanslag—you know, that old tax office that is now a squat. You were always welcome there. Hippies used to live there, and there was always a great atmosphere. Left-wingers like that don't see different colors; they were nice to everybody. They always gave me cans of cola. Anyway, I dreamed that I was there, sitting on a bench with a friend and looking across the water to Delft. In my dream, I could even smell the Netherlands. After that, I left. Just in time. When I got to the German border, I saw that my papers would expire two days later. That was Allah's will. I had allowed myself to be misled, led astray. My place was not there, but here. It was here that I had to help people—here, in The Hague.

After arriving back in the Netherlands, Fadil was arrested and extradited to Belgium, where, because he had helped his Belgian friends by giving them money and the names of contacts, he was wanted for organizing and facilitating the armed struggle.

I was detained there for three years, and rightly so. I had seen myself as chosen; that's why I'd gone. But I had been wrong. That dream that Allah

---

[26] Interview with Fadil*, March 6, 2019, The Hague.

sent me, about The Hague—that was where I was supposed to be. I am not a bad person; you can tell a bad person by his actions. I didn't want to kill anyone, not in the Netherlands and not there. At first, I wanted to help Muslims. Now, I want to help everyone, with my cycle shop here in The Hague.[27]

Fadil's story is unique in that, after conversations on the Turkish border with Syria, thanks to the wise words of an old man and, perhaps, a strong dose of stage fright, he came to the conclusion himself that devotion and struggle would not bring the redemption he had initially hoped for. He transformed his ideas of devotion and struggle into nonviolent engagement for his brothers and sisters in the Netherlands and leading a "good life" in the Netherlands. His conversations with his Turkish hosts, the death of his friend, and the dream of home opened his eyes. Fadil was able to turn his quest for meaning into a nonradical variant of social engagement in his own street and city. He rejected IS's offer just in time. Still, he was tried for giving money and clothing to Belgian jihadists and had to spend three years behind bars. His dream of redemption eventually became a dream of a nonviolent life in The Hague running a cycle shop.[28]

Most departees were not as open to good advice as Fadil. The majority of those who left to join the jihad and fight in other countries completed their journey to the caliphate, devoted themselves to the battle, and were killed or ended up in prison or in refugee camps. For this study, I mainly talked with detainees who had come back on their own initiative. That is why each of their stories is an account of deception, confusion, and demonstrable deradicalization and abandonment of former jihadist beliefs. Three of the interviewees were arrested by the Turkish authorities and deported against their will. But the die-hard jihadists, who surely retained their belief that they were fighting for radical redemption, either died or chose to stay there.

---

[27] Interview with Fadil*, March 6, 2019, The Hague.
[28] Unfortunately, Fadil was only able to enjoy his new life for a few years: at the beginning of 2020, his residence permit was revoked, and he was deported to Morocco, where he is now trying to build a new life. Fadil was given an entry ban for ten years. He instructed his lawyer to appeal against the ban and the withdrawal of his residence permit. Letter from Fadil's lawyer to me, April 7, 2020, Rotterdam.

Chaos and Infighting

By far the majority of the detainees I spoke to in the Netherlands, and a number of the Indonesians, lost their faith in radical redemption because of the constant chaos and infighting within their own groups. They did not gradually come to realize that radical redemption was flawed as a motive in itself, nor did they distance themselves from violence immediately and resolutely. Rather, it was the persistent disputes, arguments, and squabbling about logistics, arms, and food or the outbreak of armed conflict between opposition parties that caused them to doubt the value of their actions and ultimately to abandon the struggle and leave the war zone.

In the story of Syarafina Nailah and her family (see chapter 5), it was the bad hygiene and filthy conditions, the internecine arguments in the women's house, and the treachery of people in the caliphate that quite quickly undermined all faith in the redemption that IS could offer. For Syarafina, it did not take much, especially because she had always been somewhat skeptical.[29]

Male fighters needed a little more time to see that the promises of the violent jihad and the dream of the armed struggle were not as pure and holy as they had appeared on YouTube. Consider, for example, the account of Yussuf and Bilal*, friends who arrived in Syria in 2013 and joined Ahrar al-Sham. "I didn't go out there to become a martyr," Bilal told me, "but to help my brothers and sisters. If they suffer, I suffer with them. I wanted to do something for them. If I got killed in the process, so be it, but I hoped not."[30] Bilal had no military experience, so he first had to undergo training to improve his physical fitness and fighting skills. But then, all the chaos started.

> We had almost no weapons, and ammunition was very expensive. I didn't want to do that anyway—I didn't want to fight on the front, but help in some other way, in the media departments or assist with the medical care or organize and accompany aid convoys. But it was all badly organized, and there wasn't enough money. And when there was more money, IS suddenly appeared. That's when everything started to go wrong. The people wanted arms and ammunition to fight Assad themselves, but IS demanded everything for itself. They killed the leaders of our group, who were often from

---

[29] Interview with Syarafina Nailah, February 24, 2020, Jakarta.
[30] Interview with Bilal*, February 5, 2020, PI/TDU.

local communities. They suddenly monopolized all the available resources and had tanks and more weapons. How did they get all those millions of dollars?

That was the start of the chaos. We no longer knew who we should be fighting for, and what we could still do. All kinds of commanders turned out to be corrupt; I saw that with my own eyes. It was all about money and power, as usual. Islamic rhetoric was misused to achieve that. By then, I was married, in Syria, and had a small child. So in 2015, I left the front. I'd had enough.

As we saw in chapter 5, Bilal drifted around in Syria for another two years or so. He told me: "I heard and saw all kinds of things there: how corrupt people were everywhere, how territory was conquered and then sold back to the government. Opposition leaders made deals with Assad's troops that a certain area could be conquered, down to the exact longitude and latitude, in exchange for money and influence. Common Syrians were the victims. And I had been naive. What was I still doing there?"

In 2018, disillusioned and bitter, Bilal succeeded in smuggling first his family and then himself into Turkey. "I haven't lost my true faith. It is not Islam that was behind all this but foreign governments, Russia, America, and Assad who corrupted everything. It is an illusion to think that we can still accomplish anything there. One day, Assad will have to listen to his people. But when will that be? I don't know. It's no longer my problem."[31]

Ahmed, from Delft, was one of the few interviewees who still believed, even in detention, that the path of devotion and struggle is the right one and leads to radical redemption. His only regret was that, being in detention, he could not help oppressed Muslims again elsewhere. "If I could, I would leave again immediately, maybe to Burma. Muslims are being killed there, too. But this time, I would be more careful about how I could help people. I wouldn't join a jihadist group any more. That just doesn't work."[32]

Ahmed, who took a conscious decision to join IS in 2014—"I wanted to be one of the most wanted"—discovered that the life of a jihadist can also be ruled by human limitations and hypocrisy. In the months after he arrived in Syria, he found himself doubting more and more whether he was fighting for a good cause. He had no doubts about the principle of violent jihad to

---

[31] Interview with Bilal*, February 5, 2020, PI/TDU.
[32] Interview with Ahmed*, February 5, 2020, PI/TDU.

combat injustice and repression, but he did start to ask himself whether the caliphate was functioning as it should.

> I'm not going to say that I regret it or that I found it all so terrible. That's not how I am. But it was strange to be fighting for those people in Syria and Iraq, while the Muslims there were doing everything they could to get away. So, I was fighting their war for them, while they were arguing among themselves. IS was at loggerheads with other groups. People were undermining each other. And some fighters even asked me how they could best flee to the Netherlands. I was there for their struggle. It wasn't really bad, but it was pretty strange, like, "Hey, I'm here fighting for you, what are you doing?"

Ahmed and Omar*, who had left for Syria together, decided to join the Syrian opposition troops in 2015 because they thought they were more motivated and better organized. But that proved not to be the case. "We could do a lot less than we had hoped," said Ahmed. "We saved people; I have no regrets about that. But in the end, it achieved very little. And it hurt my parents. My father kept on saying that it wasn't good, and I didn't want to cause him any more sorrow."[33] In 2016, they had had enough and succeeded in returning to Turkey. After being arrested and detained there, they were eventually extradited to the Netherlands.

The rivalry between the different jihadist groups and between the anti-Assad troops led not only to chaos and frequent desertion in Syria and Iraq, but also to a loss of radical faith among confirmed jihadists in the Netherlands. For Abdelkarim*, the division between the many Syrian opposition groups, in combination with the radicalization of his friends, was reason enough to withdraw from the Salafist movement in The Hague.

> At the beginning of 2014, friction developed between IS and Jabhat al-Nusra. IS had not yet declared the caliphate but was actively undermining other groups. That upset me a lot, as I had been preaching the whole time about unity, about solidarity—that all Muslims should help each other and unite in the struggle. I was always in favor of unity. And now, we saw the same thing happening as in Afghanistan: the emergence of internal divisions, even before the enemy had been beaten. And that had consequences here, too. There were guys who had sat together with me

---

[33] Interview with Ahmed*, February 5, 2020, PI/TDU.

in a bar eating a sandwich who were now threatening to kill each other. Everyone in The Hague started taking sides, but I refused to do that. I wasn't particularly for or against IS; I was for all of us, together. But everyone started accusing each other of heresy. And that's when the disputes and arguments started. So, I decided to leave the group, saying, "Listen, guys, I'm not getting involved in all this." For me, the most important thing was to gather knowledge, propagate it, and mobilize all Muslims together. That was no longer possible.[34]

A few months later, Abdelkarim was nonetheless arrested for having tried to recruit jihadists and instigate armed violence. But during his trial, the public prosecutor and the judge concluded that he had not sworn allegiance to IS and was not a supporter of the caliphate. He was convicted for propagating hatred and recruiting jihadists and sentenced to a little under a year in prison. He now lives in the Schilderswijk again and has broken all contact with radical Salafists.

Conclusion

Of all the convicted terrorists I interviewed, only two—Ahmed and Jibran—believed that their desire for redemption had been fulfilled and that they had completed their acts of redemption with success. Their belief was, however, tempered with a degree of half-heartedness. Ahmed had no regrets that "he had wanted to help Muslims," but he felt bad about having "caused his parents too much suffering" and would never do it in that way again. And while Jibran did believe he had personally saved the Netherlands from the planned cartoon competition, he had to admit that it was ultimately Wilders himself who had abandoned the plan. In his statements, Jibran also backpedaled on his overly radical plans, saying he had "never really wanted to kill Wilders, only to warn him."

Few of the convicted terrorists indeed completed their acts of redemption. For most of them, their dreams of the desert soon turned to dust. The quest for meaning through devotion and struggle mainly resulted in disappointment. That was partly due to changes in their own understanding of the situation, but more often it was the consequence of their parents, friends, or

---

[34] Interview with Abdelkarim*, June 11, 2019, The Hague.

communities urging them to come home. Their acts of redemption were not recognized by their own constituency; quite the contrary. Most departees abandoned their quests after being confronted with the chaos and infighting on the battlefield of the holy struggle. There, where their dreams should have been fulfilled—and where they sometimes genuinely experienced something miraculous or holy—human narrow-mindedness, discord, and corruption ruled.

The infighting also led in the Netherlands and in Indonesia to doubts about the purity of the orthopraxis of radical redemption. My interviewees began to experience doubt and tried to leave the battlefield and return home, especially when recognized leaders—such as leaders within Jemaah Islamiyah or Osama bin Laden himself—stated that there was no redemption to be found in shedding innocent blood.

If we go back to the beginning, to the desire for redemption and to radical redemption as the context within which frustration and a sense of deficit were framed, it is understandable that, for almost all the interviewees, this path led to bitterness and deception, and, for some, to a change in their way of thinking. Redemption stands or falls on the belief that the deficit they feel can be removed in the here and now by devotion and struggle, as well as on the idea that they can take control of the situation and, by acting as saviors, earn points or a reward. Another pivotal point is that the people you make the sacrifice for should accept, embrace, and admire you as a savior. When you get to Syria or Iraq and discover that you are a plaything of circumstance, and that the Muslims there are not at all grateful but would rather have tips on how to get to the Netherlands themselves, the heroic image of your act of redemption is severely damaged. And when the group who made that promise and recruited you with expansive prospects and jihadist mirages proves hardly capable of achieving anything, and holy fighters begin to fight mainly among themselves, the image is shattered even further.

If an aspiring jihadist then proves to be afraid, does not dare or is unable to use weapons, and hardly lasts three days when confronted with the traumas of the battlefield, little remains of the belief in the fulfillment of the promise of redemption. The sense of deficit they felt back home then appears less intense, the opportunities for nonviolent engagement greater, the health and well-being of their families more important, and life as a "normal" Muslim in The Hague or Jakarta much more attractive. In that respect, an exaggerated and dramatic desire for redemption generates the conditions for its own negation and disillusionment. Radical saviors often proved, in the eyes of both themselves and others, to be radical losers. It takes a lot of courage, self-awareness, and time to admit that, and many of the interviewees had not, as yet, reached that stage.

So, how did it end? If validation and gratification did not materialize, they were replaced by contamination and denial. Several of my interviewees sat angry and bitter or deadened and disillusioned in their cells. Yet, other interviewees had not given up all hope of a better life than the one they led in prison. They were at least no longer in Syria or Iraq. They had not been killed, and their families, wives, and children were waiting for them. After a long time in detention, much study, and dialogue, some of them—for example, the Indonesian ex-detainees—were clearly considering different forms of engagement: though still based on their religious faith, these forms were now nonviolent. In chapter 8, we will consider the necessary conditions for such a transformation; it calls in any case for a willingness to reflect and for a great deal of support from families, friends, and religious leaders.

7
Radical Redemption Narratives in Other Contexts

By Way of Control

As the foregoing accounts show, radical redemption can function as a compelling narrative that substantially shapes thoughts, feelings, and behavior. But it is by no means a narrative exclusive to terrorists, nor is it always the one shaping the process of radicalization. At a personal level, provocation or a desire for revenge, fame, or recognition are also important factors that may tie in with other, corresponding narratives. At group level, terrorist organizations pursue very strategic, rational, and political aims; for the organization, it is about money, territory, or independence. To place this study of radical redemption as a narrative in perspective, this chapter portrays various convicted terrorists and militants who operated in the same time frame, and sometimes in the same area, but who displayed different ideological leanings and worked with different frames to articulate their actions.

In doing so, I bring together several nonredemptive narratives that are closely related in time and place to the stories of the jihadists described in chapters 4, 5, and 6. This comparative chapter is necessarily cursory and modest in scope. It operates another type of method that involves distance interviewing, using second-person perspectives in addition to first-person perspectives, and working with circumstantial materials. This was partly due to Covid-19 restrictions in Kenya and Nigeria, but I also intended to strengthen my argument by a mixed methods approach. This chapter can be considered a triangulating chapter based on indirect interviews and secondary literature in a different context, providing a focused comparison of a different sort. Rather than aiming to produce a full-fledged comparison, I just want to highlight some interesting cross-comparison points regarding militant fighters and members of terrorist organizations that differ in terms of ideological and organizational background. The contextual differences are not temporal but ideological, geographical, and organizational. Thus, they highlight both the comparable elements and the boundaries of studying radical redemption in other Middle Eastern and African contexts.

First, I portray members of armed militias in Syria who were imprisoned within the same terrorist detention facilities as my other interviewees in the Netherlands. Then, I discuss radicalization processes among members of Boko Haram, who are often seen as being driven primarily by tribal and/or socioeconomic motives. Lastly, I look at the accounts of extreme right-wing terrorists seeking meaning in their lives.

These—albeit cursory—comparisons give us some first insights into the extent to which the radical redemption narrative can be identified among members of armed militias, members of terrorist organizations in a different socioeconomic setting, such as in Africa, and nonjihadist, secular terrorists active during the same period.

Terrorism or Armed Opposition?

Since the outbreak of the civil war in Syria, thousands of Syrian asylum seekers have arrived in Europe, many of whom were followed later by family members. This influx reached a high point in 2015; for example, almost 19,000 asylum seekers came to the Netherlands, amounting to 43 percent of the total number of refugees. In 2019, 5,000 Syrians arrived in the Netherlands (CBS 2016; SER 2020). Among the refugees were asylum seekers who were identified on arrival or later as possible war criminals or members of a terrorist organization. In 2016, the Immigration and Naturalisation Service (IND) investigated 170 people on suspicion of war crimes. Sixty of them were from Syria, and sufficient evidence was found to charge ten of these Syrians.[1] In 2019, ten cases were still underway against Syrian asylum seekers and Syrians with asylum status who were suspected of being involved in war crimes or terrorism in Syria (Rosman 2020).

I spoke to several of these Syrian terrorism suspects, some of whom had in the meantime been convicted while others were still in custody awaiting trial, and was able to inspect their files. Although they were also suspected or convicted terrorists and imprisoned—according to Dutch and international

---

[1] *NOS nieuws* (2016); "Brief van de Staatssecretaris van Veiligheid en Justitie aan de Voorzitter van de Tweede Kamer der Staten-Generaal Den Haag," February 29, 2016, *Handelingen Tweede Kamer 2015–2016*, no. 2152.

law—in the same terrorist detention facility as the jihadists, what stood out was the difference in their backgrounds. The radicalization processes of the Syrians were completely different from those of the jihadists I had spoken with: among the Syrians, there was little sense of a personal or religious deficit. For them, it was more about participating in a collective struggle—which for them felt almost like an obligation—to defend or avenge their own families or communities. The accounts of the Dutch-Moroccan detainees show they were driven primarily by a desire to help, no matter how misplaced and naive such altruism sometimes proved to be. For the Syrians who had joined the armed struggle against Assad, it was often a completely different story. They did not have the opportunity of deciding for themselves—they had been attacked.

I spoke with two Syrian detainees who had come to the Netherlands as refugees but who had been charged and convicted for being members of a terrorist organization or for (alleged) war crimes.[2] Mohammed* was born in Aleppo in 1992. He was a good student and was studying medicine when the war broke out.

> I took part in demonstrations in which I and my fellow students called for freedom and democracy, transparency, and good and fair governance. Would you accept it if your country was ruled by a dictator who made up his own laws and stole all resources and property? And what would you do, as Dutch citizens, if militias invaded the Netherlands? Of course we rebelled. And you in the West supported us financially and with arms. We weren't terrorists; I was just one of the normal people who rose up against a tyrant who had been kept in the saddle by the West. For me, it wasn't about Islam or the sharia, and I was never a member of IS, nor did I ever want to be one. My brother was one of the leaders of the rebels, and it is true that he was a member of a jihadist militia. But I later distanced myself from that; I fled to Turkey and then to the Netherlands.[3]

Mohammed came to the Netherlands via Turkey and Germany: "I had heard that surgeon training here was of high quality, and I wanted to continue my studies." Because his brother was known to be a jihadist leader and a witness stated he had recognized Mohammed in a film clip in which war crimes were

---

[2] One of the cases was still pending appeal; the charges of war crimes were thus still "alleged."
[3] Interview with Mohammed*, February 5, 2020, PI/TDU.

committed, Mohammed was arrested at the asylum seekers center (AZC) where he was staying and charged with humiliating the corpses of enemies. The public prosecutor also suspected that Mohammed, rather than his brother, was a militia commandant.[4]

Like Mohammed, Arslan* was being detained on suspicion of war crimes, a charge he himself denies. Arslan was born in Idlib in about 1980 and served as an officer in the Syrian army for several years. He came to the Netherlands as an asylum seeker around 2014. With his wife and children, he quickly became integrated into the community of the small village where he had been assigned a house. His neighbors knew him as a kind man and a friendly football supporter. They were all astounded when he was arrested as a war criminal in 2018.[5]

Though the facts are still to be ascertained, and the court of appeal has not yet reached a ruling, the accounts of people like Arslan show that they clearly became involved in the war in Syria in a completely different way than the Dutch detainees. In the strongest of terms, Arslan denies being a terrorist and being motivated by the desire to become a martyr or by jihadist-Salafist convictions. He does not speak of a final battle. Nor does the public prosecutor suspect him of these sympathies.

The Syrian detainees want nothing to do with IS or the caliphate. Arslan, for instance, said: "Who determines that, when there is a caliphate? There are no grounds for that at all."[6] The files of Arslan and Mohammed confirm that neither adhered or now adhere to radical jihadist ideas or display orthodox behavior. Arslan smokes, as does Mohammed. They describe themselves, full of conviction, as members of the "armed opposition." Mohammed readily admits he supported Ahrar al-Sham, and as mentioned earlier, Arslan was an officer in the Syrian army before joining the rebels. But Ahrar al-Sham is not deemed a terrorist group by the UN or the EU—though it is by the Dutch Public Prosecution Service—and Arslan claims that he, too, did not join a terrorist group but fought with other armed opposition militias.

Arslan feels he had every right to defend his family and his country and denies all accusations of taking part in executions and war crimes. "Do you have a husband?" he asked me. "Yes? Would he protect you and your family if your house was attacked by soldiers? I was an officer in Assad's army, but

[4] Reports in the media (not specified to protect the anonymity of the interviewee).
[5] Reports in the media.
[6] Interview with Arslan*, January 16, 2020, PI/TDU.

I left when we were given orders to shoot at civilians. I may be a Sunni, but that makes no difference. There were all kinds of people from all kinds of backgrounds in the Free Syrian Army and the opposition. What held us together was the fight against Assad. And now, I am being tried as a terrorist." He wants little to do with strict Salafists. He tells me he admonishes the strict Salafist Dutch-Moroccan detainees if they intimidate other prisoners. If it was up to him, they should be able to watch football again, smoke, and play games in the terrorism unit. At the time of writing, his appeal is still pending.[7]

These portraits show that the radical redemption narrative played almost no role at all as moderator in the radicalization process of the Syrians who took part in the fighting in the country. While the Syrian detainees I talked to did speak of a collective sense of duty, of having to defend their community, that duty was not formulated in religious terms—such as purity, sacrifice, redemption, or sin—but in strictly political and military terms. They participated in the fight because of the obligation to protect the honor of the community against attacks from Assad and to avenge the injustices his troops imposed on their families and neighbors. Neither of them made any mention of earning religious points as a result of their actions or taking part in an apocalyptic final battle. Even though they were Muslims, the mold in which they cast their struggle was not religious redemption but political opposition and armed resistance. Thus, religious convictions are not necessarily the determinant in radicalization processes—the context is of equal importance. Radicalization in the context of a civil war, a context of self-defense, is significantly different from homegrown radicalization in a prosperous and peaceful country.

What was radical was the Syrians' desire to use violence to free themselves from a repressive regime and to defend their own community. It was terrorism, according to Dutch and international authorities, insofar as the Syrian militias aligned themselves with organizations the international community defined as terrorist organizations, such as Jabhat al-Nusra. Legally, that meant that many of these Syrian fighters could be convicted as terrorists—they were identified as members of known terrorist organizations. Yet, in the nontransparent context of the Syrian civil war, the dividing lines between militias, armed opposition, and terrorism were sometimes very thin and to a large extent dependent on the circumstances. What the

---

[7] Interview with Arslan*, January 16, 2020, PI/TDU; interview with prison staff, February 5, 2020, PI/TDU.

Syrian rebels' narrative did not display in any case was a desire to die as a jihadist martyr, to do penance for a life of sin, or to take part in an apocalyptic final battle or in the advent of IS. Theirs was not a narrative of redemption but one of armed resistance against an oppressor.

Ethnic-Tribal Conflict or Religious Terrorism?

Talking with Terrorists in Africa

It is relatively complex to unravel the motives and drivers of jihadist groups in Africa, such as Al-Shabaab in Kenya and Boko Haram in the African Great Lakes region, not least because it is virtually impossible to speak to perpetrators and convicted terrorists in person. The media often automatically portray African jihadists as "driven to terrorism through drought and poverty" (Vos 2020). Most of the recent articles on terrorist conflicts in Africa refer extensively to climate change, desertification, and failing agriculture (Vos 2020). They also point to increasing corruption, inequality within countries like Cameroon, Nigeria, and Kenya, and rising unemployment. While these are all important, possibly even crucial elements, such explanations of underlying causes may be insufficient to account for the success of terrorist organizations in African countries that possess substantial wealth, such as Nigeria. Boko Haram, for example, had initially, in 2009–10, only a few hundred members in the north of Nigeria; later, after severe repression by the army, numbers rose to a few thousand. Nevertheless, millions of Africans living in the same circumstances chose not to resort to armed resistance, and those who did were not always from the poorest and driest areas. There is an urgent need for in-depth studies of the individual radicalization processes of members of Boko Haram and Al-Shabaab militias to explain the success of these organizations.[8] Such explanation will have to examine their message, the deep religious and historical narrative that these sectarian organizations propagate—with the support and ideological input of Arab organizations and countries—and with which they offer a relatively small group of fighters a taste of hell and paradise and create an alternative reality of good and evil.

---

[8] The International Crisis Group (ICG) does valuable work in this respect but experiences difficulties in obtaining exact data. See, for example, ICG (2017).

For this study, I wanted to start by conducting interviews with detainees and formerly detained jihadists now reintegrating in Cameroon and Kenya, to see how their stories correlate with the accounts of jihadist detainees in the Netherlands. But that proved very difficult, for various reasons. First, the war on terror is still in full swing in Mali, Nigeria, Cameroon, and Kenya. The trenches are still there, the fighting continues, and attacks and abductions remain the order of the day. That makes it dangerous for a researcher to visit areas like northern Cameroon. Second, the authorities are very reluctant—or they reject requests outright—to grant researchers access to detention facilities. Many suspected terrorists are being detained without due process. They are locked up in detention centers that are hardly better than concentration camps, with little hope of a fair trial, or they are interrogated by the security services, who try to extract information from them about their comrades or groups. Third, unlike in Indonesia or the Netherlands, there are no accessible reintegration programs for ex-detainees that can provide valuable information to researchers. Although such programs have been announced, no details are available. And lastly, anyone talking with foreign researchers in Africa may be putting themselves at risk: they are quickly seen as hypocrites or traitors.

Importantly, gaining access to information and expressing opinions on motives for engaging in terrorism is complicated, not only for foreign researchers but also for African experts. Islamic organizations and communities that may have information on and access to detainees may be afraid of being stigmatized. Christian (Catholic, Protestant, or evangelical) organizations are afraid they may be attacked or their members may be arrested, while local governments and national or international NGOs are wary of alienating the Islamic population.[9]

Fortunately, I was able to speak with staff members of NGOs and religious organizations, acquaintances of perpetrators, and victims of Boko Haram attacks and surviving family members. Thanks to the mediation of Mensen met een Missie (People with a Mission), an organization for international peace and reconciliation, it was possible to set up the interviews on Skype. With the input of these interviews and of research conducted among

---

[9] Interviews with youth workers in Mora, Maroua (Cameroon), on Skype, April 2020. In Kenya, researchers wishing to study Al-Shabaab experience similar obstacles. See also the work of Erik Meinema (2020, 2021), who provides a detailed description of how local peacebuilding initiatives in Africa navigate past such security risks. See also Utrecht University's research program Religious Matters in an Entangled World: https://religiousmatters.nl.

more than 700 young people in Cameroon in 2015, it was possible to piece together a general picture of terrorists' motives and the role played by religion. These sections are decidedly not intended or designed to offer a full-fledged analysis of a clearly delineated focus control group. Rather, they are meant to draw a few lines of comparison and throw out some thoughts for further investigating and examining patterns of radical redemption in other contexts.

A Long History of Injustice and Deficit

Boko Haram emerged in the 1990s, when a number of young radicals distanced themselves from their moderate Islamic communities in the north of Nigeria and began to adopt increasingly fundamentalist views. Salafist preachers stirred up their followers and called on them to lead purer lives, renounce infidelity, and resist the Nigerian government, which, in their eyes, gave preferential treatment to Christians and to the people in the south of the country. The area around Lake Chad, which includes the northeast of Nigeria, the south of Niger, the northwest of Cameroon, and the southwest of Chad, was once the tribal homeland of the powerful Kanem-Bornu empire. Until well into the twentieth century, this region was governed by sovereign sultans, and it had its own language and religion. French and British colonial rule and the establishment of modern states were unable to erase the traces of this empire. Maiduguri, a regional traffic hub with influential mosques, was still a center of religious activity at the end of the twentieth century (see, e.g., Thurston 2018; MacEachern 2018; Wassouni and Gwoda 2017a, 2017b).

In this dry and not easily governed region, many groups of rebels emerged in the early years of the twenty-first century, which were united in 2002 under the leadership of radical preacher Mohammed Yusuf into the sectarian movement Boko Haram. Yusuf, a disciple of the medieval Arab scholar Ibn Tamiyyah, wished to breathe new life into the old caliphate; he called on young people to resist Western influences and called for a jihad against the apostate Nigerian government. In doing so, he made clever use of existing ethnic-tribal, religious, and geographical fault lines that divided the densely populated country of Nigeria. Of the almost 200 million inhabitants, around half are Muslims and half are Christians, but these communities are themselves divided along tribal lines. Research shows that 66 percent of Nigerians identify themselves as members of an ethnic or religious group, with tribal and religious identities being felt more strongly than socioeconomic status. Boko Haram set the Hausa-Fulani and the Kanuri in the north—who consider themselves Islamic—against Christian and traditionalist inhabitants and tribes by consciously appealing to radical purification and mobilization for the holy struggle (Çancı and Odukoya 2016).

In 2009, the Nigerian army launched an extensive operation in which hundreds of suspected Boko Haram fighters were killed, and their leader, Yusuf, was executed. His deputy, gangster-theologian Abubakar Shekau, took over as leader and inspired the movement to even more horrific acts of violence. There were rumors that Shekau had joined Al Qaeda and had received training and support from the Arab terrorist organization, but that bin Laden quickly found him too cruel and unreliable. In 2014, Boko Haram became notorious around the world with the kidnapping of 276 schoolgirls from Chibok, in the northeastern province of Borno. In a triumphant video clip, Shekau announced: "I will sell your girls as slaves on the market, by Allah" (see *Guardian* 2014). For the attentive listener, Shekau invoked memories of the mighty Islamic Kanem-Bornu empire, which owed much of its wealth to the slave trade. Like the emirs of the past, Shekau operated from the Mandara mountains in the northeast of Nigeria and led his followers to believe that, under his leadership, the Fulani and Kanuri tribes would once again establish a caliphate in the old region that was once spanned by the Kanem-Bornu empire. They would descend from the mountains—this time on small motorcycles or in pickup trucks rather than on fast horses—and attack the other tribes, subject them to their rule, enslave them, and force them to convert to Islam (see, e.g., Hare 2015).

In March 2015, Shekau—who, besides Hausa, Fulani, and Kanuri, could also speak English and Arabic—swore allegiance to IS leader Abu Bakr al-Baghdadi and launched a new wave of violence. A year later, IS distanced itself from Shekau because of his use of children as suicide terrorists. That led, in August 2016, to Abu Musab al-Barnawi taking over as leader of the Boko Haram splinter group Islamic State in West Africa (ISWA). Around that time, after a concerted effort initiated in 2015 by the armed forces of the bordering countries of Chad, Niger, and Cameroon, both groups were driven out of the borderlands. In addition, these countries called on fighters to turn themselves in in exchange for amnesty, which also paid off: from December 2015, the first groups of fighters began to desert, and in 2019, the Nigerian government claimed that Boko Haram and ISWA had technically been defeated, though both groups continued to commit regular attacks in the north in 2020 (UNDP 2022).

Exact figures on the number of rebels and Boko Haram members who turned themselves in or were arrested are not available, but hundreds of fighters are apparently being held in camps and detention facilities in Niger, Nigeria, and Cameroon. Boko Haram is still active, but the large waves of new recruits of 2014 have now petered out. NGOs estimate that 165, 150, and 250 Boko Haram fighters turned themselves in to the authorities in Cameroon in May, July, and December 2019, respectively. The government in Yaoundé has a Comité National de Désarmement, Démobilisation et Réintégration (CNDDR), set up by president Paul Biya in 2018, which houses former fighters in camps and supervises their "reintegration and education," but the committee does not publish any figures (Chahed 2019). In April 2020, NGOs reported that some 1,000 former fighters were being held in camps in the north of Cameroon. Amnesty International reported in 2015, however, that the Nigerian government had arrested 20,000 men and boys, more than 7,000 of whom had died in detention as a result of hunger or torture (Amnesty International 2015).

These figures must be seen in the context of the more than 35,000 people who were killed by Boko Haram and the 2 million Africans who fled their homes. Against this background, the tragic contours of the suffering and ongoing unrest in the African Great Lakes region are thrown into stark relief. It is clear why research and programs for detention and reintegration encounter such difficulties—the wounds are still too deep and too fresh.

Rewards on Earth and in Paradise

Despite the lack of official and regular access to detainees, more is now known about the motives and radicalization processes of Boko Haram fighters. In 2014, World Dynamics of Young People (WDYP), an NGO in Cameroon representing churches and Islamic communities, conducted a study into the scale and nature of Boko Haram's recruitment strategy and appeal among young people.[10] Anger and frustration about injustice and the appeal of sectarian, violent, and primitive redemption narratives, including the promise of gifts on earth and rewards in paradise, clearly played a crucial role.

---

[10] Interview with Dupleix Fernand Kuenzob, WDYP, Yaoundé, April 16, 2020 (on Skype).

In 2015, one in ten young people in Cameroon proved to have had some form of contact with Boko Haram, via friends and family or through recruitment activities by Boko Haram itself. The majority of them were afraid of the organization and saw it as posing a serious threat to the state and society. Nevertheless, one in ten saw it as a rebel group that was "fighting for a just cause." Boko Haram aimed its propaganda and recruitment activities mainly at people under the age of 25, sometimes even at young children, and especially at those living on the streets (WDYP 2016). From the descriptions by the young interviewees of how Boko Haram recruited them and their friends, a picture emerges of the motives that drove young people in Cameroon to join the organization. A dominant factor was the promise of money and material goods. "Boko Haram gives them presents," said one young man who did not join Boko Haram but was the victim of an attack. "First, they are given money. Then, they have two days to decide whether they want to keep it or give it back. If they keep it, they belong with the group."

The WDYP study discovered that Boko Haram also recruited young girls by getting them to go out with older members and then luring them away from their family homes. After that, they did not dare to go back due to loss of honor. Promising them a better life seemed the most successful way to attract young people. These promises included an advance in the form of money (sometimes a few hundred euros), a motorcycle, or a dowry for the girls. Boko Haram also abducted many very young children, as in the notorious case of the 276 schoolgirls from Chibok, mentioned in the previous section. Recruitment often occurred under coercion, with violence, or with recourse to "witchcraft": children and young people were told they had to go with the group because a curse had been imposed upon them or their families.[11]

At the same time, the young people interviewed in the north of Cameroon in 2015 said that, in their opinion, the choice to join Boko Haram was not always about the money. According to these interviewees—who had not been recruited themselves, but who had heard about how it went or knew people who had been recruited—it was more often about "frustration with the general situation in the country" (65%) than about material gain (37%). In other words, the reason why many young people in northern Cameroon joined

---

[11] Interviews with victims and surviving family members of Boko Haram attacks in northern Cameroon: Nana Abel, Mabi Aubin, Fadi Madeleine, Yanick Carlos, and Dalayma M. Appolos. The interviews were conducted by Kees Schilder of Mensen met een Missie, on the basis of a list of questions I had drawn up and instructions I had written for the purposes of this study. He conducted the interviews—which were later typed out and saved—on February 17, 2020, in Maroua, Cameroon. See also WDYP (2016, 33–8).

Boko Haram was anger about bad governance, a deep sense of injustice, and an experienced deficit in their own lives. Of this group of interviewees, 23 percent of those in the northern part of Cameroon and 18 percent of those in the east believed that religious motives also played a role. They felt that some of their friends and others of their age-group had been "brainwashed" and trapped into accepting the form of radical Islam that Boko Haram presented to them as the true and pure faith (WDYP 2016, 38–9).

These findings are consistent with the efforts of Abubakar Shekau to profile himself not only as a rebel commander but also as a spiritual leader, and to use that leadership to exacerbate ethnic-tribal and religious conflicts and bind Muslims to him. In a speech given in January 2012, he called on Muslims from the north to join Boko Haram and to avenge the injustice and inequality imposed on them by the "Christians." Shekau referred explicitly to earlier ethnic and religious conflicts, such as the conflict between the Hausa—the majority of whom are Muslims—and the Atyap—mainly Christians—in 1992. By doing so, he tried to cast existing tribal and economic fault lines in a religious and even eschatological light. In various speeches, he explicitly called on the archangels Gabriel, Azrael, and Michael for help and made Muslims who wished to evade their responsibility to take part in the jihad feel guilty.[12]

Unfortunately, it is difficult to draw conclusions from this study conducted in 2015, which is in essence comprehensive—partly because many young people are afraid to tell the full truth, and some of the researchers themselves come from the faith-based communities—Christian and Islamic—and wish to avoid any suggestion of religious stigmatization. Yet, it is clear from interviews with survivors and victims of Boko Haram attacks, and with those directly involved in religious reintegration programs, that religion is an important factor. "Many of the young people who joined Boko Haram knew little or nothing about their religion," Dupleix Kuenzob, an evangelical Christian youth worker in northern Cameroon, told me.[13] They were Muslims in name but could hardly read, let alone read the Koran or recite from it. These young people, especially if they were partially or fully orphaned, were extremely susceptible to the whole package offered by Boko

---

[12] The text of Shekau's speech has been translated from Arabic into English and is reproduced and explained in Apard (2015); see page 61 for the reference to the archangels, in a speech given on March 25, 2014.
[13] Interview with Dupleix Kuenzob; Pascal Djeumeugued, written information, April 2020. See also the interviews with Dalayma M. Appolos, Fadi Madeleine, and Yanick Carlos, February 17, 2020, Maroua.

Haram. They did not have to go to school because that was *haram* and, according to the group, state schools taught you the wrong things anyway. Instead, they were given access to a close rebel community. They were trained to use weapons, were paid in cash, could race around on motorcycles, and were given clear assignments to complete. They had to carry out raids, steal goats, rob convoys, and kill high-ranking officials, police officers, or military personnel. And they would not only be rewarded in the here and now but also earn points for later in paradise.

Dupleix Kuenzob and his colleague, the Catholic priest Pascal Djeumeugued, who are both involved in local initiatives to support ex-combatants, said the greatest trauma for the community in northern Cameroon was that many of their own children and young people had joined Boko Haram and then turned against their parents and families. "For Boko Haram, it was a test. Anyone who joined them had to prove that he loved the group, the emir, and Allah more than his own parents. Many Boko Haram members killed their family members or friends on the orders of the group. That gave them more points and a higher status, not only in the group but from a religious perspective. They had proved themselves."

As indicated, illiterate young people with little education and street children were very susceptible to the solidarity and the rewards on earth and in paradise that Boko Haram used to entice them. It also made them feel that they were part of a magical world of hellfire, angels, and invincible warriors. "Young people are carried along in a sectarian narrative and spiritually constrained," said Kuenzob. "They have to choose between misery or divine paradise. At the same time, they are threatened with hell, damnation, and magical spells if they do not join the group and take part in the fighting. It is almost impossible for them, once they have accepted money and have gone with the group, to escape that state of enthrallment, that brainwashing—especially because Boko Haram makes sure that they soon have blood on their hands, which means that they essentially burn their bridges behind them."[14]

Terrorism in the African Great Lakes region is a product of poverty, drought, and socioeconomic deprivation, but also of a conscious strategy by rebel leaders to mobilize historical, colonial, and religious narratives with the aim of gathering support. Boko Haram intentionally stirs up the sense of guilt, resentment, and injustice among Muslims in the area around Borno

---

[14] Interview with Dupleix Kuenzob; Pascal Djeumeugued, written information, April 2020.

and sets them against Christians and other tribes. Many young people are attracted by the prospect of a community and of food, weapons, and fast motorcycles. Here, radicalization is not so much a product of increasing frustration about a personal sense of deficit as a collective, tribal process. At the same time, the sectarian, religious, and radical element is clearly present. Devotion and struggle, reward and redemption are cast in strict, religious language. Stories of miracles are told to new recruits, and they are threatened with hell and damnation if they do not join the jihad. Thousands of young people proved susceptible to this combination of secular and divine rewards and the multilayered propaganda of worldly, historical, and religious injustice. That said, it should not be forgotten that many recruits were abducted or joined Boko Haram under coercion.

In short, for Boko Haram members, radical redemption was—and is—a narrative of highly personal desires and a sense of deficit but also clearly a substantial element in the organization's own narrative and a way of giving their socioeconomic resistance and rapacity a religious dimension and extra persuasive power. Further research is, however, required to obtain more information on their personal radicalization processes.

Right-Wing Extremist Delusions of Redemption: Saviors of Their Own Community

The Fragmented Extreme-Right Universe

When discussing present-day terrorism, we must look not only at the holy terrorism of jihadists but also at the right-wing extremist terrorism that has been responsible for several equally high-profile and widely condemned attacks in recent years. It is, however, almost impossible to say anything generally applicable about far-right terrorism: the "(ultra-)rightist galaxy" spans the whole spectrum ranging from classical fascist parties through right-conservative wings within more centrist parties to extraparliamentary, illegal, and extremist activist and terrorist groups (Mammone et al. 2012, 1). More detailed research in this area has been conducted elsewhere, but here I restrict myself to sketching a number of outlines.[15]

---

[15] In 2020, Annelotte Janse (Utrecht University) and Nikki Sterkenburg (Leiden University) conducted doctoral research into the history of right-wing extremism and far-right radicalization processes.

Since the 1980s, a clear distinction has been drawn in research between classical fascism and National Socialism (Nazism) on the one hand, and right-wing extremism on the other. But on the question as to whether that distinction lies in an ideology of racial superiority, in totalitarian tendencies, or in forms of political action or the willingness to use violence, there are as many opinions as there are researchers. Far-right extremists can be white supremacists, participants in anti-Semitic or anti-Zionist networks, or members of classical *völkische* parties. They can belong to a racial, political, cultural, or language-based national community and adhere to the accompanying variants of nationalism. Some, like the Christian Identity movement in the United States, appeal to Christian ideology, while others, like the terrorist National-Sozialistischer Untergrund in East Germany, are rabid atheists. Most researchers and security services speak of extremism when a group explicitly rejects the principles, norms, and values of democracy and the rule of law and aims to fight against them actively (Backes and Jesse 1993, 30, 40). According to the General Intelligence and Security Service (AIVD), right-wing extremism always contains one or more of the following elements: xenophobia; hatred of alien elements, such as cultural elements; and ultranationalism.[16] Extreme-right terrorists attempt to combat the principles of democracy and the rule of law by terrorist means—that is, they fight not only with legal and semilegal protests, sabotage, or vandalism, but also with terrorist crimes and actual premeditated attacks aimed at people.

The problem with such definitions, as always, is that they are strongly politically colored: what is considered as far-right terrorism or right-wing extremism depends on time, place, and public and private political opinions. This does not change the fact that they are necessary for valuable scientific and political discussions of religious and political violence and for the use of an internationally comparable terminology. Yet, they should always be seen in a historical perspective. The Bergden case, described in one of the following sections, would not have been seen as terrorism a decade or so ago. It was only the polarized and threatening climate around 2015 that left the public prosecutor no choice but to classify this attack on a mosque as an act of terrorism. In the United States, the FBI and the Department of Homeland Security have only recently qualified extreme-right violence in some cases as terrorism; before that, such cases of violence were often deemed *hate*

---

[16] See AIVD, "Rechts-extremisme": https://www.aivd.nl/onderwerpen/extremisme/rechts-extremisme.

crime, and they were thus punishable with less stringent sentences. In the United States, the debate continues on whether attacks with an extreme-right component always constitute terrorism (see, e.g., Savage et al. 2020; MacFarquhar 2020).

In such European countries as Germany and the Netherlands, there is sometimes disagreement about whether a particular outburst of violence, attack, or protest should be classified as far-right extremism, terrorism, or "rave violence." The label *terrorism* is often reserved for concrete attacks, such as those committed in Europe in the 1970s and 1980s by groups like Manfred Roeder's Deutsche Aktionsgruppen and the Wehrsportgruppe Hoffmann in Germany, and by a large number of neofascist organizations, such as Ordine Nuovo in Italy. The ideology of these groups was neofascist and neo-Nazi, aimed at driving out and wiping out "foreigners" (asylum seekers) and replacing weakened governments with a "Führer regime." If there was an element of redemption, it was focused on their own national communities, drew little inspiration from Christianity, and was often explicitly atheist. Ordine Nuovo, for example, wanted to ban all churches and Christian institutions.

The situation in the United States was different: Christian influences were explicitly visible among many white supremacist groups. Timothy McVeigh's attack in Oklahoma City in 1995, for example, could clearly be linked to the Christian Identity movement. When he was arrested, McVeigh was carrying photocopied pages from *The Turner Diaries*, the bible for white Christian supremacists in the United States. In the book, author William Luther Pierce—writing under the pseudonym Andrew Macdonald—called on white Christians to wage a race war and a final battle against the US federal government. Their acts of redemption would be seen in the light of the divine Last Judgment. McVeigh's attack appears to have acted out a passage from *The Turner Diaries*. Attacks on abortion clinics in the United States, Australia, Canada, and New Zealand are seen as instances of Christian terrorism (Cooperman 2003; Mason 2002). This kind of Christian terrorism, which is partly also far-right terrorism, was often inspired by the idea of an apocalyptic final battle and the notion that true Christians were tested and should show through their deeds that they were already preparing for Armageddon and the Second Coming—the return of Christ and the End of Days. Targets ranged from government bodies, Jewish institutions, and mosques to abortion clinics and the LGBTQ+ community (Berger 2017).

Against this background of a far-right universe that has become increasingly fluid and fragmented since the millennium, which in the new alt-right variant also dons the cloak of irony and satire, communicates in memes,[17] and embraces icons from youth culture, it is very difficult to ascertain whether redemption motives play a role of any significance (see, e.g., Ebner 2020, 21, 41–2). Clearly defined groups or parties are nowadays much less in evidence than in the past. With the advent of the Web 2.0 and 3.0, social media, and broad populist parties, all kinds of new, fluid networks have emerged.[18] Traditional anti-Semitic neo-Nazis in Europe and apocalyptic Christian Identity groups in the United States now find themselves competing with broader alt-right platforms typically propagating diffuse anti-feminist, anti-Islam, anti-elite, and anti-left ideas (see, e.g., AIVD 2018, 11). It is very difficult to draw the dividing line between legal actions and the illegal distribution of texts promoting hatred, and between sabotage and terrorist violence, partly because it is not always possible to determine the perpetrators' intentions. This is compounded by right-wing extremists inciting violence anonymously through Internet fora like 4chan and 8chan,[19] on which attacks are glorified through live streams. While some of the detainees I interviewed were convicted partly for forwarding jihadist texts and apps, this occurred much less frequently in the case of extreme-right content.

Since 9/11, violent attacks by far-right extremists against Muslims, as well as against Jews, have increased. More violence and aggression have been detected especially since the emergence of IS in 2014, the civil war in Syria, and the influx of more than a million refugees into Europe in 2015. In 2013, fifty-five violent incidents involving mosques were recorded in the Netherlands; in 2016, that number had risen to seventy-two. In December 2015, a firework bomb was set off at the house of a Somali family in the village of Pannerden. Like the Bergden case in Enschede in February 2016—see later in this chapter—this attack was condemned as a terrorism-related

---

[17] The *Oxford English Dictionary* defines a *meme* as follows: "An image, video, piece of text, etc., typically humorous in nature, that is copied and spread rapidly by internet users, often with slight variations." See also Tuters and Hagen (2020).

[18] For more background information on the links between the digital revolution, the advent of the Web 2.0 and 3.0, and terrorism, see Choudhury (2014); Conway (2017); see also Conway (2006); Stenersen (2008). With thanks to Matthijs Kock (2020).

[19] The platform 8kun, better known by its former name 8chan—and also called Infinitechan or Infinitychan—is an Internet forum originally hosted in the United States where users can anonymously participate in discussions and where every controversial standpoint can effectively be aired, no matter how racist or radical. If possible, 8chan was even more controversial than its predecessor, 4chan. See Harwood (2019).

crime of a far-right nature (Van der Valk and Törnberg 2017; see also AIVD 2018; Richards 2019). According to the National Coordinator for Counterterrorism and Security (NCTV), extreme-right sympathizers are active in the Netherlands, and it is "conceivable" that larger-scale far-right copycat attacks may be carried out (NCTV 2020, 17–18, 29). In 2019, there were two disconnected incidents in which two men, aged 55 and 59 and described as "system haters" or *Wutbürger* (angry citizens), were arrested for possession of arms and threatening to commit a terrorist act. Following the example of Brenton Tarrant, they claimed to adhere to far-right replacement theories; such far-right conspiracy theories claim that left-wing elites want to replace white citizens with nonwhite immigrants.

Since 9/11, large-scale and high-profile far-right terrorist attacks have mainly been committed by lone operators, perpetrators like Anders Behring Breivik in 2011 who, while clearly active in broad ideological networks, performed their deeds as individuals. The redemption fantasies associated with these deeds were less explicitly linked to existing far-right traditions or party standpoints, such as *The Turner Diaries*. Lone operators like Stephan Balliet or Tobias Rathjen, who committed attacks in the German cities of Halle in 2019 and Hanau in 2020, respectively, clearly fall within the extreme-right spectrum, but they gave their own very individual, idiosyncratic, sometimes highly confused and shallow interpretations to that ideology. Breivik's 2011 manifesto was a typical example of such megalomaniac cut-and-paste ideology. Nevertheless, these perpetrators, often referring to each other, did adhere to certain radical redemption narratives (Bakker and De Graaf 2010).

Far-Right Redemption Narratives

Many perpetrators of major extreme-right attacks in recent years refer to each other and try to outdo one another in spectacle and numbers of victims. Examples include the attacks by Anders Behring Breivik (Oslo, July 22, 2011, seventy-seven deaths), Dylann Roof (Charleston, June 17, 2015, nine deaths), Brenton Tarrant (Christchurch, March 15, 2019, fifty-one deaths), and Stephan Balliet (Halle, October 9, 2019, two deaths), but there are many others. These perpetrators left manifestos behind (Breivik, Tarrant, and Roof) or justified their actions either in advance on social media or afterwards in the courtroom (all four of them). Such lone operators are not necessarily lone wolves; via online communities, they surround themselves with a large group of sympathizers and followers. Their ideas contain new forms and elements but can clearly be labeled far-right: they aim to purify national or racial communities and are against perceived elites or other groups seen as posing a threat. The language they use is racist and frequently anti-Semitic. Often, after their attacks, large numbers of followers glorify them on the Internet.

Conspicuous among these perpetrators is the link between a life of perceived grievances, frustrations, and deficit, and a megalomaniac and destructive act of redemption or revenge. Before they committed those acts, they came to be convinced that their community or the world as a whole was faced with some form of existential threat and that they had been personally chosen to avert that threat, thereby eradicating the injustice in the world and the deficit in their own lives. Some also strove for a form of martyrdom. I will not examine the biographies of these perpetrators here and did not speak to them in the course of this study, but a few quotes from their texts are sufficient to point in the direction of a motive of redemption and salvation, while revenge and a desire for fame were also important motivations for them.

Anders Behring Breivik, born in 1979, suffered from psychological abuse from an early age, developed a narcissistic personality disorder, and was picked up by the police as a teenager on several occasions for minor offenses, including spraying graffiti. He devoted considerable attention to his appearance; he took anabolic steroids and underwent plastic surgery. He withdrew more and more into himself and began to develop an ideological universe in which he designated for himself a mythical role. According to Breivik, from 2002—after 9/11—he started to make plans for a major attack. The judge concluded in any case that there was sufficient evidence to show that, as of 2006, Breivik was a "man with a mission." Breivik felt that the Norwegian elites closed their eyes to the way Europe was being undermined by multiculturalism and feminism. It was his superior calling to protect the continent against being "overwhelmed by Muslims" and thus to prevent the establishment of "Eurabia." Through his deed, he would sacrifice himself—his life, or at least his freedom—and inspire his perceived constituency of white warriors to also take action (see, e.g., Gullestad 2017; Hemmingby and Bjørgo 2018). His manifesto, "2083: A European Declaration of Independence," was a 1,500-page eclectic collage of his own texts and summaries and copied passages of texts by others. He called for a "cultural war," identifying himself and his fellow warriors with the Crusaders and linking the call to intended targets, precisely categorized by type and number (Breivik 2011). He also designed medals to be awarded for heroic actions in the war, again specifically categorized according to type and numbers of victims. With his self-styled uniforms and mythical–Christian Crusader rhetoric, Breivik literally combined belief and practice and was thus an exponent par excellence of an extremely perverted redemption narrative.

Dylann Roof, born in 1994, came from a broken family (as did Breivik), was expelled from several schools, and became addicted to drugs. He was far less eloquent than Breivik and, in the months prior to the attack on the church in Charleston, he had been picked up in a shopping mall for using deranged language. Yet he had immersed himself in the history of slavery and the American Civil War, and in the statistics on "black-on-white" crimes—the notion that black people intentionally attack white people as part of a silent race war. On June 17, 2015, he entered the Emanuel African Methodist Episcopal Church in Charleston and, after sitting with the churchgoers and joining in a Bible study session for an hour, shot nine people dead. Witnesses stated that Roof had shouted he had come "to shoot black people" and that "[y]'all are raping our women and taking over the country. This must be done" (Fausset et al. 2015; Blow 2015). After the attack, it emerged that Roof had placed a manifesto on his website The Last Rhodesian, together with images of him posing with the flag of the Confederate Southern States of America and symbols of the South African apartheid regime. He had named his website after the repressive white minority regime of the unrecognized state of Rhodesia (after 1979, present-day Zimbabwe). In his manifesto, Roof displayed the same sense of calling and white supremacist beliefs, writing that white people are running "because they are too weak, scared, and brainwashed to fight." Someone had to sound the alarm and unleash a race war: "We have no skinheads, no real KKK, no one doing anything but talking on the Internet. Well someone has to have the bravery to take it to the real world, and I guess that has to be me" (Roof 2017; see also CNN 2016).

Brenton Tarrant (b. 1991) was a product of the active Internet community of white supremacists, alt-right supporters, and members of the European Identity movement. He grew up in Australia and worked there between 2009 and 2011 as a personal trainer, but in 2012, he started to travel around Europe, especially the Balkans. There, he increasingly fell under the influence of far-right ideas, writing aggressive texts and posting messages on the Internet. Tarrant claimed to have been inspired by Breivik, and after the jihadist attacks in Europe in 2015, he came to the conclusion that he himself must take action to prevent "white genocide." On March 15, 2019, Tarrant drove to the Al Noor Mosque in the Christchurch suburb of Riccarton with a car full of weapons. He opened fire on mosque visitors, killing forty-two. He then drove on to the Linwood Islamic Centre, 5 kilometers away, where he killed seven visitors. He was arrested on his way to a third mosque, before he could attack it. It emerged at his trial that he had been preparing the attack for two years. In "The Great Replacement," the 74-page manifesto that Tarrant claimed to have written, he showed himself to be obsessed with historical battles between Muslims and Christians in Europe, used swastikas, runes, and other Nazi symbols, and a Celtic cross, and referred to himself as an "ethno-nationalist" and an "eco-fascist." In his manifesto, he speaks in impassioned terms about a society that is one with nature, complete with images of cute white children dancing through a meadow of wild flowers. Through his deed, he wished to bring that ideal world closer.

Tarrant was the first to live stream his attack, and he used the nihilistic humor of the alt-right scene on the Internet in his commentary and manifesto (Tarrant 2019). Even those active in that cynical subculture flirt with the desire for that ideal state of white harmony. In countless memes, he exalted the Crusaders, who had in the distant past protected Europe from the existential danger posed by Islam. Tarrant consciously placed himself in that tradition, which he idealized. He linked his beliefs and his sense of being called to his horrific attack. He employed all kinds of stylistic figures and artifices to place his act within such a narrative of redemption and transformation, including song texts ("I Am the God of Hellfire"), military marching music (Serb battle songs, "The British Grenadiers"), symbols, and writing the names of attacks and perpetrators on his weapons. His manifesto and live stream were instantly circulated on 8chan and Twitter, even though they were quickly banned (Doyle 2019; Horton 2019). Tarrant thus inspired others, including Patrick Crusius (2019), who wrote that the Christchurch attacker's manifesto had persuaded him to select Latino Americans as a target for his own attack on the Walmart supermarket in El Paso, Texas, in August 2019, in which twenty-three people lost their lives.

The final perpetrator on this disheartening list is Stephan Balliet, born in 1992 in the state of Saxony-Anhalt, then in East Germany. On October 9, 2019, during the Jewish holiday of Yom Kippur, Balliet attempted to enter a synagogue in Halle and unleash a bloodbath. When that failed—because his self-made explosives did not work, and he was unable to open the door to the building—he shot a passerby and then entered a nearby kebab shop and killed a customer. Balliet explicitly tried to imitate his heroes: he wore battle dress, placed a manifesto online, and live streamed his attack with a camera on his helmet and rap music in the background. In the manifesto, which he posted on a message board linked to 4chan before the attack, he announced his intended "achievements" in gamer language. During the attack, he gave a sarcastic gamer commentary of his actions in English in a terrible accent. After starting the live stream, he said, "Hi, my name is Anon. And I think the holocaust never happened." Waiting at a red light on the way to the synagogue, he said, "Nobody expects the Internet SS," and when he failed to open the door, "A hundred percent fail." After failing to make more kills and thereby not making all his achievements, he apologized to his viewers, saying, "Sorry, guys; once a loser, always a loser." Five people watched the stream live, and 2,200 immediately afterwards, but no one reported the post to the police (Stritzel and Becker 2019; *Spiegel* 2019). Unlike Breivik, Tarrant, and Roof, Balliet already presented himself as a loser during his attack, as someone who did not do what his community required of him. Whether Balliet, with his rabid anti-Semitism and hatred of women, had pictured himself as the savior of a German national community was not clear. In his case, copycat behavior may have played a part, a desire for fame on the Internet or more widely, and a desire to wreak revenge on everyone who had rejected him (see Koehler 2019, 16).[20] In any case, immediately after his attack, he became world-famous on the message boards of 4chan and other platforms, albeit as the target of extreme mockery.[21]

In Louise Richardson's (2006) terminology, terrorists seek revenge, renown, and reaction. In this book, as explained in chapter 3, I add a fourth R—radical redemption—to argue for a better understanding of how the radical redemption narrative also shapes the radicalization process toward terrorism. I did not speak with the terrorists discussed here in person, and—with the exception of their manifestos or statements in court—I was unable to find any detailed explanations for their acts, for example, in interview transcripts. That makes it difficult to determine whether and how redemption as a self-reported narrative affected the way in which the perpetrators gave their actions a transcendental meaning. In the cases of Breivik and Roof, self-reflection and mythical self-glorification are more clearly present—for instance, in their manifestos—than in the case of Balliet. But one thing is

---

[20] According to Daniel Koehler (2019), Balliet was perhaps also an "incel" (involuntary celibate). Driven mainly by hatred of women, the incel movement increasingly overlaps with far-right extremism.

[21] I monitored the comments on 4chan and meguca.org myself in 2019.

certain: these extreme-right lone operators were concerned with mobilizing a constituency, pursuing a form of martyrdom (or status as saviors), and creating the conditions for a cultural or race war.

There is a striking overlap between far-right and jihadist terrorists who have committed very serious crimes and large-scale attacks: for both kinds of perpetrators, what matters is the level of preparedness and willingness to inflict mass atrocities. The Abdeslam brothers and Abdelhamid Abaaoud, who organized and led the attacks in Paris and Brussels, are good examples. In the cases of both the far-right extremists discussed here and the perpetrators of the Paris and Brussels attacks, narcissistic character traits, delusions of grandeur, and highly developed revenge fantasies were prominent elements.

At the same time, there is a clear difference: tapping into Islam and appealing to an existing, worldwide religious community and "Internet *ummah*" is not the same as propagating a far-right ideology that is very idiosyncratic in nature, is not supported by organized adherents, and resembles a bricolage rather than a systematic and recognizable theory.[22] The advocates and perpetrators of the parasitic far right are intent on creating—or invoking—a constituency and consolidating it through a wide range of fora, manifestos, and rituals. In that sense, violent jihadists have an easier task: they can plug into an existing *ummah*. They can try to appropriate and misuse existing texts, traditions, and rituals of Islam. Their fundamental account of the final battle and of the duty of a Muslim to lead a life of purity resonates with a wide-ranging narrative of how to give life meaning. The cultural repertoires and rituals that jihadists can use, or misuse, are deeply embedded in faith communities throughout the world. That makes the appeal of the jihadist narrative of radical redemption ideologically strong and coherent. Yet, it may just be a matter of time before this difference disappears. As soon as the eclectic bricolage that makes up the far-right extremist universe develops into a more mainstream and stable global (online) community and/or aligns with existing Christian nationalist ones, a right-wing extremist (Christian) narrative of radical redemption may also become a fixture in future terrorist waves.

---

[22] For a discussion on the nature of the online or virtual *ummah*, see Al-Rawi (2015), which also examines the worldwide division and sectarian polarization surrounding it.

Far-Right Redemption Narratives in the Netherlands

The narratives of the earlier-mentioned far-right terrorists had an impact on extremists in the Netherlands as well. To make a meaningful comparison between the redemption narratives of jihadist detainees and those of far-right extremists, I discuss, in the following sections, right-wing extremist cases from the Netherlands from the same period in which the jihadist detainees were active—that is, from 2010 onward. Their radicalization processes thus played out in the same time and place. I use, for instance, material from the Bergden case, which was the first instance in the Netherlands of far-right terrorists being convicted as such. I had the opportunity to speak with the attackers and was especially interested to know to what extent feelings of a moral deficit, devotion, and reward—pivotal elements in the radical redemption narrative—played a role in their actions. Whereas the attack in the Bergden case was clearly not of the same order as those of Breivik or even Balliet, and some security experts doubted whether it even was a well-considered and premeditated attack,[23] the case nevertheless led to convictions for a terrorist crime, and a coherent trajectory of radicalization could be established.

The Bergden Case

On February 27, 2016, at around 9:40 p.m., two Molotov cocktails exploded against the facade of the mosque in the Tweede Emmastraat, on the edge of Pathmos, a working-class neighborhood in Enschede.[24] There were some forty people in the mosque at the time. Shortly before, children had been playing where the explosions took place. Two passing joggers were able to stamp the fire out quickly, limiting the damage.

Meanwhile, several witnesses in the street saw three figures running away. A witness followed one of the men in his car and saw him enter a house—which later proved to be the house where Martijn* lived. The three men were Danny (b. 1991), Marco (b. 1979), and Ronald (b. 1981); their accomplices Peter* (b. 1981) and Martijn (b. 1982) were at that moment already in the

---

[23] Interviews with police and justice staff and analysts, 2019–20.
[24] This section is based on two extensive conversations and interviews with Enschede police officers involved in the Bergden case, April 13 and November 7, 2018, Enschede.

house. After their arrests, the suspects initially exercised their right to remain silent, but in custody, Martijn decided to make a statement expressing his regret, and he provided more details on the attack. He had fitted his house with a security camera, which had filmed the group leaving his house carrying the Molotov cocktails and their hasty return (the police said this was, in their experience, the first time suspects had filmed their own crime by accident). At the end of October 2016, the whole group was convicted for committing an act of a terrorist nature; it was the first conviction of its kind in the Netherlands and the first conviction of a terrorist act by far-right perpetrators.[25] The ruling emphasized the attack's "terrorist nature"—as laid out in article 83/83a of the Dutch Criminal Code—and the suspects were found guilty of conspiring, preparing, and attempting an arson attack on the mosque.

That the men would be convicted for committing an act of a terrorist nature was not a foregone conclusion. They denied any involvement, and four of them refused to say anything at all. During the process of charging and trying the suspects, not everyone agreed that the attack was an act of terrorism. Those who did not think so argued that the two Molotov cocktails could hardly have caused any serious damage to the mosque. Others, however, felt that some police officers were insufficiently aware of feelings in wider society regarding violence and intimidation aimed at Muslims. Public prosecutor Jeroen Kuipers eventually decided to prosecute the suspects on the basis of article 83/83a of the Criminal Code by referring to the general rise in anti-Islamic aggression and violence. Several other mosques in the Netherlands had been the target of abuse during that period: many had received threatening letters, and swastikas and other Nazi symbols had been daubed on their walls. Pigs' heads were deposited at AZCs. In Kuipers's eyes, the fact that the Bergden perpetrators were aware of such actions made their attack a conscious attempt to further exacerbate the already existing fear among a specific segment of the population, namely, Muslims. With their attack, they also wanted to force the Enschede authorities to drop their plans to establish a new AZC in the city. Those two elements—invoking fear among segments of the population and forcing a governmental authority to do or not do something—were, and still are, part of the definition of a terrorist crime. This, in Kuipers's opinion, meant that article 83/83a applied in the Bergden case.

[25] See H. G. Kuipers, "Requisition in the Bergden Case," ECLI:NL:RBOVE:2016:4134, October 27, 2016.

In addition, the attack proved not to be a one-off outburst by a group of men who had drunk too much. All five suspects were members of a group called Demonstrators against Municipal Governments (Demonstranten tegen Gemeenten; DTG), whose aim was to use all means at their disposal to stop the AZC from being located in Enschede; two of them were in fact leading figures in the network. The police also had information that the group wished to join the Dutch Self Defence Army (DSDA), which was more militant and violent and held a higher status in far-right circles. The attack on the mosque may have been intended as a "proof of good conduct" or part of an "initiation rite," granting the group admission to DSDA.

What bound the perpetrators in the Bergden case together—and linked them to DTG, DSDA, and other national and international far-right groups like Pegida, Voorpost, and Rechts in Verzet—was their opposition to newcomers and their fear that Islam would overwhelm the Netherlands. According to the Enschede police, Danny and Peter were ardent believers of far-right ideas—though Peter denied this. Marco was at that time an alcoholic, while Martijn seemed to be a hanger-on. Nevertheless, all five of them had for some time been involved in sending apps, had been discussing and demonstrating against the "arrival of Islam," and were afraid of perceived jihadist sleeper cells and attackers who were alleged to have arrived in the Netherlands among the influx of refugees and who would "rape their women."

The cases of Peter and Martijn allowed two clear profiles to be elaborated for participants in the new wave of fluid, non-party-aligned, far-right extremism: the inflammatory activist and the hanger-on.[26] These examples show that radical redemption as a motive is not always necessarily expressed through large-scale terrorist violence but can also play a role among individual radical activists and extremists.

Nobody Does Anything

When he was a child, Martijn's family was not very well off. His father was a laborer, his mother was a childminder, and, besides Martijn, they had two other sons to care for. When his father had to give up work for health reasons,

---

[26] Interview with Arjan Derksen, leading Enschede police officer, and two colleagues, November 7, 2018, Enschede.

his mother took on a cleaning job to make ends meet. While he was still young, Martijn was diagnosed with cancer, which impeded his education. At the age of 15, he went to work for a furniture maker. Things went well for several years. He worked as a furniture maker until 2004; then, since he was good with his hands, he got a job as a service engineer at a wastewater treatment plant. He earned enough to get a mortgage and buy a house for himself and his girlfriend Annette*. Because they wanted children but failed to conceive, they embarked on a course of IVF treatment. Then, in 2014, Martijn's life rapidly began to fall apart.[27]

> I had a daughter, José*, from an earlier relationship. Or so I thought. But in October 2014, a DNA test showed that I wasn't her father. After eight years, the child care service suddenly stopped me seeing José. I also heard for the first time that, at the age of 7, she had been abused on several occasions in a youth institution. I collapsed and spent two days in hospital because they thought I'd had a brain hemorrhage. My health deteriorated because of the stress, and I lost my job. At the same time, I had instigated proceedings to carry on seeing José. And Annette and I were still doing the IVF treatment. But there was nothing to be done about it. José lost my surname. I had bought all kinds of things for her, from when she was born to the age of 8. And I'd even made a child's bedroom for her in my house. But then I heard that the door had been closed on me seeing her. And my ex didn't even have José at home with her: she had packed her off to a care farm. I started taking drugs—I think that was around June 2015. Weed, speed, ecstasy, strong drink to get to sleep. A bottle of Safari a day. And then I would take more drugs to wake up again. That was when I lost my job. And Annette left me, too.
>
> I lost weight until I was all skin and bones. I only weighed 66 kilos. I was just a regular junkie. In December 2015, I saw that TV company RTL5 was looking for people to take part in a rehabilitation program. You would fly to South Africa and undergo the program there. I saw the dead look in my eyes in the mirror and called them. I told them my story, and they said I could take part in the program. I would be flying to South Africa in February. But that telephone call was before Christmas, so I had to get through ten weeks before I left. That's a long time for a drug addict to sit at home alone. At one point, I was up in the attic with a rope around my neck. But I called

[27] Interviews with Martijn*, May 23 and September 23, 2019, Utrecht.

the doctor and was referred to a rehab clinic. I was admitted to a Christian clinic almost immediately and spent two weeks there doing cold turkey. That went so well that I started taking an interest in the outside world again.

In the second week of January 2016, I switched my mobile telephone on and immediately heard the news from Cologne, what had happened there on New Year's Eve with the refugees and the hundreds of cases of sexual assault. It broke me up. I thought about my niece, and about José, what had already happened to her and what would happen in the future if all those refugees came to Enschede and abused our women and children. A friend of mine was already a member of DTG. Through Facebook, I asked him what was going on. He started sending me more news, and he invited me to a demonstration against the refugees. So, I went along. If there's a mass of pedophiles coming your way, of people who think differently about our norms and values, what should you do? Nothing?

When I left the clinic, I went straight to see my friend and the other guys. I went with them to demonstrate in Ede and Enschede. I wasn't smoking weed anymore, just had a beer now and again. It started going better with me; I was now part of a group. First, I had nothing; I hardly knew what was going on around me. But now, there was something real to focus on. We made plans and distributed flyers. We wanted not just to demonstrate with DTG but to really change something: that old people in homes could shower more often, that the premiums for care didn't go up again, and that the housing market opened up again—things for normal Dutch people, things that they worried about. And with good reason: Why would our government want to bring pedophiles and Muslims to the Netherlands and not have a single cent extra to help our own old people?

All the time I'd been using drugs, I could feel nothing. My parents said I looked like a devil. No one could reach me; I had closed myself off completely. When I joined the guys in DTG, I started feeling again. At first, it was mainly pain, because of what had happened with José. That's why the news of the assaults in Cologne upset me so much. Once I had left the clinic, I devoted myself to the activities of the group. The solidarity, the tension and excitement when we had confrontations with the police, as if all hell could break loose. We had on T-shirts with DTG and pictures of pit bulls, and we stood there, shoulder to shoulder, in front of the town hall. I also saw film clips of what IS fighters were doing at that time, early 2015, beheadings and stuff; we would send them to each other. And clips of Geert Wilders saying that the refugees were mainly fortune hunters and some were probably also

IS fighters. Edwin Wagensveld of Pegida, the guy with the pig's head hat, he dared to go further. I had voted for Pim Fortuyn, and later for Wilders. But Wagensveld, he wasn't afraid to say clearly what it was all about. I agreed with him. We had best bulldoze the lot of them, the AZCs and the mosques. I wanted the borders closed; I was against the EU, and still am. Political parties, they don't work anymore, and Rutte is a liar. I don't know if I felt like a far-right extremist. I was just against Muslims and pedophiles. And I was a member of DTG, but that all went through Facebook. You didn't pay a contribution or have a membership card—you could just post and like items, and you were part of the group.[28]

During another interview, Martijn continued his story.

At the beginning of 2016, in February, we decided that more needed to be done. DSDA, they were already a lot further than we were. Just demonstrating didn't achieve much at all, and those refugees, they were already coming to Enschede. In January, I had heard that hundreds of asylum seekers would be coming; some had already been housed in the old offices of the *Tubantia* newspaper, close to where I lived [*Tubantia* 2016]. I was back with Annette, and she worked in that neighborhood. From January until I was arrested, I picked her up from work every evening. I was afraid that a refugee would knock her off her bike. I was really losing it. But then, it all fell into place. Everyone had an opinion and was on the Internet or Facebook saying what they thought and what they were going to do, but they all sat at home on the couch watching the soaps. Big talk, but when it came down to it, no one dared to do anything. They were afraid of losing their jobs and all that. But not me—I had nothing left to lose.

We were going to Amersfoort on the 28th to join DSDA, so we could do something worthwhile. Peter had arranged that. On the evening of the 26th, we were all together, having a few beers and chatting. Danny told us he had just seen on the news that flyers with swastikas had been sent to mosques. He said we could do that, too, and go even further. That's when we decided to throw Molotov cocktails at a mosque. We thought if we could show that we could do that here, too, it would get things rolling, and more people would follow our example. It wasn't my idea, but we drove to

---

[28] Interview with Martijn*, May 23, 2019, Utrecht.

my house because Peter had the stuff to make the cocktails but only had beer cans to put it in. I had some bottles and a shed where we could put the things together. We were all there—Suzan*, too, Peter's girlfriend, and Annette. It had been her birthday a few days before, so we took a picture as if we were all having a party at my house to celebrate, as a kind of alibi. Then the five of us left the house in my car, but it was difficult to park, so Peter and I dropped the other three off and drove back to my house. The Molotov cocktails went off around 9:30 p.m., and the others ran back to my house. Danny was followed.

The next day, five police cars drove up to the house. The whole place was crawling with cops—no arrest team with machine guns, luckily, but it felt like the police were having an open day in my front room. I told them straight off I had a bag of ecstasy pills, and they took me in. I tried to leave the girls out in my statements. And how was I repaid for that? Annette left and took everything with her—all my things, computers, and cameras with photos of José. And she didn't tell my parents where I was and what had happened until two weeks later.

By then, I was in the PI [penitentiary institution], and because I had talked and the others had kept their mouths shut after they had been arrested, they threatened to kill me. When they came to the PI, they called me a filthy fascist and started yelling: "When you get out, we're going to set your house on fire and rip your head off." And do you know what happened then? All the foreigners, the Muslims, they took my side! Because I had been honest. They made pizzas for me. Can you imagine that? And later, they carried on cooking for me and looking out for me! I sent a letter to the mosque in Enschede. And the guys in the PI thought that was cool and said, "Martijn, we don't think you're a terrorist. You're a cool dude in your Nikes." Then I got loads of nice cards from my parents and hung them all on the walls of my cell.

I got a heavy punishment: I was in prison for two years and had another two years of probation, despite being honest about everything. I am unfit to work because I have Bechterew's disease. And it was difficult enough to get my life back on the rails after I was released. I was given a place to live elsewhere. I have to do everything anonymously. My friends and family don't know where I am. But I've been made very welcome here in my new hometown. I do voluntary work; I restore furniture and clean up gardens. In prison, I learned to make orthodox religious icons. If there's a heaven, they'll let me in now.

The most important thing is that I now have a purpose in my life. That was the cause of all the problems. I didn't care about anything, had no purpose. Then DTG came along, and I went nuts because of all those refugees. That gave me a clear focus. I had to protect my town, my girlfriend, and my daughter. I still think that the borders should be closed—there are too many criminals coming into the country. But I'm not a far-right extremist. Those people, Muslims, Jews, don't really have to die, but the pedophiles should all fuck off. I have right-wing ideas, yes. I voted Forum voor Democratie [a Dutch right-wing populist party] for a while, but now I don't vote at all. I don't want to do crazy things any more, just light up a candle now and again and find a nice girl.[29]

They Lied to Us

Peter came from a happy family and has a younger sister and brother. When he was 10, they moved from Hengelo to Enschede, where his father had a job as a manager and his mother worked in financial support services. He was smart enough but "never liked school much and couldn't sit still in class."[30] After attending secondary vocational school, he went to lower technical college.

I just wanted to have fun and do crazy things, drive around on scooters and in cars, while I didn't even have a driver's license. I hated it when people tried to tell me what to do. My parents did that, of course, but if someone doesn't want to do something, you can't force them. I was always different from the others, not like everyone expected themselves and me to be, always following the rules, you know. I wasn't like that, even though my parents tried to make me do all that. I trained to be a metal engineer but didn't finish the course. Who needs a diploma? I did get a whole load of certificates, though.

When Peter was 18, his parents got divorced. He found a job and a flat in Enschede.

---

[29] Interview with Martijn*, September 23, 2019, Utrecht.
[30] Interview with Peter*, May 15, 2019, Enschede.

Then, I could do whatever I wanted and didn't have to answer to anyone anymore. Having fun, lots of street parties—that was my motto. I had a girlfriend and a permanent job as a crane service engineer. Back then, I wasn't interested in politics, didn't read the papers or anything. I did have the idea that politicians were liars and said things in the media that weren't right. Old prime minister Wim Kok promised to give us back those 25 cents for the extra taxes on fuel, but nothing came of that. Mark Rutte [the current prime minister] made me even more skeptical. The way he presents things, that we live in a free country—that's not true. I went along with that for a few years and voted CDA [a Christian democratic party] or PVV [a populist right-wing party]. But what happened with the election results? Nothing at all. The end result no longer looks anything like what you voted for. Mark Rutte is the biggest liar in the Netherlands. And we haven't been a democracy for a long time. A lot of Dutch people think the same way. Kok talked about giving us back 25 cents, Rutte promised us 1,000 euros, but we never saw a cent of any of it. The crisis in 2008 didn't affect me personally, but it got me thinking. Decisions that affect our lives are made in Brussels. The EU was set up on the basis of false information. Everyone is sick of it. It was supposed to make us better off. But who benefited from it? The people with good educations, jobs, and contacts in high places, like Rutte and Unilever—that is mates helping mates; it's not in the interest of common people. The government is there to serve the people, not vice versa. I noticed then that a lot of people were unhappy, saw all the dishonesty. But do they dare to stand up and be counted? No. That is, of course, the safest choice. So, I asked myself: Do I dare to stand up and be counted? I knew people from all classes in society, so I saw the big difference between people living on benefits and those who earn thousands of euros a month. I have a friend who's not allowed to have a car because he's on benefits, so he has to cycle to the food bank. So, when Rutte says things are getting better, it doesn't apply to my friend. People at the bottom of the ladder should actually advance more quickly than those with lots of money, or the people in old people's homes. They can only take a shower once every two or three days. Care should be priority, shouldn't it? We're all paying more and more fines, VAT, and income taxes, but where's that money going to?

All those refugees coming here—for me, that was the moment to take action. It was the final straw. I understand them; if my country was at war, I would come to the Netherlands, too. But there are criminals among them. And what all these newcomers get when they arrive, that's not fair, is it?

Glasses, bikes, hearing aids—everything is arranged for them. But Dutch citizens living here—whether they have a Turkish, Moroccan, or Dutch background, I don't care about that—Dutch citizens living here are on benefits, too, and they can't even afford to go to the dentist. That is injustice. People daren't complain about it, but I've always been someone who's not afraid to speak his mind. This was ridiculous. We'd already had all that trouble in Cologne, and in November 2015, we heard that they'd be coming here. AZCs were being set up. I could have done voluntary work at the food bank, but I had a job. And political parties, like the Socialist Party or whatever, I just don't buy that anymore. That's how I ended up taking part in the demonstrations. And through meeting people, in one of those Nazi bars. I didn't know it was a Nazi bar. I only went once. That wasn't my kind of thing, that ideology. I'm not a fascist or a far-right extremist, but I actively oppose the arrival of the refugees. It's good that people like Pegida members do that, too, but I've got nothing in common with them. Wagensveld is a hypocritical asshole. That's why we decided to set up DTG: no ideology, but protest—that was my idea. We wanted to make our voices heard, wake people up, in different towns and provinces. Our main aim wasn't even to get rid of the refugees but to target a government that lies to us all the time; a government who calls the newcomers refugees, but they weren't families, just men on their own coming here for financial gain, and who denies that our old people are being neglected. I don't have a problem with Muslims either.

Those apps and anti-Semitic memes, that was a load of fuss about nothing. I was in an app group, and they were sent to me. It's like being on a sports team or in the Scouts: you're in a group of guys who don't all think exactly the same way. People make jokes, about Hitler, too. It might not have been very acceptable, but we never wanted that stuff to be made public. It's not on my flyers. We also made jokes about Belgians, but the public prosecutor didn't make a point of that. That brings me back to the dirty tricks played by the government. I mean, come on, I was only making a joke. Three of the high-security transport guys who took me to court told me they made the same sort of jokes. Stand-up comedians do it, too, but suddenly, I'm a fascist. What I wanted was to draw attention to what is happening, to show people that they are being screwed by the government. And it worked, too: we suddenly had 5,000 to 7,000 people supporting us on Facebook. My target was 35,000, so that we could also submit a petition. In February 2016, I also wanted to leave DTG, because they were only protesting about the refugees. I wanted to draw attention to the problems faced by children, old people, people living on benefits—a lot wider, as it were. Wagensveld was a far-right extremist, and I didn't want to work with him at all or with DTG. I wanted to set up my own chapter of DSDA and to protest on behalf of all Dutch citizens.

My wife, my mother, and my family all supported me. What did it matter that I had a permanent job if others were suffering? What sort of country are we living in? If Rutte had really given those 1,000 euros, that would have given people at the bottom a bit of self-confidence, and they would now have been more optimistic. But now, everyone had had enough. And if you say anything about it, you get labeled a racist, extremist, or terrorist. Do I look like a terrorist? No way. I just wanted to help the people in my neighborhood, who were marginalized. My granddad was the same. I think I'm like him. He was a kind of national ombudsman in Hengelo: if people were in trouble, they would go to him. He would help them out with disputes with the local council or with their employers. That dedication, that tenacity that he had, I've got that, too.

But what happens if you take action? They silence you. That business at the mosque—I had nothing to do with that. I was sitting on the couch at Martijn's house. I didn't do anything. I didn't even know about the Molotov cocktails. They're all lying. And the judges—you think they're there to find out the truth, but no, not at all. If I had really thrown something, it would have been against the town hall, not a mosque. It's the government that's screwing us, not the Muslims. Look what happened. I informed the national ombudsman, and I told the probation service that it was all wrong. Some of my complaints about unfair treatment have been declared valid. I was in prison for twenty-four months. I couldn't touch my son; that was the most difficult. I'm against the government, but I give up—the government has won. It has come out on top. No more demonstrations: DTG and other groups have fallen apart. Everyone's afraid. And my idealism is completely gone. I'm no longer going to sacrifice things for others—no time, no money, no prison sentences, nothing. If someone falls over right here on my doorstep, I'll just close the curtains. Now, I live only for myself and my family.[31]

---

[31] Interview with Peter*, May 15, 2019, Enschede.

Local Redemption or Revenue Model?

From the accounts of these two ex-detainees, it is clear that the police and the legal authorities saw all five members of the group as being active at the far-right end of the spectrum. Their ideas could also be considered right-wing extremist in terms of the AIVD's definition: they are xenophobic and ultranationalist ideas. The group members were even convicted of a terrorist crime. Nevertheless, Martijn and Peter saw themselves more as heroes of the people, as national activists, than as far-right extremists. Moreover, their radical engagement was primarily local. Unlike Pegida, which was active in both Germany and the Netherlands, Martijn and Peter were mainly concerned about the people living on the poverty line in Pathmos, their own neighborhood in Enschede. The district was originally built in the 1920s to house large numbers of poor workers from peat colonies in the Dutch province of Drenthe, who were coming to Enschede in search of employment in the textile industry. After the war, the area became increasingly impoverished, with unemployment and social problems rising enormously. Solidarity was, however, very strong. DTG mobilized that social solidarity and shared mistrust of government in its opposition to the coming of the AZCs on the edge of the district. Their protests overlapped with the demonstrations by Pegida; the civic protests and demonstrations of these new activists merged with the far-right activities of veterans from the Dutch People's Union (Nederlandse Volks-Unie; NVU) and Blood & Honour. Despite clear and important differences in terms of motivation and readiness to use violence, individuals from these groups found common ground in the far-right slogan "no immigration, our own people first."

Whereas Peter saw himself mainly—in the family tradition of his grandfather—as a kind of local trade union leader for the less well-off in his neighborhood and city, Martijn was much more concerned about the "hundreds of pedophiles" who would come to Enschede with the influx of refugees and whom he believed to have already taken up residence in the old newspaper offices. But they both felt that "the others" were not doing enough; injustice reigned, and it was up to them to take action. "I have nothing more to lose," said Martijn. "A permanent job is not the highest goal in life after all," said Peter. Someone had to do something, and sitting at home doing nothing was not an option. Both felt that they had made sacrifices and fought for a higher cause: their wives, their neighborhood, their community, and even their nation. But they achieved nothing by fighting, and afterwards, they even denied their activism and extremism. After being arrested, Peter and Martijn changed course and gave up their activism. "It's just a waste of time," said Peter. "The government has won."

Peter and Martijn were clearly motivated by a sense of deficit and opposition to injustice. They sacrificed a lot for their activism—though it is doubtful whether they were aware of the consequences the attack on the mosque would have. Both are resolute in not seeing themselves as far-right extremists, and certainly not as terrorists. They admit to being right-wing and activists—at least before they were arrested— but not to being extremist. Their accounts show that such terms as *far-right populism, far-right extremism*, and *anti-Islamism* are "slippery" in the age of Facebook and the Internet. As Martijn said, they were not official members of any group and paid no contributions. Many of the demonstrations against AZCs and other plans rested on temporary coalitions and empty talk. Nevertheless, firebombs were set off, and there were adults and children present in the mosque.

In addition, their accounts show little evidence of religious or serious metaphysical or transcendental motives. Their opinions resemble one-dimensional caricatures of Muslims rather than a fully elaborated ideology. Peter and Martijn clearly had a few bad friends and were members of an app group where anti-Semitic, racist, and right-wing extremist comments were the order of the day. They were also mainly active locally, driven by empathy for people in their immediate vicinity, and prepared to take risks. But there were no apocalyptic references to a final battle, nor was there a clearly articulated appeal to a global community. These things distinguish them clearly from both the jihadist redemption terrorists and murderous far-right extremists like Breivik, Tarrant, Balliet, and Roof, who—with premeditation, a manifesto, and an arsenal of weapons—aimed to unleash a race war.

Conclusion

The stories of detained terrorists from ethnic-tribal groups (Boko Haram, Al-Shabaab), armed resistance groups (the Syrian opposition), and right-wing extremist networks (DTG) show that radical redemption is a phenomenon, or rather an interpretative framework, that clearly has primarily religious connotations. Especially if one compares the cases from this chapter and the historical chapter (chapter 3) with the stories of jihadist terrorists told in chapters 4, 5, and 6, it becomes clear that an organized, recognizable religious framework gives far more strength and coherence to the redemption narrative. The triptych of deficit, devotion, and validation acquires much clearer contours when the perpetrators can and wish to place themselves within an existing religious tradition with a transcendent dimension and the prospect of a heaven and hell. The orthopraxis becomes more tangible as well. Jihadists in particular have a clearly defined framework within which their sense of personal deficit or the failures of their community can be placed and measured, in which devotion and struggle can be glorified as a divine calling, and where they have the promise of a reward—paradise—that no one can take away from them. Such a worldview not only focuses on the afterlife but also colors the struggle in the physical world: opponents are demons, while fighters are assisted by angels and miracles.

The situation is different for people fighting to defend themselves in a civil war. Faith differences can play a role—for example, when Sunni Muslims are fighting against Alevites or Christians—but the conflict is in the first instance a political and territorial power struggle.

The far-right extremists' situation is more complex. Their stories contain some elements of the radical redemption narrative, such as gaining redemption by earning points. White supremacists and members of the Christian Identity movement in the United States adhere to explicit eschatological ideas on the final battle and Armageddon, and feel that they need to perform and anticipate that battle in the here and now. Breivik, for instance, developed a kind of points system in his manifesto for destroying enemies and profiled himself as a modern crusader. Balliet aimed to attract a lot of followers and gain many likes for his live stream, hoping to get a "high score" and gain "achievements" while killing as many people as possible in order to impress what he believed to be a large group of virtual followers. Martijn and Peter, too, hoped to achieve acknowledgment and status.

As I have argued before, radical redemption appears to be an especially strong narrative and source of meaning when there is a constituency or support base acknowledging the redemptive act as a higher or noble deed. This requires a framework that prescribes radical, violent behavior and a large group of followers who measure themselves against each other and evaluate their actions in terms of points and reward systems. Breivik, Tarrant, Roof, and Balliet were to some extent able to create or find a framework where their achievements and associated rewards were validated—or disqualified, in Balliet's case—for example, via the 4chan and 8chan platforms, where Breivik and Tarrant in particular were glorified almost as saints. The situation for the far-right Dutch detainees I interviewed was very different. The loose nationalist and far-right Internet networks and flash mobs surrounding the anti-AZC demonstrations in 2015 and 2016 dropped their comrades immediately after they had been arrested, and dissolved almost completely.

As we have seen, Boko Haram fighters have a sectarian ideology and a strong community that facilitates the dissemination of narratives of redemption. There is a tendency to link radicalization processes in Africa quickly to such factors as poverty or deprivation. While such links may be true and evidence based, the role of religion and religious narratives as moderators in shaping these radicalization processes should not be overlooked. When young people are recruited, the promises of fast motorbikes, money, and women are tempting, and they may lack a viable alternative to make a living. But the narrative of devotion, struggle, and reward presented to them is also in itself very appealing: it immediately gives their lives new meaning, direction, and excitement. The radical redemption framework is, in this context, a model of appraisal that gives color to existing abuses and misery. The prospect of devotion and struggle and of personal redemption offers young people a meaningful, adventurous, and full life, and promises them a reward in the afterlife. Vulnerable and susceptible young people are lured into this ideological trap and, by demonic threats, are scared to such a degree that they can no longer break free.

8
Toward a Grounded Theory of Radical Redemption

The Grounded Theory Approach

In this chapter, we review our findings with respect to the threads running through the terrorists' accounts that indicate the shaping role of the narrative of radical redemption in their radicalization processes. Building on Dan McAdams's (2006) work, this study uses the notion of radical redemption as a sensitizing concept. The concept is tested against the life stories of convicted terrorists in detention. On the basis of their accounts of redemption, I develop a grounded theory approach (GTA) to give the accounts a systematic basis.[1] The GTA combines inductive and deductive research. *Inductive* means that the research has an open and flexible structure, following the accounts as the detainees give them, thus generating accessible and unstructured data. *Deductive* means that we place the data in a systematic framework (that of the narrative approach), verifying it and using it to form a theory (King et al. 2018). Historians will recognize here the iterative process of combining oral history, primary source study (legal dossiers), and secondary research (media, published texts)—going back and forth rather than working from a clearly designed set of hypotheses and conducting a fixed experiment.

With the data collected and analyzed in the previous chapters, I can now answer the research question laid out in chapter 1: To what extent does the radical redemption narrative shape radicalization toward terrorism? This question was broken down in three subquestions: (1) How does terrorism manifest itself as a praxis of radical redemption? (2) How does the redemption narrative—when we encounter it—offer individuals a framework within which they can give their lives meaning? (3) At what point and why does this

---

[1] There are many interpretations and versions of the GTA. I made use of Glaser et al. (1968) and Strauss and Corbin (2008).

narrative lose its appeal? My response is put in the form of a tentative model—tentative, because it is based on twenty-five accounts only, and is thus only a first step toward further research and further testing of the findings and hypotheses elaborated here. In the following sections, I first present some general findings on the recurring triptych-like pattern I encountered in the perpetrators' narratives that shaped their radicalization process. Then, I respond to the three subquestions.

The Recurring Pattern of the Triptych

The following three elements could be identified to some extent in the narratives of almost all individuals I interviewed for this book: (1) a sense of moral deficit and (2) a sense of calling and personal responsibility to devote oneself to (3) the physical or virtual struggle, set in motion by and channeled through immersion in the world of images and virtual reality and motivated by a desire for redemption. At the end of these steps, the redemption is validated, or the desire is contaminated (see the radical redemption model in chapter 2, figure 2.1).

Almost all the interviewees spoke of the absence of and the search for meaning in their lives. Although they were still very general experiences, these feelings of a lack of meaning or direction were, in most cases, linked to frustration about injustice and a desire to identify the people who caused it. Strikingly, more than half of the interviewees expressed the wish to transcend the experienced lack of meaning by doing something for their perceived or imagined community. Slightly less than half of them simply wanted to do something good, to create a better future for following generations, or to bring the final battle closer. All interviewees were, to a greater or lesser extent, aware of their own role, their own responsibility. They were demonstrably willing to devote themselves to a physical struggle, to fight on a real battlefield, so that spiritual landscape and physical location would come together and they could commit genuine acts of redemption—although not all of them did commit or complete these physical actions; some were arrested for planning, conspiring, and preparing to do them.

The motive of a sense of moral deficit differs from the more detached motive of injustice, as well as from the general motive of a search for meaning, which is often mentioned in the literature (Doosje et al. 2016; Moghaddam 2005; Kruglanski et al. 2009; della Porta 1995). My interviewees certainly cared strongly about the injustice experienced by those who shared their faith, and most of them were searching for meaning in their lives. But what was especially striking in their accounts was the sense of a moral deficit, seen through the lens of extreme religious—or secular—beliefs, linked to the need to do something about it themselves. Once the injustice entered their living room (via YouTube), dominated their thoughts (in the form of concern, sympathy, and anger), and got under their skin as a sense of guilt, responsibility, and the need to do something, it created in them a personal sense of deficit, and they felt they had to act.

All of the interviewees placed the often violent actions they committed because of their sense of deficit in the context of a greater project—a greater ethical or moral program such as joining the jihad, participating in the holy struggle, or protecting and purifying their national community. That often meant that, from the perspective of the overarching ethical program, they could earn points for their own actions. They told me their contributions to jihadist propaganda, their efforts to collect money, and even their departure for Syria earned them points; through those actions, they could make amends for past misdeeds, and there would be a reward waiting for them.

Despite their differences, all of the accounts thus contained recurring patterns of deficit, injustice, frustration, devotion, and the embracing of a comprehensive or even totalitarian or theocratic framework. Sometimes, they spoke of individual forms of guilt, atonement, and revenge; at other times, they talked about a collectively propagated and shared effort and desire to liberate people from injustice.

The perpetrators saw the activities for which they were ultimately convicted as things they had done to invest in a better future for themselves and/or for their perceived community, either on earth or in the afterlife. Fighting in Afghanistan or Syria and demonstrating against the arrival of an asylum seekers center were seen both as difficult tasks requiring devotion and as worthwhile activities.

Some perpetrators spoke about guilt, atonement, honor, and revenge in terms that were very similar or even identical. Others employed their own jargon. Some had devised a complete system of ideas. For most of them, radicalization occurred at a specific point in time: they were suddenly gripped— and this was supported by their dossiers—by holy notions of liberation, redemption, and oppression and the need to bring the oppression to an end. Without undergoing a further or prolonged process of radicalization, they then immediately committed ritualized acts of violence or left for the war zone. "Suddenly you get it," as Karim* told me about his brother; everything falls into place, and you only have to surrender yourself to it.[2]

A significant recurring pattern was that the interviewees were moved to act by looking at images, film clips, and videos on YouTube, which triggered the spontaneous and sudden realization just mentioned. Many of them said that, by watching IS propaganda or film clips of the struggle in Afghanistan, they not only were virtually transported to a different geographical location but also found themselves imbued with new perceptions and impressions. Through sound and vision, a spiritual landscape unfolded in front of their eyes that they were immediately invited to and in which they could play an active role. As Abdelkarim* and Fadil*, for example, told me: "The people there gave me answers and helped me to decide what I could do."[3] For the generation of detainees arrested between 2011 and 2015, who form the core group in this book, the virtual reality of the Internet and games became a genuine reality. The virtual battlefield in the film clips, the jihadist landscape they dreamed of, was "just around the corner," only a flight to Istanbul away.

I therefore conclude that the radicalization process of the individuals who radicalized after 2011 was less gradual and linear than the literature, with its schematic approach, suggests.[4] From the way in which they themselves talk about it and give meaning to the change in the course of their lives, it was, rather, a moment of epiphany, of revelation. "Suddenly you get it," and you leap into a new, alternative reality in which your own actions have a real impact. When they tapped into online offers of rewards for acts that were seen as pure, and became acquainted with people and theories that promised them points in the afterlife or likes on the fora on which they were active, the gamification of terrorism was complete. *Gamification* is the application of methods and playing patterns from computer games to nongame situations; in other words, mechanisms from the game industry are projected and enacted in the real world, including aiming for high scores and achievements and distributing likes and points among peer groups (see Brachman and Levine 2011; Evans 2019). For some detainees—who still do not understand why they were convicted as terrorists—such gamification included

---

[2] Interview with Karim*, April 17, 2020, Utrecht.
[3] Interview with Abdelkarim*, June 11, 2019, Utrecht; interview with Fadil*, March 6, 2019, The Hague.
[4] See, for example, the "staircase" presented by Moghaddam (2005) or the linear path in Gielen (2017).

the completely unrealistic expectation that they would be able to turn off the jihad computer game just as easily as they had turned it on.

Radical Redemption as an Orthopraxis

The narrative of radical redemption involves beliefs, emotions, and actions, defined here as the orthopraxis of radical redemption (see chapter 1, figure 1.4). Importantly, the element of the orthopraxis—the search for the right, pure course of action—is often neglected in discussions on the cognitive and doctrinal aspects—beliefs—that play a part in radicalization processes. By contrast, in the narrative approach used in this book, the connection between saying and doing takes center stage: it is the act of jumping into one's own script of giving meaning to one's life. Embracing and activating the sense of personal deficit, taking up responsibility for it, and engaging in action to pay off that debt are crucial to the narrative of radical redemption. The interviewees indeed told me that their decision to act was informed by an online or personal suggestion to go to Syria or Iraq and thus to fulfill their duty as pure Muslims. Terrorist contacts or organizations in the Middle East offered that jihadist solution. They portrayed the battlefield there as "the place to be" and facilitated their departure. What confirmed their radical step was that friends and comrades liked and applauded their decision. Their peers gave support, in real life or online. The jihadist interviewees reported that they dreamt dreams and saw angels on the battlefield—for them, a clear validation of their decision. The support of their friends and their dreams helped to silence their feelings of malaise, which were caused by the idea that they were doing too little and that there was too great a divide between their lives of luxury in the Netherlands and the plight of Muslim children suffering in Syria. In this sense, the orthopraxis was informed by emotions and supported by (sometimes very implicit, inarticulate) beliefs.

Another element that stood out in the interviewees' accounts of the search for pure actions was the phenomenon of earning points to validate one's actions. Within Muslim communities, on the street, in the mosque, or online, young men and women—also the radicalizing ones—often speak of earning *hasanat* or *ajr*. Pure and good deeds are discussed and allocated to specific people and their actions. Going to Syria would certainly earn someone enough points to facilitate entrance into paradise. Some of the right-wing extremists, as we saw, had a different but corresponding system of allocating points to high scores and achievements, indicating a context of gamification. Gamification was certainly a major influence in the lives of the terrorists I interviewed. Furthermore, with their search for the right, pure, and good deeds, they tapped into something that philosophy professor Thi Nguyen (2020, chapter 9) describes as *value capture*; this is a process that occurs "when our natural values are subtle, but institutions present us with simplified versions of those values and we internalize them." In short, distributing likes or points allocates a binary or at least quantitative dimension to vague and nuanced concepts such as "living a good life" and "doing the right thing." In the context of radicalization, value capture is a recipe for further dichotomous and harsh decisions and actions. It violates the complexity of the normative and moral realm, and uncertainty, conflict, and inchoate feelings of deficit are reduced to simplified judgments and corresponding actions.

It may just be the case that the immersion in the online world has triggered a series of mechanisms—such as gamification and value capture—among young potential jihadist and right-wing extremist recruits that shape their radicalization process in a novel way. For them, performance, action, and orthopraxis matter even more than for previous generations of terrorists—who had to radicalize themselves by reading long-winded texts and books. It also explains why radicalization processes sometimes occur in such a short period of time: the narrative of redemption, especially with its praxis of simplified value capture, only needs to trigger emotions, convey a superficial sense of pure beliefs, and prescribe how to earn points by engaging in specific actions.

The Role of Religion in the Radical Redemption Narrative

An overarching question for this book asked about the role of religion in the process of radicalization. I can now conclude that religion, in the individual and social aspects defined in chapter 1, has a distinctive function: it makes the framework of the radical redemption model more tangible and solid.

Take the first panel of the triptych, the sense of a deficit. This deficit can relate to a growing sense of unease or a rising feeling of frustration regarding injustices in one's own life or the lives of others. Yet, such emotions of falling short, being "bad," and leading a wrong life must be made specific and must be embedded in a broader narrative that gives direction to these emotions, translates them into actions, and connects them to beliefs regarding the right goal to fight for. This is where religious content comes in. Preachers, recruiters, texts, and websites offer specific "emotives," socially recognizable and identifiable frames that articulate inchoate individual emotions.[5] All the interviewees told me they had searched the Internet for an explanation of their sense of deficit. Abdelkarim acquired his information from Salafist preacher Anwar al-Awlaki. Noureddine*, Anwar*, and Amin* were addicted to watching film clips on the IS channels. My Indonesian interviewees had tapes, books, and texts by Sheikh Azzam. This helped them to place their personal sense of deficit into a clear and well-defined emotive of good and evil, to formulate this as a series of articulate grievances, and to embed this in a compelling narrative. One could argue that this also holds true, to some extent, for the right-wing extremists I interviewed: they found a framework for their anger in the material that Pegida and DSDA offered them, and they found a community on Facebook where they could share their emotions and discuss their beliefs. Yet, the global, historical, and recognizable outreach of religious content, frames, and narratives can be considered more pervasive as well as more accessible.

In the second panel, religious or extreme beliefs linked the articulated grievances to a sense of personal calling and moral responsibility to take action. As they came into contact—physically or digitally—with like-minded others, the necessity of engaging in the right course of action became inescapable to my interviewees. They felt called; sometimes, they were literally called upon and addressed as sinful believers, as failing patriots that needed to step up and fight for their community, belief, class, or God, and thus join the throng of fellow believers. Here, again, the presence and offer of received practices reinforced the sense of calling and the willingness to join in. It helped when other group members spoke of miracles and angels, shared dreams, or disseminated stories about martyrs who had perished on the battlefield and demanded young people to follow in their revered footsteps. The website De Ware Religie (The True Religion), for instance, disseminated such stories in the Netherlands. The presence of religious rituals, practices, and props that hailed back to acknowledged traditions and communal norms made the step toward embracing agency and preparing

---

[5] "Emotives are expressed emotions (i.e., emotional vocabulary) that are instrumental in changing, building, hiding and intensifying emotions that are accepted and recognized in a particular community" (Palm 2018, 136). For more on the "emotional turn" in history, see also Frevert (2011); Reddy (2001, 105).

to act very compelling and performative. Such performances and rituals as praying, worshipping, sacrificing, and purifying are all well aligned in existing religions. And while extremists pervert, abuse, and radicalize them, they still manage to keep these practices recognizable and appealing to potential new recruits looking for meaning, significance, and redemption.

Furthermore, facilitating organizations practically and logistically helped recruits to enter into the fight and embrace the radical struggle. The caliphate and its helpers, such as radical preachers in Indonesia or the Netherlands, acted as conveyors and trip advisers. The phenomenon of value capture featured in this stage as well: jihadists challenged and dared each other to earn more achievements, told each other about angels appearing on the battlefield, and listened to arousing battle songs composed for them by fellow Islamists. The fact that fighting could be legitimized by a belief in an eschatological final battle—which made participation in the struggle a way of earning points to enter paradise—made these instances of orthopraxis both more palatable and more meaningful, as much to the jihadists themselves as to potential followers. The fact that "he would enter paradise" and the Dutch "infidels would burn in hell" served the compelling nature of the redemptive narrative even for someone such as Gökmen Tanis, who carried out his attack in the Netherlands, survived it, and was brought to court.

Interestingly, there was less difference in orthopraxis between my Dutch and Indonesian jihadist interviewees than I expected. They often referred to similar visions and dreams, which the Indonesian perpetrators mainly had read about in books—the ones by Azzam—and their Dutch counterparts had found on the Internet. There was little difference between their descriptions of the miracles they purportedly witnessed and the battles they participated in while fighting their war. Moreover, the wider geopolitical and ideological context of the wars in Afghanistan and Syria, the advent of global jihad, and the appeal of Al Qaeda and IS ensured that young Muslims in the Netherlands and those in Indonesia could plug into a similar narrative of a jihadist holy war against the infidels and against the West, including the rituals, practices, and images used to further this cause.

Does this mean that nonreligious or not openly religious radical redemption motives are not compelling or tangible? Well, only to some extent. The triptych was also discernible in the stories right-wing extremists told me and spread on the Internet. Yet, the Dutch right-wing extremists' sense of deficit was less articulate, they felt more abandoned after their arrest, and they did not have any support base to give them gratification or a sense of validation.

On the contrary, their former right-wing compatriots betrayed and abandoned them. In other instances of right-wing extremist terrorism, a constituency may be present that offers a system of value capture and a framework of national, racial, and radical redemption. In the cases of Brenton Tarrant and Anders Behring Breivik, such a support base showed itself after their attacks. This certainly needs further investigation.

If we look back to the other examples of nonreligious radical redemption narratives discussed in this book, it might seem that some inferences could be drawn from them. Obviously, different historical contexts and dissimilar ideological situations entail a bit of a stretch in terms of discussing the notion of radical redemption deployed here. Yet, echoes and traces of this idea surfaced and were able to gain solidity and salience, especially if and when they tapped into the repertoires of received and organized religion. When Gudrun Ensslin and Ulrike Meinhof spoke convincingly of collective guilt and even sin regarding the German fascist past, they channeled the emotional vocabulary of their Lutheran upbringing. Bobby Sands's sacrifice gained such traction in the Northern Irish society and beyond because he and the Provisional Irish Republican Army (IRA) members and sympathizers very effectively used a universal Catholic language and Catholic symbols. Breivik explicitly tried to present himself to future followers as a modern crusader and savior, also tapping into deep Christian symbolism. The jury is still out on whether religion is and does something special as compared to other worldviews (Moon et al. 2023). Yet it is safe to say that, with its offer of literal immortality, a larger metaphysical and even eschatological timeline one may become a part of, and concrete rituals, practices, and prescriptions of social and moral behavior, religion provides a framework of a redemptive narrative that—even when perverted and radicalized by extremists—is hard to beat by other groups or parties and is one that can bear very strongly on the process of radicalization. It makes the mundane holy and the lowlife a savior, and it shows paradise through earthly toil.

The Rich Varieties of Religious Radical Redemption

Still, the religious version of the radical redemption narrative displays enough variations to warrant more study and research. The macrocontext provides a variety of backdrops to narratives of radical redemption: the radicalizing individual may live in a free democracy, governed by the rule of law, such as in the Netherlands, or in a situation characterized by lawlessness, such as in some places in northern Nigeria. This context directly impacts the threshold for resorting to violence and how much effort is required for a radical religious, extremist group to recruit new followers. For young people in northern Cameroon, it is far easier and—given the poverty and lack of alternatives—in some instances perhaps even more logical to adopt armed struggle and join a terrorist organization than it is for young Muslims in the Netherlands. The mesocontext also matters: a group or organization that offers a clear and compelling narrative to engage in terrorism may already be active, such as the IRA in Northern Ireland in the 1970s, or a group may have to start from scratch, such as the Red Army Faction (RAF). And the microcontext is also important: it matters whether or not the individual is already familiar with violence, has a criminal record, has experienced trauma, and has relatives and friends who have already gone to wage jihad. All these specific contexts and elements affect the way the radical redemption narrative shapes the radicalization process.

Having compared the interviewees' accounts of radical redemption, I can identify three specific manifestations of that narrative, according to a set of variables. In appendix 1, the individual accounts are placed below each other and profiled on the basis of the variables elaborated in this section. These variables relate to several elements of the triptych model of radical redemption: experiencing a sense of deficit, feeling called and feeling responsible, and taking part in the struggle.

The sense of deficit, first of all, could be considered a gliding scale ranging from a highly personal deficit—sin, *haram*, guilt—to an indirect, collective deficit experienced on behalf of one's oppressed community. Amin, for example, felt personally guilty and sinful due to his criminal past and because he felt he did not do enough for oppressed Muslims elsewhere, whereas Asaad* felt bad that so few Muslims in the West stood up for their brothers in Syria and Iraq and wanted to make up for that.

Second, the calling and feeling of responsibility could be highly personal; it could, for instance, be a calling to atone for a sinful life. Ahmed* and Abderozzak Benarabe felt such a personal responsibility. But the sense of calling could also be more general: Haroun* and Omar*, for example, felt it was their moral duty, as part of a collective, to stand up and save Muslim children in Syria. A striking finding here was that this collective sense of responsibility was often found among interviewees who reported long traditions of activist engagement in their families. Farihin and Kurnia Widodo saw their jihadist engagement as a continuation of something that just ran in their families, and Peter* referred to his grandfather, who, as a kind of informal neighborhood leader, defended the interests of the people in his area.

Third, the struggle could be waged because the perpetrators hoped to earn personal rewards with their actions, such as *hasanat* or likes on social media. But the aim of the battle or violent action could also be the liberation of a group, as part of a holy war, vis-à-vis the coming of the Mahdi or the caliph. For right-wing extremists, the equivalent could be the Great Reset.

Next, I simplified these gliding scales and turned them into a variable indicating either the one or the other end of the scale: the deficit could be personal or political, the calling/responsibility could be individual or collective, and the struggle could be personal/ethical or eschatological. In appendix 1, I accordingly indicated, where possible, the nature of each interviewee's sense of deficit (A = personal, B = political), calling/responsibility (C = individual, D = collective), and struggle (E = personal/ethical, F = eschatological). That produces three axes and several typical positions. With A, C, and E, the focus is on the personal search for meaning and atonement; with B, it is on the political aspect; with D, it is on revenge or, conversely, altruism; and with F, it is on a strong eschatological position, where the individuals concerned present themselves as zealots.

Obviously, summarizing complex life stories in a limited dataset does not do proper justice to all possible nuances and contexts of a religious radical redemption narrative. Yet, on the basis of the interviews and the variables, three profiles could be made out: narratives of (1) altruists in search of meaning, (2) individuals in search of atonement, and (3) zealots in search of revenge.

(1) The altruists were mainly those who left to join the struggle after 2011 but before June 2014, when IS declared the caliphate. They were relatively quickly disappointed in their high expectations of redemption or reward. Most returned of their own accord, and all seemed very disillusioned, frustrated, and traumatized by their discovery that their hopes of radical redemption proved mistaken.

(2) Many of the individuals seeking atonement—mostly zealots—had a criminal record; having a low violence threshold, they had committed or had planned to commit relatively serious violent crimes, including killing. They felt they had to transform their remorse for the crimes they had committed into deeds that would serve a good cause and would

earn them enough points to atone for their guilt. Their experience with crime and weapons stood them in good stead in situations of fighting and war. The crime–terror nexus emphatically applies to this category of interviewees. Among these individuals, there were also some who sought atonement for the collective guilt, out of a sense of general injustice, and not out of personal guilt.

(3) The avengers, or vengeful zealots, were the most ruthless in their actions, and in my conversations with them it was clear they still believed their deeds had been necessary. They committed the most-serious crimes—think of Gökmen Tanis, for instance—and joined IS.

In theory, far-right extremists can also be categorized as zealots if they consciously embrace notions of an ideal national community and pursue such transcendental values as purification and liberation. The Dutch far-right extremists interviewed for this study resembled the first group—the altruists—while perpetrators like Anders Breivik, Brenton Tarrant, Dylann Roof, and Stephan Balliet would more closely fit the definition of zealots with their fantasies of revenge and eternal fame. But again, we need further, more structural and encompassing research to explore the possible role of eschatology, transcendence, and the supernatural in right-wing extremist narratives.

Not Validation but Contamination

The last subquestion that needs answering is the one inquiring into the process of contamination. Put differently, this question asks when and why the narrative of radical redemption loses its appeal. It is first of all important to underscore that the belief that redemption is possible and already underway can assume various forms. The following recurring redemptive moves, which are analogous to McAdams's (2006) types of redemption, can be identified.

- Socioeconomic: from homelessness and unemployment to a job, a wife, and a higher status in society. Reasoning: "Here I am nothing, but there they need me. Here I'm homeless, but there I can work and get a motorcycle." Or: "The government does nothing; we stand up for the people

living on benefits." Fulfillment lies in achieving a new status, position, job, and/or partner.
- Medical-physical: from physical wreck to angel. Reasoning: "I failed as a boxer, was addicted to drugs, had testicular cancer, and was no longer a real man. The caliphate gave me the chance to help bring about Armageddon as an angel of vengeance." Fulfillment lies in upgrading one's body and life.
- Moral-ethical: from guilt to liberation. Reasoning: "I feel guilty about my luxury position here. I have material goods, while they have nothing. I have a criminal record and cannot appear before Allah like this. I have to do something good, to earn points for myself and for those I love." Fulfillment lies in earning points for the afterlife, in doing good deeds that will be taken into account later, by Allah, in paradise.
- Religious-eschatological: from shelf stacker in a godless land to jihadist in the caliphate. Reasoning: "Every Muslim must seize the opportunity to contribute to the holy struggle. Who wants to stay at home sitting on the couch when you know that the End of Days is drawing near? I want to fight with the winning team." Fulfillment lies in achieving victory or seeing miracles on the battlefield, gaining recognition from one's comrades, and earning points for the afterlife.

While all twenty-five interviewees reported they initially felt validated while they were "out there," only two of them said that now, after their return, they still felt they had achieved the redemption they had been looking for. Jibran* believed—and continues to believe—he had saved the people of the Netherlands. Gökmen Tanis—who was not among the interviewees but whose case I used in this study on the basis of secondary evidence—proclaimed in court that he would go to heaven while all infidels would end up in hell. Ahmed adopted a position somewhere in the middle: he initially thought that by joining IS he could contribute to the final battle, but that proved a mistake, because coalition troops ultimately conquered the territory under IS control and little was gained from the fighting. This had not, however, destroyed all hope and expectation that a new opportunity for radical redemption would present itself: "If Muslims are persecuted elsewhere, in Myanmar, for example, and my brothers there, the Rohingya, call on me to help, I'll jump on a plane in no time.... Because that's the best thing that can happen to you as a Muslim—to die for Allah. That earns you points."[6]

---

[6] Interview with Ahmed*, February 5, 2020, PI/TDU.

All the others, however, looked back on their actions with bitterness, frustration, and sadness, or were severely traumatized. They suffered from what McAdams describes as *contamination*. Twenty-two of the interviewees admitted to me that they had made a mistake, that they "should never have started it," and that "it was all for nothing." More than half of them were very resolute about only caring for themselves and their families from now on. Their narrative of redemption had become a narrative of contamination—their devotion to the holy struggle and redemption had proved a misconception, a failure, and even a crime. And none of them wanted to start the cycle of redemption (see chapter 2, figure 2.2) anew.

It is important to be aware that deradicalization and disengagement—breaking loose from an extremist network and distancing oneself from certain forms of behavior—are processes that occur one step at a time. If people have devoted themselves heart and soul to an organization in the belief that it will bring them and their family redemption and eternal life, and if this belief subsequently turns out to be false, they need time to accept that their expectations will not be met, and to find new meaning and substance for themselves and their lives. Once perpetrators are in detention, they have time to do that.

What struck me during this study was that so little advantage is taken of the opportunity to speak to detainees about their faith, hopes, and expectations, despite their clear willingness to do so. Allowing detainees to describe what they initially believed, what they were willing to do to pursue their faith, and what became of their expectations can accelerate the process of disengagement. Take, for example, what the Indonesian jihadists told me about the discovery of the Abbottabad files. They said that reading these papers was crucial in prompting a change in their thinking. Furthermore, bin Laden's notes and warnings about the errors made by Baghdadi and Al Qaeda in Iraq played a prominent role in the Indonesian government's deradicalization and exit programs. It was a great shock for my Indonesian interviewees that, after 2001, bin Laden himself criticized large-scale attacks that demanded the lives of many innocent victims. It made them doubt the value of jihadist violence, since the papers undermined and delegitimized IS and attacks like those on Bali in 2002 and 2005. Although it was not, of course, an unambiguous conversion to democracy, this was nevertheless an important step for my Indonesian interviewees.

It is helpful to identify the step in the redemption cycle where a suspect or detainee finds themself. If they were arrested before they had the opportunity to depart and commit their act of violence, they feel frustrated, and it will take much to convince them that they have been misled. If the act has already been committed, and certainly if they have returned from Syria or Iraq of their own accord, they are more open to reflection. Nevertheless, here, too, we must pay close attention to the phase in the process of increasing personal and spiritual awareness in which an individual finds themself. Research on radicalization devotes extensive attention to traumas, criminal records, and possible medical and pathological disorders. However, if we seek to really understand someone's radical potential, a better understanding of their spiritual and religious development is equally important. If a detainee has recently returned from Syria and is still coming to terms with their failed mission, interventions of a theological or religious nature have little effect. But if a detainee has discovered for themself that reward and redemption have not materialized because the ideological foundation on which that promise was based is flawed, they may be open to having a conversation on this new narrative of contamination and, perhaps, to being deradicalized.

While the leap to devotion and struggle can be taken in an instant, accepting the reality of failed redemption and false paths takes much more time. When he fled from his old comrades and rival terrorist organizations and militias, it took Haroun almost a year to reach the conclusion that he was not fighting the final battle he had dreamed of in Syria. Anwar and Noureddine hung around in Syria—under coercion or of their own free will—before deciding it could not be their promised land.

It is significant that none of the convicted terrorists I interviewed talked about their intended or actual victims. Haroun and Kurnia clearly found it difficult to live with the fact that they had taken part in the fighting and people had died as a result of their actions. Fadil, too, said that he should never have listened to the IS propaganda. But in most of my interviews with the other terrorists, their remorse or complete change of mind was implicit at best, and they were either unwilling or unable to talk about these things explicitly. While they may have modified their desire for and expectations of radical redemption and the pride they felt about their own roles in the struggle, that certainly did not automatically lead to full-scale deradicalization and abandonment of their jihadist or Salafist ideas. Nor did it mean that they had now become respectable democrats embracing the rule of law. Most of them continued to harbor resentment against the West, to be angry about injustice and Western elites, and to see the holy struggle in principle as a possibility or duty. Yet, the twenty-two interviewees felt such strong disappointment and disillusion that they completely turned their backs on the political struggle and the news from the Middle East and decided to focus exclusively on inner piety or their family lives.

An ambivalent conclusion from this study, therefore, is that in the cases of almost all the perpetrators, the narrative of radical redemption refuted itself. For those who fit the model of radical redemption—which is emphatically not all of them, particularly not ethnic-nationalist terrorists and members of the armed opposition in civil wars—the deep desire for and high expectations of their own act of redemption rarely brought the sought-after reward or fulfillment. The redemption narrative was destroyed by its own ontological inconsistences. According to almost all belief systems, true redemption is reserved for the few. Only the real Messiah, the Mahdi, saints, prophets, caliphs, and popular heroes are capable of saving others or sacrificing their lives from pure intentions. According to the legends, that path is closed to common mortals. The various holy scriptures do not convincingly validate fighting for more modest ideals, rewards, or points anywhere. So, where can one check how many points were scored with jihadist actions? Peer group confirmation is then the best option left. Jihadist fighters were, indeed, very good at upholding morale by circulating stories about corpses smelling of musk or not decomposing. Still, even those interviewees who claimed to have experienced miracles were in the end deeply disappointed in their organizations, in their own limited capacities, or in the community they had fought so hard for. It was not their caliphate after all. The final battle did not break out. The prophecies proved to be nonsense, and no one came to thank them for their efforts and their participation in the holy battle. Their exalted life story of sacrifice and redemption became a mundane narrative of failure and disappointment. Some of them, fortunately, had family members, wives, or trusted friends who were able to gradually convince them that there are other narratives to live for and other, nonradical ways to be a good Muslim, father, or son.[7]

The findings also point to the question of how the arrest and imprisonment of the interviewees relate to this sense of contamination. Significantly, most of them disengaged or returned to the Netherlands of their own accord. They were not arrested on the battlefield, but only later on. Thus, the decision to give up the fight had been their own. In addition, it is quite possible that at least some of those who died on the battlefield had entered a stage

---

[7] Family members can be particularly effective. See Sieckelinck and De Winter (2015).

of despair and contamination. Karim, for example, told me about the disappointment and despair experienced by his brother Hassan, who, before his death in battle, seemed to have lost his faith in the holy struggle. Hassan chose to die on the battlefield because he had burned all his bridges behind him and did not want to return to the Netherlands. But he had long abandoned his belief in martyrdom.[8]

As I said before, it is difficult to make general statements on the basis of a small sample. Much more research is required, especially into the experience of radical redemption among active fighters. In their situation, while they may not yet have had the opportunity to express their doubts, the redemptive sequence may have already turned into a contamination sequence. For now, I can at least point to a clear thread of doubt and disappointment running through all stories of the terrorism suspects I interviewed, including those who initially longed most earnestly for devotion and struggle.

Recidivism and Reintegration

On the basis of these observations, we can cautiously conclude that recidivism is very unlikely among adherents of the radical redemption narrative who have completed the cycle. Research appears to bear this out.

Of the approximately sixty departees who returned to the Netherlands, some twenty were still in detention in March 2020—there were, in total, thirty-six convicted terrorists in detention at that moment. Ten were deported, while the rest of them have completed their prison sentences and are now following reintegration programs. The majority of the detainees were interviewed for this study, as were some of those in reintegration programs. As stated above, only one of the detained terrorists I spoke with personally—Jibran—still explicitly believed in his mission of radical redemption. None of those who have participated in reintegration programs since 2013 have reverted to terrorism.

Despite the incompleteness of the data, it can be concluded that between 2013 and 2020, some 5 percent of convicted terrorists again committed terrorist crimes.[9] If we include three detainees from Arnhem—who are

---

[8] Interview with Karim*, April 17, 2020, Utrecht, who had been regularly speaking to Hassan on the telephone up to a few days before his death and had heard how his brother steadily became more doubtful and desperate.

[9] There is some debate about what the term *terrorist recidivism* comprises, in particular whether it includes convicted terrorists who go on to commit "normal"—that is, nonterrorist—crimes or only

suspected of preparing a terrorist attack and whose trials are still ongoing—in the group of detained terrorists arrested and convicted on appeal after 2013—a total of around fifty—we end up with six recidivists in a group of some 130 convicted terrorists in this period, which is about 5 percent (see chapter 4, table 4.1). This corresponds to the results of recent research in Belgium (see, e.g., Renard 2020).

This figure is a little higher than that from the United States (1%–2%) and lower than that from Indonesia (8%–9%). It is, however, difficult to put a value on these figures, since they reflect only the situation at a specific moment in time. Someone who seems to have reintegrated may yet revert to violent crime—as in the cases of the three suspects from Arnhem. In addition, the most fanatical jihadists are not included in the figures, because they either died or stayed in Syria or Iraq. In its most recent assessment of the terrorist threat in the Netherlands, the National Coordinator for Counterterrorism and Security (NCTV) confirms that the recidivism percentage appears to be low, at 2.5 percent. That said, the NCTV stresses that the recidivism figure is not a reliable method of measuring success in combating terrorism. Even if ex-detainees no longer commit criminal offenses, they may still play a prominent role in radical networks, acting as examples, inspirators, or communicators. And while in detention, they learn from each other—for example, by reading each other's criminal records—how to stay within the bounds of the law. That jihadists are not again arrested after completing their prison sentences may be because they have successfully undergone a learning process rather than a deradicalization process.[10]

I fully concur with these critical notes and nuances regarding the recidivism figures. Too little time has passed to be able to say anything definitive about the deradicalization and disengagement of the jihadists of the most recent wave; more research and sustained monitoring are required. Still, for the time being, we make do with the figures that are available to us, and these suggest that the recidivism percentage is very low, certainly when compared to the figure for recidivists among convicted criminals more generally, which is 40–60 percent (see Weggemans and De Graaf 2015, 27–8; 2017).

---

those who go on to commit more terrorist crimes. Here, I use the term *terrorist recidivist* to refer to previously convicted terrorists who go on to commit terrorist crimes again.

[10] NCTV (2020); background conversation with an analyst from the General Intelligence and Security Service (AIVD), July 6, 2020.

Alongside the warnings and critical explanations described earlier, I would therefore like to offer another, more hopeful explanation for the low percentage, one that is underpinned by the insights described in this study and in this chapter. Jihadists commit their acts because of their beliefs. They believe in devotion and struggle, in reward and redemption. If their beliefs are undermined through internal disputes, infighting, refutation from within their own group, or evolving insights, both the intrinsic motivation for committing violence and the encouragement and validation of a group of sympathizers dissipate. What happened to almost all of the detained terrorists I spoke with is that, just when they were closest to fulfilling their dream and had entered the envisaged landscape of the jihad, disappointment presented itself. Their jihadist dream landscape proved to be far less spiritual and harmonious than they had imagined, and fighting for Allah proved beyond their reach or led only to misery and trauma.

Strikingly, this cycle of radical redemption and contamination also applied to the accounts of the far-right extremists in Enschede. They, too, started off with a strong, reported desire to devote themselves to the struggle and to save their community, only to end up in the frustration of failure and apathy. Their community proved a mirage; no one supported them, and they landed in prison, disillusioned. They are now taking part in reintegration programs and—as far as I and the probation services can determine—have completely turned their backs on political activism.[11]

The Role of Religion in the Process of Disillusionment, Disengagement, and Reintegration

Ideological extreme beliefs played a decisive role in the lives of my interviewees and in their radicalization processes. From Africa to Asia and Europe, the desire for radical redemption proved a prominent, even dominant narrative that shaped the way they devoted their lives to the armed struggle. At the same time, it is important to point out here that religious communities can also play a crucial role in persuading radicalized young people to abandon their extremist ideas and in helping them to embrace nonviolent engagement.

---

[11] This assumption is based on conversations with and estimates by police and probation officers in 2020.

Remarkably, none of the Islamic perpetrators I spoke with had lost the basic tenets of their faith. But they had all come to realize, after talking to their parents and other family members, friends, or the imam, that their narrative of redemption and the encompassing praxis had been the result of deception. Their extreme beliefs and perceived belief community, including the bonus points that served as their reference point, ultimately proved not to offer the validation they sought. As they became disappointed in the terrorist leaders and the struggle, they began to reorient themselves toward a different form of faith-based praxis. For validation and implementation of their holy struggle, the perpetrators turned to the broader faith community, who ultimately offered them the alternative of a nonviolent praxis. Imams and spiritual leaders, as well as pious family members in the Netherlands and Indonesia, succeeded in getting through to the perpetrators—sometimes while they were still in Syria or Iraq, and sometimes only after they had been put in detention—and tried to make them see that the virtual reality on the Internet and the desert landscapes of the jihad were nothing more than an abhorrent and violent illusion.

Local mosques played an important role in the reintegration of Sofyan Tsauri, Farihin, Kurnia, Syarafina Nailah, and "Ramli" after they had been released from prison. Through the Islamic umbrella organization Muhammadiyah, Ramli was given the opportunity to give lectures. The NGO Alliance for a Peaceful Indonesia (AIDA) also works closely with Islamic community leaders and scholars to help ex-detainees re-enter society and to involve them in efforts to inform young people. "If a former gang leader or ex-terrorist tells them about the armed struggle and about the disappointments and pain it causes, this has a greater impact on secondary school pupils than if we give them boring lessons in democracy," says AIDA founder Max Boon.[12] AIDA has now organized dialogues between fifteen terrorism victims and forty-one convicted terrorists and foreign fighters. In addition, it has provided help and aftercare to fifty-two terrorism victims and set in motion a process of reconciliation with perpetrators. AIDA also gives training to prison staff, arranges dialogue sessions at schools and universities, and holds workshops for spiritual leaders and teachers. In this way, it has reached more than 10,000 pupils so far in ten provinces in Indonesia. As many as 2,764 students took part in AIDA's "victim-centric" campaign,

---

[12] Interview with Max Boon, February 26, 2020, Jakarta.

where the interests of victims are the main focus. In addition, 278 journalists have received training, and six of the country's religious leaders have been trained to use AIDA materials. Incidentally, AIDA trainers prefer not to speak of deradicalization, because from the perspective of many conservative Indonesian Muslims, being radical is a positive characteristic. Thus, they speak mainly of renouncing violence and working to achieve reconciliation. AIDA organizers report a decrease of 26 percent in the number of young people prepared to go and fight in Syria, Afghanistan, or Iraq after taking part in AIDA activities. They also see a fall of 68 percent in the number of young people who believe that taking revenge is legitimate. Confrontations with former detained terrorists telling their stories of frustration, regret, and disillusion, and conversations with the victims of earlier attacks strongly affect young people's attitudes toward violence, the holy struggle, and their own obligation to seek radical redemption.[13]

As I mentioned earlier, reintegration programs in Indonesia focus mainly on a transformation to nonviolence. Many of the interviewees in the Netherlands followed such programs. While I am by no means certain, as noted before, that the detainees I spoke with have become democrats, they have—as far as the authorities can tell—turned their backs on armed struggle, violence, and the belief that they should take violent political action. In the cases of the Islamic detainees in the Netherlands, imams have played a prominent and positive role in achieving this transformation. Talking with the imams meant a great deal to the detainees. Young men like Bilal*, Abdelkarim, and Noureddine wanted to discover through conversations with Islamic religious leaders what they should read and learn to become good Muslims, and to hear which of their ideas had been mistaken.[14] It was only in detention that they found the time and opportunity to think deeply about their religious belief, a phenomenon familiar from the literature. Both Indonesian and Dutch detainees told me they were deeply ashamed of their past ignorance and primitive beliefs, which had

---

[13] Interview with two former convicted terrorists—who wish to remain anonymous—who take part in this program, February 22, 2020, Jakarta; interview with Max Boon, February 24, 2020, Jakarta. See also Gelineau (2019) and the website for Victims' Voices, "About,": http://victimsvoices.community/about.html.

[14] Interview with Bilal*, February 5, 2020, PI/TDU; interview with Abdelkarim*, June 11, 2019, The Hague; interview with Noureddine*, November 27, 2019, and February 5, 2020, PI/TDU; interviews with TDU and probation staff.

led them to damage the reputation of their faith. The far-right extremists, by contrast, lacked the influence of a faith community; they had to rely on themselves and their families, as well as on the assistance of the probation services, to find their way back into society.

In Africa, churches and religious communities play a particularly important role. Conditions in prisons in northern Cameroon and Nigeria, for example, are so abominable that only Catholic chaplains are still willing and able to do something for detained terrorists. Various initiatives have been launched in and around Maroua, with the support of African and international NGOs and through ecumenical and interdenominational cooperation, to help ex-detainees find jobs or a little capital to set up businesses and new networks. Other initiatives are being developed through Christian churches and Islamic communities to bring reintegrating perpetrators and victims together to engage in dialogue, acknowledgment of guilt, and reconciliation.[15]

Despite repeated attempts, I was unable to speak with convicted or detained Boko Haram fighters in northern Cameroon. I did, however, have several conversations with staff of NGOs and churches, and also with the victims of terrorist attacks in the area. It was clear from their accounts that in the African Great Lakes region, hunger, drought, and unchecked anarchy—typical of failed states—gave the armed militias of Boko Haram an enormous socioeconomic boost. Young men and women here did not embrace terrorism as a result of individual radicalization processes evolving in the comfort of their own bedrooms; rather, it was dire need and the offer of money and food that made them to do so. Moreover, their need and the promise of relief were presented in strong eschatological and apocalyptic narratives that are tremendously appealing to young people living not only in physical and economic but also in spiritual deprivation. If transformation to nonviolent (religious) engagement is to be achieved here, reintegration and deradicalization programs will have to take the role of religion, religiosity, and redemption narratives seriously and address issues relating to meaning, religious identity, and responsibility (see Dawson 2021a, 2021b; Mahamat and Barka 2018).

---

[15] Information from Kees Schilder, Mensen met een Missie, The Hague, 2019.

Conclusion

In this chapter, I discussed how religion shaped my interviewees' radicalization processes with respect to orthopraxis and the three steps of the radical redemption model, as well as how it affected the contamination process of the redemption narrative. I also laid out a grounded theory of radical redemption.

Although the macro-, meso-, and microcontexts of the convicted terrorists I interviewed differ in terms of geography, political environment, and degree of violence, their radical activities all took place after 2001 and, for the most part, after 2011. The Arab Spring and the civil war in Syria, the declaration of the caliphate in 2014, and the mass movement of refugees in 2015 created an environment of geopolitical tensions and moral and cultural polarization, not only in Syria but also in Europe and Asia. The advent of the Internet, YouTube, and social media meant that jihadists in the Netherlands were exposed to the same texts and memes as jihadists in Indonesia, and that far-right extremists became just as susceptible to online propaganda as the jihadists. That makes it possible for us to compare the microhistories presented here on a number of points.

With the aid of these microhistories, I have made an initial assessment of the way in which radical redemption provided a powerful narrative in shaping the process of radicalization toward terrorism. Further research is required into other forms of terrorism and extremism, such as far-left extremism and environmental activism, which are not discussed in this study. More research is also necessary in countries like Tunisia and Turkey, where many jihadist departees came from. An interesting question to explore, for instance, would be whether individualistic ideas of deficit, guilt, and atonement play a less prominent role there.

In addition, this study devotes little attention to women. I began the research in 2017, and when I was granted access to the penitentiary institutions in 2018, there were thirty-five detainees imprisoned for terrorism-related crimes, almost all of them men. When I was able to conduct the interviews in these institutions in 2019 and 2020, only the men were initially willing to speak to me. At the time, there were two female detainees, and both were released in 2020. Three female detainees who had returned from Syria in the beginning of 2020 were as yet unable to talk about their experiences because their trials were still pending. I planned to speak with them in May 2020, but that was rendered impossible by the Covid-19 crisis, as were the conversations and visits to institutions I had planned in Cameroon and Kenya. I was, however, able to speak to Syarafina Nailah in Indonesia. From her account, it was clear that she sought redemption mainly for her family members and not so much for herself. And we can conclude from the literature that Laura H., a young Dutch woman who radicalized and fled to the caliphate in 2015, did not go to Syria to join the struggle but to seek a reward for her patience and for the setbacks and suffering she had endured (see, e.g., Rueb 2018, 100). We may need, therefore, to formulate different profiles for female terrorists, in which care and responsibility for family members and suffering as sacrifice are more important than militant martyrdom.

These reservations notwithstanding, the qualitative data collected in this book do lay a basis for a grounded theory of radical redemption, which can be used to conduct further research. This approach must always be related to the detained terrorists' macro-, meso-, and microcontexts and take account of the emotions, actions, and beliefs that constitute the radical redemption narrative. Hope lies in the realization that, although radical redemption is a powerful and dangerous motive that can force people to sacrifice their lives, it can be destroyed by its own hubris and by the ideological misinterpretation of the age-old notion of redemption. Mortals are scarcely able to redeem themselves, let alone others. Even the most seasoned jihadists among my interviewees appeared, by the end of their stories, not as angels of vengeance but as human wrecks.

9
Conclusion

Drawings of the Desert

As the reader may recall, one of the most unsettling conversations I had during the course of this study was with a detainee who, under the supervision of his guards and with the permission of the director of the terrorist detention unit (TDU), briefly showed me his cell. On one of the walls, he had hung dozens of drawings, all in shades of yellow, gray, and brown, except for one, down at the bottom, which had a few tints of clear blue. This detainee was a gifted artist. The colored-in sketches depicted scenes of the desert. There were no people, only indistinct shadows and wide panoramas of sand dunes with rocks and withered shrubs here and there. The drawing that hung at the bottom showed a glistening blue oasis. "That's how it will be after the struggle," he said. "When we no longer have to fight and there is no more sin."[1] What made this so remarkable was that this man had never been to Syria or Iraq; he was arrested before he had the opportunity to depart. His drawings were the product of his imagination, inspired by film clips and images he had found on the Internet and books he had read about the war in Afghanistan. They depicted the spiritual landscape he had constructed for himself.

At the same time, his desire to fight in Syria or Iraq had dissipated. "The caliphate, what was that all about? They announced it too soon. And it was all wrong. That's not how to do it, with all that senseless violence. I don't want anything to do with that anymore—just let me live somewhere quietly with my family, in the Netherlands or somewhere else. That was nothing but misery." This detainee's ideal image of living a pure life as a Muslim in the caliphate clashed harshly with the horrific reality. His narrative of redemption had become one of contamination. He was still looking for purity and wanted to be a good Muslim, but he had to admit he had made a series of bad

---

[1] Interview in PI/TDU, 2019; further details are omitted because this detainee did not wish my account of his drawings to be linked to his name.

choices and now had to pay the price. He found it difficult to talk about his punishment; clearly, he had not yet completed the process of acknowledging his own mistakes. In our conversations, he often still blamed his friend, who wanted to take him with him; Dutch society, which "didn't want" him; and "Assad and the Americans," who had "messed up" in the Middle East. But it was clear to him that departing and joining a terrorist organization could not provide the desired redemption. Yet, he continued to draw. His desire for purity, a life in which the everyday was aligned with the spiritual, remained.

Believers and Their Communities

That conversation, and the images of the desert landscape, stayed with me for a long time. My research showed that convicted terrorists who had a clear religious background and came from a religious community are especially susceptible to the appeal of radical redemption. Their beliefs, emotions, and actions draw from deep, rich, and imaginative religious traditions. However, as I have described here, I encountered the radical redemption narrative also in a secularized form among left-wing revolutionaries, ethnic nationalists, and far-right extremists. What has become strikingly clear is that the validation of the perpetrators' own devotion and redemption takes on greater significance when they are more deeply embedded in a political-ideological, ethnic-national, or religious community. They commit their acts according to a specific ethical program; they believe the act is "right," pure, and necessary in the context of the struggle against injustice. If the community to which they feel they belong does not recognize or validate the act or outright condemns it, the whole undertaking's footing becomes insecure. Especially for followers and potential new recruits, such public condemnation of and distancing from the act is a significant moment in breaking the narrative and the cycle of radical redemption. And at such a moment, the role of churches and religious communities is of particular importance.

Religious terrorists who act according to a narrative of radical redemption can and must be called to account by their communities. In the case of far-right extremists, this is more difficult; still, those in their immediate circles or with similar political views have a duty to deny any legitimacy to violent radical acts. Religious and political leaders should enter into dialogue with perpetrators, especially when they begin to doubt whether their act will bring the fulfillment they had expected, become confused, or find themselves in detention. Talking with perpetrators, listening to them explicitly talking about their radical beliefs, is important in terms of social and psychological processes of disengagement and deradicalization. We also need to speak more openly about the nexus between believers and communities, between extreme beliefs and the support base, which should be undermined.

This already happens, to some extent, in various countries. In Cameroon and Kenya, spiritual leaders—imams, chaplains, Christian youth workers—are the only ones willing to speak with detained or reintegrating Boko Haram and Al-Shabaab fighters and their families and to delegitimize the narrative of radical redemption. In Indonesia, Islamic foundations and communities are calling terrorists and potential recruits to account, entering into dialogue with perpetrators and victims and explaining that reconciliation is preferable to fighting. In the Netherlands, prison imams have initiated a challenging program of spiritual deradicalization and disengagement for detainees. Yet, such dialogues should not be conducted only by imams or spiritual carers—they should be part of broader intake, exit, and reintegration strategies.

Terrorism has always been with us; every ideological or religious movement brings forth its own zealots and fanatics. Nevertheless, it will always be the marginal groups that resort to violent struggle. When communities, churches, and political parties take the lead in campaigns aimed at reconciliation, compromise, and adherence to the principles of the rule of law, the flow of new recruits will slowly dry up. That is why it is so important that people acknowledge that the dangerous narrative of radical redemption can also germinate in their own community.

Radical Redemption: An Inherently Inconsistent Narrative

As we approach the end of this study, let me emphasize again that in all the stories of my interviewees, the narrative of radical redemption manifested itself, implicitly or explicitly, as an inherently inconsistent narrative. In this chapter's penultimate section, I look at the most important insights I have derived from the study and that, in my view, could be the topic of further research and, perhaps, of social scientific experiments.

This study has shown that radical redemption primarily took on a violent form in situations in which there was already a low threshold for violence. When my Indonesian interviewees became involved in ethnic conflicts and civil-war-like situations on Ambon, it turned them quickly into seasoned fighters. Similarly, untrained and naive zealots who arrived in Afghanistan in the 1980s or in Syria and Iraq after 2011 found themselves in no time involved in horrific battles and crimes, doing things that no one would have previously considered them capable of. In safe and prosperous countries, the violence threshold is a significant obstacle. There are far fewer individuals who commit attacks in such countries, and they are discovered more quickly. Still, they are often more fanatical than the young people who went to Syria in 2011 as part of a group of friends with the altruistic motive to "go and help." As will be clear from this book, I certainly do not trivialize this latter motive. This batch of departees joined jihadist groups while they could also have worked for the Red Crescent—the Islamic Red Cross. Nevertheless, there is a difference between letting out feelings of bloodlust and vengeance in a nonwarlike, peaceful society on the one hand, and taking up arms in a theater of ongoing war and general mayhem on the other.

In addition, the proximity of situations with a low violence threshold—the war in Syria for the Dutch detainees, and Ambon for the Indonesian jihadists—is a high-risk factor. Besides an individual desire, need, and push factor, an act of redemption also requires a pull factor: a relatively easily accessible supply of arms, modi operandi, action repertoires, and locations where the act can be committed. When that pull factor disappears—the caliphate has been disbanded, DTG has been wound up, or the members of the group have betrayed each other—the demand for radical redemption can no longer be met. The radical redemption narrative is, therefore, not only a transcendent but also a very worldly narrative: recognition, success, and social failure are important factors in explaining the effectiveness of the narrative's operation and its shaping of radicalization processes. In my view, the influence of and the balance between the push and pull factors of radical redemption need to be further explored. Would young people have radicalized less quickly if the battlefield had not been easily accessible and if there had not been a widespread sense of anger—not only in the Muslim community but also in society as a whole—about the crimes committed by Assad? And how important is the concrete nature of the offer of devotion and struggle in relation to the intrinsic desire to atone for a personal sense of deficit?

I have noted it before, but let me stress it here again: the act of redemption rarely has the desired effect. Almost all my interviewees initially denied in the strongest of terms that they were terrorists. As we became better acquainted with each other, they admitted to at least some of their actions, but claimed that they had been misled or their actions had failed. For an act of redemption is only effective if the perpetrator's own community considers it effective. Such an act is not something personal or individual—it has to be recognizable for family, friends, constituency, and community. It not only has practical meaning for the perpetrator but also has to acquire symbolic significance and verification. It must be a statement, and a statement needs an audience. The terrorist act must be recognizable as a religious or ideological rite and practice, both for the perpetrators and for their perceived constituency and community. If that recognition does not materialize, devotion and struggle have been for nothing and lead not to redemption but to arrest, imprisonment, and disillusion. This conclusion, based on twenty-five interviews, should also be studied further: Does it, for instance, also apply to convicted terrorists in Syria and Iraq? Is the likelihood of recidivism smaller among terrorists with altruistic religious motives than among vengeful zealots? Should we have different programs of treatment for different categories of terrorists?

Thousands of young people have been captivated by the promise of radical redemption. It started in the 1980s, through stories and texts about the worldwide jihad. "Deep histories" and repertoires of resistance against colonial rulers—whether in Indonesia or in Ireland—played an emphatic role in the revival of radical, terrorist patterns. The advent of the Internet and social media has boosted the propagation of those repertoires still further. The gamification of terrorism has combined with the ultrafast exchange of ideas on the orthopraxis of a specific ideology.[2] Through video images and memes, opponents are ridiculed, injustices identified, and feelings of anger and revenge mobilized. That can extend to a desire for more likes; to get these, one could commit an "act of redemption" against the enemies of one's own community or nation and stream it. This gamification can also manifest itself in individuals measuring themselves against each other and allocating or withholding points for the afterlife. Internet platforms like YouTube play a tremendously significant role in this respect. The instances of instantaneous conversion and embracing of radical redemption that we have seen among the post-2011 generation of terrorists should also be studied more closely, so that we can adjust existing models based on long, step-by-step processes.

Given the rise of right-wing extremism over the past years, we may ask what the difference is, in these forms of new, image-driven radicalization,

---

[2] On gamification, see, e.g., Evans (2019); see also Macklin (2019).

between jihadist and far-right extremist radicalization. Do jihadists need a more tangible arena of war and territorial promise—the caliphate—than far-right extremists, who seem to have embedded themselves almost completely in the virtual domain? Do incoherent, long-winded manifestos—such as Breivik's text—inspire a present generation of extremists in a similar way as the videos of the caliphate inspired jihadists? And are right-wing extremist fora perhaps not as good at producing striking memes, nihilistic humor, and the immediate promise of likes and followers as jihadist fora? The current generation of terrorists is in any case more affectively oriented; these terrorists focus on imagery and are less concerned with drawing up blueprints for an ideal state or writing carefully constructed manifestos. This is another element of orthopraxis among right-wing extremists that warrants more empirical research.

A Parasitic Narrative

Finally, a narrative of radical redemption feeds on the fear of its victims. Acts of radical redemption are concerned not only with the immediate victims but also with the victims-by-proxy—the society or those segments of society in which they wish to instill fear.

Our current existence and civilization are captured in what Barbara Adam refers to as a postmodern timescape: a cultural climate that, thanks to the persistent flow of images of war and misery, is characterized on the one hand by a widely felt sense of threat and impending doom, and on the other hand by the impossibility of redemption from this life, since there is no longer an afterlife, and the future is not considered open and malleable anymore (Adam 1998; see also De Graaf 2017, 74–86). Within that context of secular presentism, in which we feel the stress of the vitality culture dictating we stay young, fit, and above all alive, the act of a (suicide) terrorist is one of extreme audacity. It exposes all our nerves, because it undermines what could be considered the West's collective denial and avoidance of death. Within the horizon of understanding of a postmodern timescape, how can we bring the people's collective fear of the desire of terrorists for radical redemption back into proportion? And what can we offer the terrorist as an alternative to that desire? What does our society have to offer young people looking for meaning and personal significance? That is the challenge facing all of our open democratic societies today. And it is a question that I do not wish to answer here because, as far as I am concerned, it is one that should remain on the table for everyone who reads this book.

Terrorism—and the practice of making victims, of oneself or others—is, and will remain, a recurring phenomenon. Religion will continue to play a role in processes of radicalization. The appeal of radical redemption will not go away. Nevertheless, we can take solace in the fact that, when the religious constituencies of convicted terrorists distance themselves firmly and clearly from such extreme beliefs and acts, the impact of the radical redemption narrative can be significantly reduced. For it is, ultimately, an intrinsically inconsistent narrative that feeds parasitically on all that is good in faith and belief.

APPENDIX 1

Interviewees and Profiles

Table of Interviewees and Their Profiles

Names marked with an asterisk are pseudonyms, used at the request of the interviewee or the Custodial Institutions Agency (DJI).

Name	Bio	Nature of terrorist crime	Deficit	Calling/ Responsibility	Type of struggle	Typology
Western jihadists in the Netherlands						
Omar*	Omar was born into a Moroccan family in 1994. He grew up in Utrecht, but did not do well at school and did not complete his secondary vocational education. After his parents divorced, he became homeless and became involved in petty crime. After 2001, he began to show interest in the situation in Syria. He and his friend Ahmed became increasingly influenced by IS and ultimately left for Syria.	Omar was sentenced to seven and a half years in prison for being present in the caliphate and for war crimes committed between 2014 and 2016.	Religious/ individual (A) and political/ collective (B)	Primarily atonement/individual (C) and, to a lesser extent, shame, injustice, revenge/ collective (D)	Personal/ moral-ethical (E) but more markedly eschatological-dogmatic (F)	Zealot seeking atonement (A, C, F)
Amin*	Amin was born into a Moroccan family in 1989. He grew up in Amsterdam North. After completing a secondary vocational education, he found a job in the retail sector, but after a reorganization, he ended up working at a transport company, loading and unloading trucks. He got involved in crime and had a gun and ammunition in his cellar. Later, he became increasingly interested in the war in Syria. He was arrested in 2015.	Amin was sentenced to eight years in prison for his conduct on the Internet, spreading jihadist ideas, and possessing a Kalashnikov and ammunition.	Religious/ individual (A) and, to a lesser extent, political/ collective (B)	Shame, injustice, revenge/ collective (D)	Personal/ moral-ethical (E) and, to a lesser extent, eschatological-dogmatic (F)	Avenger in search of meaning (A, D, E)

Ilyas*	Ilyas was born in Morocco in 1976. He came to the Netherlands in 2004 and trained as a car mechanic. He found a job and married a Dutch girl; they had three children. Then, his wife divorced him, and he hardly saw his children anymore. After 2011, he became increasingly interested in the war in Syria; he started to help refugees and began to glorify IS. He was arrested at the beginning of 2018.	Ilyas's case is ongoing. The charges against him include possession of weapons and ammunition, spreading jihadist ideas, supporting the jihadist struggle, and posing with a gun as an IS fighter.	Religious/ individual (A) and political/ collective (B)	Shame, injustice, revenge/ collective (D)	Eschatological-dogmatic (F)	Avenging zealot (A, D, F)
Anwar*	Anwar was born into a Moroccan family in 1991. He grew up in The Hague and completed a vocational education in retail. In 2015, he left for Turkey and, later, Syria, with his friend Noureddine.	Anwar was arrested in 2018 and was ultimately sentenced to five years in prison for being in Syria and for membership of a terrorist organization.	Religious/ individual (A) and, to a lesser extent, political/ collective (B)	Shame, injustice, revenge/ collective (D)	Personal/ moral-ethical (E) and, to a lesser extent, eschatological-dogmatic (F)	Altruist seeking meaning (A, D, E)
Noureddine*	Noureddine was born into a Moroccan family in 1990. He grew up in The Hague, trained as a car mechanic, and found a job as a cabdriver. When the civil war in Syria reached its peak in 2014, Noureddine had had enough of his job, and his parents were getting divorced. Noureddine and his friend Anwar left for Turkey and, later, Syria.	Noureddine was arrested in 2018 and was ultimately sentenced to five years in prison for being in Syria and for membership of a terrorist organization.	Political/ collective (B)	Shame, injustice, revenge/ collective (D)	Personal/ moral-ethical (E) and, to a lesser extent, eschatological-dogmatic (F)	Political altruist (B, D, E)

Name	Bio	Nature of terrorist crime	Deficit	Calling/ Responsibility	Type of struggle	Typology
Bilal*	Bilal was born into a close Moroccan family in Rotterdam in 1989. He has two sisters. He completed his secondary vocational education and became a social worker. When the civil war broke out in Syria in 2011, he tried to help by collecting clothes. But he felt that wasn't enough. In 2013, he left for Syria and joined Ahrar Al-Sham.	Bilal was sentenced to six years in prison in 2018 for membership of a terrorist organization.	Religious/ individual (A) and, to a lesser extent, political/ collective (B)	Shame, injustice, revenge/ collective (D)	Personal/ moral-ethical (E)	Altruist seeking meaning (A, D, E)
Ahmed*	Ahmed was born in 1995 and grew up in Delft. He had behavioral problems and went to a special school. He did not finish secondary vocational school and, after working for a short time, ended up hanging around on the streets. In 2012, he was deeply affected by the images of the civil war in Syria. Shortly before the caliphate was declared, he left for Syria and ultimately joined IS.	Ahmed was sentenced to five years in prison for being present in the caliphate and for war crimes committed between 2014 and 2016.	Religious/ individual (A) and, to a lesser extent, political/ collective (B)	Atonement/individual (C)	Eschatological-dogmatic (F)	Zealot seeking atonement (A, C, F)
Abdelkarim*	Abdelkarim was born into a Moroccan family in 1997 and grew up in The Hague. He started secondary school at pre-university level but was later demoted to a lower grade level. He then studied theology at a vocational university. The war in Syria inspired him to learn more about Islam. He taught at the mosque and became a preacher on his own YouTube channel.	Abdelkarim was arrested in 2014 and sentenced to a little less than a year in prison for spreading hatred, recruiting for the armed struggle, and spreading terrorist ideas.	Religious/ individual (A) and, to a lesser extent, political/ collective (B)	Atonement/individual (C) and shame, injustice, revenge/ collective (D)	Eschatological-dogmatic (F)	Zealot seeking meaning (A, C/D, F)

Farhad*	Farhad was born in Iran in 1990. His parents fled to the Netherlands when he was 5, and he grew up in Utrecht. He completed secondary school but had trouble getting into further education and finding a job because of a personality disorder. He became unemployed and addicted to weed. After the killing of Theo van Gogh, he began to learn more about Islam. The Arab Spring came as a shock to him. In April 2016, he was arrested at Utrecht Central Station with his suitcase and ticket, on his way to Syria.	Farhad was sentenced to two and a half years in prison for preparing to join a terrorist organization (IS).	Religious/ individual (A) and, to a lesser extent, political/ collective (B)	Atonement/in-dividual (C) and shame, injustice, revenge/ collective (D)	Eschatological-dogmatic (F)	Zealot seeking meaning (A, C/D, F)
Fadil*	Fadil was born in Morocco in 1986. He moved to The Hague when he was 12. The family was not strictly religious, and he could decide for himself whether he went to the mosque or not. As a teenager, he became involved in petty crime and did not complete his vocational training in sports and physical activity management. In 2011, just as the civil war started in Syria, he was diagnosed with testicular cancer. That was a turning point for Fadil. In 2015, he decided to join the caliphate and left for Syria. But in Turkey, he changed his mind; he was arrested shortly afterwards.	Fadil was sentenced to five years in prison in Belgium for going to the caliphate.	Religious/ individual (A) and, to a lesser extent, political/ collective (B)	Atonement/ individual (C) and shame, injustice, revenge/collective (D)	Personal/ moral-ethical (E)	Altruist seeking meaning (A, C/D, E)

Name	Bio	Nature of terrorist crime	Deficit	Calling/ Responsibility	Type of struggle	Typology
Haroun*	Haroun was born in Rotterdam in 1988. He completed secondary vocational school but dropped out of the follow-up vocational course. He became homeless and ended up on the streets. In this same period, the war broke out in Syria. In 2012, urged on by a friend, he left for Syria, where he joined Ahrar al-Sham. At the end of 2013, he tried to return to the Netherlands but was arrested in Turkey.	Haroun was sentenced to four years in prison for going to Syria.	Religious/ individual (A) and, to a lesser extent, later also political/ collective (B)	Shame, injustice, revenge/ collective (D)	Eschatological-dogmatic (F)	Zealot seeking meaning (A, D, F)
Hassan (through his brother Karim*)	Hassan from Utrecht was in the commandos for a year but was sent to prison for committing an offense. Through contacts in prison, he became involved in a criminal network; at the same time, his marriage broke up. When the war started in Syria, it was a wake-up call. In May 2014, to prove himself as a Muslim and encouraged by his Internet friends, he went to Iraq and joined IS.	Hassan was killed in the battle for Fallujah on January 1, 2015.	Religious/ individual (A)	Atonement/individual (C)	Personal/ moral-ethical (E) but more strongly eschatological-dogmatic (F)	Zealot seeking meaning (A, C, F)
Asaad*	Asaad was born in the Middle East in 1989 as the son of a high-ranking army officer. His parents emigrated to northern Europe, where he grew up in a "pro-European, secular, and liberal climate" and studied civil engineering. The war in Syria was an eye-opener for him, particularly because the West—including NATO—did not intervene. He went to Iraq, where he joined the struggle, and translated and distributed IS propaganda film clips. He was arrested after flying to the Netherlands in 2017.	Asaad was sentenced to three years in prison in the Netherlands for distributing IS video clips. He was apparently also planning an attack.	Political/ collective (B)	Shame, injustice, revenge/ collective (D)	Personal/ moral-ethical (E)	Political altruist (B, D, E)

		Religious/ individual (A)	Atonement/individual (C) and shame, injustice, revenge/ collective (D)	Eschatological-dogmatic (F)	Avenging zealot (A, C/D, F)
Gökmen Tanis	Gökmen was born in Turkey in 1981. He came to the Netherlands with his family in the early 1990s. His parents divorced in 2008; after that, he had no more contact with his father. In his youth, he went more and more off the rails and ended up in the drug scene. He had no interest in school or a career, and accumulated a long record of violent crime and theft. On March 18, 2019, he committed a terrorist attack on a tram in Utrecht, in which four people died.	Gökmen was sentenced to life imprisonment in 2020 for murder, attempted murder, and posing a threat of a terrorist nature.			

Non-Western jihadists in the Netherlands

Mohammed*	Mohammed was born in 1992 in Aleppo, Syria. He was a good student and was studying medicine when the war broke out. He took part in demonstrations and joined the rebels. Eventually, he fled to the Netherlands, where he was arrested.	Mohammed was charged by the public prosecutor for "humiliating the corpses of enemies." The public prosecutor also suspects that Mohammed, rather than his brother, was a jihadist militia commandant. His trial continues on appeal.	Political/ collective (B)	Shame, injustice, revenge/ collective (D)	Neither	Armed opposition/ self-defense

Name	Bio	Nature of terrorist crime	Deficit	Calling/ Responsibility	Type of struggle	Typology
Jibran*	Jibran was born in Pakistan in 1992 in very needy circumstances. He had hardly any schooling. His father died when he was 17. He moved to Italy, where he worked as a pizza baker. He also set up his own YouTube channel and traveled throughout Europe. When Geert Wilders announced a cartoon competition about the prophet Muhammad, there were widespread protests in Pakistan. Jibran decided to go to the Netherlands, where he was arrested after posting a video clip on his social media channel announcing an attack on Wilders.	Jibran was arrested in 2018 and sentenced to ten years in prison for planning an attack on Geert Wilders.	Religious/ individual (A) and political/ collective (B)	Shame, injustice, revenge/ collective (D)	Eschatological-dogmatic (F)	Zealot seeking meaning (A/B, D, F)
Arslan*	Arslan was born in Idlib, Syria, around 1980. He served in the Syrian army for several years. When the civil war broke out in 2011, Arslan, now an army officer, joined an opposition group. Ultimately, as a deserter, he fled to the Netherlands, where he arrived in 2014 with his wife and children.	Arslan was arrested in the Netherlands in 2018 and is suspected of committing war crimes and being a member of a terrorist organization. His trial is ongoing.	Religious/ individual (A) and political/ collective (B)	Shame, injustice, revenge/ collective (D)	Neither	Armed opposition/ self-defense

Jihadist in Denmark

Abderozzak Benarabe	Abderozzak was born into a Danish-Moroccan family in Denmark in 1973. There, he became a gangster and leader of the criminal organization Blågårds Plads. He had already served eleven years in prison convicted of shootings, mutilation, drug dealing, and extortion when he heard that his brother had cancer. When his brother was cured, he turned his back on his criminal life and, in 2012, left for Syria, where he played an active part in the fighting. Shortly afterwards, he returned to Denmark, where, after some time, he resumed his activities in the criminal circuit.	As far as is known, Abderozzak has not been convicted for going to Syria.	Religious/ individual (A)	Atonement/in-dividual (C)	Personal/ moral-ethical (E) and, to a lesser extent, eschatological-dogmatic (F)	Altruist seeking atonement (A, C, E)

Jihadists in Indonesia

Sofyan Tsauri	Sofyan was born in 1976 and grew up in Depok, Jakarta. At secondary school, he became involved in petty crime. When he was 18, he became interested in Islam and the lot of Muslims. A friend in the Muslim Brotherhood gave him books. He started to dream of the final battle. After completing his police training, he joined Jemaah Islamiyah (JI) in 2007.	Sofyan was sentenced to ten years in prison in 2010 for various terrorist crimes, including giving military training, possessing weapons, preparing to take part in the jihadist struggle, and being a member of JI, a terrorist organization.	Religious/ individual (A) and political/ collective (B)	Atonement/ individual (C) and, to a greater extent, shame, injustice, revenge/ collective (D)	Personal/ moral-ethical (E) but especially eschatological-dogmatic (F)	Avenging zealot (A/B, D, F)

Name	Bio	Nature of terrorist crime	Deficit	Calling/ Responsibility	Type of struggle	Typology
Kurnia Widodo	Kurnia was born in Medang in 1974. His father worked for the government, and his mother was a member of Muhammadiyah. Just before leaving secondary school, Kurnia got involved with young men from the Muslim Brotherhood and began to feel a strong need to defend Islam. In 1992, he joined Negara Islam Indonesia (NII). He also trained to be a chemical engineer and became an expert in making bombs. He placed his findings and formulas on jihadist websites, and they were used on several occasions to commit attacks.	Kurnia was arrested in 2010 after his group had blown up a military base. He was sentenced to six years in prison for planning a terrorist attack.	Political/ collective (B)	Shame, injustice, revenge/ collective (D)	Personal/ moral-ethical (E) but especially eschatological-dogmatic (F)	Political zealot (B, D, F)
"Ramli"	Ramli was born in Lampung, South Sumatra, in 1981, as the youngest of a large family. His father had a tobacco company, and his mother had her own business. After primary school, he was sent to a secondary school run by Muhammadiyah. In 1999, he wanted to go to the prestigious University of Indonesia but narrowly failed the entrance examination. Then, everything went wrong. He took part in street races and joined a group that discussed the ethnic conflict that had arisen on Ambon. Friends went to help defend their fellow Muslims. Shortly afterwards, Ramli also decided to take part in the struggle and joined LSM Kompak in 2000.	Ramli was arrested in 2005 while transporting weapons to Indonesia. He was sentenced to seven years in prison. In 2013, he was convicted again for arms dealing.	Religious/ individual (A) and political/ collective (B)	Atonement/ individual (C) and, to a lesser extent, shame, injustice, revenge/ collective (D)	Personal/ moral-ethical (E) and, to a lesser extent, eschatological-dogmatic (F)	Altruist seeking atonement (A/B, C, E)

Syarafina Nailah	Syarafina was born on the island of Batam in 1996. Her mother was a housewife, and her father was the director general of the regional government on the island. She was studying information science at university when her sister radicalized and wanted to go to the caliphate. Her uncle supported her. After an online contact in IS had painted a very positive picture of life in the caliphate (good health care, education for women, a pure Islamic community), the whole family—eighteen persons in all—left for Syria in 2015. In 2017, completely disillusioned, the family succeeded in returning to Indonesia.	Syarafina traveled to IS territory with her family. They returned after two years, disillusioned. Her uncle and father were convicted because they had joined a terrorist organization. The rest of the family were acquitted.	Religious/ individual (A)	Shame, injustice, revenge/ collective (D)	Personal/ moral-ethical (E)	Follower seeking meaning (A, D, E)
Farihin	Farihin was born in Jakarta in 1966. He was imbued with ideas about the Islamic struggle from an early age. His father and grandfather were both active in Darul Islam. His father was imprisoned from 1957 to 1960 for being involved in a failed attack on Sukarno in Cikini; and his mother was active in Aisha, the women's section of Muhammadiyah. Farihin went off the rails at secondary school, after which the founder of Jemaah Islamiyah, who was a friend of his father and grandfather, asked him to join the jihadist struggle. He went to Afghanistan in 1987.	Farihin was imprisoned in 2002 for involvement in various attacks in Indonesia.	Religious/ individual (A) and, to a lesser extent, political/ collective (B)	Atonement/ individual C and shame, injustice, revenge/ collective (D)	Personal/ moral-ethical (E) but especially eschatological-dogmatic (F)	Zealot seeking meaning (A, C/D, F)

Name	Bio	Nature of terrorist crime	Deficit	Calling/ Responsibility	Type of struggle	Typology
Far-right extremists in the Netherlands						
Martijn*	Martijn was born in 1982. He grew up in Enschede. In his teen years, he was diagnosed with melanoma. From the age of 15, he worked as a furniture maker and, later, as a service engineer. He had a daughter. However, when he discovered in 2014 that he was not her father, he started using drugs and alcohol. He was in a rehab clinic when he heard from friends that an asylum seekers center was to be built in Enschede. He had, in the meantime, developed an aversion to refugees after the assaults in Cologne on New Year's Eve 2015. He joined Demonstranten tegen Gemeenten (DTG), which protested against the arrival of refugees. He got to know Marco, Danny, Ronald, and Peter. Together, they committed an attack on a mosque in Enschede in 2016. No one was hurt or killed.	Martijn was sentenced to four years in prison for committing an attack of a terrorist nature against the mosque in Enschede.	Religious/ individual (A) and political/ collective (B)	Shame, injustice, revenge/ collective (D)	Personal-ethical desire for redemption, reward (E)	Altruist seeking meaning (A, D, E)
Peter*	Peter was born in Hengelo in 1981. His father was a manager, and his mother worked in financial services. When he was 10, they moved to Enschede. He never liked school and preferred to hang around on the streets. He started to train as a metal engineer but did not complete the course. When he was 18, his parents got divorced, and he started to work as a crane service engineer. When he heard about the plans for an asylum seekers center, he and some of his friends set up DTG. That's where he met Marco, Danny, Ronald, and Martijn. Together, they committed an attack on a mosque in Enschede in 2016. No one was hurt or killed.	Peter was sentenced to four years in prison for committing an attack of a terrorist nature against the mosque in Enschede.	Political/ collective (B)	Shame, injustice, revenge/ collective (D)	Active for the collective community, "liberation," helping others, personally-ethically inspired (E)	Political altruist (B, D, E)

Interview List

Name	Date of interview transcriptions	Location of interview
Convicted terrorists in the Netherlands		
Omar*	December 9, 2019	Utrecht; through Utrecht City Council official
Amin*	October 30, 2019 November 27, 2019	Penitentiary institution
Ilyas*	January 16, 2020	Penitentiary institution
Anwar*	November 27, 2019	Penitentiary institution
Noureddine*	November 27, 2019 February 5, 2020	Penitentiary institution
Bilal*	February 5, 2020	Penitentiary institution
Ahmed*	February 5, 2020	Penitentiary institution
Abdelkarim*	June 11, 2019	The Hague
Farhad*	December 5, 2019	Utrecht
Fadil*	March 6, 2019	The Hague
Haroun*	January 16, 2020 February 5, 2020	Penitentiary institution
Karim* (about Hassan)	April 17, 2020	Utrecht
Asaad*	January 16, 2020	Penitentiary institution
Mohammed*	February 5, 2020	Penitentiary institution
Jibran*	February 5, 2020	Penitentiary institution

Name	Date of interview transcriptions	Location of interview
Arslan*	January 16, 2020	Penitentiary institution
Martijn*	May 23, 2019 September 23, 2019	Utrecht
Peter*	May 15, 2019	Enschede
Others in the Netherlands		
TDU staff, including Cees Kraaijveld	October 30, 2019	Penitentiary institution
TDU staff, including Yola Wanders	February 5, 2020	Penitentiary institution
Arjan Derksen (leading Enschede police officer) and two colleagues	April 13, 2018 November 7, 2018	Enschede
Probation service staff	2019	Utrecht, 's-Hertogenbosch
Utrecht City Council official	2018–20	Utrecht
Convicted terrorists in Indonesia		
Sofyan Tsauri	February 24, 2020	Jakarta
Kurnia Widodo	February 25, 2020	Jakarta
"Ramli"	February 26, 2020	Jakarta
Syarafina Nailah	February 24, 2020	Jakarta
Farihin	February 25, 2020	Jakarta
Others in Indonesia		
Max Boon, AIDA	February 24, 2020 February 26, 2020 February 27, 2020	Jakarta

AIDA staff member (anonymous)	February 22, 2020	Jakarta
Solahudin	February 26, 2020 February 27, 2020	Jakarta
BNPT staff member (anonymous)	February 27, 2020	Jakarta
Andhika Chrisnayudhanto, BNPT	February 26, 2020	Jakarta
Zainal Ahzab, BNPT	February 26, 2020	Jakarta
Others in Cameroon		
Kees Schilder	2019	The Hague/Cameroon (online)
Dupleix Fernand Kuenzob	April 16, 2020	Yaoundé (online)
Nana Abel	February 17, 2020	Maroua; conducted by Kees Schilder, at the request of the author
Mabi Aubin	February 17, 2020	Maroua; conducted by Kees Schilder, at the request of the author
Fadi Madeleine	February 17, 2020	Maroua; conducted by Kees Schilder, at the request of the author
Yanick Carlos	February 17, 2020	Maroua; conducted by Kees Schilder, at the request of the author
Dalayma M. Appolos	February 17, 2020	Maroua; conducted by Kees Schilder, at the request of the author
Pascal Djeumeugued	April 2020	Maroua (in writing); conducted by Kees Schilder, at the request of the author
Youth workers (anonymous)	April 2020	Mora, Maroua (in writing, online); conducted by Kees Schilder, at the request of the author

APPENDIX 2

Methods

Oral History as Research Method

As a terrorism researcher with a background in history, I have embedded the life histories approach of this book in the overarching tradition of oral history (see Thompson 1978).[1] In earlier work, I focused more on trajectories of organizations—the peace movement, terrorist organizations—and used participants' and actors' life stories to illustrate these histories (see De Graaf 2007, 2011, 2012a; De Graaf and Malkki 2010). In this book, by contrast, I put the perpetrators center stage and built the histories bottom-up, starting with their experiences rather than with archives or the tracing of processes of organizations. In this way, I was able to focus on what convicted terrorists themselves claim to believe, what religious and secular convictions they adhere to. I wanted to know how convicted terrorists link their worldviews, hopes, and expectations to their acts and to their current situation.

Another reason to interview convicted terrorists is that they are rarely heard in a nontheatrical setting. They have their own propaganda channels, and they communicate with manifestos and violence. They portray themselves online as martyrs. They sometimes speak during their trials, but the theater of the courtroom colors their strategies and those of their lawyers and the prosecutors. In court, it is all about the power to clarify and persuade. Only when they are in detention or are reintegrating do we have the opportunity to speak to them away from the theatrical setting of their own propaganda and the courtroom. Few people have taken this opportunity of speaking to detained terrorists systematically and in an organized, controlled setting. Research journalists—such as, in the Netherlands, Thomas Rueb, Janny Groen, and Nikki Sterkenburg—have done so on occasion, and their efforts have produced very valuable reports (e.g., Rueb 2018; Honing and Sterkenburg 2015; Groen and Kranenberg 2006). And in 2017, Edwin Bakker and Peter Grol (2017) presented six detailed life stories of Dutch jihadists. Still, while such human-interest portraits of radicals, extremists, and convicted terrorists are of inestimable value, they do not offer the systematic research into the perpetrators' ideological life histories—or rather, faith histories—that John Horgan (2012) and Lorne Dawson (2019) have called for. To date, very little of such research has been conducted. Portraits of extremists and terrorists often merely describe personal and psychological problems as

---

[1] In 1948, political scientist Alan Nevis, of Columbia University, started a program to record life histories systematically. See also Bennett (1981). In the Netherlands, Selma Leydesdorff laid the basis for this tradition. In 1979, she set up the Vereniging voor Historische Mondelinge Documentatie (VHMD); in 1996, she founded the *International Yearbook of Oral History and Life Stories*; and in 2004, she was appointed professor of oral history at the University of Amsterdam. See also Leydesdorff (2004).

the alleged causes of their radicalization, without seriously and substantially examining how and why these radicals came to adopt certain ideological or religious positions.[2]

Many studies of the motives driving extremists and terrorists that make use of interviews or profiles have been conducted from a social-scientific or governance perspective with the aim of developing models for deradicalization and disengagement. Consequently, the histories were cast in a specific mold. My book attempts, through the oral history method, to bring the qualitative, contingent, and contextual aspects of life histories more to the fore. It was not my aim to draw up a diagrammatic schema with a sample of more than 100 subjects, or to generate models based on incidents collected over a long period and from around the world. For me, it was about acquiring a better understanding of the changing and complex relationship between beliefs and violence, and between religion and terrorism, in people's life histories.

Limitations of the Life Histories Approach

The foremost pitfall of oral history is uncritically reproducing the stories related by interviewees. Even if they believe that they are telling the truth, the human memory is notoriously unreliable. Almost everyone simplifies, distorts, or mispresents events and circumstances in hindsight.[3]

Let me take up the unreliability objection mentioned in chapter 1, which is often raised when researchers deal with historical agents and perpetrators. If oral testimonies are, indeed, notoriously untrustworthy, how should we approach the stories of convicted terrorists? The advantage of interviewing convicted terrorists is that there is sufficient other material with which to compare their accounts and to calibrate them. Their cases often have received extensive attention in the media and have been documented in thick criminal dossiers. Access to these dossiers can usually be gained in consultation with lawyers, the perpetrators themselves, or the police and legal authorities. Strikingly, they contain hardly any accounts of the beliefs of the individual in question. The dossiers are compiled in line with the public prosecutor's aim of proving the suspect's involvement in a criminal offense or membership of a terrorist organization. Thus, the police and the judicial authorities are mainly concerned with finding evidence of such membership, preparations for criminal or terrorist acts, or suspicious surfing behavior on the Internet. They rarely ask or examine exactly what kinds of stories or beliefs lie behind such behavior.

Within the discipline of oral history, it is well known that facts and circumstances can be very easily concealed or distorted. Yet, if you speak to someone about their life, feelings, attitudes, and expectations chronologically and for some time, and win their confidence

---

[2] In their very interesting and inspiring (2005) article "Talking to Terrorists," Anne Speckhard and Khapta Akhmedova describe their experiences when they interviewed failed suicide terrorists. While the authors also refer to the phenomenon of guilt and the terrorists' desire to make up for a "bad boy" life, they do not describe this phenomenon as a consciously religious process or as a faith-based praxis but as a "psychodynamic" process driven possibly by traumatic experiences. Because their article is about Palestinian and Chechen suicide terrorists, and their explanatory model is strictly psychiatric and psychological, their approach is very different from the one used in this study. They appear to see their interviewees' decisions to undertake a suicide mission as the consequence of dissociative disorders or trauma.

[3] For a good discussion of the fluidity of life stories—in this case, of Islamic women—see Willemse (2007, 139–41).

as an interviewer, it is psychologically very difficult for the interviewee to cover up the emotions that are triggered by their memories and that reflect their identity. Resentment, beliefs, hope, and expectations are such primary emotions that it is very hard to convincingly relate an untruthful narrative for an extended period of time, if only because one's body language gives one away. Emotion, memory, and identity are too closely connected to maintain such a pretense.[4]

Another limitation facing historians when they record oral accounts is that there will always be a discrepancy between the actual facts and an eye witness's description of them. Everyone has their own perspective and considers some facts relevant in a completely unique way, while deliberately or unintentionally ignoring others. In the case of convicted terrorists, there is an additional limiting factor. When I spoke with them, they were either in detention or had completed their sentences. They were consequently no longer active members of terrorist networks or organizations. In most cases, my interviewees had undergone—or appeared to be undergoing at the time—a process of deradicalization and disengagement. This made it difficult for me to discover what they had believed, thought, and admitted while they were still engaged in their radical activities.

In what follows, I set out how I translated these considerations and concerns into a methodological approach.

Selection of Interviewees

For the empirical part of this study, I interviewed twenty-five convicted terrorists and another sixteen people in their immediate circle, including anti-terrorism experts, youth workers, family members, and victims. Each interview lasted on average two to three hours. In some cases, I talked to the interviewee more than once. In other cases, I spoke with them as a group. When I conducted the interviews in prison, two guards were present, either in the room or directly in the corridor with the door ajar. When interviewees were not in detention, I contacted them after the interview with additional questions, and they provided me with written answers, which I used to supplement my reports. I selected the interviewees according to the following three criteria.

First, although this book includes a historical perspective, the focus of the empirical research lies on the group of convicted terrorists arrested or detained after 2011. This allows me to explore the similarities and differences between previous waves and current forms of terrorism. Furthermore, much has been written about the first generation of jihadists from around 9/11.[5] But the post-2011 generation grew up in a world in which information flows and communication technologies were much more advanced. Facebook, Twitter (now X), Instagram, and YouTube—these were the means of communication used by radicals after 2011, while their earlier counterparts read more books and distributed videos and DVDs. The terrorists detained in the terrorist detention units (TDUs) between 2013 and 2020 all come from the post-2011 generation, which makes it a convenient and relatively homogenous group to interview. Of the thirty-six terrorists in detention in February 2020, I established contact with twenty-one and held in-depth

---

[4] For a short introduction to this theme, see Holmes (2017b) and, for example, Holmes (2017a).

[5] In the Netherlands, most members of the Hofstad Group have been interviewed or discussed. See, for example, Schuurman (2018). Another notable Dutch terrorism case, the Piranha case, has also been widely documented. I have interviewed female jihadists involved in this case myself; see De Graaf (2012a).

interviews with seventeen. Of those seventeen, fifteen were convicted on appeal, and their trials were completed. In 2020, there were only three women in detention. I tried to speak with as many of the terrorist detainees as possible, and, with seventeen out of thirty-six, I managed to achieve a fair selection, namely, almost 50 percent of the prison population and more than 80 percent of those convicted for serious terrorist offenses and sentenced for more than three years. This helped me to considerably reduce the selection bias of my sample—which therefore cannot be considered a convenience sample.

For the interviewees in Indonesia, I used my research network there and relied on the sampling my colleagues in Jakarta did for me among ex-detainees: they located seven interviewees on the basis of availability in that area in the time frame that I was there. I did not want to submit an official request, since that would have involved working with the authorities there, which could lead to opaque and uncontrollable situations both for myself and for the interviewees, such as counterterrorism officials or other officials being allocated to the interview, wanting to listen in, or wanting to edit the accounts.

Second, the focus lies on convicted jihadist terrorists simply because they account for the majority of detainees. Most attacks and terrorist acts committed between 2010 and 2020 were the work of jihadists. At the same time, I did speak to convicted far-right extremists and a well-known activist, because I wanted to test the validity of my radical redemption approach in nonreligious extremist cases. I spoke to two of these individuals directly, and I gathered secondary material and interviewed police officers and probation staff to provide a more solid foundation for the findings from my small sample of two.

Third, the choice of interviewees also depended, of course, on the interviewees themselves. For my sample in the Netherlands, I wrote to the directors of the TDUs and visited the penitentiary institutions to explain the aims and structure of my research, which I also outlined in a subsequent letter. The TDU directors showed this letter to the detainees. Almost all of the male detainees who were permitted to talk to me wished to do so. That was a significant moment, because detainees usually do not want to speak with outsiders. To my surprise, they indicated they had seen me in the media and wanted to talk to me about what I had said (see also "Positionality" in chapter 1). Another important reason for them was that I had said I was religious, took religious beliefs very seriously, and wanted to hear more about theirs. After five detainees had spoken to me, the rest indicated of their own accord that they also wished to be interviewed. Interestingly enough, of the three convicted female terrorists in detention in February 2020, only one was willing to speak with me. The women were clearly more suspicious, while the men had fewer reservations. Fortunately, I was able to make use of reports from the media and books aimed at a wider audience (Van San 2019; Rueb 2018). In addition, I could use the interviews I had held for my (2012a) book *Gevaarlijke vrouwen* (Dangerous women). Two women who had since been released were also willing to speak to me.

As indicated, I wanted to speak with detainees who had been convicted or who had been released after serving their sentences. Talking to people in detention reduces background noise. Many detainees feel the need to tell their stories, and in prison they have the peace and time to do so. Furthermore, detainees in the TDUs are closely monitored to ensure they do not hold each other captive in their radical beliefs. Ringleaders and detainees who intimidated others have been transferred to put a stop to their influence. Many interviewees were therefore willing to speak quite freely about their beliefs in the one-on-one conversations, without feeling the hot breath of their fellow detainees on their necks. The majority of them were able to reflect on the link between their religious beliefs and their past radical engagement—and to distance themselves from it.

Speaking to people who have been released from prison is equally productive. They are going through a process of reflection, rehabilitation, and reintegration, and they, too, feel a need to talk about it. The former convicted jihadists I spoke with were coming to terms with themselves and their pasts and were putting that period behind them, assisted and closely supervised by the probation services.

Source Calibration

An important risk with oral history is the danger of distortion. How can an interviewer ensure they are not being told a pack of lies? And even if the interviewees are telling the truth, it is difficult to determine whether their accounts authentically reflect their beliefs and motives from when they were radicalizing, or whether their current situation has unintentionally influenced their stories. To neutralize the pitfall of falsity or temporal distortion, I compared all the accounts with other sources. Where possible, I checked the facts in the interviewees' criminal records, examined court and media reports and interviews, and spoke to probation officials, police officers, and other judicial staff. I attempted to counteract the temporal distortion by structuring the interviews strictly chronologically and to gather in advance as much information on the interviewee as possible. By beginning the interviews with the interviewee's family, background, and place of birth, I tried to take them back in time. I devoted considerable attention to their parents, the neighborhood they grew up in, and their family traditions. That was often a way for them to put the distress of the present aside and to escape the grooves in which their accounts had often become entrenched. I would then go through their life histories step by step, asking very specific, factual questions—what mosque they attended, whether their brothers and sisters went with them, how often they saw their grandparents, and so forth. If they made a jump in time, leaping back to the present or to current feelings of anger and doubt, I tried to take them back to the past and continue the chronology, saying things like, "We were talking about your time at secondary school. What subjects did you do?" In all cases, that eventually produced a great deal of information. In these long conversations, it was clear from their body language that the interviewees had returned to a time in the past when their conviction for terrorism did not dominate their thoughts. I followed this procedure with all of my interviewees. If someone was particularly talkative, I devoted two or even three sessions to their life stories.

To compensate for this first pitfall, the interviewer must be aware that an interviewee may be consciously or unconsciously distorting their life story. A life history is by definition a subjective account. Moreover, there is the subjectivity of the interviewer themself. I had to continually remind myself that my own specific perspective and interest—the attention I wished to pay to faith and beliefs—could steer the conversations in a certain direction and encourage the interviewees to frame their answers in a particular way. The only solution was to reproduce the conversation and the way in which the interviewees talked about their emotions, motives, and identities as precisely as possible and to check the accuracy of the chronology and facts during and after the conversation—and, if necessary, to talk about them again.

By taking time, paying attention, and relating details of my own life and involvement in the theme of religion, I was able to build up a conversational relationship with the interviewees. The connection thus generated was supported by the openness I maintained as interviewer about my motives. In addition, I made it clear that there was no point in distorting or concealing facts, because I could check them in their criminal records. Moreover, they had already been convicted on appeal. Within that context of confidentiality and awareness that I had access to their criminal records, some of the interviewees entrusted me with more details and facts about their time in the caliphate than they had previously told the police.

Broadening the Perspective

Another methodological pitfall became increasingly obvious to me when I started to notice recurring patterns in my conversations with the Dutch interviewees. Almost all of them spoke of a sense of deficit and of the duty or obligation to help other Muslims. They told me about their failure to lead a meaningful life, their feeling of falling short as Muslims, and the appeal of doing something good by fighting in the war in Syria. Most of them indicated that they had not been particularly religious before they radicalized, had hardly ever visited a mosque, and had sought answers to their questions themselves on the Internet via YouTube. In listening to these stories, I strongly gained the impression of a hypermodern, highly individualized, and online-generated type of belief. There was no one between them and Allah, between their questions and the answers they found on the Internet. Could this extremely individual, almost Protestant form of personalized faith be typically Western? Would jihadists elsewhere in the world become radicalized in this same way? Were the convicted terrorists in Dutch prisons typical of the worldwide jihad, or of a variant that was specifically Dutch (or, perhaps better, Dutch-Moroccan, for many detainees had both Moroccan and Dutch passports)? Would terrorists in less individualized societies be less single-minded in seeking their own personal radical paths?

That is why I also sought out interviewees who could give me an idea of the redemption narratives in non-Western Islamic communities that were more tribal or collectively based. Here, it proved an even more complex challenge to find people I could speak with in a setting that was relatively safe, for them and for me. Ultimately, thanks to the mediation of my colleague Professor Solahudin at the University of Indonesia in Jakarta, I was able to interview convicted terrorists who had been members of Jemaah Islamiyah or who were returned departees. I held in-depth interviews with six of them. My Indonesian research assistant Chadi sat in on my interviews to translate for me if the interviewees could not speak English. With the help of the Dutch embassy in Jakarta, I was also able to speak with several staff members of the Indonesian National Counter Terrorism Agency (BNPT).

In Cameroon, with the support of Mensen met een Missie, I was able to interview people who were directly involved in the reintegration of or provision of pastoral care to detainees, or who knew perpetrators and were victims of their attacks. Unfortunately, I was only able to conduct these interviews from a distance, via Skype, because by then the Covid-19 crisis had broken out. I also asked these interviewees for permission to quote from their accounts and inquired whether they wished me to preserve their anonymity. In this way, I tried to calibrate the "Dutch" perspective on faith with the accounts of convicted terrorists in a more tribal setting (Cameroon) and in an Islamic society—Indonesia, where 85 percent of the population is Muslim and where daily life is increasingly governed by Islamic rules. In addition, I also interviewed far-right extremists in the

Netherlands to determine whether there is any overlap between their motives of resistance, rebellion, and liberation and jihadist patterns of radical redemption.

In sum, employing the method of oral history, I applied a life histories approach that focuses on jihadist terrorists but also allows for some comparisons with terrorists of other provenances—right-wing extremists—with terrorists from completely different settings—Cameroon—and with members of armed militias, in Syria. Thus, I have tried to reconstruct the role of the radical redemption narrative in shaping the radicalization process of modern jihadists and have translated the acquired insights into a grounded theory. There is enough evidence for radical redemption's significant role as moderator in radicalization processes to look for more instances of this very potent narrative. My ultimate hope is that more research will be carried out to look into the way in which this narrative manifests itself in the lives of radical young people. If we wish to break the ongoing cycle of violence and extreme beliefs, we need to better understand the link between religion and terrorism. A thorough exploration of the radical redemption narrative will significantly contribute to furthering our understanding.

APPENDIX 3

Ethics

Vulnerable Research Subjects

When interviewing a specific type of perpetrator, oral historians must be aware of the danger of stigmatizing their interviewees with their interviews and books and anchoring them in their criminal past. This also holds for interviewing terrorists. Despite their sometimes very violent histories, people in detention are a most vulnerable group. Convicted terrorists are not permitted to communicate with the outside world; they cannot send emails or stay informed about everything that is published about them, and they can certainly not respond. Their actions will haunt them for the rest of their lives, either because of the media attention they attract or because, after completing their sentences, they will remain on all kinds of blacklists. Furthermore, in the Netherlands, the Dutch citizenship of most convicted terrorists with two passports is revoked after their release, which essentially places them outside mainstream society. Thus, when researchers gain access and start talking to detained terrorists, it is crucial that they are aware of their interviewees' vulnerable position and that they do not exploit that vulnerability (see also "Positionality" in chapter 1).

Ethical Clearance

As I interviewed terrorist detainees for this study, I had to make sure I was fair in my treatment of them, considering that they are detained in the highest-security penitentiary institutions, are not permitted to write letters or send emails, and cannot, therefore, defend themselves from errors or distortions. "Do no harm" is a first principle applied especially in anthropology as a main guideline for conducting fieldwork (see, e.g., De Koning et al. 2019). In addition, I obtained advice on this issue from the ethical committee of the Faculty of Humanities at Utrecht University and from the university's privacy officer, and I pledged to uphold their guidelines.

I first and foremost walked the path of official submission and procedure regarding requests for interviewing detainees in the Netherlands. My requests to interview detainees were not initially addressed directly to the detainees or their lawyers but were submitted formally to, and processed by, the Custodial Institutions Agency (DJI) at the Ministry of Justice and Security and the prison directors. The DJI and the directors asked me to sign official statements in which I promised that, before each interview, I would explain to the detainees that they were under no obligation to answer my questions and should not expect that, by talking to me, their sentences might be reduced or moderated. I made the latter very clear to every detainee each time I spoke with them: they could not derive any benefits from talking to me.

Informed Consent

Where possible, I asked the detainees to sign an informed consent form—again, following procedures of Utrecht University—giving me permission to record the interview, make notes, and use quotations from the interviews for my research under specific conditions, allowing them to withdraw that permission at any time. Sometimes, it was impossible to personally hand them the informed consent form. In such cases, I recorded their verbal permission on tape. Three of the detainees in the Netherlands ultimately withdrew their permission to use their data, so I could not use their stories in this research. Several others asked me to modify biographical details to make it impossible to trace the details given in their accounts. These recordings and notes are stored, in consultation with Utrecht University's privacy officer, on a separate, encrypted hard disk and in my personal archive.

After consulting, again, with the same privacy officer and the DJI, I ultimately decided to modify the biographical details of all detainees who were still in prison. In practical terms this means that, while I first checked all statements and claims made by the interviewees and compared them to information from the police, media reports, and announcements relating to the terrorism sanctions list in the government gazette, I could not reference these sources explicitly in the text. Furthermore, I changed the names of the interviewees whose accounts I used for this book. Pseudonyms are marked with an asterisk on first mention and in the table. Hence, all first names for Dutch interviewees are pseudonyms.

In the cases of eight Dutch detainees who were awaiting possible deportation or an appeal ruling and were afraid of repercussions for their friends and families, I took more drastic measures. They, too, all read the interview reports and were given the opportunity to respond. Following the work of French sociologist Didier Lapeyronnie (2008) on young people living in the *banlieus*, I modified their accounts more heavily. For example, when I used their comments on their sense of deficit and atonement, I linked them to a domestic situation, educational history, or work situation from a different interview. That produced portraits that were substantially closely related to the actual accounts but in which factual details and coordinates had been changed such that only the interviewees themselves would recognize some of the comments (see Lapeyronnie 2008, 34–44).[1]

Those who have been released from detention, including all the former detainees in Indonesia, permitted me to use their real names. I asked them, too, for their (written or oral) permission to use their accounts for my research, which they all gave. I operated here again in line with the requirements of Utrecht University's ethical committee. All ex-detainees received a typed-out copy of my report, were allowed to respond to it, and approved the texts via mail or WhatsApp.

---

[1] I thank Luuk Slooter for this tip.

References

Abadie, Alberto. 2006. "Poverty, Political Freedom, and the Roots of Terrorism." *American Economic Review* 96: pp. 50–6.
Abels, Romana, and Kustaw Bessems. 2002. "Eindhovenaren plotseling naar Kashmir." *Trouw*, January 15. https://www.trouw.nl/nieuws/eindhovenaren-plotseling-naar-kashmir~b3e6d374/.
Abu-Zahra, Nadia. 1997. *The Pure and Powerful: Studies in Contemporary Muslim Society*. Reading: Ithaca.
Adam, Barbara. 1998. *Timescapes of Modernity: The Environment & Invisible Hazards*. London: Routledge.
AIVD (General Intelligence and Security Service). 2002. *Rekrutering in Nederland voor de jihad: Van incident naar trend*. The Hague: AIVD.
AIVD. 2016. *Leven bij ISIS, de mythe ontrafeld*. The Hague: AIVD.
AIVD. 2018. *Rechts-extremisme in Nederland: Een fenomeen in beweging*. The Hague: AIVD.
Almond, Gabriel A., R. Scott Appleby, and Emmanuel Sivan. 2003. *Strong Religion: The Rise of Fundamentalisms around the World*. Chicago: University of Chicago Press.
Al-Rawi, Ahmed. 2015. "Online Reactions to the Muhammad Cartoons: YouTube and the Virtual Ummah." *Journal for the Scientific Study of Religion* 54 (2): pp. 261–76.
Amnesty International. 2015. "Nigeria: Horror in Numbers." Amnesty International. June 3. https://www.amnesty.org/en/latest/news/2015/06/nigeria-horror-in-numbers/.
Apard, Élodie. 2015. "Les mots de Boko Haram: Décryptages de discours de Mohammed Yusuf et d'Abubakar Shekau." *Afrique Contemporaine* 255 (3): pp. 41–69. https://www.cairn-int.info/article-E_AFCO_255_0043--the-words-of-boko-haram.htm.
Armstrong, Karen. 2014. *Fields of Blood: Religion and the History of Violence*. New York: Knopf.
Arnaz, Farouk. 2013. "Permintaan maaf Ramli si penjual senjata." Berita Satu. September 3. https://www.beritasatu.com/nasional/135758/permintaan-maaf-ramli-si-penjual-senjata.
Atran, Scott. 2010. *Talking to the Enemy: Violent Extremism, Sacred Values, and What It Means to Be Human*. London: Penguin.
Atran, Scott. 2016. "The Devoted Actor: Unconditional Commitment and Intractable Conflict across Cultures." *Current Anthropology* 57: pp. 192–203.
Aust, Stefan. 2008. "Terrorism in Germany: The Baader-Meinhof Phenomenon." *German Historical Institute Bulletin* 43: pp. 45–57.
Awan, Imran. 2017. "Cyber-Extremism: Isis and the Power of Social Media." *Social Science and Public Policy* 54 (2): pp. 138–49.
Azzam, Abdullah. n.d. *Signs of ar-Rahman in the Jihad of Afghan*. Birmingham: Maktabah.
Backes, Uwe, and Eckhard Jesse. 1993. *Politischer Extremismus in der Bundesrepublik Deutschland*. Bonn: Bundeszentrale für Politische Bildung.
Badara, Mohamed, and Masaki Nagata. 2017. "Modern Extremist Groups and the Division of the World: A Critique from an Islamic Perspective." *Arab Law Quarterly* 31 (4): pp. 305–35.
Bahara, Hassan. 2013. "Jihadisten in Nederland: 'Wat zeg je tegen je moeder?'" *De Groene Amsterdammer*, April 10.
Bailey, Holly. 2017. "The Unabomber's Not-So-Lonely Prison Life." *Yahoo News*, October 11.

Bakker, Edwin, and Beatrice de Graaf. 2010. *Lone Wolves: How to Prevent this Phenomenon?* The Hague: International Centre for Counter-Terrorism. https://www.icct.nl/sites/default/files/2023-02/ICCT-Bakker-deGraaf-EM-Paper-Lone-Wolves.pdf.

Bakker, Edwin, and Peter Grol. 2017. *Nederlandse jihadisten: Van naïeve idealisten tot geharde terroristen.* Amsterdam: Hollands diep.

Baron, R. M., and D. A. Kenny. 1986. "The Moderator-Mediator Variable Distinction in Social Psychology Research." *Journal of Personality and Social Psychology* 51 (6): pp. 1173–82.

Basra, Rajan, Peter R. Neumann, and Claudia Brunner. 2016. *Criminal Pasts, Terrorist Futures: European Jihadists and the New Crime-Terror Nexus.* London: ICSR. https://icsr.info/wp-content/uploads/2016/10/ICSR-Report-Criminal-Pasts-Terrorist-Futures-European-Jihadists-and-the-New-Crime-Terror-Nexus.pdf.

Baurmann, Michael. 2007. "Rational Fundamentalism? An Explanatory Model of Fundamentalist Beliefs." *Episteme* 4 (2): pp. 150–66.

Baurmann, Michael, Gregor Betz, and Rainer Cramm. 2018. "'Führer befiehl, wir folgen dir!' Charismatic Leaders in Extremist Groups." In *Morality, Governance, and Social Institutions*, edited by Thomas Christiano, Ingrid Creppell, and Jack Knight, pp. 259–87. Cham: Palgrave Macmillan.

Beam, Louis. 1992. "Leaderless Resistance." *The Seditionist* 12: pp. 1–7. https://websites.umich.edu/~satran/Ford%2006/Wk%202-1%20Terrorism%20Networks%20leaderless-resistance.pdf.

Beatty, Andrew. 2014. "Anthropology and Emotion." *Journal of the Royal Anthropological Institute* 20 (3): pp. 545–63.

Becker, Ernest. 1971. *The Birth and Death of Meaning: An Interdisciplinary Perspective on the Problem of Man.* 2nd revised edition. New York: Free Press.

Becker, Ernest. 1973. *The Denial of Death.* New York: Free Press.

Becker, Ernest. 1975. *Escape from Evil.* New York: Free Press.

Beek, Johan van de, and Claire van Dyck. 2017. *Sultan en de lokroep van de jihad.* Amsterdam: Balans.

Bennett, James. 1981. *Oral History and Delinquency: The Rhetoric of Criminology.* Chicago: University of Chicago Press.

Berger, J. M. 2017. *Extremist Construction of Identity: How Escalating Demands for Legitimacy Shape and Define In-Group and Out-Group Dynamics.* The Hague: International Centre for Counter-Terrorism. https://www.icct.nl/sites/default/files/2022-12/ICCT-Berger-Extremist-Construction-of-Identity-April-2017-2.pdf.

Berger, J. M. 2018. *Extremism.* Cambridge, MA: MIT Press.

Berkelder, Nadia. 2018. "Celstraffen voor Rotterdammers die naar Syrië reisden." *Algemeen Dagblad*, August 2. https://www.ad.nl/rotterdam/celstraffen-voor-rotterdammers-die-naar-syrie-reisden~a76bbfcd/.

Berkowitz, Leonard. 1993. *Aggression: Its Causes, Consequences, and Control.* New York: McGraw-Hill.

Bessems, Kustaw. 2005. "Scholier vulde web met dreigementen." *Trouw*, January 31.

Bjørgo, Tore, ed. 2005. *Root Causes of Terrorism: Myths, Reality and Ways Forward.* London: Routledge.

Bloom, Mia, Hicham Tiflati, and John Horgan. 2019. "Navigating ISIS's Preferred Platform: Telegram." *Terrorism and Political Violence* 31 (6): pp. 1242–54.

Blow, Charles M. 2015. "In Charleston, a Millennial Race Terrorist." *New York Times*, June 21. https://www.nytimes.com/2015/06/22/opinion/charles-blow-in-charleston-a-millennial-race-terrorist.html.

Blumer, Herbert. 1969. *Symbolic Interactionism: Perspective and Method.* Englewood Cliffs, NJ: Prentice Hall.

Boff, Clodovis. 1987. *Theology and Praxis: Epistemological Foundations.* Maryknoll: Orbis Books.

Bortolotti, Lisa. 2021. "Extreme Beliefs: An Interview with Rik Peels." *Imperfect Cognitions* blog. November 2. http://imperfectcognitions.blogspot.com/2021/11/extreme-beliefs-interview-with-rik-peels.html.

Bortolotti, Lisa, Anna Ichino, and Matteo Mameli. 2021. "Conspiracy Theories and Delusions." *Reti, Saperi, Linguaggi: Italian Journal of Cognitive Sciences* 8 (2): pp. 183–200.

Borum, Randy. 2011. "Radicalization into Violent Extremism I: A Review of Social Science Theories." *Journal of Strategic Security* 4 (4): pp. 7–36.

Bos, Kees van den. 2018. *Why People Radicalize: How Unfairness Judgments Are Used to Fuel Radical Beliefs, Extremist Behaviors, and Terrorism*. Oxford: Oxford University Press.

Bos, Kees van den. 2020a. *Empirical Legal Research: A Primer*. Northampton, MA: Edward Elgar.

Bos, Kees van den. 2020b. "Injustice and Violent Extremism: Methodological Directions for Future Justice Research." In *Social Psychology and Justice*, edited by E. Allan Lind, pp. 162–80. New York: Routledge.

Bos, Kees van den. 2020c. "Unfairness and Radicalization." *Annual Review of Psychology* 71: pp. 563–88.

Bos, Kees van den, Marijn Poortvliet, Marjolein Maas, Joost Miedema, and Ernst-Jan van den Ham. 2005. "An Enquiry Concerning the Principles of Cultural Norms and Values: The Impact of Uncertainty and Mortality Salience on Reactions to Violations and Bolstering of Cultural Worldviews." *Journal of Experimental Social Psychology* 41 (2): pp. 91–113.

Boterman, Frits. 2005. *Moderne geschiedenis van Duitsland, 1800–heden*. Amsterdam: De Arbeiderspers.

Boterman, Frits. 2013. *Cultuur als macht: Cultuurgeschiedenis van Duitsland, 1800–heden* Amsterdam: De Arbeiderspers.

Bowen, Glenn A. 2006. "Grounded Theory and Sensitizing Concepts." *International Journal for Qualitative Methods* 5 (3): pp. 12–23.

Brachman, Jarret, and Alix Levine. 2011. "The World of Holy Warcraft." *Foreign Policy*, April. https://foreignpolicy.com/2011/04/13/the-world-of-holy-warcraft/.

Breivik, Anders Behring [Andrew Berwick]. 2011. "2083: A European Declaration of Independence." Unpublished manuscript.

Brown, Colin, ed. 1981. *The New International Dictionary of New Testament Theology*. Vol. 3. 6th edition. Grand Rapids, MI: Zondervan.

Bruinessen, Martin van. 1996. "Islamic State or State Islam? Fifty Years of State-Islam Relations in Indonesia." In *Indonesien am Ende des 20. Jahrhunderts*, edited by Ingrid Wessel, pp. 19–34. Hamburg: Abera-Verlag.

Bruinessen, Martin van. 2002. "Genealogies of Islamic Radicalism in Post-Suharto Indonesia." *Southeast Asia Research* 10 (2): pp. 117–54.

Buenting, Joel, and Jason Taylor. 2010. "Conspiracy Theories and Fortuitous Data." *Philosophy of the Social Sciences* 40 (4): pp. 567–78.

Buitelaar, Marjo. 2014. "Dialogical Constructions of a Muslim Self through Life Story Telling." In *Religious Stories We Live By: Narrative Approaches in Theology and Religious Studies*, edited by R. Ruard Ganzevoort, Maaike de Haardt, and Michael Scherer-Rath, pp. 143–55. Leiden: Brill.

Burgoon, Brian. 2006. "On Welfare and Terror: Social Welfare Policies and Political-Economic Roots of Terrorism." *Journal of Conflict Resolution* 50: pp. 176–203.

Calvert, John. 2010. *Sayyid Qutb and the Origins of Radical Islamism*. New York: Columbia University Press.

Çancı, Haldun, and Opeyemi Adedoyin Odukoya. 2016. "Ethnic and Religious Crises in Nigeria: A Specific Analysis upon Identities (1999–2013)." *African Journal on Conflict Resolution* 16 (1). https://www.accord.org.za/ajcr-issues/ethnic-religious-crises-nigeria.

Carson, Jennifer Varriale, and Matthew Suppenbach. 2018. "The Global Jihadist Movement: The Most Lethal Ideology?" *Homicide Studies* 22 (1): pp. 8–44.

Cassam, Quassim. 2018. "The Epistemology of Terrorism and Radicalisation." *Royal Institute of Philosophy Supplement* 84: pp. 187–209.
Cassam, Quassim. 2019. *Conspiracy Theories*. Cambridge: Polity Press.
Cassam, Quassim. 2021a. "Epistemic Vices, Ideologies and False Consciousness." In *The Routledge Handbook of Political Epistemology*, edited by Michael Hannon and Jeroen de Ridder, pp. 301–11. London: Routledge.
Cassam, Quassim. 2021b. *Extremism: A Philosophical Analysis*. London: Routledge.
Cavanaugh, William T. 2009. *The Myth of Religious Violence: Secular Ideology and the Roots of Modern Conflict*. Oxford: Oxford University Press.
CBS (Centraal Bureau voor de Statistiek). 2016. "In 2015 twee keer zo veel asielzoekers en nareizigers als in 2014." Centraal Bureau voor de Statistiek. January 27. https://www.cbs.nl/nl-nl/nieuws/2016/04/in-2015-twee-keer-zo-veel-asielzoekers-en-nareizigers-als-in-2014.
Chahed, Nadia. 2019. "Cameroun: Plus de 250 ex-combattants démobilisés depuis fin janvier 2019 (officiel)." *Anadolu Agency*, December 3. https://www.aa.com.tr/fr/afrique/cameroun-plus-de-250-ex-combattants-d%C3%A9mobilis%C3%A9s-depuis-fin-janvier-2019-officiel-/1662621.
Choudhury, Nupur. 2014. "World Wide Web and Its Journey from Web 1.0 to Web 4.0." *International Journal of Computer Science and Information Technologies* 5 (6): pp. 8096–100.
CNN. 2016. "Dylann Roof Confession Video." December 10. https://edition.cnn.com/videos/justice/2016/12/10/dylann-roof-church-massacre-confession-ekr-orig-vstop.cnn.
Cohler, B. J. 1982. "Personal Narrative and the Life Course." In *Life-Span Development and Behavior*. Vol. 4, edited by Paul Baltes and Orville G. Brim, pp. 205–41. New York: Academic Press.
Conway, Maura. 2006. "Terrorism and the Internet: New Media – New Threat?" *Parliamentary Affairs* 59 (2): pp. 283–98.
Conway, Maura. 2017. "Determining the Role of the Internet in Violent Extremism and Terrorism: Six Suggestions for Progressing Research." *Studies in Conflict & Terrorism* 40 (1): pp. 77–98.
Cook, David B. 2007. *Martyrdom in Islam*. Cambridge: Cambridge University Press.
Cook, David B. 2017. "Contemporary Martyrdom: Ideology and Material Culture." In *Jihadi Culture: The Art and Social Practices of Militant Islamists*, edited by Thomas Hegghammer, pp. 151–70. Cambridge: Cambridge University Press.
Cooperman, Alan. 2003. "Is Terrorism Tied to Christian Sect?" *Washington Post*, June 2. https://www.washingtonpost.com/archive/politics/2003/06/02/is-terrorism-tied-to-christian-sect/7510f762-4ac6-43b5-9b15-479a8cef16d4/.
Crenshaw, Martha. 1981. "The Causes of Terrorism." *Comparative Politics* 13 (4): pp. 379–99.
Crenshaw, Martha. 1987. "Theories of Terrorism: Instrumental and Organization Approaches." *Journal of Strategic Studies* 10 (4): pp. 13–31.
Crenshaw, Martha, ed. 1995. *Terrorism in Context*. University Park, PA: Pennsylvania State University Press.
Crenshaw, Martha. 2007. "Explaining Suicide Terrorism: A Review Essay." *Security Studies* 16 (1): pp. 133–62.
Crenshaw, Martha. 2011. *Explaining Terrorism: Causes, Processes, and Consequences*. London: Routledge.
Crone, Manni. 2016. "Radicalization Revisited: Violence, Politics and the Skills of the Body." *International Affairs* 92 (3): pp. 587–604.
Crusius, Patrick. 2019. "The Inconvenient Truth." Unpublished manuscript.
Curtis, Glenn E., and Tara Karacan. 2002. *The Nexus among Terrorists, Narcotics Traffickers, Weapons Proliferators, and Organized Crime Networks in Western Europe*. Washington, DC: Federal Research Division, Library of Congress. https://apps.dtic.mil/sti/pdfs/ADA439844.pdf.
Dahhan, Ghassan, and Milena Holdert. 2019. "OM botst in de rechtszaal met Buitenlandse Zaken over Syrische strijdgroepen." *Trouw*, March 1. https://www.trouw.nl/nieuws/

om-botst-in-de-rechtszaal-met-buitenlandse-zaken-over-syrische-strijdgroepen~b5356495/?referrer=https://www.google.com/.
Dawson, Lorne L. 2009. "The Study of New Religious Movements and the Radicalization of Home-Grown Terrorists: Opening a Dialogue." *Terrorism and Political Violence* 22 (1): pp. 1–21.
Dawson, Lorne L. 2017. "Discounting Religion in the Explanation of Homegrown Terrorism." In *The Cambridge Companion to Religion and Terrorism*, edited by James R. Lewis, pp. 32–45. Cambridge: Cambridge University Press.
Dawson, Lorne L. 2019. "Taking Terrorist Accounts of Their Motivations Seriously: An Exploration of the Hermeneutics of Suspicion." *Perspectives on Terrorism* 13 (5): pp. 74–89.
Dawson, Lorne L. 2021a. "Bringing Religiosity Back In: Critical Reflection on the Explanation of Western Homegrown Religious Terrorism (Part I)." *Perspectives on Terrorism* 15 (1): pp. 2–16.
Dawson, Lorne L. 2021b. "Bringing Religiosity Back In: Critical Reflection on the Explanation of Western Homegrown Religious Terrorism (Part II)." *Perspectives on Terrorism* 15 (2): pp. 2–22.
Day, Abby. 2009. "Believing in Belonging: An Ethnography of Young People's Constructions of Belief." *Culture and Religion* 10 (3): pp. 263–78.
Deeb, Mary-Jane. 1992. "Militant Islam and the Politics of Redemption." *The Annals of the American Academy of Political and Social Science* 524 (1): pp. 52–65.
Del Cid Gómez, Juan Miguel. 2010. "A Financial Profile of the Terrorism of Al-Qaeda and Its Affiliates." *Perspectives on Terrorism* 4 (4): pp. 3–27.
Della Porta, Donatella. 1995. *Social Movements, Political Violence, and the State: A Comparative Analysis of Italy and Germany*. Cambridge: Cambridge University Press.
Della Porta, Donatella. 2008. "Research on Social Movements and Political Violence." *Qualitative Sociology* 31: pp. 221–30.
Della Porta, Donatella. 2009. "Recruitment Processes in Clandestine Political Organizations: Italian Left-Wing Terrorism." In *Psychology of Terrorism: Classic and Contemporary Insights*, edited by Jeff Victoroff and Arie W. Kruglanski, pp. 307–16. New York: Psychology Press.
Demant, Froukje, and Beatrice de Graaf. 2010. "How to Counter Radical Narratives: Dutch Deradicalization Policy in the Case of Moluccan and Islamic Radicals." *Studies in Conflict & Terrorism* 33 (5): pp. 408–28.
"De Nederlandse Mujahideen in Bilaad As-Shaam." 2013. *De banier*. Unpublished manuscript.
Dentith, M R. X. 2014. *The Philosophy of Conspiracy Theories*. London: Palgrave Macmillan.
Dentith, M R. X. 2023. "*Some* Conspiracy Theories." *Social Epistemology* 37 (4): pp. 522–34.
Dershowitz, Alan M. 2002. *Why Terrorism Works: Understanding the Threat, Responding to the Challenge*. New Haven: Yale University Press.
Deursen, Alexander van, Jan van Dijk, and Peter ten Klooster. 2015. "Increasing Inequalities in What We Do Online: A Longitudinal Cross Section Analysis of Internet Activities among the Dutch Population (2010 to 2013) over Gender, Age, Education, and Income." *Telematics and Informatics* 32: pp. 259–72.
Devji, Faisal. 2005. *Global Landscapes of Jihad: Militancy, Morality, Modernity*. Ithaca, NY: Cornell University Press.
Devji, Faisal. 2009. *The Terrorist in Search of Humanity: Militant Islam and Global Politics*. New York: Columbia University Press.
Dingley, James, and Marcello Mollica. 2007. "The Human Body as a Terrorist Weapon: Hunger Strikes and Suicide Bombers." *Studies in Conflict & Terrorism* 30 (6): pp. 459–92.
Dobbin, Christine. 1983. *Islamic Revivalism in a Changing Peasant Economy: Central Sumatra 1784–1847*. London: Routledge.
Doornbos, Harald, and Jenan Moussa. 2016. "Present at the Creation." *Foreign Policy*, August 16. https://foreignpolicy.com/2016/08/16/present-at-the-creation/.

Doosje, Bertjan, Fathali M. Moghaddam, Arie W. Kruglanski, Arjan de Wolf, Liesbeth Mann, and Allard R. Feddes. 2016. "Terrorism, Radicalization and De-radicalization." *Current Opinion in Psychology* 11: pp. 79–84.

"Dossier radicale verlossing." 2023. Special issue, *Tijdschrift Sociologie* 4.

Doyle, Gerry. 2019. "New Zealand Mosque Gunman's Plan Began and Ended Online." Reuters. March 15. https://www.reuters.com/article/us-newzealand-shootout-internet-idUSKC N1QW1MV.

Durkheim, Émile. 2008. *The Elementary Forms of Religious Life*. Oxford: Oxford University Press.

Ebner, Julia. 2020. *Going Dark: The Secret Social Lives of Extremists*. London: Bloomsbury.

Edgar, Ian R., and Gwynned de Looijer. 2017. "The Islamic Dream Tradition and Jihadi Militancy." In *Jihadi Culture: The Art and Social Practices of Militant Islamists*, edited by Thomas Hegghammer, pp. 128–50. Cambridge: Cambridge University Press.

Eerten, Jan-Jaap van, Bertjan Doosje, Elly Konijn, Beatrice de Graaf, and Mariëlle de Goede. 2017. *Developing a Social Media Response to Radicalization: The Role of Counter-Narratives in Prevention of Radicalization and De-radicalization*. The Hague: Wetenschappelijk Onderzoek- en Documentatiecentrum.

EFSAS (European Foundation for South Asian Studies). 2020. *Guilty until Proven Innocent: The Sacrilegious Nature of Blasphemy Laws in Pakistan*. Amsterdam: EFSAS.

Eliraz, Giora. 2004. *Islam in Indonesia: Modern Radicalism and the Middle East Dimension* Brighton: Sussex Academic Press.

Ensslin, Gudrun, and Andreas Baader. 2010. "August 1968." In *Gudrun Ensslin, Bernward Vesper, »Notstandsgesetze von Deiner Hand« Briefe 1968/1969*, edited by Caroline Harmsen, Ulrike Meyer, and Johannes Ullmaier, pp. 163, 173. Berlin: Suhrkamp.

English, Richard. 2003. *Armed Struggle: The History of the IRA*. Oxford: Oxford University Press.

Esposito, John I. 2002. *What Everyone Needs to Know about Islam*. Oxford: Oxford University Press.

Evans, Robert. 2019. "The El Paso Shooting and the Gamification of Terror." Bellingcat. August 4. https://www.bellingcat.com/news/americas/2019/08/04/the-el-paso-shooting-and-the-gamification-of-terror/.

Farwell, James P. 2014. "The Media Strategy of ISIS." *Survival* 56 (6): pp. 49–55.

Faulkner, Brian. 1971. "Press Release: Statement by the Prime Minister, Mr Brian Faulkner DL MP at 11 15 AM on Monday 9 August 1971." PRONI Public Records pm/5/169/14. http://cain.ulst.ac.uk/proni/1971/proni_PM-5-169-14_1971-08-09.pdf.

Fausset, Richard, John Eligon, Jason Horowitz, and Frances Robles. 2015. "A Hectic Day at Charleston Church, and Then a Hellish Visitor." *New York Times*, June 20. https://www.nytimes.com/2015/06/21/us/a-day-at-the-statehouse-and-a-night-of-slaughter.html.

Feddes, Allard R., Lars Nickolson, Liesbeth Mann, and Bertjan Doosje. 2020. *Psychological Perspectives on Terrorism*. London: Routledge.

Ferguson, Neil, and Eve Binks. 2015. "Understanding Radicalization and Engagement in Terrorism through Religious Conversion Motifs." *Journal of Strategic Security* 8 (1–2): pp. 16–26.

Fierke, Karin M. 2012. "The Warden's Dilemma: Self-Sacrifice and Compromise in Asymmetric Interactions." *Government and Opposition* 47 (3): pp. 321–41.

Fishbein, Martin, and Icek Ajzen. 1975. *Belief, Attitude, Intention, and Behavior: An Introduction to Theory and Research*. Reading, MA: Addison-Wesley.

Folger, Robert. 1977. "Distributive and Procedural Justice: Combined Impact of 'Voice' and Improvement of Experienced Inequity." *Journal of Personality and Social Psychology* 35 (2): pp. 108–19.

Fox, Jonathan. 2004. "The Rise of Religious Nationalism and Conflict: Ethnic Conflict and Revolutionary Wars, 1945–2001." *Journal of Peace Research* 41 (6): pp. 715–31.

Frankl, Viktor E. 2000. *Man's Search for Ultimate Meaning*. New York: Perseus Books.

REFERENCES 317

Frevert, Ute. 2011. *Emotions in History: Lost and Found*. Budapest: CEU Press.
Friis, Simone Molin. 2015. "'Beyond Anything We Have Ever Seen': Beheading Videos and the Visibility of Violence in the War against ISIS." *International Affairs* 91 (4): pp. 725–46.
Gadher, Dipesh, David Leppard, Hala Jaber, Toby Harnden, and Laura Molyneaux. "'We Need to Start Taking Heads Off': The YouTube Jihadists Who Pose a Risk to Britain." *Sunday Times*, January 12. https://www.thetimes.com/article/we-need-to-start-taking-heads-off-the-youtube-jihadists-who-pose-a-risk-to-britain-b0tfb008b76.
Gall, Terry Lynn, Claire Charbonneau, Neil Henry Clarke, Karen Grant, Anjali Joseph, and Lisa Shouldice. 2005. "Understanding the Nature and Role of Spirituality in Relation to Coping and Health: A Conceptual Framework." *Canadian Psychology* 46 (2): pp. 88–104.
Gartenstein-Ross, Daveed, Colin P. Clarke, and Samuel Hodgson. 2020. "Foreign Terrorist Fighters from Southeast Asia: What Happens Next?" International Centre for Counter-Terrorism. February 17. https://www.icct.nl/publication/foreign-terrorist-fighters-southeast-asia-what-happens-next.
GeenStijl. 2019. "030-verdachte Gokmen Tanis is 'Haatdemocraat' uit GeenStijlTV video uit 2011." GeenStijl blog. March 18. https://www.geenstijl.nl/5146785/030-verdachte-gokmen-tanis-is-haatdemocraat/.
Gehrig, Sebastian. 2011. "Sympathizing Subcultures? The Milieus of West German Terrorism." In *Between Prague Spring and French May: Opposition and Revolt in Europe, 1960–1980*, edited by Martin Klimke, Jacco Pekelder, and Joachim Scharloth, pp. 233–50. New York: Berghahn Books.
Gelineau, Kristen. 2019. "Bali Bombers' Brother, Bomb Widow Become Friends, Seek Peace." *AP News*, December 27. https://apnews.com/f8f8dc3b07ee1dd116aab04eaa1a7b7f.
Gergen, Kenneth J. 1973. "Social Psychology as History." *Journal of Personality and Social Psychology* 26 (2): pp. 309–20.
Gergen, Kenneth J. 1980. "Towards Intellectual Audacity in Social Psychology." In *The Development of Social Psychology*, edited by Robin Gilmour and Steve Duck, pp. 239–70. London: Academic Press.
Gielen, Amy-Jane. 2017. "Countering Violent Extremism: A Realist Review for Assessing What Works, for Whom, in What Circumstances, and How?" *Terrorism and Political Violence* 31 (6): pp. 1149–67.
Girard, René, and Robert Doran. 2008. "Apocalyptic Thinking after 9/11: An Interview with René Girard." *SubStance* 37: pp. 20–32.
Githens-Mazer, Jonathan. 2008. "Islamic Radicalisation among North Africans in Britain." *British Journal of Politics and International Relations* 10 (4): pp. 550–70.
Glaser, Barney G., Anselm L. Strauss, and Elizabeth Strutzel. 1968. "The Discovery of Grounded Theory: Strategies for Qualitative Research." *Nursing Research* 17 (4): pp. 364–5.
Gobée, E., and C. Adriaanse, eds. 1957–65. *Ambtelijke adviezen van C. Snouck Hurgronje 1889–1936*. 3 vols. Rijks Geschiedkundige Publicatiën, Kleine Serie 33, 34, 35. The Hague: Martinus Nijhoff.
Graaf, Beatrice de. 2007. *Über die Mauer: Die DDR, die niederländischen Kirchen und die Friedensbewegung*. Münster: Agenda Verlag.
Graaf, Beatrice de. 2010. *Theater van de angst: De strijd tegen terrorisme in Nederland, Duitsland, Italië en Amerika*. Amsterdam: Boom.
Graaf, Beatrice de. 2011. *Evaluating Counterterrorism Performance: A Comparative Study*. New York: Routledge.
Graaf, Beatrice de. 2012a. *Gevaarlijke vrouwen: Tien militante vrouwen in het vizier*. Amsterdam: Boom.
Graaf, Beatrice de. 2012b. "Van 'helsche machines' en Russische provocateurs: De strijd tegen het anarchisme in Nederland." *Tijdschrift voor Geschiedenis* 125 (3): pp. 314–31.
Graaf, Beatrice de. 2014. "The Van Gogh Murder and Beyond." In *The Evolution of the Global Terrorist Threat: From 9/11 to Osama bin Laden's Death*, edited by Bruce Hoffman and Fernando Reinares, pp. 144–87. New York: Columbia University Press.

Graaf, Beatrice de. 2017. *Heilige strijd: Het verlangen naar veiligheid en het einde van het kwaad*. Utrecht: Boekencentrum.
Graaf, Beatrice de. 2019. "Foreign Fighters on Trial: Sentencing Risk, 2013–2017." In *Radicalization in Belgium and the Netherlands: Critical Perspectives on Violence and Security*, edited by Nadia Fadil, Martijn de Koning, and Francesco Ragazzi, pp. 97–130. London: Bloomsbury.
Graaf, Beatrice de. 2021. *Radicale verlossing: Wat terroristen geloven*. Amsterdam: Prometheus.
Graaf, Beatrice de, and Kees van den Bos. 2021. "Religious Radicalization: Social Appraisals and Finding Radical Redemption in Extreme Beliefs." *Current Opinion in Psychology* 40: pp. 56–60.
Graaf, Beatrice de, Kees van den Bos, and Liesbeth Hulst. 2019. "Vergis je niet, Gökmen T. staat niet alleen." *NRC Handelsblad*, July 2. https://www.nrc.nl/nieuws/2019/07/02/vergis-je-niet-gokmen-t-staat-niet-alleen-a3965828.
Graaf, Beatrice de, and Leena Malkki. 2010. "Killing It Softly? Explaining the Early Demise of Left-Wing Terrorism in the Netherlands." *Terrorism and Political Violence* 22 (4): pp. 623–40.
Greig, Charlotte. 2012. *Criminal Masterminds: Evil Geniuses of the Underworld*. London: Arcturus.
Groen, Janny, and Annieke Kranenberg. 2006. *Strijdsters van Allah: Radicale moslima's en het Hofstadnetwerk*. Amsterdam: Meulenhoff.
Guardian. 2014. "Boko Haram Leader: 'We Will Sell the Girls on the Market'—video." May 6. https://www.theguardian.com/world/video/2014/may/06/boko-haram-sell-girls-market-video.
Gullestad, Siri Erika. 2017. "Anders Behring Breivik, Master of Life and Death: Psychodynamics and Political Ideology in an Act of Terrorism." *International Forum of Psychoanalysis* 26 (4): pp. 207–16.
Gurr, Ted R. 1970. *Why Men Rebel*. Princeton, NJ: Princeton University Press.
Gutiérrez, Gustavo. 1974. *Theologie van de bevrijding*. Baarn: Ten Have.
Hafez, Mohammed M. 2007. "Martyrdom Mythology in Iraq: How Jihadists Frame Suicide Terrorism in Videos and Biographies." *Terrorism and Political Violence* 19 (1): pp. 95–115.
Harambam, Jaron. 2020. *Contemporary Conspiracy Culture: Truth and Knowledge in an Era of Epistemic Instability*. London: Routledge.
Haraway, Donna. 1988. "Situated Knowledge: The Science Question in Feminism and the Privilege of Partial Perspective." *Feminist Studies* 14 (3): pp. 575–99.
Hardin, Russell. 2002. "The Crippled Epistemology of Extremism." In *Political Extremism and Rationality*, edited by Albert Breton, Gianluigi Galeotti, Pierre Salmon, and Ronald Wintrobe, pp. 3–22. Cambridge: Cambridge University Press.
Harding, Sandra. 1991. *Whose Science? Whose Knowledge? Thinking from Women's Lives*. Ithaca, NY: Cornell University Press.
Hare, John Neville. 2015. "How Northern Nigeria's Violent History Explains Boko Haram." *National Geographic*, March 14. https://www.nationalgeographic.com/history/article/150314-boko-haram-nigeria-borno-rabih-abubakar-shekau.
Harris, Keith. 2018. "What's Epistemically Wrong with Conspiracy Theorising?" *Royal Institute of Philosophy Supplement* 84: pp. 235–57.
Hart van Nederland. 2019. "Tien jaar cel voor Pakistaan die dreigde met aanslag op Wilders." November 18. https://www.hartvannederland.nl/nieuws/tien-jaar-cel-voor-pakistaan-die-dreigde-met-aanslag-op-wilders.
Harwood, Elizabeth T. 2019. "Terrorism and the Digital Right-Wing." *Contexts* 18 (3): pp. 60–2.
Hatina, Meir. 2014. *Martyrdom in Modern Islam: Piety, Power, and Politics*. Cambridge: Cambridge University Press.
Hegghammer, Thomas. 2019. *The Caravan: Abdallah Azzam and the Rise of Global Jihad*. Cambridge: Cambridge University Press.

Helden, Berrie van. 2018. "Arnhemse jihadstrijder Marouane B. roept op tot het plegen van aanslagen in Europa." *De Gelderlander*, April 4. https://www.gelderlander.nl/arnhem-e-o/arnhemse-jihadstrijder-marouane-b-roept-op-tot-het-plegen-van-aanslagen-in-europa~a6edbe47/.

Hemmingby, Cato, and Tore Bjørgo. 2018. "Terrorist Target Selection: The Case of Anders Behring Breivik." *Perspectives on Terrorism* 12 (6): pp. 164–76.

Het Parool. 2012. "200 lijken aangetroffen in Daraya." August 25. https://www.parool.nl/nieuws/200-lijken-aangetroffen-in-daraya~b31ac52b/.

Hildermeier, Manfred. 2000. *The Russian Socialist Revolutionary Party before the First World War*. Münster: Lit Verlag.

Hofstede Insights. n.d. "Country Comparison." Hofstede Insights. Accessed September 6, 2023. https://www.hofstede-insights.com/country-comparison/indonesia/.

Hogg, Michael A., Janice R. Adelman, and Robert D. Blagg. 2010. "Religion in the Face of Uncertainty: An Uncertainty-Identity Theory Account of Religiousness." *Personality and Social Psychology Review* 14 (1): pp. 72–83.

Holbrook, Donald, and John Horgan. 2019. "Terrorism and Ideology: Cracking the Nut." *Perspectives on Terrorism* 13 (6): pp. 2–15.

Holmes, Katie. 2017a. "Does It Matter If She Cried? Recording Emotion and the Australian Generations Oral History Project." *The Oral History Review* 44 (1): pp. 56–76.

Holmes, Katie. 2017b. "Learning to Read Emotions in Oral History." OUP blog. May 16. https://blog.oup.com/2017/05/oral-history-emotions/.

Honing, Dennis Abdelkarim, and Nikki Sterkenburg. 2015. *Ongeloofwaardig: Hoe ik mezelf radicaliseerde en daarvan terugkwam*. Amsterdam: Singel.

Horgan, John. 2003. "The Search for the Terrorist Personality." In *Terrorists, Victims, and Society*, edited by Andrew Silke, pp. 3–27. Chichester: John Wiley.

Horgan, John. 2008. "From Profiles to Pathways and Roots to Routes: Perspectives from Psychology on Radicalization into Terrorism." *The Annals of the American Academy of Political and Social Science* 618: pp. 80–94.

Horgan, John. 2012. "Interviewing the Terrorists: Reflections on Fieldwork and Implications for Psychological Research." *Behavioral Sciences of Terrorism and Political Aggression* 4 (3): pp. 195–211.

Horgan, John. 2014. *The Psychology of Terrorism*. 2nd revised edition. London: Routledge.

Horgan, John. 2024. *Terrorist Minds: The Psychology of Violent Extremism from Al-Qaeda to the Far Right*. New York: Columbia University Press.

Horton, Alex. 2019. "With Strobe Lights and Guns Bearing Neo-Nazi Slogans, New Zealand Gunman Plotted a Massacre." *Washington Post*, March 15. https://www.washingtonpost.com/world/2019/03/15/with-strobe-lights-guns-bearing-neo-nazi-slogans-new-zealand-gunman-plotted-massacre/.

Hough, Andrew. 2011. "Norway Shooting: Anders Behring Breivik Plagiarised 'Unabomber.'" *Daily Telegraph*, July 24. https://www.telegraph.co.uk/news/worldnews/europe/norway/8658269/Norway-shooting-Anders-Behring-Breivik-plagiarised-Unabomber.html.

Houterman, Karlijn, and Jeroen Wetzels. 2020. "Dit stond op het wapen dat Gökmen T. gebruikte bij de tramaanslag in Utrecht." *RTL nieuws*, March 1. https://www.rtl.nl/nieuws/nederland/artikel/5040301/gokmen-aanslag-utrecht-tram-wapen-tekst-sharia-allah.

Huisman, Charlotte. 2020. "Een kusmondje, een middelvinger, een klodder spuug, maar geen berouw van tramschutter Gökmen T." *De Volkskrant*, March 2. https://www.volkskrant.nl/nieuws-achtergrond/een-kusmondje-een-middelvinger-een-klodder-spuug-maar-geen-berouw-van-tramschutter-gokmen-t~b25fad3b/.

Hutchinson, Steven, and Pat O'Malley. 2007. "A Crime-Terror Nexus? Thinking on Some of the Links between Terrorism and Criminality." *Studies in Conflict & Terrorism* 30 (12): pp. 1095–1107.

ICG (International Crisis Group). 2004. *Indonesia Backgrounder: Why Salafism and Terrorism Mostly Don't Mix.* Asia Report no. 83. Brussels: ICG. https://icg-prod.s3.amazonaws.com/83-indonesia-backgrounder-why-salafism-and-terrorism-mostly-don-t-mix.pdf.

ICG. 2009a. *Indonesia: The Hotel Bombings.* Asia Briefing no. 94. Brussels: ICG. https://icg-prod.s3.amazonaws.com/b94-indonesia-the-hotel-bombings.pdf.

ICG. 2009b. *Indonesia: Noordin Top's Support Base.* Asia Briefing no. 95. Brussels: ICG. https://icg-prod.s3.amazonaws.com/b95-indonesia-noordin-top-s-support-base.pdf.

ICG. 2017. *Niger and Boko Haram: Beyond Counter-insurgency.* Africa Report no. 245. Brussels: ICG. https://icg-prod.s3.amazonaws.com/245-niger-and-boko-haram-beyond-counter-insurgency.pdf.

Inayat, Naila. 2018. "Geert Wilders' Muhammad Cartoon Contest Sparks Pakistani-Dutch Diplomatic Rift." *Washington Times*, October 14. https://www.washingtontimes.com/news/2018/oct/14/geert-wilders-muhammad-cartoon-contest-sparks-paki/.

Ingram, Haroro J. 2017. "An Analysis of *Inspire* and *Dabiq*: Lessons from AQAP and Islamic State's Propaganda War." *Studies in Conflict & Terrorism* 40 (5): pp. 357–75.

Jackson, Richard. 2015. "The Epistemological Crisis of Counterterrorism." *Critical Studies on Terrorism* 8 (1): pp. 33–54.

James, William. 1902. *The Varieties of Religious Experience: A Study in Human Nature.* Auckland: Floating Press.

Janse, Annelotte, and Rosa de Jong. 2016. "'Terrorisme is nooit ons ding geweest': De geschiedenis van de *Rote Armee Fraktion* vanuit een oorspronkelijk perspectief; Interview met oud-lid Ronald Augustin." *Skript Historisch Tijdschrift* 38 (3): pp. 202–7.

Jarboe, James F. 2002. "Congressional Testimony: The Threat of Eco-terrorism," February 12. Federal Bureau of Investigation (FBI) Archives. https://archives.fbi.gov/archives/news/testimony/the-threat-of-eco-terrorism.

Jenkins, Brian Michael. 2006. *Unconquerable Nation: Knowing Our Enemy, Strengthening Ourselves.* Santa Monica, CA: RAND.

Jensen, Richard Bach. 2014. *The Battle against Anarchist Terrorism: An International History, 1878–1934.* Cambridge: Cambridge University Press.

Juergensmeyer, Mark. 2017. *Terror in the Mind of God: The Global Rise of Religious Violence.* 4th edition. Berkeley, CA: University of California Press.

Kaczynski, Theodore J. 1995. "Industrial Society and Its Future." Supplement published in the *Washington Post*, September 22. https://www.washingtonpost.com/wp-srv/national/longterm/unabomber/manifesto.text.htm.

Kaczynski, Theodore J. 2010. *Technological Slavery: The Collected Writings of Theodore J. Kaczynski, a.k.a. "The Unabomber."* With an introduction by David Skrbina. Washington, DC: Feral House.

Kahn, Paul W. 2008. *Sacred Violence: Torture, Terror, and Sovereignty.* Ann Arbor, MI: University of Michigan Press.

Karazsia, Bryan T., and Kristoffer S. Berlin. 2018. "Can a Mediator Moderate? Considering the Role of Time and Change in the Mediator–Moderator Distinction." *Behavior Therapy* 49 (1): pp. 12–20.

Katsafanas, Paul. 2019. "Fanaticism and Sacred Values." *Philosophers' Imprint* 19 (17): pp. 1–20.

Keatinge, Tom. 2014. "Finances of Jihad: How Extremist Groups Raise Money." *BBC News*, December 12. https://www.bbc.co.uk/news/world-middle-east-30393832.

Kester, Sacha. 2014. "Deense gangsterbaas vertrekt als jihadist naar Syrië en neemt filmmaker mee." *De Volkskrant*, July 8. https://www.volkskrant.nl/nieuws-achtergrond/deense-gangsterbaas-vertrekt-als-jihadist-naar-syrie-en-neemt-filmmaker-mee~b94234e1/.

Khaja, Nagieb. 2014. "On the Frontline in Syria: The Danish Gangster Who Turned Jihadi." *Guardian*, July 7. https://www.theguardian.com/world/2014/jul/07/european-jihadi-danish-gangster-frontline-syria.

Khalil, James, and Lorne L. Dawson. 2023. "Understanding Involvement in Terrorism and Violent Extremism: Theoretical Integration through the ABC Model." *Terrorism and Political Violence*. https://doi.org/10.1080/09546553.2023.2190413.

Khalil, James, John Horgan, and Martine Zeuthen. 2022. "The Attitudes-Behaviors Corrective (ABC) Model of Violent Extremism." *Terrorism and Political Violence* 34 (3): pp. 425-50.

Kindermann, Nora, Rik Peels, and Anke Liefbroer. Forthcoming. "The Fundamentalism Matrix: A Tool for Defining, Mapping, and Operationalizing Fundamentalism." In *Conceptualizing Extreme Beliefs and Behaviors: Definitions and Relations*, edited by Rik Peels and John Horgan. New York: Oxford University Press.

King, Anya H. 2017. *Scent from the Garden of Paradise: Musk and the Medieval Islamic World*. Leiden: Brill.

King, Nigel, Christine Horrocks, and Joanna Brooks. 2018. *Interviews in Qualitative Research*. London: Sage.

Kintz, Theresa. 1999. "Interview with Ted Kaczynski, Administrative Maximum Facility Prison, Florence, Colorado, USA." *Earth First! Journal* (June). https://web.archive.org/web/20090318135703/http://www.insurgentdesire.org.uk/tedk.htm.

Klem, Wouter. 2020. "Founded on Fear: Transnational Police Cooperation against the Anarchist Conspiracy, 1880s-1914." PhD dissertation, Utrecht University.

Kock, Matthijs. 2020. "Updating Terrorism: The Changing Uses of the Internet by Terrorists in the West." MA thesis, Utrecht University.

Koehler, Daniel. 2019. "The Halle, Germany, Synagogue Attack and the Evolution of the Far-Right Terror Threat." *CTC Sentinel* 12 (11): pp. 14-20.

Komitees gegen Folter an politischen Gefangenen in der BRD. 1974. "Flugblatt zum Tod von Holger Meins," November 18. International Institute of Social History (IISH).

Koning, Martijn de. 2018. "'I'm a Weak Servant': The Question of Sincerity and the Cultivation of Weakness in the Lives of Dutch Salafi Muslims." In *Straying from the Straight Path: How Senses of Failure Invigorate Lived Religion*, edited by Daan Beekers and David Kloos, pp. 37-54. New York: Berghahn Books.

Koning, Martijn de. 2020. "Reaching the Land of Jihad: Dutch Syria Volunteers, Hijra and Counter-conduct." Unpublished manuscript.

Koning, Martijn de, Carmen Becker, and Ineke Roex. 2020. *Islamic Militant Activism in Belgium, the Netherlands and Germany: "Islands in a Sea of Disbelief."* Cham: Palgrave Macmillan.

Koning, Martijn de, Birgit Meyer, Annelies Moors, and Peter Pels. 2019. "Guidelines for Anthropological Research: Data Management, Ethics, and Integrity." *Ethnography* 20 (2): pp. 170-4.

Koning, Martijn de, Joas Wagemakers, and Carmen Becker. 2013. *Salafisme: Utopische idealen in een weerbarstige praktijk*. Almere: Parthenon.

Kouwenhoven, Andreas. 2014. "'Daar waren we dan, in het gezegende land.'" *NRC Handelsblad*, July 5. https://www.nrc.nl/nieuws/2014/07/05/daar-waren-we-dan-in-het-gezegende-land-1398422-a216815.

Kraushaar, Wolfgang. 2008. "Mythos RAF: Im Spannungsfeld von terroristischer Herausforderung und populistischer Bedrohungsphantasie." In *Die RAF: Entmythologisierung einer terroristischen Organisation*, edited by Wolfgang Kraushaar, pp. 15-49. Bonn: Bundeszentrale für Politische Bildung.

Krueger, Alan B., and Jitka Malecková. 2003. "Education, Poverty and Terrorism: Is There a Causal Connection?" *Journal of Economic Perspectives* 17: pp. 119-44.

Kruglanski, Arie W., Xiaoyan Chen, Mark Dechesne, Shira Fishman, and Edward Orehek. 2009. "Fully Committed: Suicide Bombers' Motivation and the Quest for Personal Significance." *Political Psychology* 30 (3): pp. 331-57.

Kruglanski, Arie W., Catalina Kopetz, and Ewa Szumowska, eds. 2021. *The Psychology of Extremism: A Motivational Perspective*. London: Routledge.

Kruglanski, Arie W., James Y. Shah, Ayelet Fischbach, Ron Friedman, Woo Young Chun, and David Sleeth-Keppler. 2002. "A Theory of Goal Systems." In *Advances in Experimental Social Psychology*. Vol. 34, edited by Mark P. Zanna, pp. 331–78. San Diego, CA: Academic Press.

Kwantes, R. C., ed. 1975. *De ontwikkeling van de nationalistische beweging in Nederlands-Indië: Bronnenpublicatie, eerste stuk, 1917–medio 1923*. Groningen: Tjeenk Willink.

Laan, Servaas van der, and Nikki Sterkenburg. 2015. "Dit zijn de personen op de nationale terroristenlijst." *Elsevier Weekblad*, July 30. https://www.ewmagazine.nl/nederland/article/2015/07/dit-zijn-de-personen-op-de-nationale-terroristenlijst-2664668W/.

Lakoff, George. 2002. *Moral Politics: How Liberals and Conservatives Think*. 2nd edition. Chicago: University of Chicago Press.

Lange, Christian. 2016. *Paradise and Hell in Islamic Traditions*. Cambridge: Cambridge University Press.

Lankford, Adam. 2013. *The Myth of Martyrdom: What Really Drives Suicide Bombers, Rampage Shooters, and Other Self-Destructive Killers*. New York: Palgrave Macmillan.

Lapeyronnie, Didier. 2008. *Ghetto Urbain: Ségrégation, Violence, Pauvreté en France Aujourd'hui*. Paris: Robert Laffont.

Lazarus, Richard S., and Susan Folkman. 1984. *Stress, Appraisal and Coping*. New York: Springer.

Lei, Ryan F., Emily Foster-Hanson, and Jin X. Goh. 2023. "A Sociohistorical Model of Intersectional Social Category Prototypes." *Nature Reviews Psychology* 2: pp. 297–308.

Leydesdorff, Selma. 2004. *De mensen en de woorden: Geschiedenis op basis van verhalen*. Amsterdam: Meulenhoff.

Litvak, Meir. 1998. "The Islamization of the Palestinian-Israeli Conflict: The Case of Hamas." *Middle Eastern Studies* 34 (1): pp. 148–63.

Lyotard, Jean-François. 1984. *The Postmodern Condition: A Report on Knowledge*. Translated by Geoff Bennington and Brian Massumi. Manchester: Manchester University Press.

MacEachern, Scott. 2018. *Searching for Boko Haram: A History of Violence in Central Africa*. Oxford: Oxford University Press.

MacFarquhar, Neil. 2020. "As Domestic Terrorists Outpace Jihadists, New U.S. Law Is Debated." *New York Times*, February 25. https://www.nytimes.com/2020/02/25/us/domestic-terrorism-laws.html.

Macklin, Graham. 2019. "The Christchurch Attacks: Livestream Terror in the Viral Video Age." *CTC Sentinel* 12 (6): pp. 18–29.

Mahamat, Mbarkoutou, and Bana Barka. 2018. *Understanding Boko Haram Reintegration in Cameroon*. USAID report. Washington, DC: USAID.

Makarenko, Tamara. 2004. "The Crime-Terror Continuum: Tracing the Interplay between Transnational Organised Crime and Terrorism." *Global Crime* 6 (1): pp. 129–45.

Mammone, Andrea, Emmanuel Godin, and Brian Jenkins. 2012. "Introduction: Mapping the 'Right of the Mainstream Right' in Contemporary Europe." In *Mapping the Extreme Right in Contemporary Europe*, edited by Andrea Mammone, Emmanuel Godin, and Brian Jenkins, pp. 1–14. New York: Routledge.

Marshall, Douglas A. 2002. "Behavior, Belonging, and Belief: A Theory of Ritual Practice." *Sociological Theory* 20 (3): pp. 360–80.

Martinez, J. Michael. 2012. *Terrorist Attacks on American Soil: From the Civil War Era to the Present*. Plymouth: Rowman & Littlefield.

Maslow, Abraham H. 1965. "Some Basic Propositions of a Growth and Self-Actualization Psychology." In *Theories of Personality: Primary Sources and Research*, edited by Gardner Lindzey and Calvin Hall, pp. 307–16. New York: Wiley.

Mason, Carol. 2002. *Killing for Life: The Apocalyptic Narrative of Pro-Life Politics*. Ithaca, NY: Cornell University Press.

Massoud, Mark Fathi. 2022. "The Price of Positionality: Assessing the Benefits and Burdens of Self-Identification in Research Methods." *Journal of Law and Society* 49 (S1): pp. 64–86.

Masud, Muhammad K. 1990. "The Obligation to Migrate: The Doctrine of *hijrah* in Islamic Law." In *Muslim Travellers: Pilgrimage, Migration, and the Religious Imagination*, edited by Dale F. Eickelman and James Piscatori, pp. 29–49. London: Routledge.

Maynard, Elizabeth A., Richard L. Gorsuch, and Jeff P. Bjorck. 2001. "Religious Coping Style, Concept of God, and Personal Religious Variables in Threat, Loss, and Challenge Situations." *Journal for the Scientific Study of Religion* 40 (1): pp. 65–74.

McAdams, Dan P. 2006. *The Redemptive Self: Stories Americans Live By*. Oxford: Oxford University Press.

McAdams, Dan P., Jeffrey Reynolds, Martha Lewis, Allison H. Patten, and Phillip J. Bowman. 2001. "When Bad Things Turn Good and Good Things Turn Bad: Sequences of Redemption and Contamination in Life Narrative and Their Relation to Psychosocial Adaptation in Midlife Adults and in Students." *Personality and Social Psychology Bulletin* 27 (4): pp. 474–85.

McCauley, Clark. 2012. "Testing Theories of Radicalization in Polls of U.S. Muslims." *Analyses of Social Issues and Public Policy* 12 (1): pp. 296–311.

McCauley, Clark, and Sophia Moskalenko. 2017a. *Friction: How Conflict Radicalizes Them and Us*. Revised and expanded edition. New York: Oxford University Press.

McCauley, Clark, and Sophia Moskalenko. 2017b. "Understanding Political Radicalization: The Two-Pyramids Model." *American Psychologist* 72 (3): pp. 205–16.

McFadden, Robert D. 1996. "Prisoner of Rage: A Special Report; From a Child of Promise to the Unabom Suspect." *New York Times*, May 26. https://www.nytimes.com/1996/05/26/us/prisoner-of-rage-a-special-report-from-a-child-of-promise-to-the-unabom-suspect.html.

McKenna, Robin. 2023. *Non-Ideal Epistemology*. Oxford: Oxford University Press.

Mead, George Herbert. 1934. *Mind, Self, and Society: From the Standpoint of a Social Behaviorist*. Chicago: University of Chicago Press.

Meinema, Erik. 2020. "'Idle Minds' and 'Empty Stomachs': Youth, Violence and Religious Diversity in Coastal Kenya." *Africa* 90 (5): pp. 890–913.

Meinema, Erik. 2021. "Regulating Religious Coexistence: The Intricacies of 'Interfaith' Cooperation in Coastal Kenya." PhD dissertation, Utrecht University.

Meins, Holger. 1974a. "Letzter Brief von Holger Meins im Info," October 31. International Institute of Social History (IISH). Rote Armee Fraktion Collection, mappe 2. English translation retrieved from https://socialhistoryportal.org/sites/default/files/raf/en/0019741031%2520EN_2.pdf.

Meins, Holger. 1974b. "Notiz für den Fall . . .," March 9. International Institute of Social History (IISH). Rote Armee Fraktion Collection, mappe 2.

Merriman, John. 2009. *The Dynamite Club: How a Bombing in Fin-de-Siècle Paris Ignited the Age of Modern Terror*. New Haven: Yale University Press.

Moen, Ole Martin. 2019. "The Unabomber's Ethics." *Bioethics* 33 (2): pp. 223–9.

Moghaddam, Fathali M. 2005. "The Staircase to Terrorism: A Psychological Exploration." *American Psychologist* 60 (2): pp. 161–9.

Moon, Jordan W., Adam B. Cohen, Kristin Laurin, and David P. MacKinnon. 2023. "Is Religion Special?" *Perspectives on Psychological Science* 18 (2): pp. 340–57.

Morton, Adam. 2011. "Empathy for the Devil." In *Empathy: Philosophical and Psychological Perspectives*, edited by Amy Coplan and Peter Goldie, pp. 318–30. Oxford: Oxford University Press.

Mossière, Géraldine. 2020. "Embracing Islam to Improve and Restore the Vulnerable Subject: Religious Conversion as Hermeneutics of the Self; A Case in Prison." In *Lived Religion, Conversion and Recovery: Negotiation of Self, the Social and the Sacred*, edited by Srdjan Sremac and Ines W. Jindra, pp. 147–69. Cham: Palgrave Macmillan.

Müller, Mathias. 2019. "Signs of the Merciful: Abdullah Azzam (d. 1989) and the Sacralization of History in Jihadist Literature, 1982–2002." *Journal of Religion and Violence* 7 (2): pp. 91–127.

Muthuswamy, Moorthy S. 2021. "Does Sharia Act as Both a Mediator and Moderator in Salafi Radicalism?" SSRN. August 29. https://dx.doi.org/10.2139/ssrn.3914083.

Nanninga, Pieter. 2019. *Branding a Caliphate in Decline: The Islamic State's Video Output (2015–2018)*. The Hague: International Centre for Counter-Terrorism. https://www.icct.nl/sites/default/files/2022-12/ICCT-Nanninga-Branding-a-Caliphate-in-Decline-April2019.pdf.

Napolitano, M. Giulia. 2021. "Conspiracy Theories and Evidential Self-Insulation." In *The Epistemology of Fake News*, edited by Sven Bernecker, Amy K. Flowerree, and Thomas Grundmann, pp. 82–106. Oxford: Oxford University Press.

NCTV (National Coordinator for Counterterrorism and Security). 2020. *Dreigingsbeeld Terrorisme Nederland 52*. The Hague: NCTV.

Neiman, Susan. 2008. *Moral Clarity: A Guide for Grown-Up Idealists*. Orlando, FL: Harcourt.

Newton, A. Taylor, and Daniel McIntosh. 2010. "Specific Religious Beliefs in a Cognitive Appraisal Model of Stress and Coping." *International Journal for the Psychology of Religion* 20 (1): pp. 39–58.

New York Times. 1894. "The Guillotine's Sure Work: Details of the Execution of Vaillant, the Anarchist." February 6. https://www.nytimes.com/1894/02/06/archives/the-guillotines-sure-work-details-of-the-execution-of-vaillant-the.html.

Nguyen, C. Thi. 2020. *Games: Agency as Art, Thinking Art*. New York: Oxford University Press.

Noor, Farish A., Yoginder Sikand, and Martin van Bruinessen, eds. 2008. *The Madrasa in Asia: Political Activism and Transnational Linkages*. Amsterdam: Amsterdam University Press.

NOS nieuws. 2016. "Vorig jaar dertig verdachte asielzoekers naar Nederland." February 29. https://nos.nl/artikel/2089758-vorig-jaar-dertig-verdachte-asielzoekers-naar-nederland.

NOS nieuws. 2018. "De cartoonwedstrijd van Wilders, wat houdt die precies in?" August 29. https://nos.nl/artikel/2248092-de-cartoonwedstrijd-van-wilders-wat-houdt-die-precies-in.

NOS nieuws. 2019a. "Cel voor terreurverdachten Rotterdam, maar geen bewijs voor plannen aanslag." January 14. https://nos.nl/artikel/2267477-cel-voor-terreurverdachten-rotterdam-maar-geen-bewijs-voor-plannen-aanslag.

NOS nieuws. 2019b. "Gökmen T.: 'Ik laat niemand met ons geloof spotten.'" July 1. https://nos.nl/artikel/2291463-gokmen-t-ik-laat-niemand-met-ons-geloof-spotten.

NRC Handelsblad. 2012. "Beelden van oorlogsmisdaad Syrië." August 27. https://www.nrc.nl/nieuws/2012/08/27/beelden-van-oorlogsmisdaad-syrie-12376970-a1061718.

NU.nl. 2020. "Gökmen T. schreef verwijzingen naar islam en de sharia op wapen." March 1. https://www.nu.nl/binnenland/6034409/gokmen-t-schreef-verwijzingen-naar-islam-en-de-sharia-op-wapen.html.

Oleson, J. C. 2005. "Evil the Natural Way: The Chimerical Utopias of Henry David Thoreau and Theodore John Kaczynski." *Contemporary Justice Review* 8 (2): pp. 211–28.

Ortiz-Ospina, Esteban. 2019. "The Rise of Social Media." Our World in Data. September 18. https://ourworldindata.org/rise-of-social-media.

Palm, Trineke. 2018. "Interwar Blueprints of Europe: Emotions, Experience and Expectation." *Politics and Governance* 6 (4): pp. 135–43.

Panorama. 2019. "Buurtgenoten: 'Gökmen Tanis geen terrorist.'" March 19. https://panorama.nl/artikel/178531/buurtgenoten-gokmen-tanis-geen-terrorist.

Passmore, Leith. 2009. "The Art of Hunger: Self-Starvation in the Red Army Faction." *German History* 27 (1): pp. 32–59.

Peels, Rik. 2020. "Responsibility for Fundamentalist Belief." In *Epistemic Duties: New Arguments, New Angles*, edited by Kevin Ray McCain and Scott Stapleford, pp. 221–38. Oxford: Routledge.

Peels, Rik. 2023a. "On Defining 'Fundamentalism.'" *Religious Studies* 59 (4): pp. 729–47.

Peels, Rik. 2023b. "Vice Explanations for Conspiracy Theorizing, Extremism, and Fundamentalism." *Review of Philosophy and Psychology*. https://doi.org/10.1007/s13164-023-00685-x.

Peels, Rik. 2023c. "What Is It to Explain Extremism?" *Terrorism and Political Violence*. https://doi.org/10.1080/09546553.2023.2255902.

Peels, Rik. 2024. *Monotheism and Fundamentalism*. Cambridge: Cambridge University Press.

Peels, Rik, and Nora Kindermann. 2022. "What Are Fundamentalist Beliefs?" *Journal of Political Ideologies*. https://doi.org/10.1080/13569317.2022.2138294.

Peels, Rik, and Nora Kindermann. 2023. "Een kritische evaluatie van Beatrice de Graafs model van radicale verlossing." *Tijdschrift Sociologie* 4 (issue "Dossier radicale verlossing"): pp. 75–85.

Peels, Rik, Nora Kindermann, and Chris Ranalli. 2023. "Normativity in Studying Conspiracy Theory Belief: Seven Guidelines." *Philosophical Psychology* 36 (6): pp. 1125–59.

Peels, Rik, Ruth Tietjen, J. M. Berger, and John Horgan. Forthcoming. "Extremism, Fanaticism, Fundamentalism, Terrorism: A Conceptual Map." In *Conceptualizing Extreme Beliefs and Behaviors: Definitions and Relations*, edited by Rik Peels and John Horgan, Forthcoming. New York: Oxford University Press.

Pekelder, Jacco. 2007. "Links slachtofferschap: De RAF als afrekening met de Duitse schuld." In *Duitsers als slachtoffers: Het einde van een taboe?*, edited by Patrick Dassen, Ton Nijhuis, and Krijn Thijs, pp. 305–35. Amsterdam: Duitsland Instituut.

Pekelder, Jacco. 2012. "The RAF and the Left in West-Germany: Communication Processes between Terrorists and Their Constituency in the Early 1970s." In *Gewalt ohne Ausweg? Terrorismus als Kommunikationsprozess in Europa seit dem 19. Jahrhundert*, edited by Klaus Weinhauer and Jörg Requate, pp. 203–22. Frankfurt am Main: Campus Verlag.

Pickel, Gert, Cemal Öztürk, Verena Schneider, Susanne Pickel, and Oliver Decker. 2022. "Covid-19-Related Conspiracy Myths, Beliefs, and Democracy-Endangering Consequences." *Politics and Governance* 10 (4): pp. 177–91.

Pigden, Charles. 1995. "Popper Revisited, or What Is Wrong with Conspiracy Theories?" *Philosophy of the Social Sciences* 25 (1): pp. 3–34.

Prelooker, Jaakoff. 1908. *Heroes and Heroines of Russia: Builders of a New Commonwealth*. London: Simpkin, Marshall, Hamilton, Kent.

Pringle, Robert. 2010. *Understanding Islam in Indonesia: Politics and Diversity*. Honolulu, HI: University of Hawaii Press.

Prooijen, Jan-Willem van, André P. M. Krouwel, and Thomas V. Pollet. 2015. "Political Extremism Predicts Belief in Conspiracy Theories." *Social Psychological and Personality Science* 6 (5): pp. 570–8.

Prucha, Nico. 2016. "IS and the Jihadist Information Highway: Projecting Influence and Religious Identity via Telegram." *Perspectives on Terrorism* 10 (6): pp. 48–58.

RAF (Red Army Faction). 1997. "Hungerstreikerklärung vom 8. Mai 1973, 8. Mai bis 29. Juni 1973." In *Texte und Materialien zur Geschichte der RAF*, edited by M. Hoffmann, pp. 187–9. Berlin: ID-Verlag.

Rapoport, David. 2004. "The Four Waves of Modern Terrorism." In *Attacking Terrorism: Elements of a Grand Strategy*, edited by Audrey Kurth Cronin and James M. Ludes, pp. 46–73. Washington, DC: Georgetown University Press.

Rapoport, David. 2017. "Terrorism as a Global Wave Phenomenon: An Overview." *Oxford Research Encyclopedia of Politics*. https://oxfordre.com/politics/display/10.1093/acrefore/9780190228637.001.0001/acrefore-9780190228637-e-299.

Reddy, William M. 2001. *The Navigation of Feeling: A Framework for the History of Emotions*. Cambridge: Cambridge University Press.

Renard, Thomas. 2020. "Overblown: Exploring the Gap between the Fear of Terrorist Recidivism and the Evidence." *CTC Sentinel* 13 (4): pp. 19–29.

Richards, Imogen. 2019. "A Dialectical Approach to Online Propaganda: Australia's United Patriots Front, Right-Wing Politics, and Islamic State." *Studies in Conflict & Terrorism* 42 (1–2): pp. 43–69.

Richardson, Louise. 2006. *What Terrorists Want: Understanding the Enemy, Containing the Threat.* New York: Random House.

Ricklefs, Merle C. 2001. *A History of Modern Indonesia since c. 1200.* 3rd edition. Stanford, CA: Stanford University Press.

Ritchie, Hannah, Edouard Mathieu, Max Roser, and Esteban Ortiz-Ospina. 2023. "Internet." Our World in Data. https://ourworldindata.org/internet#the-internet-s-history-has-just-begun.

Roberts, Michael. 2005. "Saivite Symbols, Sacrifice, and Tamil Tiger Rites." *Social Analysis: The International Journal of Anthropology* 49 (1): pp. 67–93.

Roberts, Skye Riddell. 2016. "The Crime-Terror Nexus: Ideology's Misleading Role in Islamist Terrorist Groups." E-International Relations. April 23. https://www.e-ir.info/2016/04/23/the-crime-terror-nexus-ideologys-misleading-role-in-islamist-terrorist-groups/.

Roex, Ineke, Sjef van Stiphout, and Jean Tillie. 2010. *Salafisme in Nederland: Aard, omvang en dreiging.* Amsterdam: Instituut voor Migratie en Etnische Studies.

Rome, Adam. 2003. "Give Earth a Chance: The Environmental Movement and the Sixties." *The Journal of American History* 90 (2): pp. 525–54.

Roof, Dylann. 2017. "Manifesto." Unpublished manuscript.

Rosman, Cyril. 2019. "Broer aanslagpleger in verband gebracht met deze Turkse extremistenclub." *Algemeen Dagblad*, March 19. https://www.tubantia.nl/binnenland/broer-aanslagpleger-in-verband-gebracht-met-deze-turkse-extremistenclub~a302bb95/.

Rosman, Cyril. 2020. "Al 7 zaken tegen Syrische vluchtelingen: 'Vuile handen' komen alsnog voor de rechter." *Algemeen Dagblad*, February 11. https://www.ad.nl/binnenland/al-7-zaken-tegen-syrische-vluchtelingen-vuile-handen-komen-alsnog-voor-de-rechter~ac904f06/.

Roussinos, Aris. 2014. "Behead First, Ask Questions Later: The Disturbing Social Media of British Jihadists." *Vice News*, April 15. https://www.vice.com/en/article/4387em/behead-first-ask-questions-later-the-disturbing-social-media-of-british-jihadists.

RTL nieuws. 2015. "Afscheidsvideo opgedoken van Nederlandse zelfmoordterroristen." February 10. https://www.rtlnieuws.nl/nieuws/nederland/artikel/1353871/afscheidsvideo-opgedoken-van-nederlandse-zelfmoordterroristen.

Rueb, Thomas. 2018. *Laura H.: Het kalifaatmeisje uit Zoetermeer.* Amsterdam: Das Mag.

Rumiya. 2017a. "Among the Believers Are Men: Abu Mujahid Al-Faransi." *Rumiyah* 11 (July): pp. 44–52.

Rumiya. 2017b. "The Kafir's Wealth Is Halal for You, So Take It." *Rumiyah* 8 (April): pp. 12–15.

Sageman, Marc. 2004. *Understanding Terror Networks.* Philadelphia: University of Pennsylvania Press.

Sageman, Marc. 2014. "The Stagnation in Terrorism Research." *Terrorism and Political Violence* 26 (4): pp. 565–80.

San, Marion van. 2019. *Kalifaatontvluchters.* Amsterdam: Prometheus.

Sandelin, Magnus, and Daniel Olsson. 2019. "IS-mannen hade gått fri i Sverige." *Expressen/GT*, March 24. https://www.expressen.se/gt/is-mannen-hade-gatt-fri-i-sverige/.

Sands, Bobby. 1981. *The Diary of Bobby Sands.* Dublin: Sinn Fein Publicity Department.

Sarat-St. Peter, Hilary A. 2019. "From *Hijrah* to *Khilafah*: Rhetoric, Redemption, and ISIL's Recruitment Strategy." *International Journal of Communication* 13: pp. 510–27.

Satria, Alif. 2019. "The Neo-JI Threat: Jema'ah Islamiyah's Resurgence in Indonesia Follows an Old Playbook." *New Mandala*, August 16. https://www.newmandala.org/the-neo-ji-threat-jemaah-islamiyahs-resurgence-in-indonesia-follows-an-old-playbook/.

Savage, Charlie, Adam Goldman, and Eric Schmitt. 2020. "U.S. Will Give Terrorist Label to White Supremacist Group for First Time." *New York Times*, April 6. https://www.nytimes.

com/2020/04/06/us/politics/terrorist-label-white-supremacy-Russian-Imperial-Movement.html.
Schmid, Alex P. 2013. *Radicalisation, De-Radicalisation, Counter-radicalisation: A Conceptual Discussion and Literature Review*. The Hague: International Centre for Counter-Terrorism. https://www.icct.nl/sites/default/files/import/publication/ICCT-Schmid-Radicalisation-De-Radicalisation-Counter-Radicalisation-March-2013_2.pdf.
Schmid, Alex. 2016. "The Trial of Vera Zasulich." In *Terrorists on Trial: A Performative Perspective*, edited by Beatrice de Graaf and Alex P. Schmid, pp. 51–92. Leiden: Leiden University Press.
Schoen, Tom. 2019. "Theodore Kaczynski: A Radical Redeemer?" Unpublished manuscript.
Schubert, Ingrid. 1977. "Bericht zur Kontaktsperre im Gefängnis München-Stadelheim," October. International Institute of Social History (IISH). Rote Armee Fraktion Collection, file 6.I.
Schulten, Norah, Bertjan Doosje, Ramón Spaaij, and Jan Henk Kamphuis. 2019. *Psychopathologie en terrorisme: Stand van zaken, lacunes en prioriteiten voor toekomstig onderzoek*. WODC report. Amsterdam: Wetenschappelijk Onderzoek- en Documentatiecentrum (WODC).
Schuurman, Bart. 2018. *Becoming a European Homegrown Jihadist: A Multilevel Analysis of Involvement in the Dutch Hofstadgroup, 2002–2005*. Amsterdam: Amsterdam University Press.
Schuurman, Bart, and John Horgan. 2016. "Rationales for Terrorist Violence in Homegrown Jihadist Groups: A Case Study from the Netherlands." *Aggression and Violent Behavior* 27: pp. 55–63.
Scull, Margaret M. 2016. "The Catholic Church and the Hunger Strikes of Terence MacSwiney and Bobby Sands." *Irish Political Studies* 31 (2): pp. 282–99.
SER (Social and Economic Council of the Netherlands). 2020. "Aantallen & herkomst." SER. Updated April 2023. https://www.ser.nl/nl/thema/werkwijzer-vluchtelingen/feiten-en-cijfers/aantallen-herkomst.
Shah, James Y., Ron Friedman, and Arie W. Kruglanski. 2002. "Forgetting All Else: On the Antecedents and Consequences of Goal Shielding." *Journal of Personality and Social Psychology* 83 (6): pp. 1261–80.
Sheikh, Mona Kanwal, and Mark Juergensmeyer, eds. 2019. *Entering Religious Minds: The Social Study of Worldviews*. London: Routledge.
Shelley, Louise I., and John T. Picarelli. 2005. "Methods and Motives: Exploring Links between Transnational Organized Crime and International Terrorism." *Trends in Organized Crime* 9 (2): pp. 52–67.
Sieckelinck, Stijn, and Micha de Winter, eds. 2015. *Formers & Families: Transitional Journeys in and out of Extremisms in the United Kingdom, Denmark and the Netherlands*. The Hague: NCTV.
Sikand, Yoginder. 2001. "The Changing Course of the Kashmiri Struggle: From National Liberation to Islamist Jihad?" *Muslim World* 91: pp. 229–56.
Sisk, Timothy, ed. 2011. *Between Terror and Tolerance: Religious Leaders, Conflict, and Peacemaking*. Washington, DC: Georgetown University Press.
Sizoo, Bram, Bertjan Doosje, and Berno van Meijel. 2022. "Percepties over radicalisering en psychiatrie in de relatie tussen ggz en veiligheidsdomein." *Tijdschrift voor Psychiatrie* 64 (1): pp. 12–17.
Snouck Hurgronje, Christiaan. 1888. *Mekka*. Vol. 1. The Hague: Martinus Nijhoff.
Snouck Hurgronje, Christiaan. 1893. *De Atjehers*. Vol. 1. Batavia: Landsdrukkerij; Leiden: Brill.
Snouck Hurgronje, Christiaan. 2006. *Mekka in the Latter Part of the 19th Century: Daily Life, Customs and Learning; The Moslims of the East-Indian Archipelago*. Leiden: Brill.
Solahudin. 2013. *The Roots of Terrorism in Indonesia: From Darul Islam to Jema'ah Islamiyah*. Singapore: NewSouth.

Solomon, Erika, and Guy Chazan. 2015. "Isis Inc: How Oil Fuels the Jihadi Terrorists." *Financial Times*, October 14. https://www.ft.com/content/b8234932-719b-11e5-ad6d-f4ed76f0900a.
Solomon, Erika, Robin Kwong, and Steven Bernard. 2016. "Inside Isis Inc.: The Journey of a Barrel of Oil." *Forbes*, February 29. https://ig.ft.com/sites/2015/isis-oil/?.
Speckhard, Anne, and Khapta Akhmedova. 2005. "Talking to Terrorists." *Journal for Psychohistory* 33 (2): pp. 125–56.
Spiegel. 2019. "Deadly Attack Exposes Lapses in German Security Apparatus." October 11. https://www.spiegel.de/international/germany/far-right-terrorism-in-germany-shooting-exposes-lapses-in-security-apparatus-a-1291075.html.
Stampnitzky, Lisa. 2013. *Disciplining Terror: How Experts Invented "Terrorism."* Cambridge: Cambridge University Press.
Steenbrink, Karel A. 1991. *De islam bekeken door koloniale Nederlanders*. Utrecht: Interuniversitair Instituut voor Missiologie en Oecumenica.
Stekelenburg, Jacquelien van. 2017. "Radicalization and Violent Emotions." *Political Science and Politics* 50 (4): pp. 936–9.
Stenersen, Anne. 2008. "The Internet: A Virtual Training Camp?" *Terrorism and Political Violence* 20 (2): pp. 215–33.
Sterkenburg, Nikki. 2014. "Dit zijn de gezichten van de jihad in Nederland." *Elsevier Weekblad*, September 8. https://www.ewmagazine.nl/nederland/article/2014/09/dit-zijn-de-gezichten-van-de-jihad-in-nederland-1593919W/.
Stokes, Patrick. 2018. "Conspiracy Theory and the Perils of Pure Particularism." In *Taking Conspiracy Theories Seriously*, edited by M R. X. Dentith, pp. 25–37. London: Rowman and Littlefield.
Stoter Boscolo, Brenda. 2016. "The Making of an Islamic State Terrorist." Brenda Stoter Boscolo. May 8. http://www.brendastoter.nl/the-making-of-an-islamic-state-terrorist/.
Strack, Fritz, and Roland Deutsch. 2014. "The Reflective-Impulsive Model." In *Dual-Process Theories of the Social Mind*, edited by Jeffrey W. Sherman, Bertram Gawronski, and Yaacov Trope, pp. 92–104. New York: Guilford.
Strauss, Anselm, and Juliet Corbin. 2008. *Basics of Qualitative Research: Techniques and Procedures for Developing Grounded Theory*. 3rd edition. Los Angeles, CA: Sage.
Stritzel, Björn, and Robert Becker. 2019. "Was uns das Video über den Killer-Nazi sagt." *Bild*, October 10. https://www.bild.de/politik/ausland/politik-ausland/halle-neonazi-stephan-balliet-streamte-den-gesamten-anschlag-was-uns-das-video-s-65246702.bild.html.
Suminto, Husnul Aqib. 1985. *Politik Islam Hindia Belanda: Het Kantoor voor Inlandsche Zaken*. Jakarta: Lembaga Penelitian pendidikan dan Penerangan Ekonomi dan Sosial.
Sweeney, George. 1993a. "Irish Hunger Strikes and the Cult of Self-Sacrifice." *Journal of Contemporary History* 28 (3): pp. 421–37.
Sweeney, George. 1993b. "Self-Immolation in Ireland: Hunger Strikes and Political Confrontation." *Anthropology Today* 9 (5): pp. 10–14.
Sweeney, George. 2004. "Self-Immolative Martyrdom: Explaining the Irish Hunger Strike Tradition." *Studies: An Irish Quarterly Review* 93 (371): pp. 337–48.
Tahir, Roohi. 2018. "Repentance, Redemption, & Salvation: An Islamic Framework." Yaqeen Institute for Islamic Research. February 5. https://yaqeeninstitute.org/roohi-tahir/repentance-redemption-salvation-an-islamic-framework/.
Tarrant, Brenton. 2019. "The Great Replacement." Unpublished manuscript.
Taylor, Bron. 1998. "Religion, Violence and Radical Environmentalism: From Earth First! to the Unabomber to the Earth Liberation Front." *Terrorism and Political Violence* 10 (4): pp. 297–336.
Terhoeven, Petra. 2007. "Opferbilder – Täterbilder: Die Fotografie als Medium linksterroristischer Selbstermächtigung in Deutschland und Italien während der 70er Jahre." *Geschichte in Wissenschaft und Unterricht* 58 (7–8): pp. 380–99.

REFERENCES

Thatcher, Margaret. 1981. "Speech in Belfast," March 5. Margaret Thatcher Foundation. http://www.margaretthatcher.org/document/104589.
Thijs, Fabienne, Elanie Rodermond, and Frank Weerman. 2018. *Verdachten van terrorisme in beeld: Achtergrondkenmerken, "triggers" en eerdere politiecontacten*. The Hague: Sdu.
Thijssen, Gaby, Erik Masthoff, Jelle Sijtsema, and Stefan Bogaerts. 2023. "Understanding Violent Extremism: Socio-demographic, Criminal, and Psychopathological Background Characteristics of Detainees Residing in Dutch Terrorism Wings." *Criminology and Criminal Justice* 23 (2): pp. 290–308.
Thompson, Paul. 1978. *The Voice of the Past: Oral History*. Oxford: Oxford University Press.
Thurston, Alexander. 2018. *Boko Haram: The History of an African Jihadist Movement*. Princeton: Princeton University Press.
Tieleman, Yelle, and Cyril Rosman. 2017. "Proces tegen jihadist begonnen terwijl verdachte in Syrië zit." *Algemeen Dagblad*, March 23. https://www.ad.nl/utrecht/proces-tegen-jihadist-begonnen-terwijl-verdachte-in-syrie-zit~a4771f9b/#.
Tietjen, Ruth. 2021. "Religious Zeal as an Affective Phenomenon." *Phenomenology and the Cognitive Sciences* 20 (1): pp. 75–91.
Trip, Simona, Carmen Hortensia Bora, Mihai Marian, Angelica Halmajan, and Marius Ioan Drugas. 2019. "Psychological Mechanisms Involved in Radicalization and Extremism: A Rational Emotive Behavioral Conceptualization." *Frontiers in Psychology* 10: art. no. 437.
Tubantia. 2016. "COA kiest voor noodopvang vluchtelingen in voormalig pand *Tubantia* in Enschede." January 12.
Tuters, Marc, and Sal Hagen. 2020. "(((They))) Rule: Memetic Antagonism and Nebulous Othering on 4chan." *New Media & Society* 22 (12): pp. 2218–37.
UNDP (United Nations Development Programme). 2022. *Conflict Analysis in the Lake Chad Basin 2020–2021*. Chad: UNDP. https://www.undp.org/sites/g/files/zskgke326/files/2022-08/Conflict%20Analysis%20in%20the%20Lake%20Chad%20Basin.pdf.
Uscinski, Joseph E., and Joseph M. Parent. 2014. *American Conspiracy Theories*. New York: Oxford University Press.
Vaillant, Auguste. 1894. "Courtroom Speech." The Anarchist Library. https://theanarchistlibrary.org/library/auguste-vaillant-courtroom-speech.
Valk, Ineke van der, and Peter Törnberg. 2017. *Derde monitor moslimdiscriminatie*. Amsterdam: Instituut voor Migratie en Etnische Studies.
Varon, Jeremy P. 2004. *Bringing the War Home: The Weather Underground, the Red Army Faction, and Revolutionary Violence in the Sixties and Seventies*. Berkeley, CA: University of California Press.
Velde, Koert van der. 2011. "Bonuspunten halen om in het paradijs te komen." *Trouw*, August 17. https://www.trouw.nl/nieuws/bonuspunten-halen-om-in-het-paradijs-te-komen~b424830b/.
Versteegt, Inge, Vanja Ljujic, Fatima El Bouk, Frank Weerman, and Floor van Maanen. 2018. *Terrorism, Adversity and Identity: A Qualitative Study on Detained Terrorism Suspects in Comparison to Other Detainees*. Amsterdam: NSCR/VU.
Vesper, Bernward, and Gudrun Ensslin. 2010a. "2. Mai 1968." In *Gudrun Ensslin, Bernward Vesper, »Notstandsgesetze von Deiner Hand« Briefe 1968/1969*, edited by Caroline Harmsen, Ulrike Meyer, and Johannes Ullmaier, pp. 51–2. Berlin: Suhrkamp.
Vesper, Bernward, and Gudrun Ensslin. 2010b. "21. oder 28.7.1968." In *Gudrun Ensslin, Bernward Vesper, »Notstandsgesetze von Deiner Hand« Briefe 1968/1969*, edited by Caroline Harmsen, Ulrike Meyer, and Johannes Ullmaier, p. 121. Berlin: Suhrkamp.
Victoroff, Jeff. 2005. "The Mind of the Terrorist: A Review and Critique of Psychological Approaches." *Journal of Conflict Resolution* 49 (1): pp. 3–42.
Vos, Carlijne. 2020. "Jihadisten lijken uit op een nieuw Kalifaat in de Sahel en het gaat hen voor de wind." *De Volkskrant*, February 5. https://www.volkskrant.nl/nieuws-achtergrond/jihadisten-lijken-uit-op-een-nieuw-kalifaat-in-de-sahel-en-het-gaat-hen-voor-de-wind~bb16a04b/.

Wagemakers, Joas. 2012. *A Quietist Jihadi: The Ideology and Influence of Abu al-Maqdisi.* Cambridge: Cambridge University Press.

Wagemakers, Joas. 2016. "What Should an Islamic State Look Like? Jihadi-Salafi Debates on the War in Syria." *The Muslim World* 106 (3): pp. 501–22.

Wal, Simon L. van der, ed. 1967. *De opkomst van de nationalistische beweging in Nederlands-Indië.* Groningen: Wolters.

Wassouni, François, and Adder Abel Gwoda. 2017a. *Boko Haram au Cameroun: Dynamiques plurielles.* Brussels: Peter Lang.

Wassouni, François, and Adder Abel Gwoda. 2017b. *Regards croisés sur Boko Haram au Cameroun.* Yaoundé: Les Éditions du Schabel.

WDYP (World Dynamics of Young People), ed. 2016. *Recruitment of Young People in Armed Groups in Cameroon.* Yaoundé: WDYP. https://www.ziviler-friedensdienst.org/sites/default/files/media/file/2020/recruitment-young-peoplewebpdf-4421.pdf.

Weber, Max. 1922. *Wirtschaft und Gesellschaft.* Tübingen: Mohr.

Weggemans, Daan J., and Beatrice de Graaf. 2015. *Na de vrijlating: Een exploratieve studie naar recidive en re-integratie van jihadistische ex-gedetineerden.* Amsterdam: Reed Business.

Weggemans, Daan, and Beatrice de Graaf. 2017. *Reintegrating Jihadist Extremist Detainees: Helping Extremist Offenders Back into Society.* New York: Routledge.

Weimann, Gabriel. 2010. "Terror on Facebook, Twitter, and YouTube." *The Brown Journal of World Affairs* 16 (2): pp. 45–54.

White, Robert W. 1993. *Provisional Irish Republicans: An Oral and Interpretive History.* Westport, CT: Greenwood.

Wilhelmsen, Julie. 2004. *When Separatists Become Islamists: The Case of Chechnya.* Kjeller: Norwegian Defence Research Establishment.

Wilkinson, Benedict. 2020. *Scripts of Terror: The Stories Terrorists Tell Themselves.* Oxford: Oxford University Press.

Willemse, Karin. 2007. *One Foot in Heaven: Narratives on Gender and Islam in Darfur, West-Sudan.* Leiden: Brill.

Wilson, Tim. 2010. *Frontiers of Violence: Conflict and Identity in Ulster and Upper Silesia 1918–1922.* Oxford: Oxford University Press.

Wiltermuth, Scott S., and David T. Newman. 2018. "Moral Clarity." In *Atlas of Moral Psychology*, edited by Kurt Gray and Jesse Graham, pp. 493–504. New York: Guilford.

Wintour, Patrick. 2019. "Erdoğan Shows Christchurch Attack Footage at Rallies." *Guardian*, March 18. https://www.theguardian.com/world/2019/mar/18/erdogan-shows-christchurch-attack-footage-at-rallies.

Wood, Simon A., and David Harrington Watt, eds. 2014. *Fundamentalism: Perspectives on a Contested History.* Columbia, SC: University of South Carolina Press.

Wright, Joanne. 1991. *Terrorist Propaganda: The Red Army Faction and the Provisional IRA, 1968–86.* London: Palgrave Macmillan.

Zehorai, Itay. 2018. "The Richest Terror Organizations: #4 - Al-Qaeda." *Forbes Israel*, January 1. http://e.forbes.co.il/4-al-qaeda/.

Zeilstra, Eva. 2018. "Blessed Are Those Who Hunger for Justice? A Comparative Analysis of the Functioning of the Discourse of Christian Martyrdom in the Cases of the Political Hunger Strikes of the Women's Social and Political Union (1909) and the Irish Republican Army (1981)." MA thesis, Utrecht University.

Index

For the benefit of digital users, indexed terms that span two pages (e.g., 52–53) may, on occasion, appear on only one of those pages.

Tables and figures are indicated by an italic *t* and *f* following the page number.

Abaaoud, Abdelhamid, 186–87, 238
Abbey, Edward, 100–1
Abbottabad files, 204, 205, 267
ABC (Attitudes-Behaviors Corrective) model, 16–17
Abdelkarim (interviewee), 152–54, 212–13, 257, 259–60, 274–75, 286
Abdeslam, Brahim, 186–87, 238
Abdeslam, Salah, 186–87, 238
Abroujui, Macreme (Abu Mujahid al-Faransi), 189–90
Adam, Barbara, 283
affective (emotional) dimension, 4, 10, 282–83
   See also contamination; validation and reward
Afghanistan, war in, 111–12, 138–40
   accessible conflict zone, 137
   accounts and images of, 111–12, 115–16, 124, 127, 138–39, 140, 145–46, 257, 278
   decrease in number of youths prepared to depart for, 273–74
   departing for and fighting in, 137, 138, 142–43, 179, 273–74, 280–81
   miraculous experiences, 142–43
   veterans of, 139, 143–44, 145, 146, 147, 170, 203, 204
afterlife, earning points for, 134, 135–37, 162–63, 194, 256, 258–59, 266
Ahmed (interviewee), 161–64, 183, 211–12, 213, 263–64, 266, 286
Ahrar al-Sham, 147, 156–57, 159–60, 160n.40, 197–98, 210, 219
Aisha, 137–38
AIVD (General Intelligence and Security Service), 25, 33, 70n.14, 141n.13, 154–55, 184, 184*t*, 230, 250
ajr, 135–36, 258–59. *See also* afterlife, earning points for; validation and reward
Akhmedova, Khapta, 302n.2
Al-Awlaki, Anwar, 153, 153n.30, 259–60

Alexander II (tsar), 77–78
Al-Ittihad al-Islami, 142–43
Al Jazeera, 111–12, 117, 155–56
Alliance for a Peaceful Indonesia (AIDA), 206, 206n.24, 273–74
Almond, Gabriel, 16–17
Al-Mukmin school, 130–31, 138
Al Qaeda, 24, 109, 144, 153n.30, 170
   Al Qaeda in Iraq, 202, 205, 267
   Boko Haram and, 224
   financial support for, 185–86
   Jemaah Islamiyah and, 139–40, 147
   9/11, 60–61, 112
   Tahrir al-Sham and, 184
   universal jihad, 111–12, 261
   variation in ideas of application of jihad, 147
Al-Qibla Mosque, 23–24
Al-Shabaab, 48, 221, 280
alt-right, 232, 235–36
Amin (interviewee), 118–20, 136, 151–52, 154, 196–97, 198–99, 259–60, 263, 286
Amnesty International, 225
Amri, Anis, 173
anarchist terrorism wave (1880–1914), 74–75, 77–84
   Auguste Vaillant, 78–80, 83
   Zinaida Konopliannikova, 78, 80–84
Annette (girlfriend of Martijn), 241–42, 244–45
anti-colonial terrorism wave (1920s–1960s), 74–75. *See also* Irish Republican Army
anti-Semitism and anti-Zionism, 230, 232, 233–34, 236–37, 248–49, 251
Anwar (interviewee), 170–73, 196–97, 259–60, 268, 286
Appleby, R. Scott, 2, 16–17
appraisal, 39–40, 134, 135
   Christian redemption narrative, 54–55
   as component of radical redemption narrative, 60

332 INDEX

appraisal (*cont.*)
   personal, emotional appraisal of injustice, 61–62
   radical redemption as cultural worldview for, 56–57, 253
   reappraisal of convictions, 183, 202–3
Arab Spring, 113–14, 117, 118, 122–23, 132, 148–49, 165, 276
Ar-Rohmah.com, 146
Arslan (interviewee), 219–20, 286
Asaad (interviewee), 173–75, 263, 286
Ashraf (friend of Fadil), 208
Assad, Bashar al-, 62, 132, 135, 148–49, 151, 153–55, 156–57, 158, 160, 161–62, 169, 174, 180–81, 191, 192, 198, 210–11, 212, 217–18, 219–20, 278–79, 281. *See also* Syria, war in
As-Soennah Mosque, 23–24
atonement, 32–33, 72–73, 85, 104, 182, 256–57, 263–65
   concepts of redemption, 54–55, 62–64
   martyrdom, 64–65
At-Taubah.net, 146
Attitudes-Behaviors Corrective (ABC) model, 16–17
Augustin, Ronald, 87
Ayaturahman fi jihadil Afghan (*Signs of ar-Rahman in the Jihad of Afghan*) (Azzam), 139
Azzam, Abdullah Yusuf, 109, 111–12, 115–16, 129, 140–42, 144, 145–46, 259–60, 261
   writings of, 138–39, 140

Baader, Andreas, 85–86, 87, 90, 91–92, 93, 188–89
Baader-Meinhof Group, 85–86. *See also* Red Army Faction
Baghdadi, Abu Bakr al-, 131–32, 154–55, 199, 224–25, 267
Bakker, Edwin, 301–2
Bakunin, Michael, 77
Bali bomb attacks (2002/2005), 123–24, 145, 146, 147, 203, 206, 267
Balliet, Stephan, 233–34, 236–38, 237n.20, 251, 252, 265
Banna, Hassan al-, 138
Banner of God (Rayat al-Tawheed), 186, 186n.4
Barnawi, Abu Musab al-, 224–25
Bashir, Abu Bakar, 137–38, 143
Basra, Rajan, 186–87
Baurmann, Michael, 8–9
Beam, Louis, 68
Beatty, Andrew, 33–34

Becker, Ernest, 56
behavioral dimension, 4. *See also* devotion and struggle
Behind Bars, 23–24, 24n.2, 68, 195–96, 200–1
Benarabe, Abderozzak (Big A) (interviewee), 190–92, 263–64, 286
Bergden case (2016), 232–33, 239–51
Berlin Christmas market attack (2016), 173, 186–87
Berlin Wall, fall of, 48, 201–2
Berzel, Sultan, 180–81, 180n.66
Bilal (interviewee), 157–61, 210–11, 274–75, 286
Bin Laden, Osama, 109, 111–12, 114, 115–16, 131–32, 142–43, 144, 147, 202, 204–5, 206, 214, 224, 267
Biya, Paul, 225
Blågårds Plads, 190–91
Blood & Honour, 250
Bloody Sunday, 94–95
BNPT (Indonesian National Counter Terrorism Agency), 169–70, 306
Boko Haram, 44, 48, 221–29, 253, 275, 280
   desertion and amnesty, 224–25
   difficulty in researching, 222–23, 225, 227–28
   origin of, 223–24
   recruitment strategies and appeal of, 225–29
   schoolgirl abductions, 224, 226
Bonjol, Tuanku Imam, 129, 145–46
Boon, Max, 206n.24, 273–74
Bos, Kees van den, 7–9, 26–27, 30, 61–62, 62n.7, 69, 71
Bos, Wouter, 117
Boterman, Frits, 85–86
Bouyeri, Mohammed, 141n.13, 150, 150nn.24–25, 165n.45
Breivik, Anders Behring, 60–61, 61n.5, 103–4, 233–36, 237–38, 251, 252–53, 261–62, 265, 282–83
Brunner, Claudia, 186–87
Buddhism
   concept of redemption, 63–64
   in Indonesia, 123–24
Budi Utomo, 129 .

caliphate
   crime-terror nexus, 190
   declaration of, 44, 151, 154–55, 162, 264, 276
   fall of, 48, 199, 202, 281
   propaganda about, 114–15, 155n.35, 167, 168, 207
   See also Iraq, war in; Syria, war in

INDEX   333

calling and choosing, 55–56, 71–73, 72f, 77–78, 79, 84, 104, 110, 142–43, 165, 234–35, 236, 260–61, 263–64
Carnot, Sadi, 80
Caserio, Sante Geronimo, 80
Cassam, Quassim, 8–9, 11–12
Catholicism, 94–96, 98–99, 104–5, 123–24, 201, 222, 262, 275
Cavanaugh, William, 67
Charleston church shooting (2015), 233–34, 235
Chekatt, Chérif, 186–87
Chrisnayudhanto, Andhika, 170
Christchurch mosque shootings (2019), 60–61, 61n.5, 176, 233–34, 235–36
Christian Identity movement, 230, 231–32, 252
Christianity
   Catholicism, 94–96, 98–99, 104–5, 123–24, 201, 222, 262, 275
   concept of redemption, 54–55, 62–63
   in Indonesia, 123–24
   Protestantism, 26, 49–50, 85, 113–14, 123–24, 222
Circle of Peace, 205
civil rights movements, 11–12
CNDDR (Comité National de Désarmement, Démobilisation et Réintégration), 225
cognitive dimension, 4, 10, 68
   injustice and 'cold/hot cognition,' 62n.7
   See also contamination; validation and reward
cognitive openings, 69, 191, 191n.7
Comité National de Désarmement, Démobilisation et Réintégration (CNDDR), 225
conative dimension, 4
Confucianism, 123–24
conspiracy theorizing, 4, 160–61, 193
   defined, 13–14
   far-right extremism, 232–33
   generalism versus particularism, 12–13
   overlap with extremism, 14
   role of religion in, 26, 45
constituency concept, 200–1, 200n.16, 234–35, 237–38, 252–53
contamination, 3, 53–54, 60, 71–72, 73, 182–83, 255, 265, 267–68, 269–70, 272, 276, 278–79
   accepting good advice, 207–8, 209
   constituency concept, 200–1, 200n.16
   counternarratives, 201, 203–6
   denial, 195–99
   disappointment, 199

infighting, 210–13
internal criticism, 202–4
lack of recognition and sanction, 201
need for communities to help deradicalize, 279–80
refutation and reappraisal, 200–15
reorientation, 202–3, 205, 206
spontaneous events in global history, 201–2
transformation to other forms of engagement, 202–3, 205, 206, 209
coping mechanisms and strategies, 34–35, 39, 40, 54–55, 57, 60, 61–62, 62n.7, 71–73, 72f, 75–77, 79, 80–81, 84, 89, 99, 102–3, 104, 105–6, 188
Coulibaly, Amedy, 186–87
counternarratives, 201, 202, 203–6
Covid-19 pandemic, 14, 26, 216–17, 276–77
Crenshaw, Martha, 8, 31–32, 54, 59
crime-terror nexus, 183–92
   criminals recruited and transformed to terrorists, 186–87, 188–89
   criminals transformed into terrorists and back to criminals, 190–92
   offer and confirmation of redemption, 189–90
   profit-versus-ideology dichotomy, 185–86
Crone, Manni, 7
cross-domain study, 2, 3, 13–15
   defining, conceptualizing, and operationalizing phenomena, 14–15
   explaining extreme behavior, 15
   overlap between conspiracy theorizing and extremism, 14
   provisional definitions of phenomena, 13–14
Cruijff, Johan, 65n.10
Crusaders, 234–36
Crusius, Patrick, 236
Custodial Institutions Agency (DJI), 32n.12, 309, 310

Dabiq (magazine), 114, 200–1
Danny (Bergden case participant), 239–40, 241, 244–45
dar al-Dawa, 146–47
dar al-Harb, 107n.1, 143, 145–47
dar al-Islam, 107n.1, 124n.22
dar al-Kufr, 107n.1
Darul Islam, 123–24, 124n.22, 127–28, 129, 137–38
dawah (dakwah), 130, 130n.33, 143, 144, 147, 203–4, 205
Dawson, Lorne, 7–9, 16–17, 27, 32, 35–36, 41, 67, 71, 301–2

334 INDEX

De Atjehers (Snouck Hurgronje), 129
deductive research, 254
defensive jihad concept, 141, 143
deficit, sense of, 61–62, 71–73, 72f, 107–33, 135–36, 166, 172–73, 177–78, 214–15, 217–18, 251–52, 255–56, 258, 259–60, 263, 264
   dealing with through armed struggle, 181
   desire for purity and action, 107, 109, 120–23
   dream images, 107, 109–11, 115–16
   far-right extremism, 234, 239, 251, 261–62
   gliding scale of, 263, 264
   identification with suffering people, 107, 117–18, 122–23, 126
   individual awareness, indigenous traditions, and universal jihad, 128–30
   Indonesian Muslims, 123–31, 125t
   mass and social media, 111–16
   new-left terrorism, 84–85
   sense of personal responsibility and duty, 117–18, 120, 127
   transition from local to global nature of jihad, 111–12
   turning points, 109, 117–20, 122–23, 126
De Graaf, Beatrice, 3, 7–9, 49–52
Della Porta, Donatella, 34, 36
Demonstrators against Municipal Governments (Demonstranten tegen Gemeenten [DTG]), 241, 243–44, 246, 247–50, 281
Dentith, M R. X., 12–13
deradicalization. *See* contamination
Deutsche Aktionsgruppen, 231
Devji, Faisal, 112, 131–32
devotion and struggle, 72f, 134–81, 255, 260–61, 263–64
   accessible conflict zones, 134, 137, 148, 281
   appealing organizations, 134, 138, 139–40, 145–46, 148, 151–52, 154–55, 164, 167–68, 261
   appraisal, 134, 135
   Azzam's writings, 138–39, 140–42, 144
   departing for and fighting in Syria, 154–57, 159–60, 162–63, 164, 166–70
   dream images, 139–40, 144, 162–63, 179–80
   earning points for afterlife, 134, 135–37, 162–63, 194
   gliding scale of, 263–64
   Islamization of ethnic and separatist conflicts, 140
   miraculous experiences, 142–43, 144, 159
   in own countries, 173–75
   practical, even physical manifestation, 179
   preaching, 153, 154
   pursuit of purity, 134, 135–40, 144, 161–62, 194
   search for meaning and better life, 134, 149, 161–62, 164, 182, 183
   sense of calling and choosing, 142–43, 165, 264
   sense of deficit, 135–36, 181
   sense of guilt and shame, 160, 161–62
   sense of personal responsibility and duty, 142, 145–47, 149, 155–56, 158–59, 160, 174, 194
   strong religious theme, 179
   taking up arms after giving the country in question opportunity to perform their sacred duty, 146–47
   variation in ideas of application of jihad, 147
   volunteer and charity work, 151–52, 154, 158–59
De Ware Religie (The True Religion) (website), 260–61
Diaryofmuhajirah (blog), 167
Dilah (girlfriend of Noureddine), 171–72
Diponegoro (prince), 129
distance interviewing, 216–53
Djeumeugued, Pascal, 228
DJI (Custodial Institutions Agency), 32n.12, 309, 310
drawings, inspired by film clips and images, 110, 278
dream images, 107, 109–11, 115–16, 139–40, 144, 162–63, 179–80, 182, 200, 208–9, 258, 260–61
DTG (Demonstranten tegen Gemeenten [Demonstrators against Municipal Governments]), 241, 243–44, 246, 247–50, 281
Dulmatin (Joko Pitoyo), 139–40, 147
Durkheim, Emile, 26–27, 67–68, 108
Dutch People's Union (Nederlandse Volks-Unie [NVU]), 250
Dutch Self Defence Army (DSDA), 241, 244–45, 248–49, 259–60
duty and personal responsibility, 117–18, 120, 127, 142, 145–47, 149, 155–56, 158–59, 160, 174, 194, 263–64

Earth First! movement, 100–1
ecoterrorism, 100–1, 103
8chan, 232, 232n.19, 236, 251
Elisabeth (empress), 77–78
Ellul, Jacques, 100–1
El Paso Walmart attack (2019), 236
emancipation, 83, 83n.2, 99, 103, 114

emotion transformation theory, 39
emotives, 259–60, 260n.5
Enschede mosque attack (2016), 232–33, 239–41, 244–45
Ensslin, Felix, 86–87
Ensslin, Gudrun, 85–87, 90, 105t, 262
Erdoğan, Recep Tayyip, 176
Esposito, John, 112n.10
ethical opportunities and programs, 134, 134n.1, 140, 160–61, 256, 279
European Identity movement, 235–36
Euskadi Ta Askatasuna (ETA), 185–86
existentialism, 66
Extinction Rebellion, 11–12
extreme belief and behavior
 conceptualizing and operationalizing, 5
 defining, 4–5
 examples of, 5
 hypotheses underlying study of, 1–2, 3, 6–18
 paradigm for studying, 1–2
 purpose of book series, 1
 purpose of this volume, 3, 19
 structure of book series, 18–22
 See also radical redemption; terrorism
extremism, 4
 conceptualization of, 11–12
 defined, 13–14, 25, 70n.14
 overlap with conspiracy theorizing, 14
 process of radicalization, 26f

Facebook, 113, 165, 194–96, 207, 243–44, 248–49, 259–60
Fadil (interviewee), 109–10, 116–18, 132, 135, 207–9, 209n.28, 257, 268–69, 286
fanaticism, 4, 13–14
Faransi, Abu Mujahid al- (Macreme Abroujui), 189–90
FARC (Revolutionary Armed Forces of Colombia), 59, 185–86, 188–89, 201
fard, 135–36, 141
fard ayn, 130, 145–47, 156
Farhad (interviewee), 165–66, 199, 286
Farihin (interviewee), 137–38, 142–44, 146–47, 166n.48, 203–4, 263–64, 273–74, 286
far-right extremism, 229–51, 252–53
 Bergden case (2016), 239–51
 constituency concept, 234–35, 237–38
 desire for fame, 234, 236–37
 elements of, 230
 fluid and fragmented nature of, 232
 gamification, 258–59

increase in attacks against Muslims and Jews, 232–33
inflammatory activists and the hangers-on, 241
jihadist terrorists versus, 238
perceived threats and injustices, 234–36, 241, 243–44, 247–48, 249, 251
qualifying as terrorism, 230–31
referring to and outdoing each other, 233–34
religious component, 230, 231
revenge, 234, 236–37, 265
sacrifice and martyrdom, 234–35, 237–38, 250–51
search for meaning and better life, 246
sense of calling and choosing, 234–35, 236
sense of deficit, 250–51, 261–62
triptych model, 261–62
fascism, 84–86, 229–30, 231, 235–36, 262
Fassi, Soufian El, 24
Feby (Bali attack survivor), 206
female terrorists, lack of research into, 276–77. *See also* Nailah, Syarafina
fida, 64–65
first-person approach, 1, 3, 7–10, 15, 41
 challenges to, 9–10
 motivational agency, 7–8
 philosophical and anthropological idea underlying, 9
 third-person approaches versus, 7–8, 10
 variation in, 8–9
First World War, 94
Fortuyn, Pim, 243–44
Forum Jihad, 146–47
4chan, 232, 236–37, 251
Free Syrian Army, 154–55, 171–72, 191, 219–20
French Revolution, 79
fundamentalism, 4
 defined, 13–14, 46
 use of term, 11
Fundamentalism Project (Marty and Appleby), 2

Gaddafi, Muammar, 199
gamification, 236–37, 257–59, 282
Gardens of the Righteous, The (Uthaymeen), 119, 119n.18
GeenStijl (blog), 176
Geertz, Clifford, 67–68
General Intelligence and Security Service (AIVD), 25, 33, 70n.14, 141n.13, 154–55, 184, 184t, 230, 250
generalism, 12–13

generativity and generative personalities/life stories, 53–61, 67–68, 134
  defined, 53–54
  identifying generativity in life stories of terrorists, 55–61, 75–76
  recurring patterns, 54–55
  redemption sequences, 53–54
Gergen, Kenneth, 36
Gevaarlijke vrouwen (De Graaf), 304
global jihad. *See* universal/global jihad
goal pursuit and achievement, 39–40, 57–59, 65–66, 102–3, 134
goal shielding, 39–40, 57
goal systems theory, 39–40
Gogh, Theo van, 141n.13, 165, 165n.45
"Great Replacement, The" (Tarrant), 235–36
Groen, Janny, 301–2
Grol, Peter, 301–2
grounded theory approach (GTA), 53n.1, 254–55, 277
Guevara, Che, 87, 113–14
guilt and shame, 75, 152, 153, 154, 160, 161–62, 179, 182, 183, 185, 188–89, 192, 255–57, 263, 264–65
  contamination, disappointment, and denial, 205, 206
  individual versus collective, 73
  moral-ethical redemption, 266
  owning injustice, 61–62, 62n.7

Habibi, B. J., 126
halal, 135–36, 189
Halle synagogue shooting (2019), 233–34
Halsema, Femke, 117
Hanafi school, 142–43
Hanief, Abu (Lotfi S.; Abu Abdurahman al-Hollandi), 180–81, 180n.66
haram, 135–36, 227–28, 263
Hardin, Russell, 8
Haroun (interviewee), 111, 155–57, 181, 197–98, 263–64, 268–69, 286
hasanat, 64, 135–36, 258–59, 264
Hassan (brother of Karim), 120–22, 269–70, 286
Henry, Emile, 106n.10
Herman, Benjamin, 186–87
hijra, 110, 110n.7, 132, 136, 137, 148, 156, 188–89, 190
Hinduism
  in Indonesia, 123–24
  Tamil Tigers and, 66
historical perspectives, 35–36, 40, 74–106
  anarchist terrorism, 74–75, 77–84

anti-colonial terrorism, 74–75
Auguste Vaillant, 78–80, 83
breakdown of redemption narratives, 105*t*
holy/religious terrorism, 74–75, 111
Irish Republican Army, 88–90, 94–96, 97–99
new-left terrorism, 74–75, 84–99
Red Army Faction, 84–94, 97, 98–99
Unabomber, 99–104
wave model of terrorism, 74–77
Zinaida Konopliannikova, 78, 80–84
Hoffman, Bruce, 8
Hofstad Group, 141, 141n.13, 148–49, 303n.5
Hofstede, Geert, 123–24
Holbrook, Donald, 27
Hollandi, Abu Abdurahman al- (Lotfi S.; Abu Hanief), 180–81, 180n.66
Holocaust, 86
Horgan, John, 2, 6, 7–8, 27, 35–36, 41, 301–2
Hume, David, 70–71
hunger strikes, 76–77, 88–90, 91–93, 94–96, 97, 98–99, 201
Hussein, Saddam, 199

Ibn Rusdi, 205
Ibn Tamiyyah, 223–24
ICG (International Crisis Group), 130–31
ICSR (International Centre for the Study of Radicalisation), 40, 188
Ilyas (interviewee), 149–51, 150n.25, 154, 286
Immigration and Naturalisation Service (IND), 217
incel movement, 237n.20
Indonesian National Counter Terrorism Agency (BNPT), 169–70, 306
inductive research, 254
Industrial Revolutions, 77, 113–14, 113n.13
"Industrial Society and Its Future" (Kaczynski), 102–3
inherent normativity, 1–2, 3, 11–13
inqadh, 64, 65
Inspire (magazine), 114, 153n.30
International Centre for the Study of Radicalisation (ICSR), 40, 188
International Crisis Group (ICG), 130–31
Internet and social media, 44, 64–65, 110–11, 120, 121, 122–23, 124, 132, 133, 136, 145–46, 149–50, 151–53, 155, 161–62, 163–64, 165–66, 167, 170, 174–75, 179–80, 181, 192–95, 196, 198–99, 205, 207, 257, 259–60, 261–62, 278, 303–4
  Abbottabad files, 204, 205
  app groups, 248–49, 251
  earning points for afterlife, 135–36

emergence and growth of, 111, 112–16, 276, 282
far-right extremism, 232, 233–34, 235–37, 238, 244, 251, 252–53
fora, 126, 135–36, 146–47, 232
gamification, 258–59
livestreaming attacks, 236–37
memes, 232, 232n.17, 236, 248–49, 276, 282–83
reward of likes, 264
IRA (Irish Republican Army), 11–12, 33, 59, 76–77, 88–90, 94–96, 97–99, 185–86, 201, 262–63
Iraq, war in, 23, 24, 44, 116, 132, 174–75, 199, 202, 207, 212, 214, 215, 263, 273, 278–79, 280–81
  decrease in number of youths prepared to depart for, 273–74
  departees, 40, 122, 135, 136, 137, 148, 162–63, 166, 174–75, 198, 258, 267–68
  number of adults who departed for, 184, 184t
  profit-versus-ideology dichotomy, 185–86
Irish Republican Army (IRA), 11–12, 33, 59, 76–77, 88–90, 94–96, 97–99, 185–86, 201, 262–63
IS. See Islamic State
islah, 64, 65
Islam
  categories of action, 135–36
  concepts of redemption, 63–65
  history of in Indonesia, 123–24
  Muslim population in Netherlands versus in Indonesia, 123–24
  Shia Islam, 172–73
  Sufism, 172–73
  Sunni Islam, 64, 109, 156, 172–73, 174, 219–20, 252
  Wahhabism, 109–10, 130
  See also Salafism
Islamic State (IS), 24, 40, 121, 122, 131–32, 147, 148, 150–52, 154–55, 155n.35, 159, 160–61, 163, 164–66, 167–68, 169, 171–72, 173, 174–75, 180–81, 183–85, 193, 195, 198–99, 200–1, 203, 205, 206, 207, 210–13, 219, 224–25, 232, 261, 264, 265, 266, 267
  counternarratives against, 201, 202
  crime-terror nexus, 188–90
  profit-versus-ideology dichotomy, 185–86
  propaganda, 64–65, 110, 114–15, 120, 150, 151, 165–66, 174–75, 176, 186, 197, 198, 243–44, 257, 259–60, 268–69
  Rumiyah (magazine), 189–90
Islamic State in West Africa (ISWA), 224–25

Islam Indonesia (NII), 144, 145–46
Islamization of ethnic and separatist conflicts, 140
ISWA (Islamic State in West Africa), 224–25

Jabhat al-Nusra, 24, 153–55, 172, 180–81, 212–13, 220–21
Jakarta bomb attacks (2004/2009), 108n.2, 123–24, 147–48
Jakarta Charter, 127–28
James, William, 26–27
Jandal, Abu, 24
Jemaah Anshorut Tauhid (JAT), 146
Jemaah Islamiyah (JI), 108n.2, 123–24, 130–31, 137–38, 139–40, 143, 144, 145, 146–47, 203–4, 214
Jibran (interviewee), 192–96, 213, 266, 270, 286
"jihad and the rifle alone" motto, 141, 142
Jneid, Fawaz, 23–24
José (stepdaughter of Martijn), 242, 243, 245
Judaism
  anti-Semitism and anti-Zionism, 230, 232, 233–34, 236–37, 248–49, 251
  concept of redemption, 63–64
  increase in far-right attacks against Jews, 232–33
Juergensmeyer, Mark, 8–9, 38

Kaczynski, David, 102
Kaczynski, Ted (Unabomber), 76–77, 99–105, 103n.9, 105t
kaffarah, 64
Kant, Immanuel, 70–71
Kaplancilar, 176
Karim (interviewee), 120–22, 256–57, 269–70, 286
Kartosuwiryo, 137–38
Kasasbeh, Muath al-, 163
Kaya, Ayhan, 7–8
Khalil, James, 16–17
Kindermann, Nora, 33–34
King, Martin Luther, Jr., 11–12
Kok, Wim, 247
Komite Aksi Penanggulangan Akibat Krisis (LSM Kompak), 145, 204
Konopliannikova, Zinaida, 78, 80–84, 88, 105t
Kouachi, Chérif, 186–87
Kouachi, Saïd, 186–87
Kraushaar, Wolfgang, 85–86
Kropotkin, Peter, 77
Kruglanski, Arie, 8–9, 39–40, 54, 56–57
Kuenzob, Dupleix, 227–28
Kuipers, Jeroen, 240
Kurnia. See Widodo, Kurnia

Lakdim, Redouane, 186–87
Lankford, Adam, 6
Lapeyronnie, Didier, 310
Last Rhodesian, The (website), 235
Laura H. (departee), 276–77
Lei, Ryan, 36, 74
Les Révoltes, 78–79
Leydesdorff, Selma, 301n.1
life histories approach, 35–36, 41–45, 48, 107–8, 301–7, 301n.1
  broadening the perspective, 306–7
  interviewees and methods, 41–45, 107–8, 303–5
  limits of, 35–36, 302–3
  reason for choosing, 41
  source calibration, 305–6
London city bus bombings (2005), 5
Lotfi S. (Abu Hanief; Abu Abdurahman al-Hollandi), 180–81, 180n.66
LSM Kompak (Komite Aksi Penanggulangan Akibat Krisis), 145, 204
LTTE (Tamil Tigers), 66

Maanaoui, Abdel, 23
makrooh, 135–36
Maliki, Nouri al-, 174
Mandela, Nelson, 11–12, 113–14
Maqdisi, Abu Muhammad al-, 153, 153n.30
Marco (Bergden case participant), 239–40, 241
Marouane B. (departee), 189
Marshall, Douglas A., 32
Martijn (interviewee), 239–40, 241–46, 249–51, 252, 286
Marty, Martin E., 2
martyrdom, 24, 66, 74–75, 122, 133, 144, 163, 177–78, 180–81, 182, 183–84, 189–90, 260–61, 276–77
  anarchist terrorism, 80, 105–6
  dying for beliefs under persecution, 66n.11
  far-right extremism, 103, 234–35, 237–38, 250–51
  Islamic concepts of redemption, 64–65
  new-left terrorism, 89–90, 93–94, 98–99
  psychodynamics, 56–57
  validation and reward, 60
Massali, Choukrie, 24
Massali, Mourad, 24
mass media, 111–12, 117, 148–49, 155–56. See also Internet and social media
McAdams, Dan, 35–36, 47–48, 53–56, 55n.2, 61, 67–68, 102–3, 134, 197, 265, 267
McCauley, Clark, 10, 16–17
McIntosh, Daniel, 39

McKinley, William, 77–78
McVeigh, Timothy, 11–12, 103–4, 146, 231
meaning and significance, quest for, 3, 28, 33, 35–36, 42–43, 55–56, 65–66, 128, 134, 149, 161–62, 164, 179, 181, 182, 183, 188, 209, 213–14, 217, 238, 252–53, 255, 257–58, 260–61, 264, 283–84
  far-right extremism, 246
  generativity, 56–57, 59
  guidelines for what is meaningful, 57–58
  new-left terrorism, 76–77
  redemption as sacred praxis, 68–69
Meinhof, Ulrike, 85, 88–89, 90, 262
Meins, Holger, 90, 91–93, 97, 98–99, 201
Melville, Herman, 91–92
memes, 232, 232n.17, 236, 248–49, 276, 282–83
Mensen met een Missie (People with a Mission), 222–23, 306–7
Merah, Mohamed, 173, 186–87
MILF (Moro Islamic Liberation Front), 145
Min, Georgiy, 82
miraculous experiences, 49–50, 140, 142–43, 144, 159, 179–80, 200, 213–14, 228–29, 251–52, 258, 260–61, 266, 269
Moby Dick (Melville), 91–92, 93
Moghaddam, Fathali, 69
Mohammed (interviewee), 218–19, 286
Mohammed VI, 201
Monkey Wrench Gang, The (Abbey), 100–1
Moro Islamic Liberation Front (MILF), 145
Morsi, Mohammed, 174
Moskalenko, Sophia, 10, 16–17
Muhajirun.com, 146
Muhammadiyah, 124–26, 126n.24, 130, 137–38, 273–74
multilevel approach (macro-, meso-, and microfactors), 16–17, 37–40, 46–47, 262–63, 276, 277
Muslim Brotherhood, 108–9, 111–12, 127, 129, 130, 131–32, 139

Naik, Zakir, 193, 194
Nailah, Syarafina (interviewee), 166–71, 210, 273–74, 276–77, 286
Narodnaya Volya (People's Will), 81–82
narratives
  as component of radical redemption, 60
  counternarratives, 201, 202, 203–6
  cross-comparison of redemptive with nonredemptive narratives, 216–53
  cycle of radical redemption narrative, 72–73, 73f

generative personalities and creation of narrative identity, 53
inconsistency of, 280–83
narrative analysis of radical redemption, 30–37, 40–41, 42–43, 47f
parasitic nature of, 283–84
of redemption, 24, 34
redemption as, 34
role of religion in radical redemption narrative, 259–62
as storyline and temporal construct, 34–35
Syrian detainees' narrative of armed resistance against an oppressor, 217–21
See also radical redemption; religion-and-radicalization puzzle
Nasser, Gamel, 109
National Coordinator for Counterterrorism and Security (NCTV), 25, 176, 195–96, 232–33, 271
National Socialism (Nazism), 86, 90, 97, 230
National-Sozialistischer Untergrund, 230
nation-states, emergence and consolidation of, 74–75
Nederlandse Volks-Unie (NVU; Dutch People's Union), 250
Nemmouche, Mehdi, 173
Neo-JI, 203–4
Neumann, Peter, 186–87
Nevis, Alan, 301n.1
new-left terrorism wave (1960s–1990s), 74–75, 84–99
 Irish Republican Army, 88–90, 94–96, 97–99
 Red Army Faction, 84–94, 97, 98–99
Newton, Taylor, 39
Nguyen, Thi, 258–59
Nigeria schoolgirl abductions, 5, 224, 226
NII (Islam Indonesia), 144, 145–46
9/11, 7, 58, 60–61, 112, 115–16, 147, 193, 232, 233, 234–35, 303–4
Nobel, Alfred, 77–78
nonideal epistemology, 6
normalcy (normality) hypothesis, 1, 3, 6–7, 58
 nonideal epistemology, 6
 psychopathological explanations versus, 6–7
 rationality, 6
Noureddine (interviewee), 132, 170–73, 196–97, 259–60, 268, 274–75, 286
NVU (Nederlandse Volks-Unie; Dutch People's Union), 250

objective rationality, 6
Oklahoma City bombing (1995), 103–4, 231
Omar (interviewee), 132, 163–64, 212, 263–64, 286
Omar (second caliph), 64
Orange Revolution, 113–14
Ordine Nuovo, 231
orthopraxis, 68–69, 105t, 106, 132, 251–52, 282–83
 cycle of radical redemption narrative, 73f
 defined, 3, 46
 Dutch versus Indonesian jihadist interviewees, 261
 ethical opportunities, 134n.1
 gamification, 282
 lack of validation, 201
 neo-orthodoxy, 112n.10
 radical redemption as, 45–47, 47f, 258–59
 religious praxis, 46
 value capture, 258–59, 261–62
 See also triptych model
Oslo Accords, 127
Oslo bombing and Utøya mass shooting (2011), 60–61, 61n.5, 233–34

Padri movement, 123–24, 138, 145–46
Paltalk, 207
pan-Islamism, 130
Paradise Gate Boys, 23–24, 31–32, 185–86, 187
Paris *Charlie Hebdo* attacks (2015), 151–52, 173, 186–87
particularism, 12–13
Patek, Umar, 145
Peels, Rik, 33–34, 41–71
Pegida, 241, 243–44, 247–48, 250, 259–60
People's Will (Narodnaya Volya), 81–82
People with a Mission (Mensen met een Missie), 222–23, 306–7
pesantren, 115–16, 130–31, 133, 137–38, 139, 143, 170, 179–80
Peshmerga, 150
Peter (interviewee), 239–40, 241, 244–45, 246–51, 252, 263–64, 286
pidyon haben, 63–64
Pigden, Charles, 12–13
Piranha case, 303n.5
Pitoyo, Joko (Dulmatin), 139–40, 147
Prāyaścitta, 63–64
Prevention of Terrorism Act, 95
Project A (Facebook group), 195–96
Protestantism, 26, 49–50, 85, 113–14, 123–24, 222
Proudhon, Pierre-Joseph, 77
Provisional Irish Republican Army (Provisional IRA), 89–90, 94–96, 262

psychodynamics, 56–57, 302n.2
psychopathological explanations, 6–7, 18, 178n.62
purity, pursuit of, 32, 45, 66, 72, 134, 135–40, 142, 144, 147, 160–61, 170–71, 179, 186, 190, 191, 192, 194, 197, 223–24, 238, 256, 258–59, 278–79
   accessible conflict zone, 137
   earning points for afterlife, 136
   far-right extremism, 233–34, 265
   Islamic concepts of redemption, 64, 65
   orthopraxis, 46
   sense of deficit, 107, 109, 120–23
   Tatidealismus, 85–86
push and pull factors, 134, 148, 179, 281

QAnon, 14, 26
Qutb, Sayyid, 109, 111–12, 115–16, 129, 138

radicalization. *See* radical redemption; religion-and-radicalization puzzle
radical redemption, 9, 9n.9, 30–37
   author's positionality, 49–52
   components of, 60
   cross-comparison with nonredemptive narratives, 216–53
   as cultural worldview, 56–57, 253
   cycle of, 72–73, 73*f*, 267–68, 270, 272, 279
   disillusionment and disengagement, 267, 268–70
   grounded theory approach, 53n.1, 254–55, 277
   historical perspective of, 74–106
   implication of "radical," 34, 43
   inconsistency of narrative, 280–83
   intersection of social psychology, religious studies, and history, 35–36
   interviewees and methods, 41–45, 107–8, 303–5
   lack of systematic investigation of, 33–35
   life histories approach, 35–36, 41–45, 48, 301–7, 301n.1
   narrative analysis of, 30–37, 40–41, 42–43, 47*f*
   as orthopraxis, 45–47, 47*f*, 258–59
   parasitic nature of narrative, 283–84
   purpose of this volume, 3, 19
   recidivism and reintegration, 268–72
   recurring redemptive moves, 265–66
   redemption as sacred praxis, 67–68
   as religious and cultural theme, 62–66
   religious framework, 251–52
   research question and subquestions, 30, 254–55
   role of redemption in radicalization process, 31–34
   role of religion in disillusionment, disengagement, and reintegration, 272–75
   role of religion in radical redemption narrative, 259–62
   as sacred praxis, 67–71
   sand glass model for research design, 30, 31*f*
   scope of this volume, 47–49
   as sensitizing concept, 53
   three Rs and fourth R, 9n.9, 29–30, 75–76, 177, 237–38
   triptych model, 8–9, 71–73, 72*f*, 105–6, 107, 135, 182, 251–52, 255–58, 259–60, 261–62, 263
   variation in religious radical redemption, 262–65
   worldly nature of, 281
   See also appraisal; calling and choosing; coping mechanisms and strategies; deficit, sense of; devotion and struggle; meaning and significance, quest for; narratives; orthopraxis; religion-and-radicalization puzzle; sacrifice; validation and reward
RAF (Red Army Faction), 11–12, 33, 76–77, 84–94, 97, 98–99, 105–6, 188–89, 201–2, 262–63
Ramli (interviewee), 124–27, 124n.23, 129, 130, 144–45, 146–47, 204–5, 204n.20, 273–74, 286
Rapoport, David, 74–75, 83, 94, 111
Rathjen, Tobias, 233
Rayat al-Tawheed (Banner of God), 186, 186n.4
recidivism, 270–72, 270–71n.9
Red Army Faction (RAF), 11–12, 33, 76–77, 84–94, 97, 98–99, 105–6, 188–89, 201–2, 262–63
Red Brigades, 33
Red Crescent, 280–81
redemption, 29–30, 33–34
   Buddhist concept, 63–64
   Christian religious concept, 54–55, 62–63
   defined, 53–54, 62–63, 102–3
   Indian religious concepts, 63–64
   Islamic concepts, 63–65
   Judaic concept, 63–64
   metaphorical meaning, 63
   as narrative, 34
   role in radicalization process, 31–34
   See also radical redemption
redemptive self, 3

Redemptive Self, The (McAdams), 53–54
Reformation, 113–14
religion-and-radicalization puzzle, 23–52, 192–93, 251–52, 253, 266, 267–68, 281–82, 284
  current literature on, 37–40
  defining radicalization, 25
  difficulty in conceptualizing and defining religion, 26–27
  disillusionment, disengagement, and reintegration, 272–75
  ethnic-tribal conflict versus religious terrorism, 221–29
  holy/religious terrorism wave, 74–75
  identifying generativity in life stories of terrorists, 55–61
  interviewees and methods, 41–45, 107–8, 303–5
  lack of religious background, 108, 116, 118, 121, 124–26, 130–31, 158, 161–62, 164, 166–67, 174, 177–78, 179, 187
  multilevel approach to (macro-, meso-, and microfactors), 37–40, 46–47, 262–63, 276, 277
  need for communities to help deradicalize, 279–80, 284
  non-religious waves of terrorism, 75, 85, 94, 98–99, 104–6
  process of radicalization, 25–30, 26f, 69
  redemption as religious and cultural theme, 62–66
  redemption as sacred praxis, 67–71
  religion as moderator in radicalization process, 26–30, 29f
  religiosity versus religion, 27, 67
  religious versus political-ideological motives, 59–60
  role of religion in disillusionment, disengagement, and reintegration, 272–75
  role of religion in radical redemption narrative, 259–62
  strong religious theme manifested in practical way, 179
  sudden "seeing-the-light" character of radicalization, 32, 69–70, 256–58
  taking terrorists' religious beliefs seriously, 24, 32, 71, 267–68
  use of terminology "radicals" or "radicalizing youth," 43
  varieties of religious radical redemption, 262–65
  See also orthopraxis; radical redemption
religiosity, 27, 67
religious (sacred) praxis, 46, 46n.24, 67–71, 194

revenge, 33, 60–61, 71–73, 104, 163, 173, 174–75, 176–78, 181, 182, 265, 266, 273–74
  anarchist terrorism, 80
  far-right extremism, 234, 236–37, 265
  new-left terrorism, 84–85, 94
  three Rs and fourth R, 9n.9, 29–30, 75–76, 177, 237–38
  Unabomber, 101, 102–4
Revolutionary Armed Forces of Colombia (FARC), 59, 185–86, 188–89, 201
reward. *See* validation and reward
Richardson, Louise, 9n.9, 29–30, 75–76, 176, 237–38
Roeder, Manfred, 231
Ronald (Bergden case participant), 239–40
Roof, Dylann, 233–34, 235, 237–38, 251, 252–53, 265
root cause theories, 24–25, 38
Rote Armee Fraktion. *See* Red Army Faction
Rueb, Thomas, 301–2
Rumiyah (magazine), 189–90, 200–1
Rutte, Mark, 243–44, 247

sacrifice, 31–32, 60–61, 65–66, 72–73, 74–75, 76–77, 78, 104, 105t, 183, 220, 234–35, 250–51, 269, 276–77
  anarchist terrorism, 83
  as component of radical redemption, 60
  devotion and struggle, 133, 135, 136, 141, 155–56, 164, 177, 180–81
  Islamic concepts of redemption, 64–65
  Judaic concept of redemption, 63
  new-left terrorism, 84–85, 86, 87, 89, 92–93, 96, 97–99, 262
  psychodynamics, 56–57
  transcendental element of, 60
  Unabomber, 102–4
  validation, 214
Salafism, 24n.2, 115–16, 128, 130, 131–32, 142–43, 152–53, 156, 160–61, 164, 172–73, 193, 205, 212–13, 219–20, 223, 259–60
  categories of action, 135–36, 137
  concept of redemption, 65
  orthopraxis, 112n.10
  persuasive power of jihadist-Salafist narrative, 160–61, 170
  See also martyrdom
Samir A. (convicted terrorist), 141
Samudra, 146–47
sand glass model for research design, 30, 31f
Sands, Bobby, 95–97, 98–99, 104–5, 105t, 201, 262
Sands, Gerry, 99

Sarekat Islam, 129, 129n.29, 130, 145–46
Sawlat al-fida (film), 64–65
Sayyaf, Rasul, 142–43
school shooters, 100n.8
Schubert, Ingrid, 90
Search for Common Ground (SFCG), 206
second-person approaches, 216–17
Second World War, 113–14, 117
secular presentism, 283
self-actualization, 71n.15, 85–86
sensitizing concepts, 53, 53n.1, 254
SFCG (Search for Common Ground), 206
shahid, 64–65, 144
sharia, 26, 127–28, 142, 146, 176, 178–79, 203, 218
Shari A4Belgium, 200–1
Shekau, Abubakar, 224–25, 227
Shia Islam, 172–73
Sinn Féin, 99
Sisi, Abdel Fattah el-, 174
Sivan, Emmanuel, 16–17
Sneijder, Jeffrey, 120–21
Sneijder, Wesley, 120–21
Snouck Hurgronje, Christiaan, 50–51, 129
Socialist Revolutionary Party, 81–82
social media. *See* Internet and social media
social-psychological theory, 10, 28, 35, 36, 38, 40, 46–47, 74, 75, 135n.2, 178n.62, 279–80
Sofyan. *See* Tsauri, Sofyan
Solahudin, 169–70, 204
Speckhard, Anne, 302n.2
Stampnitzky, Lisa, 10
Stasi, 201–2
Stekelenburg, Jacquelien van, 39
Sterkenburg, Nikki, 301–2
Stokes, Patrick, 12–13
Straat Dawah, 23–24, 24n.2, 200–1
Strasbourg Christmas market attack (2018), 186–87
structure-chance-choice framework, 16–17
subjective rationality, 6
Sufism, 172–73
Suharto, 123–24, 126, 130
Sukarno, 123–24, 127–28, 130, 137–38
Sunata, Abdullah, 145
Sungkar, Abdullah, 138, 143
sunna, 135–36
Sunni Islam, 64, 109, 156, 172–73, 174, 219–20, 252
Suzan (girlfriend of Peter), 244–45
Syarafina. *See* Nailah, Syarafina
Syria, war in, 44, 122–23, 174, 210–13, 232–33, 276

accessible conflict zone, 132, 148
asylum seekers, 217
decrease in number of youths prepared to depart for, 273–74
departees, 23, 24, 32, 40, 111, 122, 124, 135, 137, 154–57, 158–60, 162–64, 166, 168–73, 179, 180–81, 183, 189, 190–92, 197–98, 200, 208, 210–12, 268, 277, 280–81
earning points for afterlife and pursuit of purity, 135, 136, 256, 258–59
identification with people of Syria, 149–51, 162
members of armed militias, 217–21
number of adults who departed for, 184, 184*t*
perceived injustice and sense of deficit and duty, 61–62, 110, 117–18, 119–20, 121–22, 132, 148–53, 156, 171, 174, 179, 207, 210, 258, 263–64

Tahrir al-Sham, 184
takfir, 204, 204n.19, 205, 206
Talbi, Mohamed, 23–24
Taliban, 149–50, 152–53, 185–86
"Talking to Terrorists" (Speckhard and Akhmedova), 302n.2
Tamil Tigers (LTTE), 66
Tanis, Gökmen, 150, 150nn.24–25, 175–79, 183–84, 261, 265, 266, 286
Tarrant, Brenton, 60–61, 61n.5, 176, 232–33, 235–36, 251, 261–62, 265
Tatidealismus, 85–86
tawba, 64
tazkiah, 64
Technological Society, The (Ellul), 100–1
Telegram app, 114–15, 121
terrorism, 4
crime-terror nexus, 183–92
defined, 13–14, 25
female terrorists, 166–71, 276–77
generativity and, 53–61, 67–68, 75–76
historical perspective of, 74–106
interviewees and methods, 41–45, 107–8, 303–5
number of convicted terrorists/detainees in Indonesia/Netherlands, 125*t*
process of radicalization, 25, 26*f*
taking terrorists' religious beliefs seriously, 24, 32, 71, 267–68
territory, 107, 107n.1
three Rs and fourth R, 9n.9, 29–30, 75–76, 177, 237–38
use of terms "terrorists" or "convicted terrorists," 43

victim-perpetrator dynamic, 60–61
wave model of, 74–77
See also radical redemption; religion-and-radicalization puzzle
Thatcher, Margaret, 96–97
Thijssen, Gaby, 6
third-person approaches, 1, 7–8, 10, 15
Top, Noordin, 146–47, 206
transactional model, 39
transcendental dimension, 24, 26–27, 35, 41, 45, 66, 71, 71n.15, 103, 105–6, 107–8, 281
defined, 60
far-right extremism, 237–38, 251, 265
reward, 60
triptych model, 8–9, 71–73, 72f, 105–6, 107, 135, 182, 251–52, 255–58, 259–60, 261–62, 263
true interdisciplinarity, 2, 3, 16–18
defining "true," 17–18
integration of results, 18
multidisciplinarity versus, 17
multilevel explanations (macro-, meso-, and microfactors), 16–17
relevant disciplines, 16
True Religion, The (De Ware Religie) (website), 260–61
Tsauri, Sofyan (interviewee), 108–10, 108n.2, 127, 129, 138–40, 146–48, 205, 273–74, 286
Tubantia (newspaper), 244
Tumblr, 167
Turner Diaries, The, 231, 233
"2083" (Breivik), 234–35
Twitter (X), 113, 113n.12, 165–66, 236

Unabomber (Ted Kaczynski), 76–77, 99–105, 103n.9, 105t
Union of Concerned Scientists, 100–1
universal/global jihad, 109, 110–12, 130, 131–32, 145–46, 261
US Capitol insurrection (2021), 5, 14
ustads, 129, 129n.28, 206
Uthaymeen, Muhammad ibn Saalih al-, 119n.18
Utrecht tram shooting (2019), 176, 177, 178n.63

Vaillant, Auguste, 78–80, 83, 88, 105t, 106n.10
Vaillant, Sidonie, 80
validation and reward, 55, 60, 66, 71–72, 72f, 73, 88, 103–5, 105t, 182–215, 255, 261–62, 264, 281–82
as components of radical redemption, 60

crime-terror nexus, 183–84, 185
deliverance, 182, 192, 195
deradicalization and abandonment of ideals, 200–13
greater metaphysical battle between good and evil, 182
individual versus collective narratives, 182, 200–1
insistence on innocence, 195–96
Rumiyah (magazine), 189–90
worldly nature of redemption narrative, 281
See also contamination
value capture, 258–59, 261–62
Versteegt, Inge, 187–88
Vesper, Bernward, 86–87
Viol, Virginie, 78–79

Wagensveld, Edwin, 243–44
Wahhabism, 109–10, 130
Wahid, Abdurrahman, 126
Washington Post, 102–3
wave model of terrorism, 74–77
WDYP (World Dynamics of Young People), 225–26
Weather Underground, 31–32, 33
Weber, Max, 63–64
Wehrsportgruppe Hoffmann, 231
white supremacy, 61n.5, 230, 231, 235–36, 252
Widodo, Kurnia (interviewee), 129, 132, 136, 145–47, 205, 206, 263–64, 268–69, 273–74, 286
Wie baue ich einen Molotow-Cocktail? (film), 91–92
Wilders, Geert, 192, 193–96, 213, 243–44
World Dynamics of Young People (WDYP), 225–26
World Trade Center bombing (1993), 103–4. *See also* 9/11

X (Twitter), 113, 113n.12, 165–66, 236

Yehya K. (convicted terrorist), 141
Yom Kippur scapegoat ritual, 63–64
Yousef, Ramzi, 103–4
YouTube, 110–11, 114–15, 121, 122–23, 126, 149–50, 161, 210, 255–56, 257, 276, 282
Yussuf (friend of Bilal), 210
Yusuf, Mohammed, 223–24

Zarqawi, Abu Musab al-, 202